Beginner SQL Programming Using Microsoft SQL Server 2016

Kalman Toth

Beginner SQL Programming
Using Microsoft SQL Server 2016
Copyright © 2016 by Kalman Toth

Contact: kalmantoth@gmail.com

ISBN-13: 978-1535311762
ISBN-10: 1535311762

Trademark Notices

Warning and Disclaimer

Beginner SQL Programming

Using Microsoft SQL Server 2016

Contents at a Glance

ABOUT THE AUTHOR

Kalman Toth currently working on the development of Artificial General Intelligence.

Kalman Toth has been working with relational database technology since 1990. One day his boss at a commodity brokerage firm in Greenwich, Connecticut, had to leave early. He gave his SQL Server login and password to Kalman along with a small SQL task. Kalman was a C/C++ developer fascinated by SQL. Therefore, he studied a Transact-SQL manual 3 times from start to finish "dry", without any server access. His boss was satisfied with the results of the SQL task and a few days later Kalman's dream came true: he got his very own SQL Server login.

Kalman's relational database career since then includes database design, database development, database administration, OLAP architecture, and Business Intelligence development. Applications have included enterprise-level general ledger and financial accounting, bond funds auditing, international stock market feeds processing, broker-dealer firm risk management, derivative instruments analytics, consumer ecommerce database management for online dating, personal finance, physical fitness, and diet and health. His MSDN forum participation in the Transact-SQL and SQL Server Tools was rewarded with the Microsoft Community Contributor award. Kalman has a Master of Arts degree in Physics from Columbia University and a Master of Philosophy degree in Computing Science, also from Columbia. Additionally, he has Microsoft certifications in database administration, development, and Business Intelligence. His dream SQL career took him across the United States and Canada as well as to South America and Europe. SQL also involved him in World History. At one time he worked for Deloitte and Touche on the 96th floor of World Trade Center North. On September 11, 2001, he was an RDBMS consultant at Citibank on 111 Wall Street. After escaping at 10:30 on that fateful Tuesday morning in the heavy dirt and smoke, it took 10 days before he could return to his relational database development job just 1/2 mile from the nearly three thousand victims buried under steel.

What Kalman loves about SQL is that the same friendly, yet powerful, commands can process 2 records or 2 million records or 200 million records in the same easy way. Currently, he is Principal Trainer at www.sqlusa.com. His current interest is Artificial Intelligence. He is convinced that machine intelligence will not only replace human intelligence, but will even surpass it by millions of times in the near future. Kalman's hobby is flying gliders and vintage fighter planes. Kalman is moderator on the following MSDN forums: Database Design, Transact-SQL and Getting Started with SQL Server.

OTHER BOOKS & EBOOKS BY THE AUTHOR:

SQL Server 2016 Database Design

SQL Server 2016 Design & Programming

Exam 70-461 Bootcamp: Querying Microsoft SQL Server 2012

SQL CAREERS: SQL Server Developer jobs on monster.com (global online employment portal).

SQL Server Developer Jobs

1000+ Jobs Found

Featured Job
Pure Michigan Talent Connect
Find the career that is right for you!

PURE MICHIGAN
Talent Connect

SQL Server Developer

Veredus Inc

Irving , TX

SQL SERVER DEVELOPER – PERM – IRVING, TX Involved in implementing mission-critical solutions which consist of 70% coding functional

07/14/2016

SQL Server Database Developer

Responsive Search

Chicago , IL

Candidates should possess a bachelor's degree or equivalent experience and 1-3 years' experience in the following areas: · SQL Server (2008R2,

07/08/2016

MS SQL Server Developer

Aditi Staffing Private Limited

nt

y Language)

p)

SHOW MORE

SQL CAREERS: Microsoft SQL Server Developer jobs on dice.com (technical employment portal).

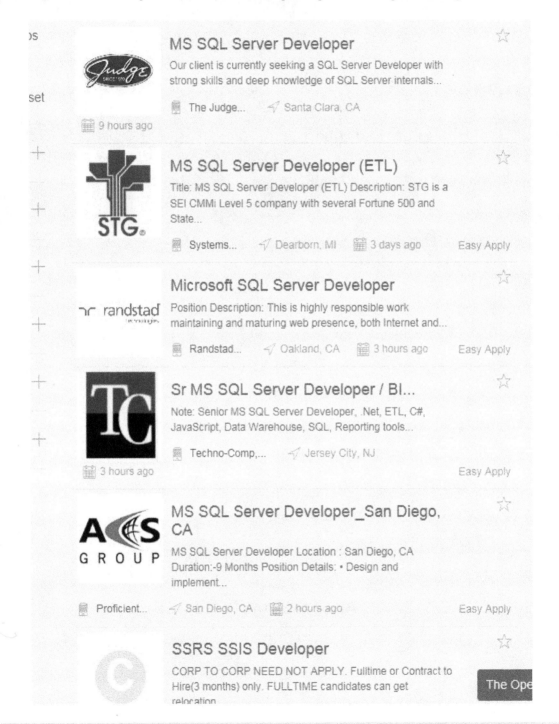

CONTENTS

SQL CAREERS: SQL Server Developer jobs on linkedin.com/jobs (employment portal).

9,351 Sql Server Developer jobs in United States

SQL Server Developer
TenDelta

Los Angeles, California

3-5 years' experience working as a SQL Server database developer. Strong SQL Server experience.Competitive salary, in-line with experience.

Apply

SQL Server Developer
HireVergence

Tampa, Florida

Possess strong Microsoft SQL Server and SQL services skills. Strong SSIS/ETL Developmen experience. Experince in SSRS or SSAS is preferred.

Apply

SQL Server Developer
Solomon Page Group

New York, New York

A Big 4 Management Consulting firm is seeking Junior-Mid level SQL Server Developer in N 2-5 years experience in SQL Server 2012/2008.

Apply

SQL Server Developer
JMD Partners Inc

New York, New York

You would be the primary SQL Reporting & BI Engineer for a 1,000 user firm that offers a gr work experience, training, & true autonomy...

Apply

SQL CAREERS: Microsoft SQL Server Developer jobs on cybercoders.com (technical employment portal).

SQL Server Database Developer (Up to around $95k/yr)

Madison, WI   Full-time $85k - $95k   Posted 05/23/2016

If you are a SQL Server Database Developer with experience, please read on!Based in Madison, WI, we are a well established company (established in 1998) helping one million people a day to compare hea...

MS SQL Server   t-sql   SSIS

Database Developer - SQL Server, SQL, T-SQL

New York, NY   Full-time $90k - $130k   Posted 07/12/2016

If you are a Database Developer with very strong SQL experience, please read on! Located in New York, NY, we have built and managed global financial portfolios and related vehicles for over 15 years. W...

SQL Server   SQL   t-sql   ETL   SSIS

SQL Server / ETL Developer - C#

Nashville, TN   Full-time $75k - $95k   Posted 07/14/2016

If you are Software Developer who has experience developing ETL applications to interface data between company, clients and vendors.. please read on!!Located in Nashville, TN we're a Privately Held Fi...

INTRODUCTION

SQL Server 2016 programming builds on achievements of decades in advanced relational database technology. Among the new SQL Server 2016 features is prominent: the stretch database whereby inactive records automatically pushed into the cloud. Programming SQL Server 2016 is fun due to the host of marvelous tools available for the developer in SQL Server Management Studio and Visual Studio. Graphical query designer, for example, helps the developer to develop the JOIN structure of a complex query. SQL Server 2016 provides a highly productive environment for database software development.

The previous version, SQL Server 2014, introduced 3 new database design features: in-memory OLTP tables, inline index declaration in CREATE TABLE statement and updateable clustered columnstore indexes. In-memory OLTP aims to boost performance by reducing disk io as memory capacities are expanding frequently beyond the size of the database. SQL Server 2012 columnstore indexes are static. Updateable columnstore index expands the applicability of the performance feature. Inline index declaration elevates indexes to the level of PRIMARY KEY, FOREIGN KEY, CHECK constraint and DEFAULT constraint which can be declared inline.

Developers across the world face database issues daily. While immersed in procedural languages with loops, RDBMS forces them to think in terms of sets without loops. It takes transition. It takes training. It takes experience. Developers are exposed also to Excel worksheets, or spreadsheets, as they were called in the not so distant past. So, if you know worksheets, how hard can databases be? After all, worksheets look pretty much like database tables, don't they? The big difference is the connections among well-designed tables. A database is a set of connected tables, which represent entities in the real world. A database can be 100 connected tables or 3000. The connection is very simple: row A in table Alpha has affiliated data with row B in table Beta. However, even with 200 tables and 300 connections (FOREIGN KEY references), it takes a good amount of time to become familiar to the point of having an acceptable working knowledge.

"The Cemetery of Computer Languages" is expanding. You can see tombstones like PL/1, Forth, Ada, Pascal, LISP, RPG, APL, SNOBOL, JOVIAL, Algol – the list goes on. For some, the future is in question: PowerBuilder, ColdFusion, FORTRAN and COBOL. On the other hand, SQL is running strong after 3 decades of glorious existence. What is the difference? The basic difference is that SQL can handle large datasets in a consistent manner based on mathematical foundations. You can throw together a computer language easily: assignment statements, looping, if-then conditional, 300 library functions, and voila! Here is the new language: Mars/1, named after the red planet to be fashionable with NASA's new Mars robot. However, can Mars/1 JOIN a table of 1 million rows with a table of 10 million rows in a second? The success of SQL language is so compelling that other technologies are tagged onto it like XML/XQuery, which deals with semi-structured information objects. In SQL you are thinking at a high level. In C# or Java, you are dealing with details – lots of them. That is the major difference.

Why is so much of the book dedicated to database design? Why not plunge into SQL coding and eventually the developer will get a hang of the design? Because high-level thinking requires thinking at the database design level. A farmer has six mules. H how do we model it in the database? We design the

Farmer and FarmAnimal tables, and then connect them with FarmerID FOREIGN KEY in FarmAnimal referencing the FarmerID PRIMARY KEY in the Farmer table. What is the big deal about it? It looks so simple. In fact, how about just calling the tables Table1 and Table2 to be more generic. Ouch! Meaningful naming is the very basis of good database design. Relational database design is truly simple for simple well-understood models. The challenge starts in modeling complex objects such as financial derivative instruments, airplane passenger scheduling, or a social network website. When you need to add 5 new tables to a 1000 table database and hook them in (define FOREIGN KEY references) correctly, it is a huge challenge. To begin with, some of the five new tables may already be redundant, but you don't know that until you understand what the 1000 tables are really storing. Frequently, learning the application area is the biggest challenge for a developer when starting a new job.

The SQL language is simple to program and read even when touching 10 tables. Complexities abound though. The very first one: does the SQL statement touch the right data set – 999 records and 1000 or 998? T-SQL statements are turned into Transact-SQL scripts, stored procedures, and user-defined functions, and trigger server-side database objects. They can be short 5 statement programs or long 1000 statement programs. The style of Transact-SQL programming is different from the style in procedural programming languages. There are no arrays, only tables or table variables. Typically, there is no looping, only set-based operation. Error control is different. Testing and debugging is relatively simple in Transact-SQL due to the interactive environment and the magic of selecting and executing a part without recompiling the whole.

WHOM THIS BOOK IS FOR

Developers, programmers, and systems analysts who are new to relational database technology will find this book of value. It is also applicable for developers, designers, and administrators, who know some SQL programming and database design, but wish to expand their RDBMS design and development technology horizons. Familiarity with another computer language is assumed. The book has lots of queries, lots of T-SQL scripts, and plenty to learn. The best way to learn it is to type in the query in your own SQL Server copy and test it, examine it, change it. Wouldn't it be easier just to copy and paste it? It would, but the learning value would diminish. You need to feel the SQL language in your fingers. SQL queries must "pour" out from your fingers into the keyboard. Why is that so important? After all, everything can be found on the web and just be copied and pasted? Well, not exactly. If you want to be an expert, it has to be in your head not on the web. Second, when your supervisor is looking over your shoulder, "Charlie, can you tell me what the total revenue is for March." you have to be able to type in the query without a web search and provide the results to your superior promptly.

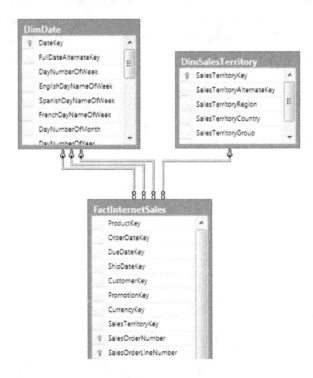

ABOUT THIS BOOK

Beginning Transact-SQL Programming is not a reference manual. Rather you will learn by examples: there are over 1,100 SELECT queries in the book. Instead of imaginary tables, the book uses the SQL Server sample databases for explanations and examples: pubs (PRIMARY KEYs 9, FOREIGN KEYs 10), Northwind (PRIMARY KEYs 13, FOREIGN KEYs 13) and the AdventureWorks family. Among them: AdventureWorks, AdventureWorks2008, AdventureWorks2012 (PRIMARY KEYs 71, FOREIGN KEYs 90), and AdventureWorksDW2012 (PRIMARY KEYs 27, FOREIGN KEYs 44). The book introduces relational database design concepts, and then reinforces them again and again, not to bore the reader, but rather to indoctrinate with relational database design principles. Light weight SQL starts at the beginning of the book, because working with database metadata (not the content of the database, rather data which describes the database) is essential for understanding database design. By the time the reader gets to T-SQL programming, he already knows basic SQL programming from the database design section of the book. The book was designed to be readable in any environment, even on the beach, laptop available or no laptop in sight at all. All queries are followed by results row count and/or full/partial results listing in tabular (grid) format. For full benefits though, the reader should try out the T-SQL queries and scripts as he progresses from page to page, topic to topic. Example for SQL Server 2014 T-SQL query and results presentation:

```
SELECT          V.Name                                   AS Vendor,
                FORMAT(SUM(POH.TotalDue), 'c', 'en-US')  AS [Total Purchase],
                FORMAT(AVG(POH.TotalDue), 'c', 'en-US')  AS [Average Purchase]
FROM AdventureWorks.Purchasing.Vendor AS V
   INNER JOIN AdventureWorks.Purchasing.PurchaseOrderHeader AS POH
       ON V.VendorID = POH.VendorID
GROUP BY V.Name  ORDER BY Vendor;
-- (79 row(s) affected) - Partial results.
```

Vendor	Total Purchase	Average Purchase
Advanced Bicycles	$28,502.09	$558.86
Allenson Cycles	$498,589.59	$9,776.27
American Bicycles and Wheels	$9,641.01	$189.04
American Bikes	$1,149,489.84	$22,539.02

CONVENTIONS USED IN THIS BOOK

- The Transact-SQL queries and scripts (sequence of statements) are shaded.
- The number of resulting rows is displayed as a comment line: -- (79 row(s) affected).
- The results of the queries are usually displayed in grid format.
- Less frequently, the results are enclosed in comment markers: /*...... */.
- When a query is a trivial variation of a previous query, no result is displayed.

While the intention of the book is database design and database development, SQL Server installation and some database administration tasks are included.

SQL CAREERS: Microsoft SQL Server Developer jobs on careerjet.com (technical employment portal).

NET/SQL Server Developer - Cloud Integration Platform

Cognizant - Nashua, NH

Senior C#, **SQL** Server **Developer** - Cloud Integration Technologies Cognizant is leading the charge i application technology... **developer**, you will code, test, and analyze software programs and applicatic developing a new market-leading Cloud Integration...

www.cognizant.com - July 15 - Save - Send to a friend

SQL Developer needed for a Contract to Perm opportunity

Jacksonville, FL

Description: My client is looking for a **SQL Developer** that will create and maintain database environn permissions, and job schedules..., including backup and maintenance plans, SSRS and SSIS job cont deployment of **SQL** scripts and SSIS packages to various environments...

www.roberthalf.com - July 14 - Save - Send to a friend

SQL Developer

U.S. Bank - USA

U.S. Bank is hiring a **SQL Developer** at our Headquarters in Minneapolis. Our team is looking for a D enjoys process automation... to specific requirements) Project Management Programming/Developme Oracle, Excel VBA Systems integration testing (IT) and review...

www.usbank.com - July 14 - Save - Send to a friend

Needed: Senior SQL Database Developer in Scottsdale

Scottsdale, AZ

Description: Robert Half Technology is seeking a Senior **SQL** Database **Developer** for our client. The for a Senior **SQL**... Database **Developer** to work with existing team to build and assist in the database this growing company. The Senior **SQL** Database...

www.roberthalf.com - July 14 - Save - Send to a friend

Sr SQL Developer for Non-Profit Organization

Los Angeles, CA

Description: Sr **SQL Developer** For immediate consideration send resume to Toni.Anzalone @rht.cor Technology is seeking a Sr... **SQL Developer** to join our client a stable non-profit organization locatec CA. This is a contract-to-hire opportunity for a Sr...

www.roberthalf.com - July 14 - Save - Send to a friend

SQL CAREERS: Microsoft SQL Server Developer jobs on glassdoor.com (technical employment portal).

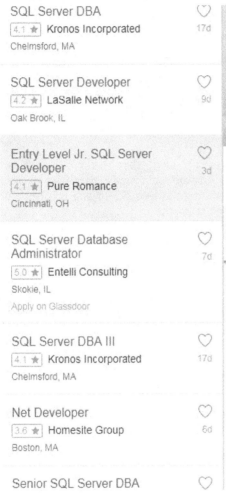

SQL Server DBA
4.1 ★ Kronos Incorporated   17d
Chelmsford, MA

SQL Server Developer
4.2 ★ LaSalle Network   9d
Oak Brook, IL

Entry Level Jr. SQL Server Developer
4.1 ★ Pure Romance   3d
Cincinnati, OH

SQL Server Database Administrator
5.0 ★ Entelli Consulting   7d
Skokie, IL
Apply on Glassdoor

SQL Server DBA III
4.1 ★ Kronos Incorporated   17d
Chelmsford, MA

Net Developer
3.6 ★ Homesite Group   6d
Boston, MA

Senior SQL Server DBA

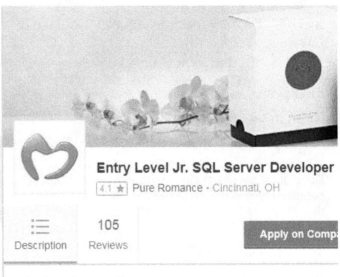

Entry Level Jr. SQL Server Developer
4.1 ★ Pure Romance · Cincinnati, OH

≡   105
Description   Reviews   **Apply on Comp**

Title: Jr. SQL Server Developer
Classification: Full Time
Reports to: Manager of Database Systems
Pure Romance is the largest direct seller of relationship enhancement
premiere line of products is marketed through a distinctive network of
20,000 independent sales Consultants.
You will find a challenging and rewarding career working with a group
States, Canada, Australia, Puerto Rico, and South Africa. Our staff en
onsite gym with full-time trainers, free parking in our garage, flexible w
throughout the year to boost friendship and camaraderie between dep
exceptional performance with accelerated salary increases and promc
Summary: We are looking for a Jr SQL Server Developer with at leas
or above who is looking for an extremely challenging role working in a
successful applicant will work closely with the Manager of Database S

SQL Server 2016 New Features

FORMATMESSAGE (Transact-SQL 2016)

In previous versions, FORMATMESSAGE built a message from strings located in sys.messages. In SQL Server 2016 you can also supply a format string. Examples in SQL Server 2016 Management Studio:

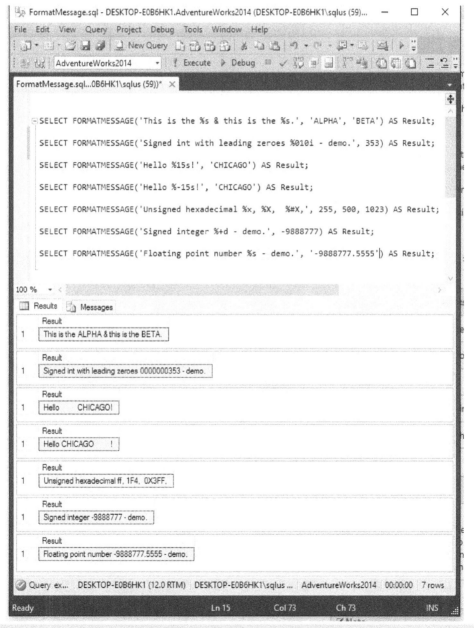

COMPRESS, DECOMPRESS (Transact-SQL 2016)

COMPRESS compresses the input expression using the GZIP algorithm. The output is byte array of type varbinary(max). DECOMPRESS restores the information to the uncompressed format.

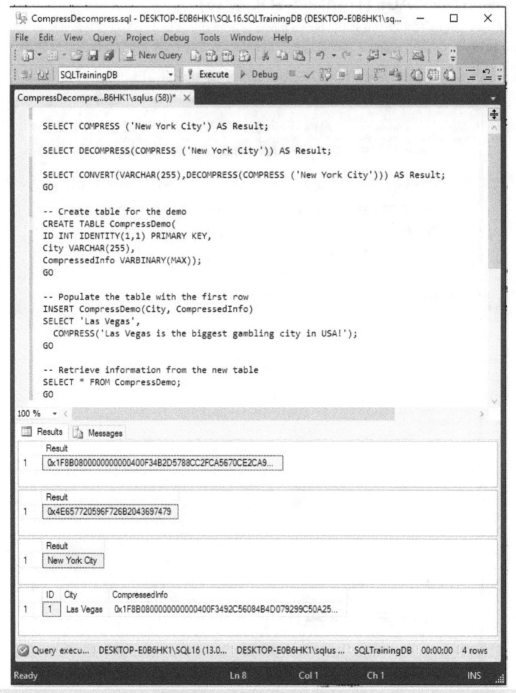

DATEDIFF_BIG, AT TIME ZONE (Transact-SQL 2016)

DATEDIFF_BIG returns the count (BIGINT) of the specified datepart boundaries crossed in the specified date range. DATEDIFF returns INT only. AT TIME ZONE converts an inputdate to the corresponding datetimeoffset value in the target time zone.

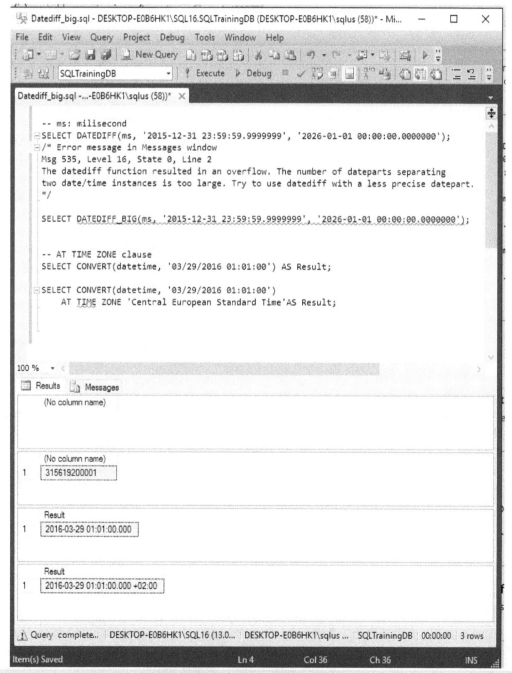

STRING_SPLIT (Transact-SQL 2016)

STRING_SPLIT function splits a list with separators to its members.

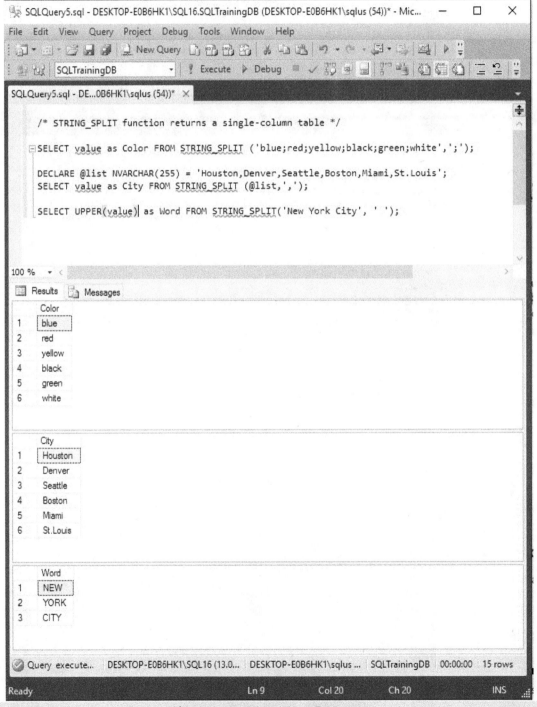

SET COMPATIBILITY LEVEL TO SQL SERVER 2016

Compatibility level should be 130 for a SQL Server 2016 database.

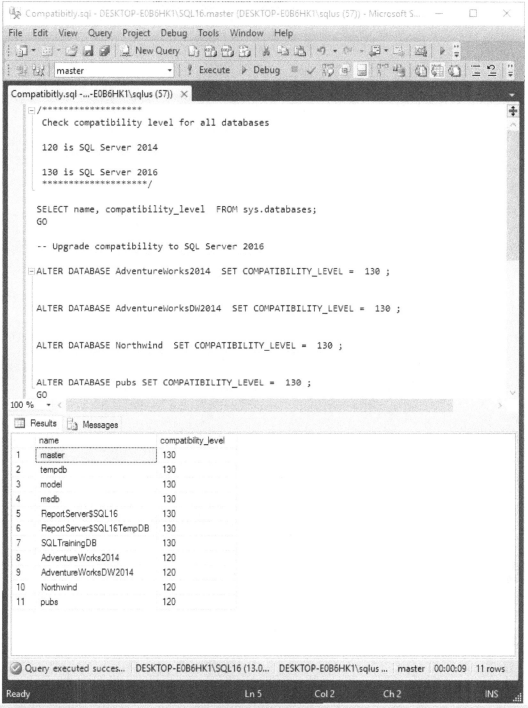

DROP TABLE IF EXISTS (Transact-SQL 2016)

DROP TABLE throws an error if the table does not exist. The new command is rerunnable.

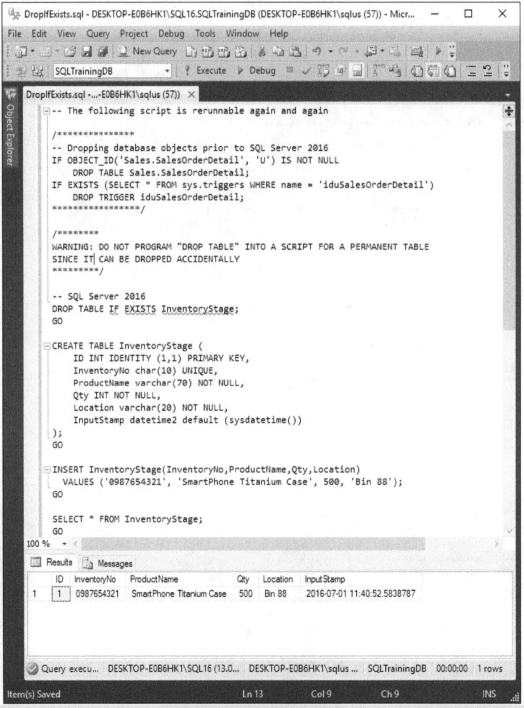

Dynamic Data Masking (SQL Server 2016)

Information in tables can be hidden partially from designated users.

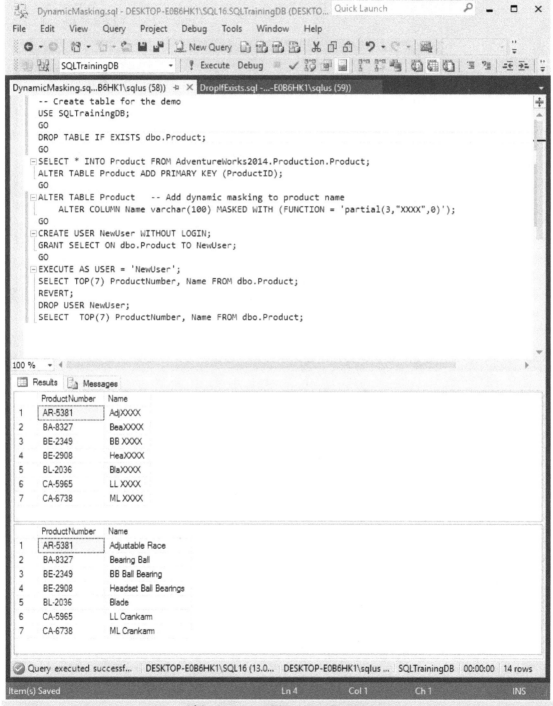

Dynamic Data Masking with email() Mask

email() is a predefined mask function.

Temporal Tables (SQL Server 2016)

Temporal table data changes are automatically logged into an associated history table.

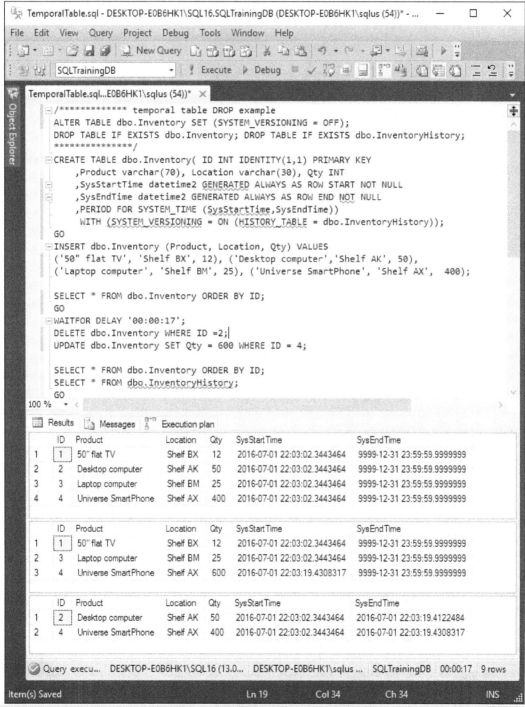

Object Explorer view of the temporal table Inventory with history table InventoryHistory.

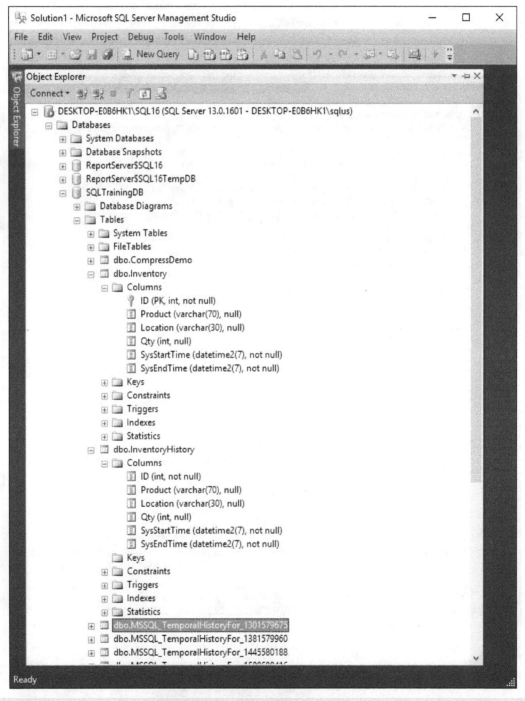

The regular table Product can be altered into a temporal (system-versioned) table.

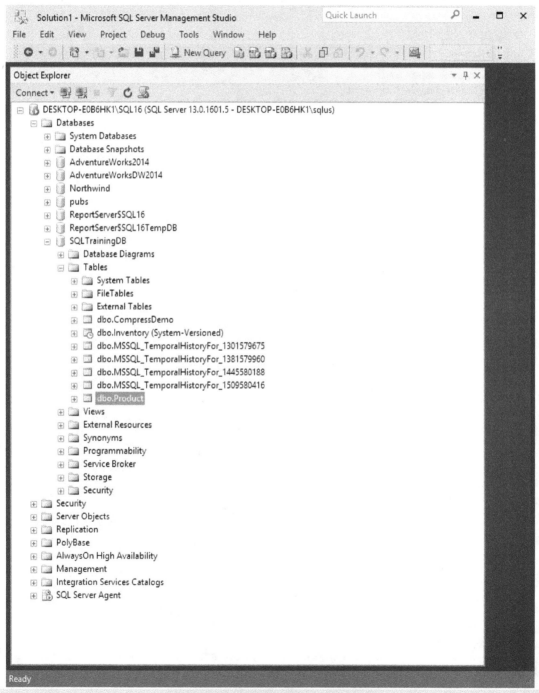

ALTER TABLE to temporal table (Transact-SQL 2016)

Demo of altering the Product table to a temporal table with history log in ProductHistory.

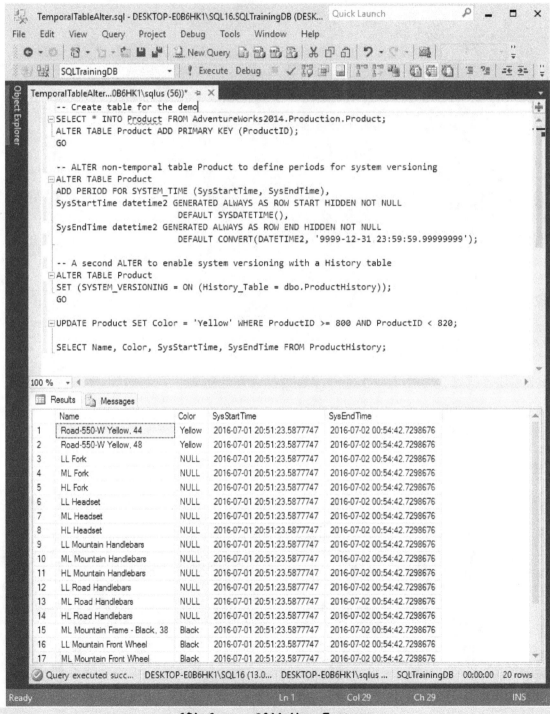

Object Explorer view of the Product table after system versioning (altering it to temporal).

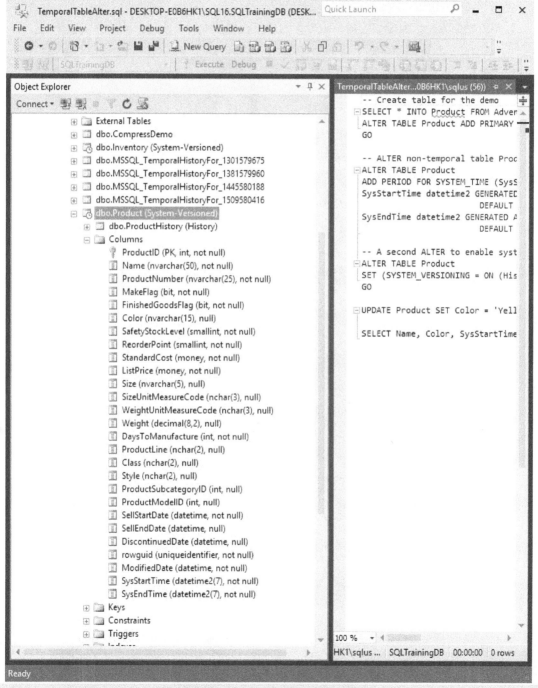

Create Temporal Table with Template (SQL Server 2016)

New System-Versioned Table creation can be launched from Object Explorer.

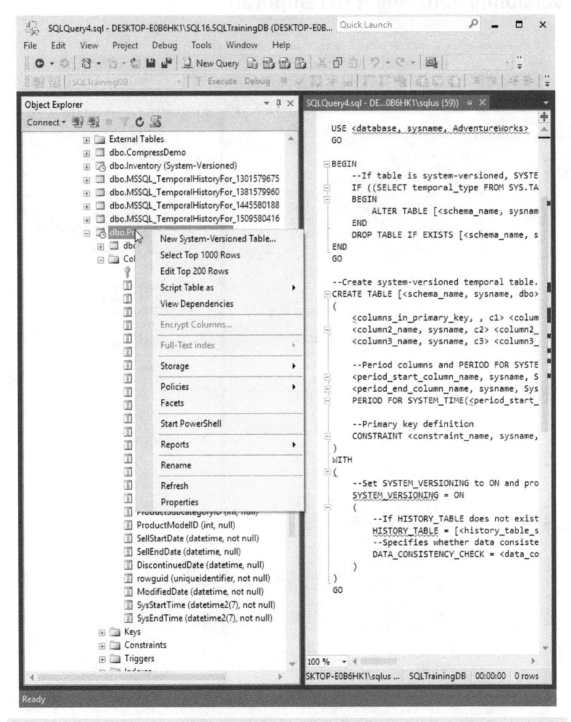

On the Query drop-down menu choose the Template Parameters option to start the creation.

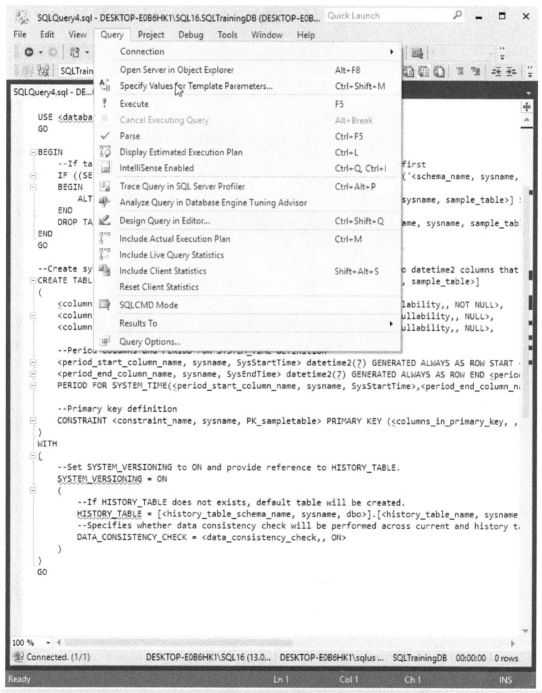

Specify the values for the parameters in the data entry window.

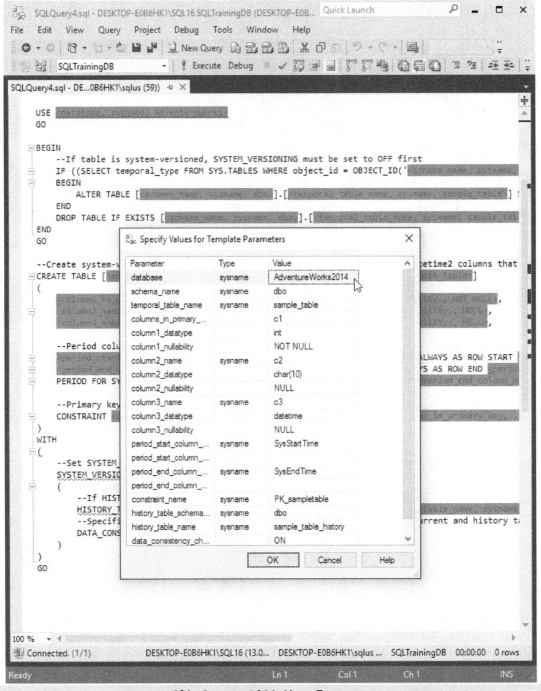

STRETCH DATABASE (SQL Server 2016)

Inactive records in the database moved into the cloud (Azure). No query changes are necessary. No application software changes necessary. The cloud records are available the same way as the local database records.

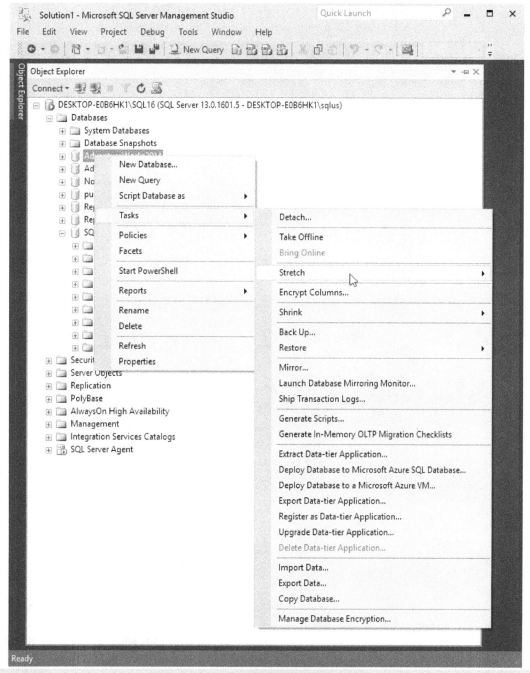

ANSI NULLS Setting (Transact-SQL 2016)

See demo below. Reference BOL article: https://msdn.microsoft.com/en-us/library/ms188048.aspx .

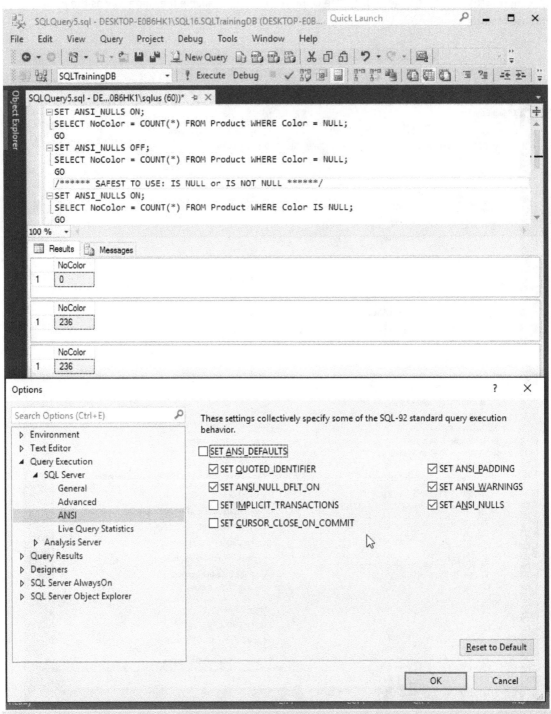

CHAPTER 1: SQL Server Sample & System Databases

AdventureWorks Series of OLTP Databases

AdventureWorks sample On Line Transaction Processing (OLTP) database has been introduced with SQL Server 2005 to replace the previous sample database Northwind, a fictional gourmet food items distributor. The intent of the AdventureWorks sample database is to support the business operations of AdventureWorks Cycles, a fictitious mountain, touring and road bike manufacturer. The company sells through dealer (reseller) network and directly online on the web. In addition to bikes, it sells frames and parts as well as accessories such as helmets, biking clothes and water bottles. The AdventureWorks2012 database image of "Touring-1000 Blue, 50" bike in the Production.ProductPhoto table.

T-SQL query to generate the list of tables of AdventureWorks2012 in 5 columns (instead of 1 column). The core query is simple. Presenting the results in 5 columns instead of 1 column adds a bit of complexity.

```
;WITH cteTableList  AS
(   SELECT CONCAT(SCHEMA_NAME(schema_id), '.', name)                                  AS TableName,
   (( ROW_NUMBER() OVER( ORDER BY CONCAT(SCHEMA_NAME(schema_id),'.', name)) ) % 5)   AS Remainder,
   (( ROW_NUMBER() OVER( ORDER BY CONCAT(SCHEMA_NAME(schema_id),'.', name)) - 1 )/ 5)  AS Quotient
                        FROM AdventureWorks2012.sys.tables),
CTE AS (   SELECT TableName, CASE WHEN Remainder=0 THEN 5 ELSE Remainder END AS Remainder, Quotient
        FROM cteTableList)
SELECT    MAX(CASE WHEN Remainder = 1 THEN TableName END),
          MAX(CASE WHEN Remainder = 2 THEN TableName END),
          MAX(CASE WHEN Remainder = 3 THEN TableName END),
          MAX(CASE WHEN Remainder = 4 THEN TableName END),
          MAX(CASE WHEN Remainder = 5 THEN TableName END)
FROM  CTE
GROUP  BY Quotient
ORDER  BY Quotient;
GO
```

The query result set in grid format: tables in AdventureWorks2012

dbo.AWBuildVersion	dbo.DatabaseLog	dbo.ErrorLog	HumanResources.Department	HumanResources.Employee
HumanResources.EmployeeDepartmentHistory	HumanResources.EmployeePayHistory	HumanResources.JobCandidate	HumanResources.Shift	Person.Address
Person.AddressType	Person.BusinessEntity	Person.BusinessEntityAddress	Person.BusinessEntityContact	Person.ContactType
Person.CountryRegion	Person.EmailAddress	Person.Password	Person.Person	Person.PersonPhone
Person.PhoneNumberType	Person.StateProvince	Production.BillOfMaterials	Production.Culture	Production.Document
Production.Illustration	Production.Location	Production.Product	Production.ProductCategory	Production.ProductCostHistory
Production.ProductDescription	Production.ProductDocument	Production.ProductInventory	Production.ProductListPriceHistory	Production.ProductModel
Production.ProductModelIllustration	Production.ProductModelProductDescriptionCulture	Production.ProductPhoto	Production.ProductProductPhoto	Production.ProductReview
Production.ProductSubcategory	Production.ScrapReason	Production.TransactionHistory	Production.TransactionHistoryArchive	Production.UnitMeasure
Production.WorkOrder	Production.WorkOrderRouting	Purchasing.ProductVendor	Purchasing.PurchaseOrderDetail	Purchasing.PurchaseOrderHeader
Purchasing.ShipMethod	Purchasing.Vendor	Sales.CountryRegionCurrency	Sales.CreditCard	Sales.Currency
Sales.CurrencyRate	Sales.Customer	Sales.PersonCreditCard	Sales.SalesOrderDetail	Sales.SalesOrderHeader
Sales.SalesOrderHeaderSalesReason	Sales.SalesPerson	Sales.SalesPersonQuotaHistory	Sales.SalesReason	Sales.SalesTaxRate
Sales.SalesTerritory	Sales.SalesTerritoryHistory	Sales.ShoppingCartItem	Sales.SpecialOffer	Sales.SpecialOfferProduct
Sales.Store	NULL	NULL	NULL	NULL

CHAPTER 1: SQL Server Sample & System Databases

Diagram of Person.Person & Related Tables

The database diagram below displays the Person.Person and related tables. PRIMARY KEYs are marked with a gold (in color monitor display) key. The "oo-------->" line is interpreted as many-to-one relationship. For example a person (one) can have one or more (many) credit cards. The "oo" side is the table with **FOREIGN KEY** (child table) referencing the gold key side table with the **PRIMARY KEY** (parent table).

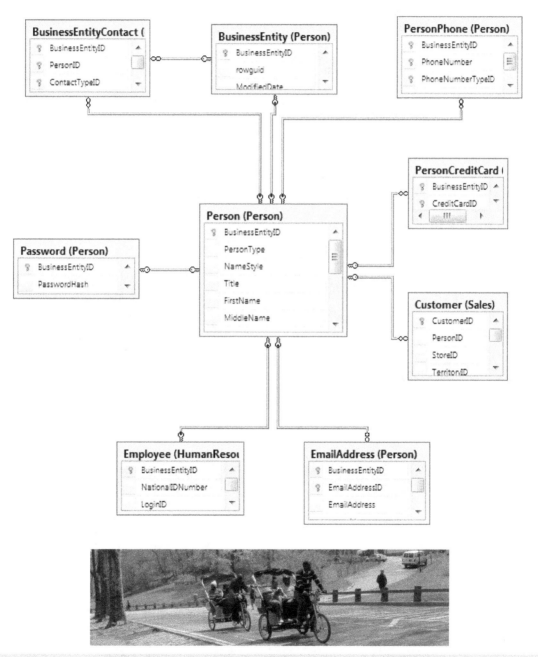

CHAPTER 1: SQL Server Sample & System Databases

Diagram of Sales.SalesOrderHeader and Related Tables

The database diagram below displays Sales.SalesOrderHeader and all tables related to it with **FOREIGN KEY** constraints. The SalesOrderHeader table stores the general information about each order. Line items, e.g. 5 Helmets at $30 each, are stored in the SalesOrderDetail table. SalesOrderHeader & SalesOrderDetail tables represent exclusive parent-child relationship also referred to as master-detail relationship.

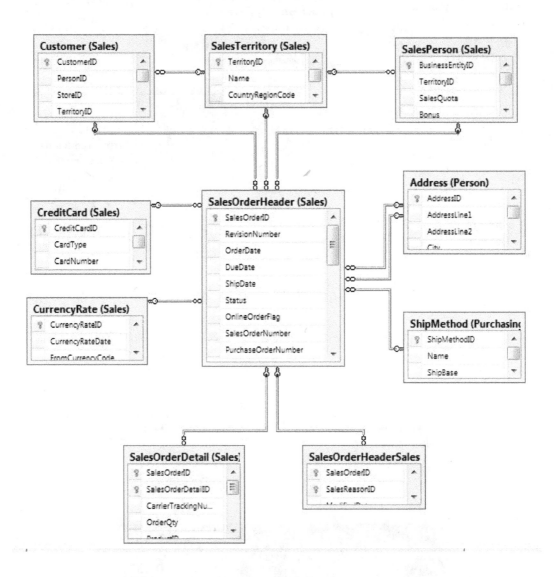

SELECT Query Basics

We have to use "light-weight" SQL (Structured Query Language) in the database design lessons. The reason is that rather difficult to discuss any database related topic without demonstration T-SQL scripts, in fact it would not make sense. **Relational database** and the **SQL language** are "married" to each other forever and ever.

The Simplest SELECT Statement

The simplest SELECT statement is "SELECT * FROM TableNameX" as demonstrated following. The "*" means wildcard inclusion of all columns in the table. Since there is no any other clause in the SELECT statement, it means also to retrieve all rows in the **table in no particular order**. Small tables which were populated in order are usually retrieved in order even though there is no ORDER BY clause. But this behaviour is purely coincidental. **Only ORDER BY clause can guarantee a sorted output.**

```
SELECT * FROM AdventureWorks2012.HumanResources.Department;
-- (16 row(s) affected)
```

DepartmentID	Name	GroupName	ModifiedDate
1	Engineering	Research and Development	2002-06-01 00:00:00.000
2	Tool Design	Research and Development	2002-06-01 00:00:00.000
3	Sales	Sales and Marketing	2002-06-01 00:00:00.000
4	Marketing	Sales and Marketing	2002-06-01 00:00:00.000
5	Purchasing	Inventory Management	2002-06-01 00:00:00.000
6	Research and Development	Research and Development	2002-06-01 00:00:00.000
7	Production	Manufacturing	2002-06-01 00:00:00.000
8	Production Control	Manufacturing	2002-06-01 00:00:00.000
9	Human Resources	Executive General and Administration	2002-06-01 00:00:00.000
10	Finance	Executive General and Administration	2002-06-01 00:00:00.000
11	Information Services	Executive General and Administration	2002-06-01 00:00:00.000
12	Document Control	Quality Assurance	2002-06-01 00:00:00.000
13	Quality Assurance	Quality Assurance	2002-06-01 00:00:00.000
14	Facilities and Maintenance	Executive General and Administration	2002-06-01 00:00:00.000
15	Shipping and Receiving	Inventory Management	2002-06-01 00:00:00.000
16	Executive	Executive General and Administration	2002-06-01 00:00:00.000

When tables are JOINed, SELECT * returns all the columns with all the data in the participant tables.

```
SELECT TOP 3 * FROM Sales.SalesOrderHeader H
            INNER JOIN Sales.SalesOrderDetail D
                ON H.SalesOrderID = D.SalesOrderID;
-- 121,317 rows in the JOIN
```

Query Result Set In Text Format

If no grid format available, text format can be used. While it works, it is a challenge to read it, but computer geeks are used to this kind of data dump.

```
/* SalesOrderID RevisionNumber OrderDate        DueDate         ShipDate        Status
OnlineOrderFlag SalesOrderNumber      PurchaseOrderNumber     AccountNumber CustomerID
SalesPersonID TerritoryID BillToAddressID ShipToAddressID ShipMethodID CreditCardID
CreditCardApprovalCode CurrencyRateID SubTotal        TaxAmt         Freight        TotalDue
Comment                                                                   rowguid
ModifiedDate        SalesOrderID SalesOrderDetailID CarrierTrackingNumber   OrderQty ProductID
SpecialOfferID UnitPrice       UnitPriceDiscount   LineTotal               rowguid
ModifiedDate
----------- -------------- ----------------------- ----------------------- ----------------------- ------ -------------- -------------------
------ ---------------------- ----------------------- -------------- ----------------------- --------------- -------------- -----------
- ---------------------- -------------- ----------------------- ----------------------- ----------------------- ----------------------- --------------------
----------------------------------------------------------------------------------------------------- -----------------------
--------- ---------------------- -------------- ----------------------- ----------------------- -------- ---------- -------------- -------------
-------- ----------------------

43735    3          2005-07-10 00:00:00.000 2005-07-22 00:00:00.000 2005-07-17 00:00:00.000 5     1
SO43735         NULL           10-4030-016522 16522    NULL     9      25384      25384
1      6526      1034619Vi33896    119     3578.27        286.2616       89.4568
3953.9884       NULL                                                     98F80245-
C398-4562-BDAF-EA3E9A0DDFAC 2005-07-17 00:00:00.000 43735      391       NULL          1
749    1       3578.27       0.00        3578.270000        74838EF7-FDEB-4EB3-8978-
BA310FBA82E6 2005-07-10 00:00:00.000
43736    3          2005-07-10 00:00:00.000 2005-07-22 00:00:00.000 2005-07-17 00:00:00.000 5     1
SO43736         NULL           10-4030-011002 11002    NULL     9      20336      20336
1      1416      1135092Vi7270     119     3399.99        271.9992       84.9998
3756.989        NULL                                                     C14E29E7-
DB11-44EF-943E-143925A5A9AE 2005-07-17 00:00:00.000 43736      392       NULL          1
773    1       3399.99       0.00        3399.990000        3A0229FA-0A03-4126-
97CE-C3425968B670 2005-07-10 00:00:00.000
43737    3          2005-07-11 00:00:00.000 2005-07-23 00:00:00.000 2005-07-18 00:00:00.000 5     1
SO43737         NULL           10-4030-013261 13261    NULL     8      29772      29772
1      NULL      NULL          136     3578.27        286.2616       89.4568        3953.9884
NULL                                                     0B3E274D-E5A8-4E8C-A417-
0EAFABCFF162 2005-07-18 00:00:00.000 43737      393       NULL          1    750    1
3578.27       0.00        3578.270000        65AFCCE8-CA28-41C4-9A07-0265FB2DA5C8
2005-07-11 00:00:00.000

(3 row(s) affected)  */
```

SELECT Query with WHERE Clause Predicate

Query to demonstrate how can we be selective with columns, furthermore, filter returned rows (WHERE clause) and sort them (ORDER BY clause).

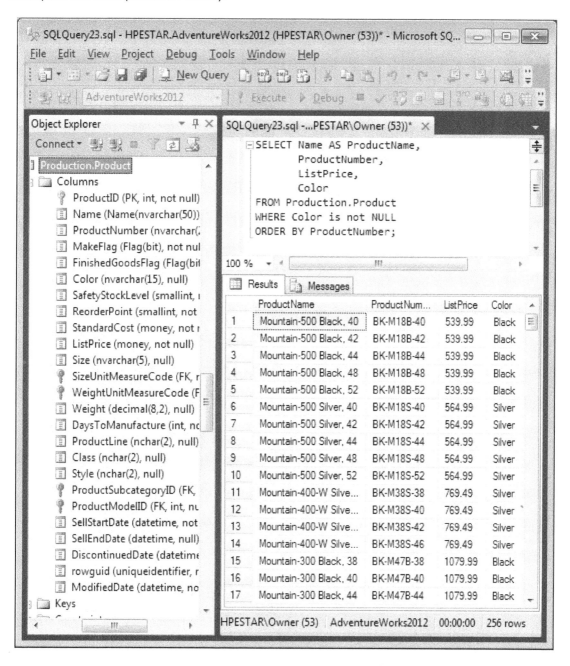

Aggregating Data with GROUP BY Query

The second basic query is GROUP BY aggregation. It can be used to survey data at a high level.

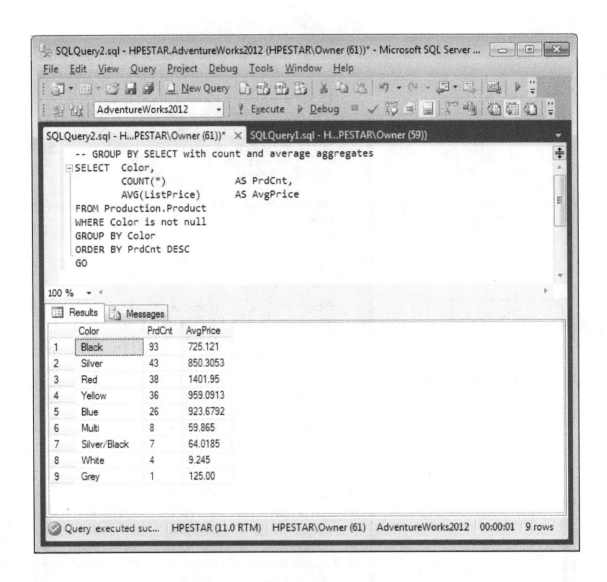

NOTE
GROUP BY aggregate queries can efficiently "fingerprint" (profile) data in tables, even millions of rows.
GROUP BY aggregates form the computational base of Business Intelligence.

GROUP BY Query with 2 Tables & ORDER BY for Sorting

JOINing two tables on matching KEYs, FOREIGN KEY to PRIMARY KEY, to combine the data contents in a consistent fashion.

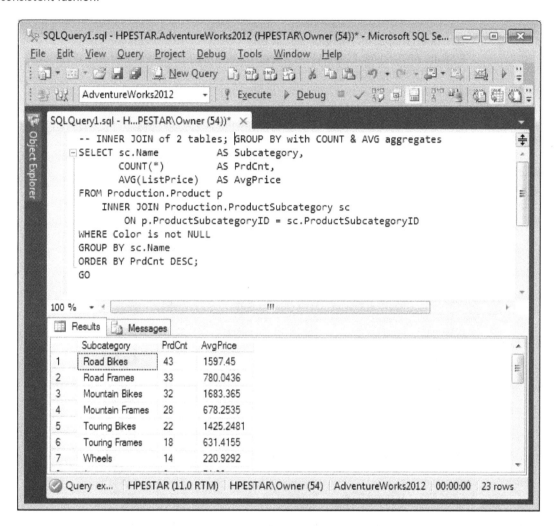

LEN(), DATALENGTH(), LTRIM() & RTRIM() Functions

The LEN() function counts characters without the trailing spaces. DATALENGTH() counts storage bytes including trailing spaces. LTRIM() trims leading spaces, RTRIM() trims trailing spaces.

```
DECLARE @W varchar(32)= CHAR(32)+'Denver'+CHAR(32);
DECLARE @UW nvarchar(32) = CHAR(32)+N'MEGŐRZÉSE'+CHAR(32);  -- UNICODE 2 bytes per character
SELECT Length=LEN(@W), DLength=DATALENGTH (@W);                              -- 7  8
SELECT Length=LEN(@UW), DLength=DATALENGTH (@UW);                           -- 10 22
SELECT Length=LEN(LTRIM(RTRIM(@W))), DLength=DATALENGTH (LTRIM(RTRIM(@W)));  -- 6  6
SELECT Length=LEN(LTRIM(RTRIM(@UW))), DLength=DATALENGTH (LTRIM(RTRIM(@UW))); -- 9 18
```

CHAPTER 1: SQL Server Sample & System Databases

Finding All Accessories in Production.Product Table

Query to list all accessories (a category) for sale.

```
USE AdventureWorks2012;

SELECT          UPPER(PC.Name) AS Category, PSC.Name        AS Subcategory,
                P.Name AS Product, FORMAT(ListPrice, 'c', 'en-US')   AS ListPrice,
                FORMAT(StandardCost, 'c', 'en-US')           AS StandardCost
FROM Production.Product AS P
   INNER JOIN Production.ProductSubcategory AS PSC
            ON PSC.ProductSubcategoryID = P.ProductSubcategoryID
   INNER JOIN Production.ProductCategory AS PC
            ON PC.ProductCategoryID = PSC.ProductCategoryID
WHERE PC.Name = 'Accessories'
ORDER BY Category, Subcategory, Product;
```

Category	Subcategory	Product	ListPrice	StandardCost
ACCESSORIES	Bike Racks	Hitch Rack - 4-Bike	$120.00	$44.88
ACCESSORIES	Bike Stands	All-Purpose Bike Stand	$159.00	$59.47
ACCESSORIES	Bottles and Cages	Mountain Bottle Cage	$9.99	$3.74
ACCESSORIES	Bottles and Cages	Road Bottle Cage	$8.99	$3.36
ACCESSORIES	Bottles and Cages	Water Bottle - 30 oz.	$4.99	$1.87
ACCESSORIES	Cleaners	Bike Wash - Dissolver	$7.95	$2.97
ACCESSORIES	Fenders	Fender Set - Mountain	$21.98	$8.22
ACCESSORIES	Helmets	Sport-100 Helmet, Black	$34.99	$13.09
ACCESSORIES	Helmets	Sport-100 Helmet, Blue	$34.99	$13.09
ACCESSORIES	Helmets	Sport-100 Helmet, Red	$34.99	$13.09
ACCESSORIES	Hydration Packs	Hydration Pack - 70 oz.	$54.99	$20.57
ACCESSORIES	Lights	Headlights - Dual-Beam	$34.99	$14.43
ACCESSORIES	Lights	Headlights - Weatherproof	$44.99	$18.56
ACCESSORIES	Lights	Taillights - Battery-Powered	$13.99	$5.77
ACCESSORIES	Locks	Cable Lock	$25.00	$10.31
ACCESSORIES	Panniers	Touring-Panniers, Large	$125.00	$51.56
ACCESSORIES	Pumps	Minipump	$19.99	$8.25
ACCESSORIES	Pumps	Mountain Pump	$24.99	$10.31
ACCESSORIES	Tires and Tubes	HL Mountain Tire	$35.00	$13.09
ACCESSORIES	Tires and Tubes	HL Road Tire	$32.60	$12.19
ACCESSORIES	Tires and Tubes	LL Mountain Tire	$24.99	$9.35
ACCESSORIES	Tires and Tubes	LL Road Tire	$21.49	$8.04
ACCESSORIES	Tires and Tubes	ML Mountain Tire	$29.99	$11.22
ACCESSORIES	Tires and Tubes	ML Road Tire	$24.99	$9.35
ACCESSORIES	Tires and Tubes	Mountain Tire Tube	$4.99	$1.87
ACCESSORIES	Tires and Tubes	Patch Kit/8 Patches	$2.29	$0.86
ACCESSORIES	Tires and Tubes	Road Tire Tube	$3.99	$1.49
ACCESSORIES	Tires and Tubes	Touring Tire	$28.99	$10.84
ACCESSORIES	Tires and Tubes	Touring Tire Tube	$4.99	$1.87

How Can SQL Work without Looping?

Looping is implicit in the SQL language. The commands are set oriented and carried out for each member of the set be it 5 or 500 millions in an unordered manner.

SELECT * FROM AdventureWorks2012.Sales.SalesOrderDetail;   (121317 row(s) affected)

SQL Server database engine looped through internally on all rows in SalesOrderDetail table in an unordered way. In fact the database engine may have used some ordering for efficiency, but that behaviour is a blackbox as far as programming concerned. Implicit looping makes SQL statements so simple, yet immensely powerful for information access from low level to high level.

Single-Valued SQL Queries

Single-valued SQL queries are very important because **we can use them where ever the T-SQL syntax requires a single value just by enclosing the query in parenthesis**. The next T-SQL query returns a single value, a cell from the table which is the intersection of a row and a column.

SELECT ListPrice FROM AdventureWorks2012.Production.Product WHERE ProductID = 800;
-- (1 row(s) affected)

ListPrice
1120.49

The ">" comparison operator requires a single value on the right hand side so we plug in the single-valued query. The WHERE condition is evaluated for each row (implicit looping).

SELECT ProductID, Name AS ProductName, ListPrice
FROM AdventureWorks2012.Production.Product   -- 504 rows
WHERE ListPrice > 2 *   (
                SELECT ListPrice FROM AdventureWorks2012.Production.Product
                WHERE ProductID = 800
)
ORDER BY ListPrice DESC, ProductName;
-- (35 row(s) affected) - Partial results.

ProductID	ProductName	ListPrice
750	Road-150 Red, 44	3578.27
751	Road-150 Red, 48	3578.27
752	Road-150 Red, 52	3578.27
753	Road-150 Red, 56	3578.27
749	Road-150 Red, 62	3578.27
771	Mountain-100 Silver, 38	3399.99

Data Dictionary Description of Tables in the Sales Schema

It is not easy to understand a database with 70 tables, even harder with 2,000 tables. Documentation is very helpful, if not essential, for any database. SQL Server provides Data Dictionary facility for documenting tables and other objects in the database. Data which describes the design & structure of a database is called **metadata**. Here is the high level documentation of tables in the Sales schema using the fn_listextendedproperty system function.

```
SELECT   CONCAT('Sales.', objname COLLATE DATABASE_DEFAULT)      AS TableName,
         value                                                   AS [Description]
FROM fn_listextendedproperty (NULL, 'schema', 'Sales', 'table', default, NULL, NULL)
ORDER BY TableName;
```

TableName	Description
Sales.ContactCreditCard	Cross-reference table mapping customers in the Contact table to their credit card information in the CreditCard table.
Sales.CountryRegionCurrency	Cross-reference table mapping ISO currency codes to a country or region.
Sales.CreditCard	Customer credit card information.
Sales.Currency	Lookup table containing standard ISO currencies.
Sales.CurrencyRate	Currency exchange rates.
Sales.Customer	Current customer information. Also see the Individual and Store tables.
Sales.CustomerAddress	Cross-reference table mapping customers to their address(es).
Sales.Individual	Demographic data about customers that purchase Adventure Works products online.
Sales.SalesOrderDetail	Individual products associated with a specific sales order. See SalesOrderHeader.
Sales.SalesOrderHeader	General sales order information.
Sales.SalesOrderHeaderSalesReason	Cross-reference table mapping sales orders to sales reason codes.
Sales.SalesPerson	Sales representative current information.
Sales.SalesPersonQuotaHistory	Sales performance tracking.
Sales.SalesReason	Lookup table of customer purchase reasons.
Sales.SalesTaxRate	Tax rate lookup table.
Sales.SalesTerritory	Sales territory lookup table.
Sales.SalesTerritoryHistory	Sales representative transfers to other sales territories.
Sales.ShoppingCartItem	Contains online customer orders until the order is submitted or cancelled.
Sales.SpecialOffer	Sale discounts lookup table.
Sales.SpecialOfferProduct	Cross-reference table mapping products to special offer discounts.
Sales.Store	Customers (resellers) of Adventure Works products.
Sales.StoreContact	Cross-reference table mapping stores and their employees.

CHAPTER 1: SQL Server Sample & System Databases

NULL Values in Tables & Query Results

NULL means no value. If so why do we capitalize it? We don't have to. Somehow, it became a custom in the RDBMS industry, nobody knows anymore how it started. Since the U.S. default collation for server and databases are case insensitive, we can just use "null" as well. **NULL value is different from empty string (") or 0 (zero) which can be tested by the "=" or "!=" operators.** If a database table does not have a value in a cell for whatever reason, it is marked (flagged) as NULL by the database engine. When a value is entered, the NULL marking goes away. **NULL values can be tested by "IS NULL" or "IS NOT NULL" operators, but not the "=" or "!=" operators.**

The likelihood is high that the color attribute is not applicable to items like tire tube, that is the reason that some cell values were left unassigned (null).

```
SELECT TOP 5    Name                        AS ProductName,
                ProductNumber,
                ListPrice,
                Color
FROM AdventureWorks2012.Production.Product  WHERE Color IS NULL
ORDER BY ProductName DESC;
```

ProductName	ProductNumber	ListPrice	Color
Water Bottle - 30 oz.	WB-H098	4.99	NULL
Touring Tire Tube	TT-T092	4.99	NULL
Touring Tire	TI-T723	28.99	NULL
Touring Rim	RM-T801	0.00	NULL
Touring End Caps	EC-T209	0.00	NULL

We can do random selection as well and get a mix of products with color and null value.

```
SELECT TOP 5    Name AS ProductName, ProductNumber, ListPrice, Color
FROM AdventureWorks2012.Production.Product
ORDER BY NEWID();        -- Random sort
```

ProductName	ProductNumber	ListPrice	Color
Touring-1000 Yellow, 46	BK-T79Y-46	2384.07	Yellow
HL Spindle/Axle	SD-9872	0.00	NULL
ML Mountain Tire	TI-M602	29.99	NULL
Road-650 Red, 60	BK-R50R-60	782.99	Red
Pinch Bolt	PB-6109	0.00	NULL

NULL Values Generated by Queries

NULL values can be generated by queries as well. Typically, LEFT JOIN, RIGHT JOIN and some functions generate NULLs. The meaning of OUTER JOINs: include no-match rows from the left or right table in addition to the matching rows.

```
SELECT TOP 5
            PS.Name                          AS Category,
            P.Name                           AS ProductName,
            ProductNumber,
            ListPrice,
            Color
FROM AdventureWorks2012.Production.Product P
  RIGHT JOIN AdventureWorks2012.Production.ProductSubcategory PS
        ON PS.ProductSubcategoryID = P.ProductSubcategoryID
    AND ListPrice >= 3500.0
ORDER BY newid();
GO
```

Category	ProductName	ProductNumber	ListPrice	Color
Road Bikes	Road-150 Red, 62	BK-R93R-62	3578.27	Red
Road Bikes	Road-150 Red, 52	BK-R93R-52	3578.27	Red
Bib-Shorts	NULL	NULL	NULL	NULL
Socks	NULL	NULL	NULL	NULL
Cranksets	NULL	NULL	NULL	NULL

Some system functions, like the brand new TRY_CONVERT(), can generate NULL values as well. If the PostalCode cannot be converted into an integer, TRY_CONVERT() returns NULL.

```
SELECT TOP 5    ConvertedZip = TRY_CONVERT(INT, PostalCode),
            AddressLine1,    City, PostalCode
FROM Person.Address
ORDER by newid();
```

ConvertedZip	AddressLine1	City	PostalCode
91945	5979 El Pueblo	Lemon Grove	91945
NULL	7859 Green Valley Road	London	W1V 5RN
3220	6004 Peabody Road	Geelong	3220
NULL	6713 Eaker Way	Burnaby	V3J 6Z3
NULL	5153 Hackamore Lane	Shawnee	V8Z 4N5

The SOUNDEX() Function to Check Sound Alikes

The soundex() function is very interesting for testing different spelling of words such as names.

```
USE AdventureWorks2012;
GO
```

```
SELECT DISTINCT LastName FROM Person.Person
WHERE soundex(LastName)  = soundex('Steel');
GO
```

LastName
Seidel
Sotelo
Stahl
Steel
Steele

```
SELECT DISTINCT LastName FROM Person.Person
WHERE soundex(LastName)  = soundex('Brown');
GO
```

LastName
Bourne
Brian
Brown
Browne
Bruno

```
SELECT DISTINCT FirstName FROM Person.Person
WHERE soundex(FirstName)  = soundex('Mary');
GO
```

FirstName
Mari
Maria
María
Mariah
Marie
Mario
Mary
Mary Lou
Mayra

Building an FK-PK Diagram in AdventureWorks2012

The **FOREIGN KEY - PRIMARY KEY** diagram of AdventureWorks2012 database with over 70 tables can be built just by adding the tables to the diagram. The FK-PK lines are automatically drawn. An FK-PK line represents a predefined referential constraint.

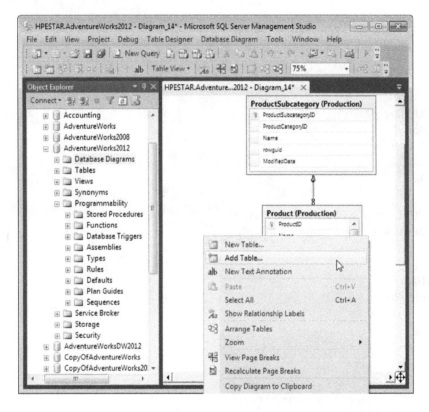

While all tables are important in a database, tables with the most connections play central roles, in a way analogous to the Sun with planets around it.

```
-- PRIMARY KEY tables with the most FOREIGN KEY references
SELECT              schema_name(schema_id)        AS SchemaName,
                    o.name                        AS PKTable,
                    count(*)                      AS FKCount
FROM sys.sysforeignkeys s    INNER JOIN sys.objects o      ON s.rkeyid = o.object_id
GROUP BY schema_id, o.name    HAVING count(*) >= 5    ORDER BY FKCount DESC;
```

SchemaName	PKTable	FKCount
Production	Product	14
Person	Person	7
HumanResources	Employee	6
Person	BusinessEntity	5
Sales	SalesTerritory	5

AdventureWorksDW Data Warehouse Database

AdventureWorksDW contains second hand data only since it is a Data Warehouse database. All the data originates from other sources such as the AdventureWorks OLTP database and Excel worksheets. The tables in the data warehousing database are divided between two groups: dimension tables and fact tables.

Diagram of a Star Schema in AdventureWorksDW2012

The high level star schema diagram in AdventureWorksDW2012 Data Warehouse database with FactResellerSales fact table and related dimension tables. The temporal dimension table DimDate plays a central role in Business Intelligence data analytics.

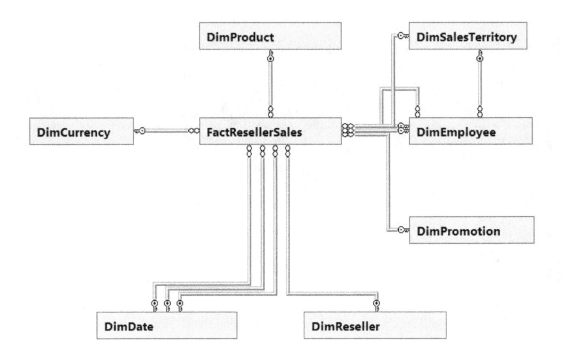

Distribution of **PRIMARY KEY - FOREIGN KEY** relationships can be generated from metadata (system views) for the entire Data Warehouse.

SELECT   schema_name(schema_id) AS SchemaName, o.name AS PKTable, count(*) AS FKCount
FROM sys.sysforeignkeys s   INNER JOIN sys.objects o   ON s.rkeyid = o.object_id
GROUP BY schema_id, o.name HAVING COUNT(*) > 2 ORDER BY FKCount DESC;

SchemaName	PKTable	FKCount
dbo	DimDate	12
dbo	DimCurrency	4
dbo	DimSalesTerritory	4
dbo	DimEmployee	3
dbo	DimProduct	3

AdventureWorks2008 Sample Database

There were substantial changes made from the prior version of the sample database. Among them demonstration use of the **hierarchyid** data type which has been introduced with SS 2008 to support sophisticated tree hierarchy processing. In addition employee, customer and dealer PRIMARY KEYs are pooled together and called BusinessEntityID.

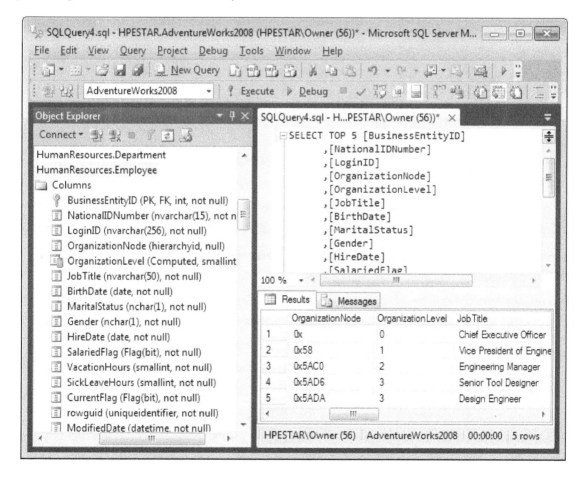

AdventureWorks2012 Sample Database

There were no apparent design changes made from the prior version of the sample database. A significant content change: dates were advanced 4 years. An OrderDate (Sales.SalesOrderHeader table) of 2004-02-01 in previous versions is now 2008-02-01.

The OrderDate statistics in the two sample databases.

```
SELECT  [Year]           = YEAR(OrderDate),       OrderCount      = COUNT(*)
FROM AdventureWorks2008.Sales.SalesOrderHeader GROUP BY YEAR(OrderDate)
ORDER BY [Year];
```

Year	OrderCount
2001	1379
2002	3692
2003	12443
2004	13951

```
SELECT  [Year]          = YEAR(OrderDate),       OrderCount      = COUNT(*)
FROM AdventureWorks2012.Sales.SalesOrderHeader GROUP BY YEAR(OrderDate)
ORDER BY [Year];
```

Year	OrderCount
2005	1379
2006	3692
2007	12443
2008	13951

Starting with SQL Server 2014, numeric figures, among others, can be formatted with the FORMAT function.

```
SELECT  [Year]           = YEAR(OrderDate),
            OrderCount       = FORMAT(COUNT(*), '###,###')
FROM AdventureWorks2012.Sales.SalesOrderHeader
GROUP BY YEAR(OrderDate)  ORDER BY [Year];
```

Year	OrderCount
2005	1,379
2006	3,692
2007	12,443
2008	13,951

Production.Product and Related Tables

The Product table is the "center" of the database. The reason is that AdventureWorks Cycles is a product base company selling through dealers and directly to consumers through the internet. You may wonder why are we pushing **FOREIGN KEY - PRIMARY KEY** relationship so vehemently? Because there is nothing else to a database just **well-designed tables and their connections which are FK-PK constraints**.

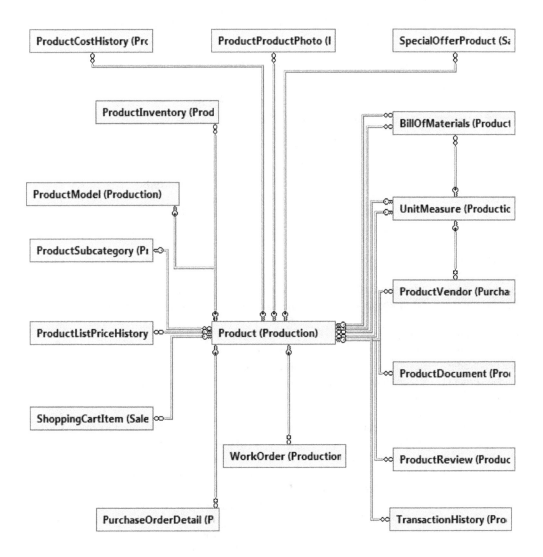

Descriptions of Columns in Production.Product Table

Queries to list the description of table and columns from Extended Property (data dictionary).

```
USE AdventureWorks2012;
SELECT          objname AS TableName, value        AS [Description]
FROM fn_listextendedproperty(    NULL, 'schema', 'Production', 'table', 'Product', NULL, NULL);
```

TableName	Description
Product	Products sold or used in the manfacturing of sold products.

```
SELECT          'Production.Product'              AS TableName,           -- String literal
                objname                           AS ColumnName,
                value                             AS [Description]
FROM fn_listextendedproperty(    NULL, 'schema', 'Production', 'table',
                                 'Product', 'column', default);
```

TableName	ColumnName	Description
Production.Product	ProductID	Primary key for Product records.
Production.Product	Name	Name of the product.
Production.Product	ProductNumber	Unique product identification number.
Production.Product	MakeFlag	0 = Product is purchased, 1 = Product is manufactured in-house.
Production.Product	FinishedGoodsFlag	0 = Product is not a salable item. 1 = Product is salable.
Production.Product	Color	Product color.
Production.Product	SafetyStockLevel	Minimum inventory quantity.
Production.Product	ReorderPoint	Inventory level that triggers a purchase order or work order.
Production.Product	StandardCost	Standard cost of the product.
Production.Product	ListPrice	Selling price.
Production.Product	Size	Product size.
Production.Product	SizeUnitMeasureCode	Unit of measure for Size column.
Production.Product	WeightUnitMeasureCode	Unit of measure for Weight column.
Production.Product	Weight	Product weight.
Production.Product	DaysToManufacture	Number of days required to manufacture the product.
Production.Product	ProductLine	R = Road, M = Mountain, T = Touring, S = Standard
Production.Product	Class	H = High, M = Medium, L = Low
Production.Product	Style	W = Womens, M = Mens, U = Universal
Production.Product	ProductSubcategoryID	Product is a member of this product subcategory. Foreign key to ProductSubCategory.ProductSubCategoryID.
Production.Product	ProductModelID	Product is a member of this product model. Foreign key to ProductModel.ProductModelID.
Production.Product	SellStartDate	Date the product was available for sale.
Production.Product	SellEndDate	Date the product was no longer available for sale.
Production.Product	DiscontinuedDate	Date the product was discontinued.
Production.Product	rowguid	ROWGUIDCOL number uniquely identifying the record. Used to support a merge replication sample.
Production.Product	ModifiedDate	Date and time the record was last updated.

Mountain Bikes in Production.Product Table

Query to list all mountain bikes offered for sale by AdventureWorks Cycles with category, subcategory, list price and standard cost information.

```
USE AdventureWorks2012;
GO
SELECT   UPPER(PC.Name) AS Category, PSC.Name AS Subcategory,
         P.Name AS Product, FORMAT(ListPrice, 'c', 'en-US') AS ListPrice,
         FORMAT(StandardCost, 'c', 'en-US') AS StandardCost
FROM Production.Product AS P
  INNER JOIN Production.ProductSubcategory AS PSC
          ON PSC.ProductSubcategoryID = P.ProductSubcategoryID
  INNER JOIN Production.ProductCategory AS PC
          ON PC.ProductCategoryID = PSC.ProductCategoryID
WHERE PSC.Name = 'Mountain Bikes'
ORDER BY Category, Subcategory, Product;
```

Category	Subcategory	Product	ListPrice	StandardCost
BIKES	Mountain Bikes	Mountain-100 Black, 38	$3,374.99	$1,898.09
BIKES	Mountain Bikes	Mountain-100 Black, 42	$3,374.99	$1,898.09
BIKES	Mountain Bikes	Mountain-100 Black, 44	$3,374.99	$1,898.09
BIKES	Mountain Bikes	Mountain-100 Black, 48	$3,374.99	$1,898.09
BIKES	Mountain Bikes	Mountain-100 Silver, 38	$3,399.99	$1,912.15
BIKES	Mountain Bikes	Mountain-100 Silver, 42	$3,399.99	$1,912.15
BIKES	Mountain Bikes	Mountain-100 Silver, 44	$3,399.99	$1,912.15
BIKES	Mountain Bikes	Mountain-100 Silver, 48	$3,399.99	$1,912.15
BIKES	Mountain Bikes	Mountain-200 Black, 38	$2,294.99	$1,251.98
BIKES	Mountain Bikes	Mountain-200 Black, 42	$2,294.99	$1,251.98
BIKES	Mountain Bikes	Mountain-200 Black, 46	$2,294.99	$1,251.98
BIKES	Mountain Bikes	Mountain-200 Silver, 38	$2,319.99	$1,265.62
BIKES	Mountain Bikes	Mountain-200 Silver, 42	$2,319.99	$1,265.62
BIKES	Mountain Bikes	Mountain-200 Silver, 46	$2,319.99	$1,265.62
BIKES	Mountain Bikes	Mountain-300 Black, 38	$1,079.99	$598.44
BIKES	Mountain Bikes	Mountain-300 Black, 40	$1,079.99	$598.44
BIKES	Mountain Bikes	Mountain-300 Black, 44	$1,079.99	$598.44
BIKES	Mountain Bikes	Mountain-300 Black, 48	$1,079.99	$598.44
BIKES	Mountain Bikes	Mountain-400-W Silver, 38	$769.49	$419.78
BIKES	Mountain Bikes	Mountain-400-W Silver, 40	$769.49	$419.78
BIKES	Mountain Bikes	Mountain-400-W Silver, 42	$769.49	$419.78
BIKES	Mountain Bikes	Mountain-400-W Silver, 46	$769.49	$419.78
BIKES	Mountain Bikes	Mountain-500 Black, 40	$539.99	$294.58
BIKES	Mountain Bikes	Mountain-500 Black, 42	$539.99	$294.58
BIKES	Mountain Bikes	Mountain-500 Black, 44	$539.99	$294.58
BIKES	Mountain Bikes	Mountain-500 Black, 48	$539.99	$294.58
BIKES	Mountain Bikes	Mountain-500 Black, 52	$539.99	$294.58
BIKES	Mountain Bikes	Mountain-500 Silver, 40	$564.99	$308.22
BIKES	Mountain Bikes	Mountain-500 Silver, 42	$564.99	$308.22
BIKES	Mountain Bikes	Mountain-500 Silver, 44	$564.99	$308.22
BIKES	Mountain Bikes	Mountain-500 Silver, 48	$564.99	$308.22
BIKES	Mountain Bikes	Mountain-500 Silver, 52	$564.99	$308.22

Prior SQL Server Sample Databases

There are two other sample databases used in the releases of SQL Server: **Northwind** and **pubs**. Northwind has been introduced with SQL Server 7.0 in 1998. That SQL Server version had very short lifetime, replaced with SQL Server 2000 in year 2000. The pubs sample database originates from the time Microsoft & Sybase worked jointly on the database server project around 1990. Despite the relative simplicity of pre-2005 sample databases, they were good enough to demonstrate basic RDBMS SQL queries.

Book sales summary GROUP BY aggregation query.

```
USE pubs;

SELECT pub_name              AS Publisher,
    au_lname                 AS Author,
    title                    AS Title,
    SUM(qty)                 AS SoldQty
FROM   authors
    INNER JOIN titleauthor
        ON authors.au_id = titleauthor.au_id
    INNER JOIN titles
        ON titles.title_id = titleauthor.title_id
    INNER JOIN publishers
        ON publishers.pub_id = titles.pub_id
    INNER JOIN sales
        ON sales.title_id = titles.title_id
GROUP  BY pub_name,    au_lname,      title
ORDER BY Publisher, Author, Title;
-- (23 row(s) affected) - Partial results.
```

Publisher	Author	Title
Algodata Infosystems	Bennet	The Busy Executive's Database Guide
Algodata Infosystems	Carson	But Is It User Friendly?
Algodata Infosystems	Dull	Secrets of Silicon Valley
Algodata Infosystems	Green	The Busy Executive's Database Guide
Algodata Infosystems	Hunter	Secrets of Silicon Valley
Algodata Infosystems	MacFeather	Cooking with Computers: Surreptitious Balance Sheets
Algodata Infosystems	O'Leary	Cooking with Computers: Surreptitious Balance Sheets
Algodata Infosystems	Straight	Straight Talk About Computers
Binnet & Hardley	Blotchet-Halls	Fifty Years in Buckingham Palace Kitchens
Binnet & Hardley	DeFrance	The Gourmet Microwave

Northwind Sample Database

The Northwind sample database contains well-prepared sales data for a fictitious company called Northwind Traders, which imports & exports specialty gourmet foods & drinks from wholesale suppliers around the world. The company's sales offices are located in Seattle and London. Among the gourmet food item products: Carnarvon Tigers, Teatime Chocolate Biscuits, Sir Rodney's Marmalade, Sir Rodney's Scones, Gustaf's Knäckebröd, Tunnbröd & Guaraná Fantástica.

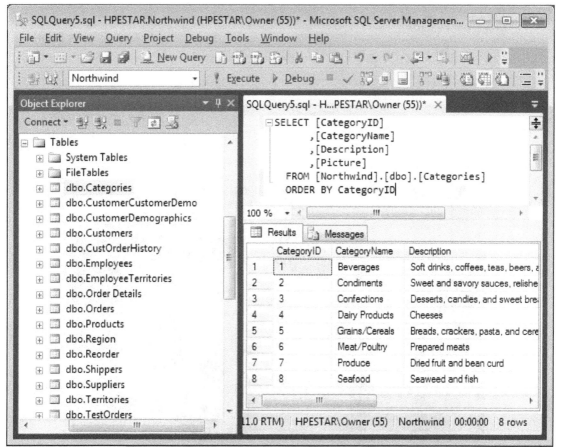

Diagram of Northwind Database

The basic diagram of Northwind database excluding a few ancillary tables. The Orders table is central since the business is wholesale distribution (reselling) of high-end food products.

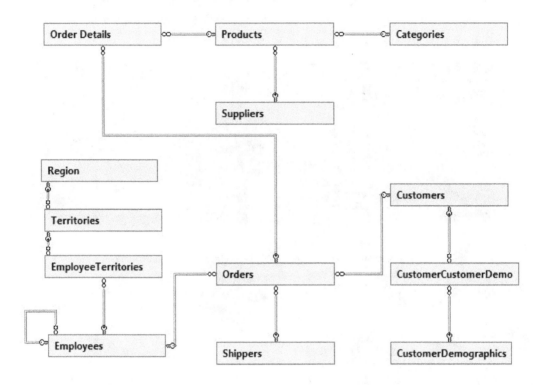

pubs Sample Database

The pubs database is a very small and simple publishing database, yet it demonstrates the main features of database design such as PRIMARY KEYs, FOREIGN KEYs, and junction table reflecting many-to-many relationship. The main entities (tables) are: (book) titles, authors, titleauthor (junction table), publishers, sales & royalties.

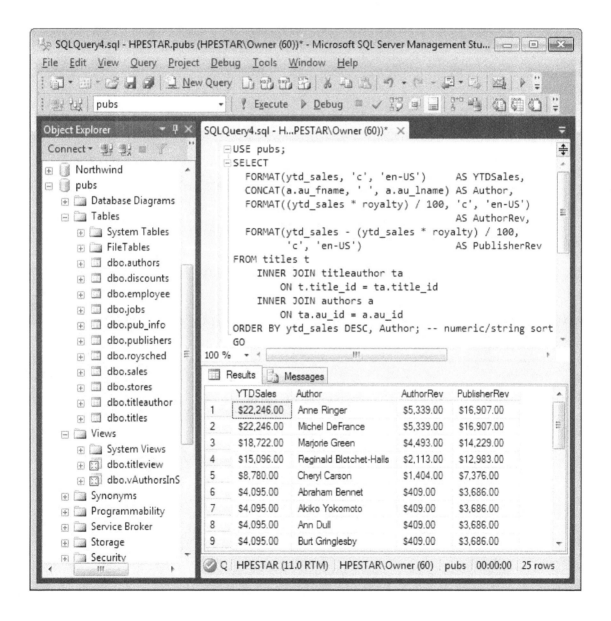

Book Titles in pubs Database

The titles table has the most interesting content in the pubs database as demonstrated by the following T-SQL query.

```
SELECT  TOP 4 title_id AS TitleID, title AS Title, type              AS Type,
        pub_id AS PubID, FORMAT(price, 'c','en-US')                  AS Price,
        FORMAT(advance, 'c','en-US')                                 AS  Advance,
        FORMAT(royalty/100.0, 'p') AS Royalty, FORMAT(ytd_sales, 'c', 'en-US')  AS YTDSales,
        Notes
FROM pubs.dbo.titles ORDER BY title;
```

TitleID	Title	Type	PubID	Price	Advance	Royalty	YTDSales	Notes
PC1035	But Is It User Friendly?	popular_comp	1389	$22.95	$7,000.00	16.00 %	$8,780.00	A survey of software for the naive user, focusing on the 'friendliness' of each.
PS1372	Computer Phobic AND Non-Phobic Individuals: Behavior Variations	psychology	0877	$21.59	$7,000.00	10.00 %	$375.00	A must for the specialist, this book examines the difference between those who hate and fear computers and those who don't.
BU1111	Cooking with Computers: Surreptitious Balance Sheets	business	1389	$11.95	$5,000.00	10.00 %	$3,876.00	Helpful hints on how to use your electronic resources to the best advantage.
PS7777	Emotional Security: A New Algorithm	psychology	0736	$7.99	$4,000.00	10.00 %	$3,336.00	Protecting yourself and your loved ones from undue emotional stress in the modern world. Use of computer and nutritional aids emphasized.

Diagram of pubs Database

Since pubs is a small database, the diagram conveniently fits on a page.

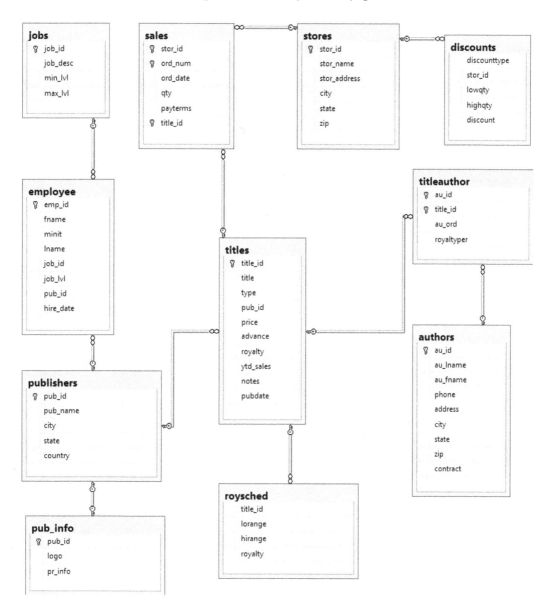

SQL Server System Databases

The master, model, tempdb and msdb are system databases for special database server operations purposes.

SSMS Object Explorer drill-down listing of system databases.

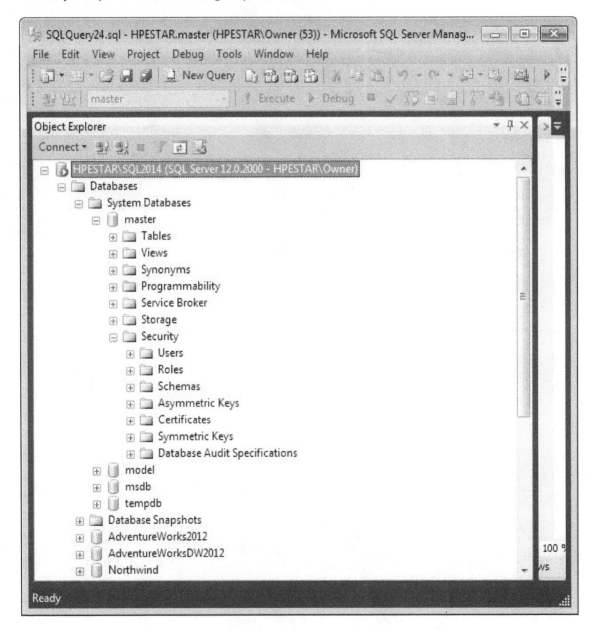

The master Database

The master system database is the nerve center of SQL Server. It contains tables and db objects essential for server operations. System tables are accessible only through read-only views, they cannot be changed by users. A subset of the system views are called Dynamic Management Views (DMV) which return server state information for monitoring the operational aspects of a SQL Server instance, diagnosing problems, and performance tuning. Dynamic Management Functions (DMF) are applied in conjunction with DMVs.

```
SELECT TOP 5 ST.text, EQS.*
FROM master.sys.dm_exec_query_stats AS EQS              -- DMV
CROSS APPLY master.sys.dm_exec_sql_text(EQS.sql_handle) as ST     -- DMF
ORDER BY last_worker_time DESC;
```

Object Explorer display of some objects in the master database and query listing of databases.

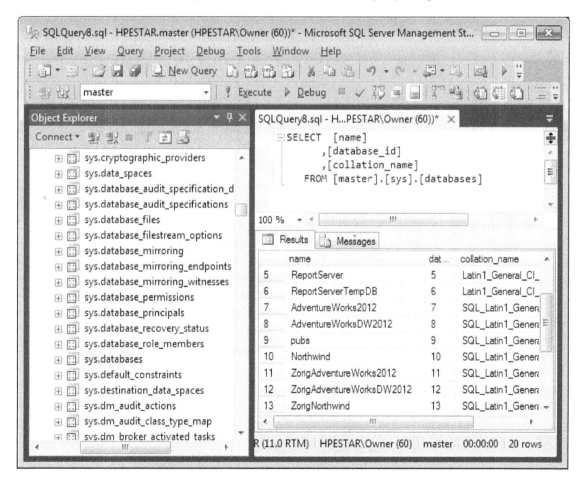

An Important System View In master Database: sys.databases

SELECT TOP (10) name, database_id FROM master.sys.databases ORDER BY database_id;

name	database_id
master	1
tempdb	2
model	3
msdb	4
ReportServer	5
ReportServerTempDB	6
AdventureWorks2012	7
AdventureWorksDW2012	8
pubs	9
Northwind	10

The spt_values table in the master database can be used for integer sequence with a range of 0 - 2047.

-- End of the range - BOTTOM
SELECT TOP 5 number FROM master.dbo.spt_values WHERE TYPE='P' ORDER BY number DESC;

number
2047
2046
2045
2044
2043

Example for using the sequence in spt_values to generate DATE and MONTH sequences.

SELECT TOP 5 number,   dateadd(day, number, '20000101')   AS "Date",
               dateadd(mm, number, '20000101')   AS "Month"
FROM **master.dbo.spt_values** WHERE type = 'P' ORDER BY number;

number	Date	Month
0	2000-01-01 00:00:00.000	2000-01-01 00:00:00.000
1	2000-01-02 00:00:00.000	2000-02-01 00:00:00.000
2	2000-01-03 00:00:00.000	2000-03-01 00:00:00.000
3	2000-01-04 00:00:00.000	2000-04-01 00:00:00.000
4	2000-01-05 00:00:00.000	2000-05-01 00:00:00.000

The model Database

The model database serves as prototype for a new database and tempdb when the SQL Server instance started. Upon server shutdown or restart everything is wiped out of tempdb, it starts with a clean slate as a copy of the model database.

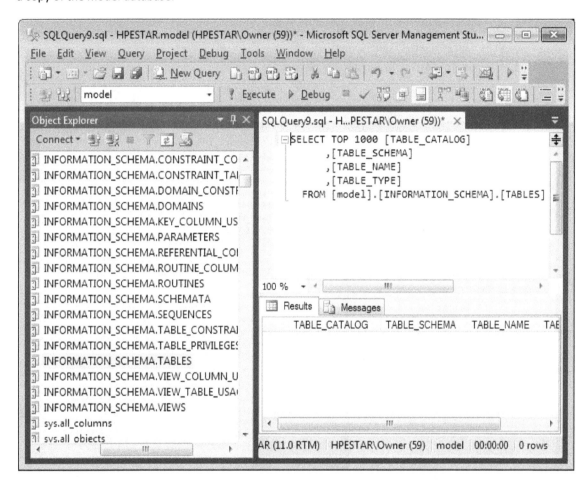

The msdb Database

The msdb database is used for server internal operations such as support for SQL Server Agent job scheduling facility or keeping track of database the all important backups and restores.

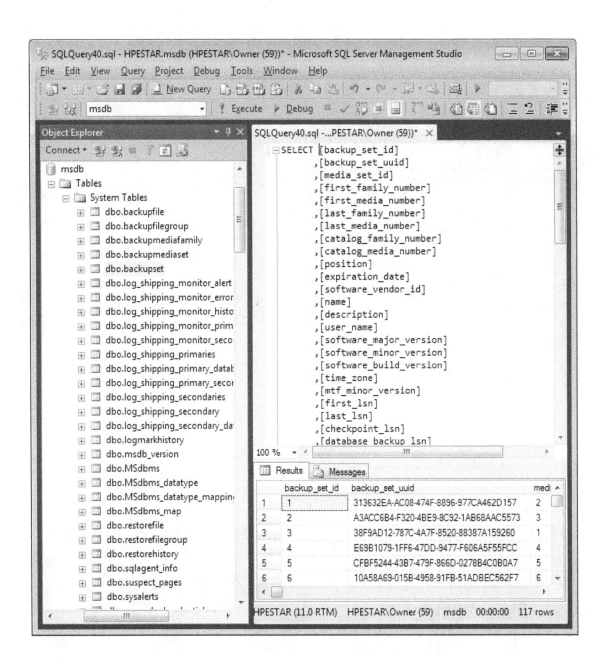

The tempdb Database

The tempdb serves as temporary database for system operations such as sorting. Temporary tables (#temp1) and global temporary tables (##globaltemp1) are stored in the tempdb as well. "Permanent" tables can be created in tempdb with a short lifetime which lasts till shutdown or restart.

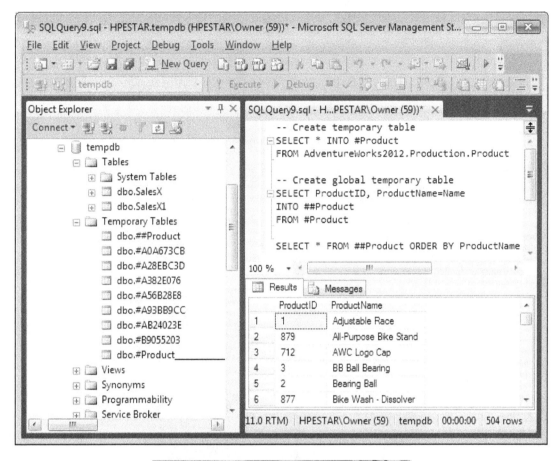

Sudden Death in tempdb When Server Restarts

Even though a temporary table and a global temporary table are created and queried in the context
setting for AdventureWorks2012 database, they are placed into tempdb automatically. Same
consideration when a temporary table is created from a stored procedure which is compiled in an
application database. Upon server restart everything is wiped out of tempdb, rebirth follows as a copy of
model db.

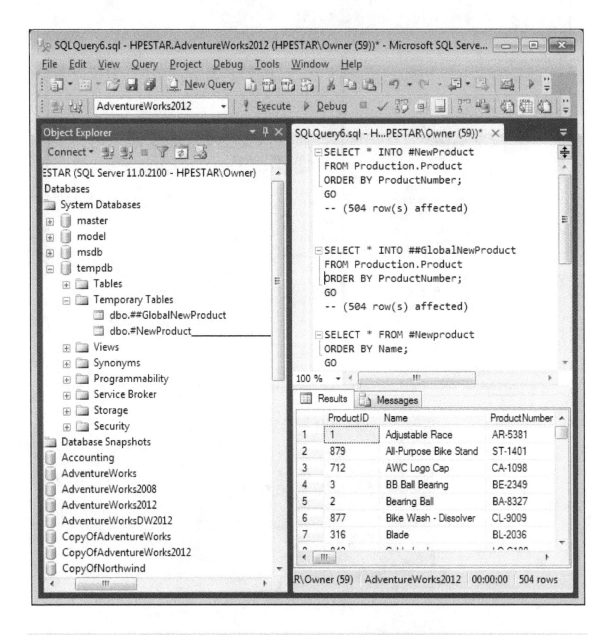

CHAPTER 2: Installing SQL Server 2016

SQL Server 2016 Express Edition Installation

The **Express Edition** is free. It can be installed from the following webpage.

https://www.microsoft.com/en-us/download/details.aspx?id=52679

Installation instructions provided.

SQL Server 2016 Evaluation Edition Installation

The **Evaluation Edition** is free for a certain time period like 6 months. It can be installed from the following webpage.

https://www.microsoft.com/en-us/evalcenter/evaluate-sql-server-2016

Installation instructions provided.

SQL Server 2016 Developer Edition Installation

The **Developer Edition** is free (in previous version the cost was around $50). It can be installed from the following webpage.

https://www.visualstudio.com/en-us/products/visual-studio-dev-essentials-vs.aspx

After joining Visual Studio Dev Essentials, a download screen appears.

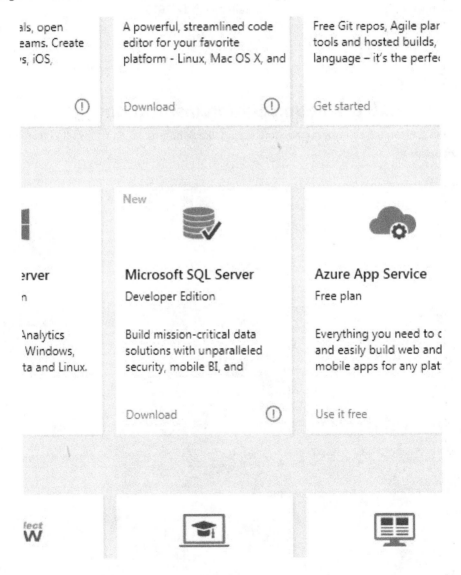

Installation instructions provided.

SQL Server 2016 Pay Edition Installation

The installation process from the distribution DVD is fairly automatic. Product key (4 x 5 alphanumeric) entry is required near the beginning of the installation.

Planning tab has the preparation steps.

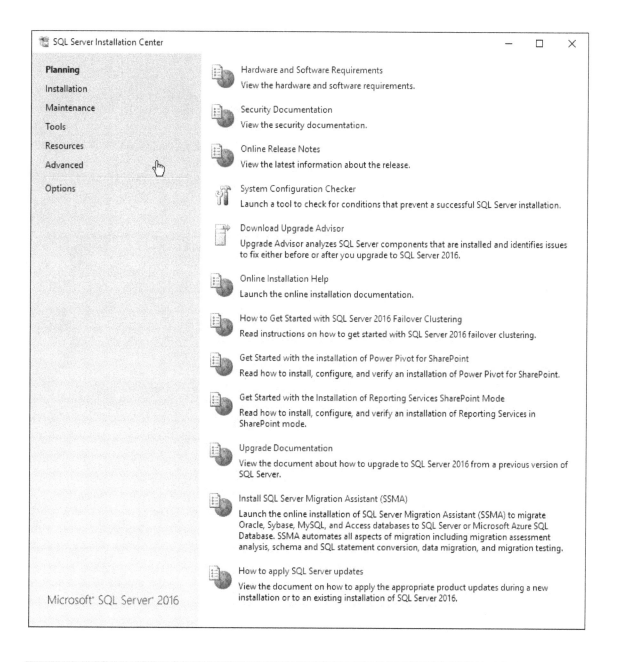

The Resources tab has a list of important resources.

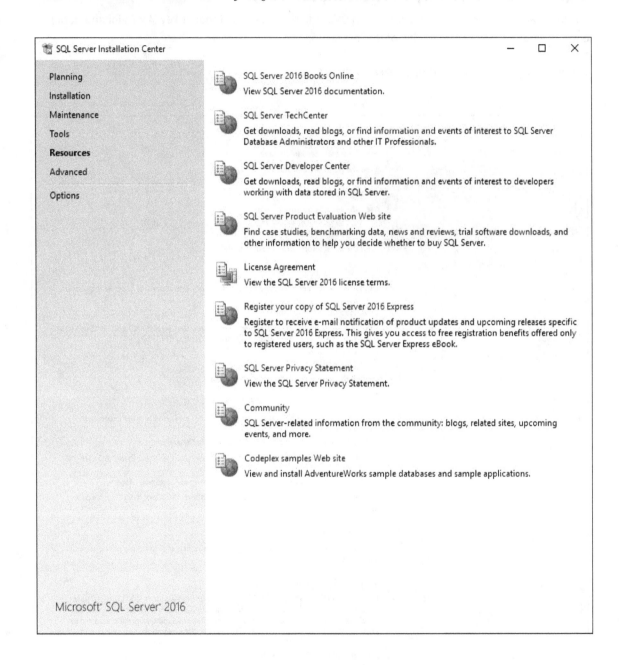

The Maintenance, Tools & Advanced tabs with list of SQL Server resources.

Planning
Installation
Maintenance
Tools
Resources
Advanced

Options

 Edition Upgrade
Launch a wizard to change your edition of SQL Server 2016, like changing from Developer to Enterprise.

 Repair
Launch a wizard to repair a corrupt SQL Server 2016 installation.

 Remove node from a SQL Server failover cluster
Launch a wizard to remove a node from an existing SQL Server 2016 failover cluster.

 Launch Windows Update to search for product updates
Launch the Windows Update application to search for updates that are available for your existing SQL Server installations and your system. To obtain updates for SQL Server ensure you Windows Updates settings are set to received updates for Microsoft products.

Planning
Installation
Maintenance
Tools
Resources
Advanced

Options

 System Configuration Checker
Launch a tool to check for conditions that prevent a successful SQL Server installation.

 Installed SQL Server features discovery report
View a report of all SQL Server products and features that are installed on the local server.

 Microsoft Assessment and Planning (MAP) Toolkit for SQL Server
The Microsoft Assessment and Planning (MAP) Toolkit can help with your migration to SQL Server by giving you a complete network inventory of SQL Server, Oracle, MySQL, and Sybase installations, as part of a comprehensive process for planning and migrating legacy database instances to SQL Server 2016.

 PowerPivot Configuration Tool
Use the PowerPivot Configuration Tool to deploy PowerPivot for SharePoint in a SharePoint farm.

Planning
Installation
Maintenance
Tools
Resources
Advanced

Options

 Install based on configuration file
Use an existing configuration file to install SQL Server 2016.

 Advanced cluster preparation
Launch a wizard to prepare a SQL Server 2016 failover cluster installation.

 Advanced cluster completion
Launch a wizard to complete a SQL Server 2016 failover cluster from a list of cluster-prepared SQL Server 2016 instances.

 Image preparation of a stand-alone instance of SQL Server
Launch a wizard to prepare an imaged instance of SQL Server 2016.

 Image completion of a prepared stand-alone instance of SQL Server
Launch a wizard to configure a prepared imaged instance of SQL Server 2016.

CHAPTER 2: Installing SQL Server 2016

The Installation tab has the SQL Server and Client Tools (SS Management Studio is a client tool) install options.

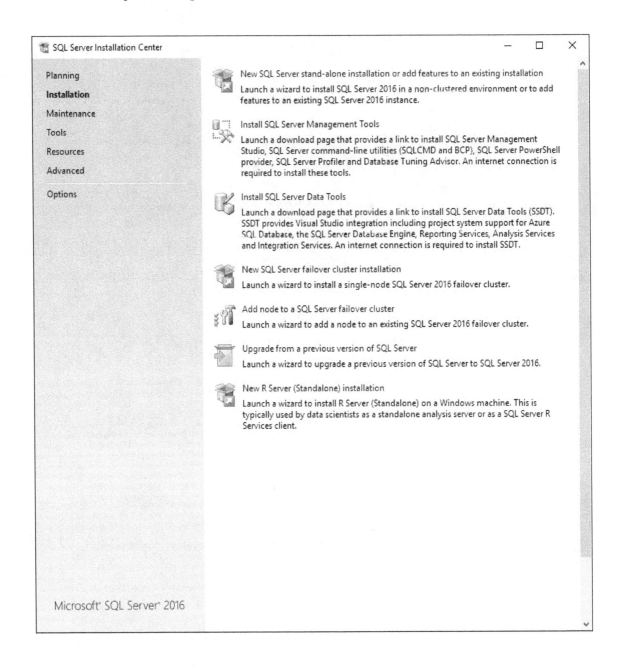

Installation Wizard first page: Install Rules page shows the results of preliminary checks for installation readiness. Failed issues require fix.

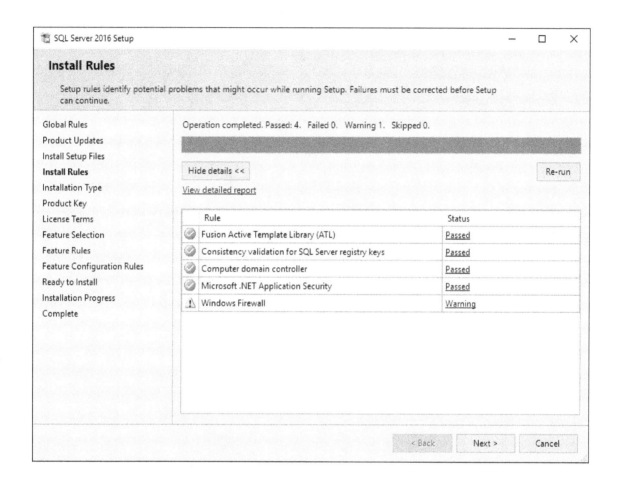

Installation Wizard second page: Installation Type can be new or an upgrade of existing installation.

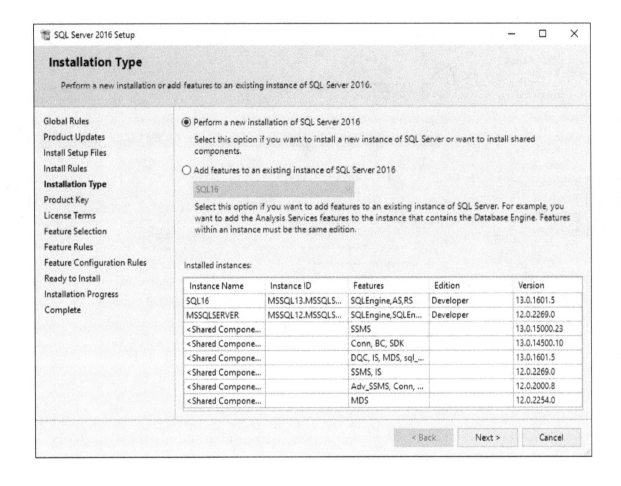

The Product Key page follows when selecting new installation.

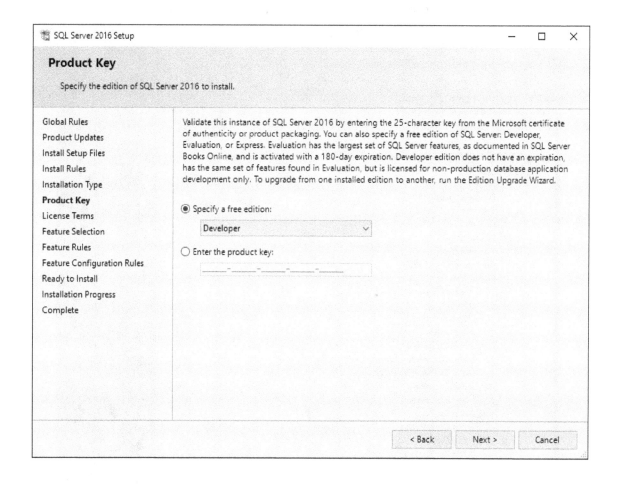

The Installation Wizard will guide you through the installation process step by step. At the end of the process, you can initiate the installation of SQL Server 2016 which may take several minutes.

SQL Server Management Studio 2016

SSMS is used by developers and database administrators to program and manage SQL Server. The following screen image shows the Object Explorer.

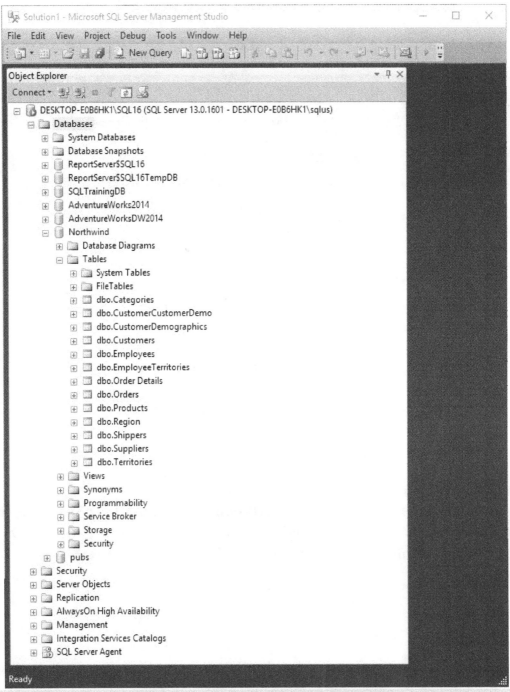

Query & Results Windows in SSMS

Queries are typed into the query window. Upon pressing the Execute button the query is executed and the results returned in the results window.

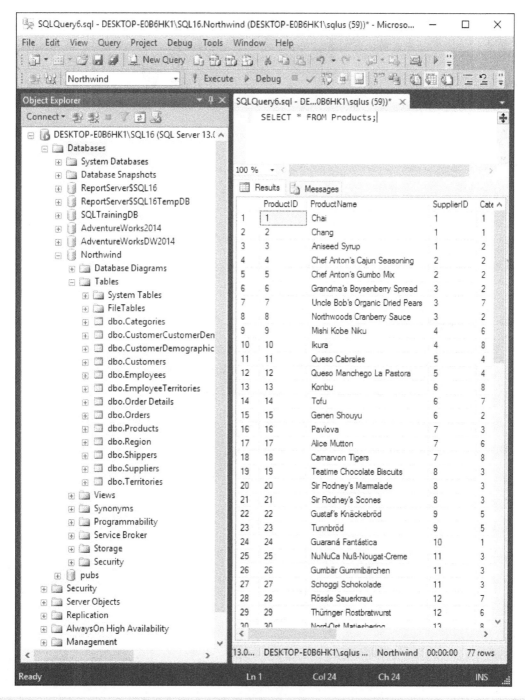

Server Dashboard in SSMS

Server Dashboard displays information related to the operation of the server.

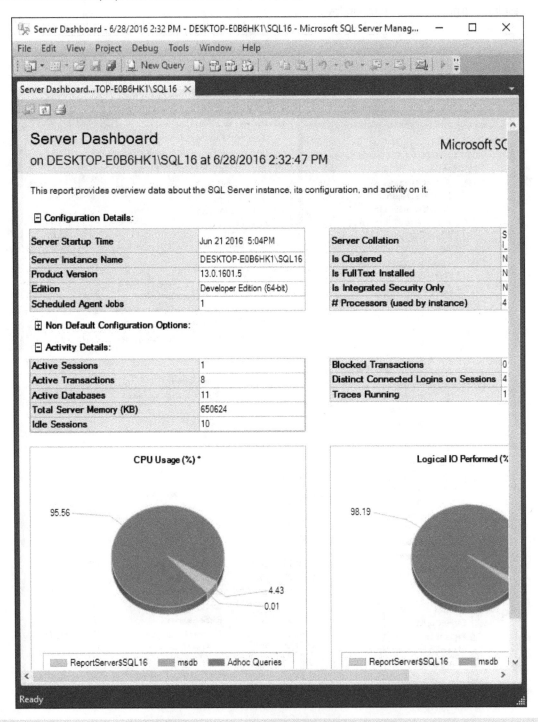

Activity Monitor in SSMS

The Activity Monitor displays information about the operation and performance of the server.

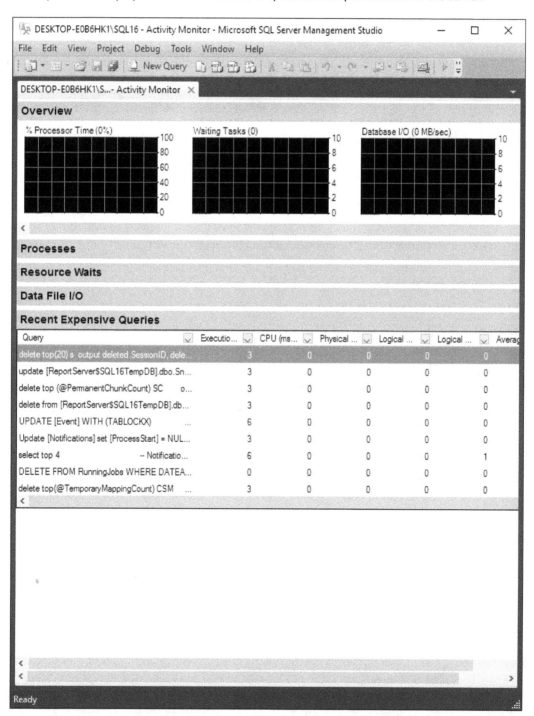

Investigating the New SQL Server Instance

We can start discovering the new SQL Server instance in Query Editor & Object Explorer.

Connecting to 2 SQL Server Instances Simultaneously

SSMS Object Explorer support multiple SS instances connections. Warning: **Production, QA and Development SS instances may look similar, an opportunity to get confused and carry out actions on the wrong server**. Best prevention: **take regular database backups and connect only to one SQL Server instance at one time**.

The first connection is the named instance, the second is the default instance.

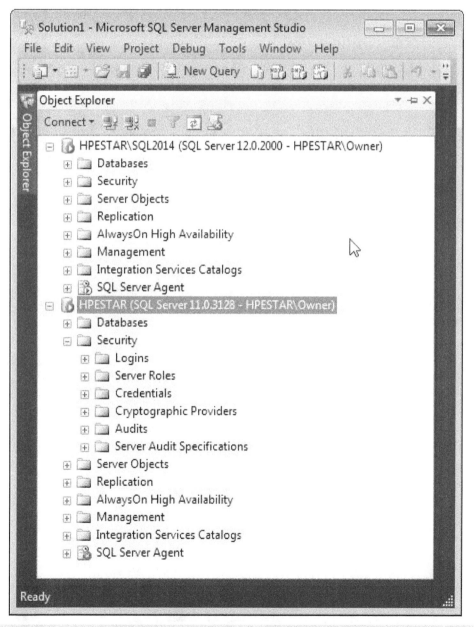

BACKUP DATABASE Command

Database backup command; the backup filename can be changed at will to reflect the backup date.

```
BACKUP DATABASE [AdventureWorks2012] TO  DISK = N'F:\data\backup\AW20161023.bak';
```

```
-- Dynamic backup filename with datestamp
DECLARE @Filename nvarchar(64) = CONCAT(N'F:\data\backup\AW', CONVERT(varchar, CONVERT(DATE, getdate())),'.bak');
BACKUP DATABASE [AdventureWorks2012] TO  DISK = @Filename;
-- AW2018-08-23.bak
```

Installing Books Online - BOL

Books Online can be installed from the web or from the distribution DVD. Books Online is also available on the web: https://msdn.microsoft.com/en-us/library/ms130214.aspx

▼ SQL Server 2016 Technical
  Documentation

    SQL Server 2016 Release Notes

    What's New in SQL Server 2016

  ▶ SQL Server 2016 Resources

  ▶ SQL Server Installation

  ▶ Database Engine

  ▶ Analysis Services

  ▶ Integration Services

  ▶ Data Quality Services

  ▶ Replication

  ▶ Reporting Services

  ▶ Master Data Services

  ▶ R Services

  ▶ SQL Server Configuration Manager
    Help

    Glossary

▶ Developer Reference for SQL
  Server 2016

▶ Tutorials for SQL Server 2016

▶ Technical Articles

SQL Server 2016 Technical Documentation

SQL Server 2016 | Other Versions ▾

Updated: June 11, 2016

Documentation to help you install, configure, and use SQL Server 2016 featu includes end-to-end examples, code samples, and videos. For the latest rele Release Notes. For the latest information on what is new, see What's New in

Try it out:

- ⊕ Download SQL Server 2016 from the **Evaluation Center**

- Have an Azure account? Then go **Here** to spin up a Virtual Machine v installed.

- ⊕ To get the latest version of SQL Server Management Studio, see **Management Studio (SSMS)**.

SQL Server Technologies

	Technology
	Database Engine

Searching Books Online Index Mode

In the Index Mode, items are listed alphabetically. When you click on an item, the corresponding article pops up in the right pane.

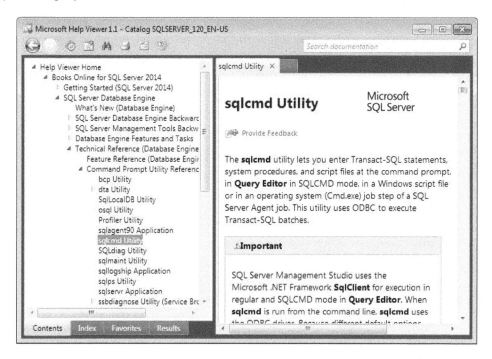

Searching the Web for SQL Server MSDN Articles

When searching the web for SS documentation use the prefix "SQL SERVER" or "T-SQL" before the keyword.

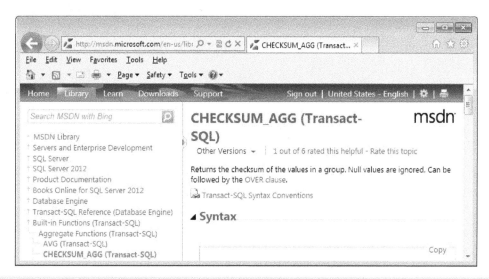

Books Online on the Web

Books Online is available on the web:

https://technet.microsoft.com/en-us/library/ms130214(v=sql.130).aspx

▷ TechNet Library
▷ SQL Server
▷ SQL Server 2016
▷ SQL Server 2016 Technical Documentation
▷ Database Engine
    ◂ Technical Reference
       Feature Reference
       ▷ Command Prompt Utility Reference (Database Engine)
       ▷ Database Engine PowerShell Reference
       ▷ Errors and Events Reference
       Showplan Logical and Physical Operators Reference
       ▷ SQL Server Event Class Reference

Feature Re
Engine)

SQL Server 2016   Other

Applies To: SQL Server 201

The SQL Server Database E
create, manage, and view c
use to monitor and trouble
features, services, and netw
dialog boxes of these tools

To access a user interface t
while the dialog box, Web

◂ In This Section

Start and Use the Database
Provides help for Database

Provides help for the tools,
Studio

Installing AdventureWorks2014 Sample Database

At the writing of this book, no AdventureWorks2016 available. AdventureWorks2014 and other related databases can be installed from the following webpage: http://msftdbprodsamples.codeplex.com/releases/view/125550

Community Projects & Samples from the Start Menu will bring up the following site: http://sqlserversamples.codeplex.com/

Installing Northwind & pubs Sample Databases

Here is the download website with instructions. http://www.microsoft.com/en-us/download/details.aspx?displaylang=en&id=23654

CHAPTER 2: Installing SQL Server 2016

CHAPTER 3: Structure of the SELECT Statement

The SELECT Clause

The SELECT clause is the only required clause in a SELECT statement, all the other clauses are optional. The SELECT columns can be literals (constants), expressions, table columns and even subqueries. Lines can be commented with "--".

```
SELECT 15 * 15;                              -- 225
```

```
SELECT Today = convert(DATE, getdate());    -- 2016-07-27
```

```
SELECT          Color,
                ProdCnt           = COUNT(*),
                AvgPrice          = FORMAT(AVG(ListPrice),'c','en-US')
FROM AdventureWorks2012.Production.Product p
WHERE Color is not null
GROUP BY Color   HAVING count(*) > 10
ORDER BY AvgPrice DESC;
GO
```

Color	ProdCnt	AvgPrice
Yellow	36	$959.09
Blue	26	$923.68
Silver	43	$850.31
Black	93	$725.12
Red	38	$1,401.95

```
-- Equivalent with column aliases on the right
SELECT          Color,
                COUNT(*)                                  AS ProdCnt,
                FORMAT(AVG(ListPrice),'c','en-US')        AS AvgPrice
FROM AdventureWorks2012.Production.Product p
WHERE Color is not null  GROUP BY Color
HAVING count(*) > 10
ORDER BY AvgPrice DESC;
GO
```

SELECT with Search Expression

SELECT statement can have complex expressions for text or numbers as demonstrated in the next T-SQL query for finding the street name in AddressLine1 column.

```
SELECT  AddressID,
        SUBSTRING(AddressLine1, CHARINDEX(' ', AddressLine1+' ', 1) +1,
        CHARINDEX(' ', AddressLine1+' ', CHARINDEX(' ', AddressLine1+' ', 1) +1) -
        CHARINDEX(' ', AddressLine1+' ', 1) -1)                                      AS StreetName,
        AddressLine1,
        City
FROM AdventureWorks2012.Person.Address
WHERE ISNUMERIC (LEFT(AddressLine1,1))=1
  AND City = 'Seattle'
ORDER BY AddressLine1;
-- -- (141 row(s) affected)- Partial results.
```

AddressID	StreetName	AddressLine1	City
13079	boulevard	081, boulevard du Montparnasse	Seattle
859	Oak	1050 Oak Street	Seattle
110	Slow	1064 Slow Creek Road	Seattle
113	Ravenwood	1102 Ravenwood	Seattle
95	Bradford	1220 Bradford Way	Seattle
32510	Steven	1349 Steven Way	Seattle
118	Balboa	136 Balboa Court	Seattle
32519	Mazatlan	137 Mazatlan	Seattle
25869	Calle	1386 Calle Verde	Seattle
114	Yorba	1398 Yorba Linda	Seattle
15657	Book	151 Book Ct	Seattle
105	Stillman	1619 Stillman Court	Seattle
18002	Carmel	1635 Carmel Dr	Seattle
19813	Acardia	1787 Acardia Pl.	Seattle
16392	Orchid	1874 Orchid Ct	Seattle
18053	Green	1883 Green View Court	Seattle
13035	Mt.	1887 Mt. Diablo St	Seattle
29864	Valley	1946 Valley Crest Drive	Seattle
13580	Hill	2030 Hill Drive	Seattle
106	San	2144 San Rafael	Seattle

SELECT Statement with Subquery

Two Northwind category images, Beverages & Dairy Products, from the dbo.Categories table.

The following SELECT statement involves a subquery which is called a derived table. It also demonstrates that INNER JOIN can be performed with a GROUP BY subquery as well not only with another table or view.

```
USE Northwind;
SELECT   c.CategoryName                          AS Category,
               cnum.NoOfProducts                 AS CatProdCnt,
               p.ProductName                     AS Product,
               FORMAT(p.UnitPrice,'c', 'en-US')  AS UnitPrice
 FROM    Categories c
               INNER JOIN Products p
                     ON c.CategoryID = p.CategoryID
               INNER JOIN (     SELECT   c.CategoryID,
                                     NoOfProducts = count(* )
                          FROM    Categories c
                          INNER JOIN Products p
                                ON c.CategoryID = p.CategoryID
                          GROUP BY c.CategoryID
                          ) cnum                         -- derived table
                     ON c.CategoryID = cnum.CategoryID
ORDER BY Category, Product;
-- (77 row(s) affected) - Partial results.
```

Category	CatProdCnt	Product	UnitPrice
Dairy Products	10	Mozzarella di Giovanni	$34.80
Dairy Products	10	Queso Cabrales	$21.00
Dairy Products	10	Queso Manchego La Pastora	$38.00
Dairy Products	10	Raclette Courdavault	$55.00
Grains/Cereals	7	Filo Mix	$7.00
Grains/Cereals	7	Gnocchi di nonna Alice	$38.00
Grains/Cereals	7	Gustaf's Knäckebröd	$21.00
Grains/Cereals	7	Ravioli Angelo	$19.50
Grains/Cereals	7	Singaporean Hokkien Fried Mee	$14.00
Grains/Cereals	7	Tunnbröd	$9.00

Creating Delimited String List (CSV) with XML PATH

The XML PATH clause , the text() function and correlated subquery is used to create a comma delimited string within the SELECT columns. Note: it cannot be done using traditional (without XML) SQL single statement, it can be done with multiple SQL statements only. STUFF() string function is applied to replace the leading comma with an empty string

.

```
USE AdventureWorks;

SELECT   Territory = st.[Name],
         SalesYTD =  FORMAT(floor(SalesYTD), 'c', 'en-US'), -- currency format
         SalesStaffAssignmentHistory =

         STUFF((SELECT CONCAT(', ', c.FirstName, SPACE(1), c.LastName)      AS [text()]
              FROM   Person.Contact c
              INNER JOIN Sales.SalesTerritoryHistory sth
              ON c.ContactID = sth.SalesPersonID
              WHERE  sth.TerritoryID =   st.TerritoryID
              ORDER  BY StartDate
              FOR XML Path ('')), 1, 1, SPACE(0))

FROM   Sales.SalesTerritory st
ORDER  BY SalesYTD DESC;
GO
```

Territory	SalesYTD	SalesStaffAssignmentHistory
Southwest	$8,351,296.00	Shelley Dyck, Jauna Elson
Canada	$6,917,270.00	Carla Eldridge, Michael Emanuel, Gail Erickson
Northwest	$5,767,341.00	Shannon Elliott, Terry Eminhizer, Martha Espinoza
Central	$4,677,108.00	Linda Ecoffey, Maciej Dusza
France	$3,899,045.00	Mark Erickson
Northeast	$3,857,163.00	Maciej Dusza, Linda Ecoffey
United Kingdom	$3,514,865.00	Michael Emanuel
Southeast	$2,851,419.00	Carol Elliott
Germany	$2,481,039.00	Janeth Esteves
Australia	$1,977,474.00	Twanna Evans

Logical Processing Order of the SELECT Statement

The results from the previous step will be available to the next step. The logical processing order for a SELECT statement is the following. Actual processing by the database engine may be different due to performance and other considerations.

1.	FROM
2.	ON
3.	JOIN
4.	WHERE
5.	GROUP BY
6.	WITH CUBE or WITH ROLLUP
7.	HAVING
8.	SELECT
9.	DISTINCT
10.	ORDER BY
11.	TOP

As an example, it is logical to filter with the WHERE clause prior to applying GROUP BY. It is also logical to sort when the final result set is available.

```
SELECT Color, COUNT(*) AS ColorCount  FROM AdventureWorks2012.Production.Product
WHERE Color is not NULL  GROUP BY Color ORDER BY ColorCount DESC;
```

Color	ColorCount
Black	93
Silver	43
Red	38
Yellow	36
Blue	26
Multi	8
Silver/Black	7
White	4
Grey	1

The TOP Clause

The TOP clause filters results according the sorting specified in an ORDER BY clause, otherwise random filtering takes place.

Simple TOP usage to return 10 rows only.

SELECT TOP 10 SalesOrderID, OrderDate, TotalDue
FROM AdventureWorks2012.Sales.SalesOrderHeader ORDER BY TotalDue DESC;

SalesOrderID	OrderDate	TotalDue
51131	2007-07-01 00:00:00.000	187487.825
55282	2007-10-01 00:00:00.000	182018.6272
46616	2006-07-01 00:00:00.000	170512.6689
46981	2006-08-01 00:00:00.000	166537.0808
47395	2006-09-01 00:00:00.000	165028.7482
47369	2006-09-01 00:00:00.000	158056.5449
47355	2006-09-01 00:00:00.000	145741.8553
51822	2007-08-01 00:00:00.000	145454.366
44518	2005-11-01 00:00:00.000	142312.2199
51858	2007-08-01 00:00:00.000	140042.1209

Complex TOP function usage: not known in advance how many rows will be returned due to "TIES".

SELECT   TOP 1 WITH TIES coalesce(Color, 'N/A')   AS Color,
         FORMAT(ListPrice, 'c', 'en-US')   AS ListPrice,
         Name   AS ProductName,
         ProductID
FROM   AdventureWorks2012.Production.Product
ORDER BY ROW_NUMBER() OVER(PARTITION BY Color ORDER BY ListPrice DESC);

Color	ListPrice	ProductName	ProductID
N/A	$229.49	HL Fork	804
Black	$3,374.99	Mountain-100 Black, 38	775
Red	$3,578.27	Road-150 Red, 62	749
Silver	$3,399.99	Mountain-100 Silver, 38	771
Blue	$2,384.07	Touring-1000 Blue, 46	966
Grey	$125.00	Touring-Panniers, Large	842
Multi	$89.99	Men's Bib-Shorts, S	855
Silver/Black	$80.99	HL Mountain Pedal	937
White	$9.50	Mountain Bike Socks, M	709
Yellow	$2,384.07	Touring-1000 Yellow, 46	954

The DISTINCT Clause to Omit Duplicates

The DISTINCT clause returns only unique results, omitting duplicates in the result set.

```
USE AdventureWorks2012;
SELECT DISTINCT Color FROM Production.Product
WHERE Color is not NULL
ORDER BY Color;
GO
```

Color
Black
Blue
Grey
Multi
Red
Silver
SIlver/Black
White
Yellow

```
SELECT DISTINCT ListPrice
FROM Production.Product
 WHERE ListPrice > 0.0
ORDER BY ListPrice DESC;
GO
-- (102 row(s) affected) - Partial results.
```

ListPrice
3578.27
3399.99
3374.99
2443.35

```
-- Using DISTINCT in COUNT - NULL is counted
SELECT          COUNT(*)                 AS TotalRows,
                COUNT(DISTINCT Color)    AS ProductColors,
                COUNT(DISTINCT Size)     AS ProductSizes
FROM AdventureWorks2012.Production.Product;
```

TotalRows	ProductColors	ProductSizes
504	9	18

The CASE Conditional Expression

The CASE conditional expression evaluates to a **single value of the same data type**, therefore **it can be used anywhere in a query where a single value is required.**

```
SELECT   CASE ProductLine
                    WHEN 'R' THEN 'Road'
                    WHEN 'M' THEN 'Mountain'
                    WHEN 'T' THEN 'Touring'
                    WHEN 'S' THEN 'Other'
                    ELSE 'Parts'
              END                        AS Category,
              Name                       AS ProductName,
              ProductNumber
FROM AdventureWorks2012.Production.Product
ORDER BY ProductName;
GO
-- (504 row(s) affected) - Partial results.
```

Category	ProductName	ProductNumber
Touring	Touring-3000 Blue, 62	BK-T18U-62
Touring	Touring-3000 Yellow, 44	BK-T18Y-44
Touring	Touring-3000 Yellow, 50	BK-T18Y-50
Touring	Touring-3000 Yellow, 54	BK-T18Y-54
Touring	Touring-3000 Yellow, 58	BK-T18Y-58
Touring	Touring-3000 Yellow, 62	BK-T18Y-62
Touring	Touring-Panniers, Large	PA-T100
Other	Water Bottle - 30 oz.	WB-H098
Mountain	Women's Mountain Shorts, L	SH-W890-L

Query to return different result sets for repeated execution due to newid().

```
SELECT  TOP 3 CompanyName,    City=CONCAT(City, ', ', Country),          PostalCode,
        [IsNumeric] =  CASE      WHEN PostalCode like '[0-9][0-9][0-9][0-9][0-9]'
                                 THEN '5-Digit Numeric'    ELSE 'Other' END
FROM    Northwind.dbo.Suppliers
ORDER BY NEWID();                       -- random sort
GO
```

CompanyName	City	PostalCode	IsNumeric
PB Knäckebröd AB	Göteborg, Sweden	S-345 67	Other
Gai pâturage	Annecy, France	74000	5-Digit Numeric
Heli Süßwaren GmbH & Co. KG	Berlin, Germany	10785	5-Digit Numeric

CHAPTER 3: Structure of the SELECT Statement

*Same query as above expanded with ROW_NUMBER() and another CASE
expression column.*

```
SELECT   ROW_NUMBER() OVER (ORDER BY Name)            AS RowNo,
            CASE ProductLine
              WHEN 'R' THEN 'Road'
              WHEN 'M' THEN 'Mountain'
              WHEN 'T' THEN 'Touring'
              WHEN 'S' THEN 'Other'
              ELSE 'Parts'
            END                                        AS Category,
            Name                                       AS ProductName,
            CASE WHEN Color is null THEN 'N/A'
                    ELSE Color END                     AS Color,
            ProductNumber
FROM Production.Product   ORDER BY ProductName;
-- (504 row(s) affected) - Partial results.
```

RowNo	Category	ProductName	Color	ProductNumber
1	Parts	Adjustable Race	N/A	AR-5381
2	Mountain	All-Purpose Bike Stand	N/A	ST-1401
3	Other	AWC Logo Cap	Multi	CA-1098
4	Parts	BB Ball Bearing	N/A	BE-2349
5	Parts	Bearing Ball	N/A	BA-8327
6	Other	Bike Wash - Dissolver	N/A	CL-9009
7	Parts	Blade	N/A	BL-2036
8	Other	Cable Lock	N/A	LO-C100
9	Parts	Chain	Silver	CH-0234
10	Parts	Chain Stays	N/A	CS-2812

Testing PostalCode with ISNUMERIC and generating a flag with CASE expression.

```
SELECT  TOP (4) AddressID,   City,   PostalCode                AS Zip,
          CASE WHEN ISNUMERIC(PostalCode) = 1 THEN 'Y' ELSE 'N'  END    AS IsZipNumeric
FROM    AdventureWorks2008.Person.Address  ORDER BY NEWID();
```

AddressID	City	Zip	IsZipNumeric
16704	Paris	75008	Y
26320	Grossmont	91941	Y
27705	Matraville	2036	Y
18901	Kirkby	KB9	N

CHAPTER 3: Structure of the SELECT Statement

The OVER Clause

The OVER clause defines the partitioning and sorting of a rowset (intermediate result set) preceding the application of an associated window function, such as ranking. Window functions are also dubbed as ranking functions.

```
USE AdventureWorks2012;
-- Query with three different OVER clauses
SELECT   ROW_NUMBER() OVER ( ORDER BY SalesOrderID, ProductID)            AS RowNum
         ,SalesOrderID, ProductID, OrderQty
         ,RANK() OVER(PARTITION BY SalesOrderID ORDER BY OrderQty DESC)   AS Ranking
         ,SUM(OrderQty) OVER(PARTITION BY SalesOrderID)                   AS TotalQty
         ,AVG(OrderQty) OVER(PARTITION BY SalesOrderID)                   AS AvgQty
         ,COUNT(OrderQty) OVER(PARTITION BY SalesOrderID)  AS "Count"  -- T-SQL keyword, use "" or []
         ,MIN(OrderQty) OVER(PARTITION BY SalesOrderID)                   AS "Min"
         ,MAX(OrderQty) OVER(PARTITION BY SalesOrderID)                   AS "Max"
FROM Sales.SalesOrderDetail
WHERE SalesOrderID BETWEEN 61190 AND 61199  ORDER BY RowNum;
-- (143 row(s) affected) - Partial results.
```

RowNum	SalesOrderID	ProductID	OrderQty	Ranking	TotalQty	AvgQty	Count	Min	Max
1	61190	707	4	13	159	3	40	1	17
2	61190	708	3	18	159	3	40	1	17
3	61190	711	5	8	159	3	40	1	17
4	61190	712	12	2	159	3	40	1	17
5	61190	714	3	18	159	3	40	1	17
6	61190	715	5	8	159	3	40	1	17
7	61190	716	5	8	159	3	40	1	17
8	61190	858	4	13	159	3	40	1	17
9	61190	859	7	6	159	3	40	1	17
10	61190	864	8	4	159	3	40	1	17
11	61190	865	3	18	159	3	40	1	17
12	61190	870	9	3	159	3	40	1	17
13	61190	876	4	13	159	3	40	1	17
14	61190	877	5	8	159	3	40	1	17
15	61190	880	1	34	159	3	40	1	17
16	61190	881	5	8	159	3	40	1	17
17	61190	883	2	26	159	3	40	1	17
18	61190	884	17	1	159	3	40	1	17
19	61190	885	3	18	159	3	40	1	17
20	61190	886	1	34	159	3	40	1	17
21	61190	889	2	26	159	3	40	1	17
22	61190	892	4	13	159	3	40	1	17
23	61190	893	3	18	159	3	40	1	17
24	61190	895	1	34	159	3	40	1	17

FROM Clause: Specifies the Data Source

The FROM clause specifies the source data sets for the query such as tables, views, derived tables and table-valued functions. Typically the tables are JOINed together. The most common JOIN is INNER JOIN which is based on equality between FOREIGN KEY and PRIMARY KEY values in the two tables.

PERFORMANCE NOTE
All FOREIGN KEYs should be indexed. PRIMARY KEYs are indexed automatically with unique index.

```
USE AdventureWorks2012;
GO
SELECT
  ROW_NUMBER() OVER(ORDER BY SalesYTD DESC)                          AS RowNo,
  ROW_NUMBER() OVER(PARTITION BY PostalCode ORDER BY SalesYTD DESC)  AS SeqNo,
              CONCAT(p.FirstName, SPACE(1), p.LastName)              AS SalesStaff,
              FORMAT(s.SalesYTD,'c','en-US')                         AS YTDSales,
              City,
              a.PostalCode                                           AS ZipCode
FROM Sales.SalesPerson AS s
  INNER JOIN Person.Person AS p
    ON s.BusinessEntityID = p.BusinessEntityID
  INNER JOIN Person.Address AS a
    ON a.AddressID = p.BusinessEntityID
WHERE  TerritoryID IS NOT NULL   AND SalesYTD <> 0 ORDER BY ZipCode, SeqNo;
```

RowNo	SeqNo	SalesStaff	YTDSales	City	ZipCode
1	1	Linda Mitchell	$4,251,368.55	Issaquah	98027
3	2	Michael Blythe	$3,763,178.18	Issaquah	98027
4	3	Jillian Carson	$3,189,418.37	Issaquah	98027
8	4	Tsvi Reiter	$2,315,185.61	Issaquah	98027
12	5	Garrett Vargas	$1,453,719.47	Issaquah	98027
14	6	Pamela Ansman-Wolfe	$1,352,577.13	Issaquah	98027
2	1	Jae Pak	$4,116,871.23	Renton	98055
5	2	Ranjit Varkey Chudukatil	$3,121,616.32	Renton	98055
6	3	José Saraiva	$2,604,540.72	Renton	98055
7	4	Shu Ito	$2,458,535.62	Renton	98055
9	5	Rachel Valdez	$1,827,066.71	Renton	98055
10	6	Tete Mensa-Annan	$1,576,562.20	Renton	98055
11	7	David Campbell	$1,573,012.94	Renton	98055
13	8	Lynn Tsoflias	$1,421,810.92	Renton	98055

The WHERE Clause to Filter Records (Rows)

The WHERE clause filters the rows generated by the query. Only rows satisfying (TRUE) the WHERE clause predicates are returned.

PERFORMANCE NOTE
All columns in WHERE clause should be indexed.

USE AdventureWorks2012;

String equal match predicate - equal is TRUE, not equal is FALSE.

SELECT ProductID, Name, ListPrice, Color
FROM Production.Product WHERE Name = 'Mountain-100 Silver, 38' ;

ProductID	Name	ListPrice	Color
771	Mountain-100 Silver, 38	3399.99	Silver

-- Function equality predicate
SELECT * FROM Sales.SalesOrderHeader WHERE YEAR(OrderDate) = 2008;
-- (13951 row(s) affected)

PERFORMANCE NOTE
When a column is used as a parameter in a function (e.g. YEAR(OrderDate)), index (if any) usage is voided.
Instead of random SEEK, all rows are SCANned in the table. The predicate is not SARGable.

-- String wildcard match predicate
SELECT ProductID, Name, ListPrice, Color
FROM Production.Product WHERE Name LIKE ('%touring%');

-- Integer range predicate
SELECT ProductID, Name, ListPrice, Color
FROM Production.Product WHERE ProductID >= 997 ;

-- Double string wildcard match predicate
SELECT ProductID, Name, ListPrice, Color
FROM Production.Product WHERE Name LIKE ('%bike%') AND Name LIKE ('%44%');

-- String list match predicate
SELECT ProductID, Name, ListPrice, Color FROM Production.Product
WHERE Name IN ('Mountain-100 Silver, 44', 'Mountain-100 Black, 44');

The GROUP BY Clause to Aggregate Results

The GROUP BY clause is applied to partition the rows and calculate aggregate values. An extremely powerful way of looking at the data from a summary point of view.

```
SELECT
            V.Name                              AS Vendor,
            FORMAT(SUM(TotalDue), 'c', 'en-US')  AS TotalPurchase,
            A.City,
            SP.Name                             AS State,
            CR.Name                             AS Country
FROM Purchasing.Vendor AS V
   INNER JOIN Purchasing.VendorAddress AS VA
            ON VA.VendorID = V.VendorID
   INNER JOIN Person.Address AS A
            ON A.AddressID = VA.AddressID
   INNER JOIN Person.StateProvince AS SP
            ON SP.StateProvinceID =  A.StateProvinceID
   INNER JOIN Person.CountryRegion AS CR
            ON CR.CountryRegionCode = SP.CountryRegionCode
   INNER JOIN Purchasing.PurchaseOrderHeader POH
            ON POH.VendorID = V.VendorID
GROUP BY V.Name, A.City, SP.Name, CR.Name
ORDER BY SUM(TotalDue) DESC,  Vendor;   -- TotalPurchase does a string sort instead of numeric
GO
-- (79 row(s) affected) - Partial results.
```

Vendor	TotalPurchase	City	State	Country
Superior Bicycles	$5,034,266.74	Lynnwood	Washington	United States
Professional Athletic Consultants	$3,379,946.32	Burbank	California	United States
Chicago City Saddles	$3,347,165.20	Daly City	California	United States
Jackson Authority	$2,821,333.52	Long Beach	California	United States
Vision Cycles, Inc.	$2,777,684.91	Glendale	California	United States
Sport Fan Co.	$2,675,889.22	Burien	Washington	United States
Proseware, Inc.	$2,593,901.31	Lebanon	Oregon	United States
Crowley Sport	$2,472,770.05	Chicago	Illinois	United States
Greenwood Athletic Company	$2,472,770.05	Lemon Grove	Arizona	United States
Mitchell Sports	$2,424,284.37	Everett	Washington	United States
First Rate Bicycles	$2,304,231.55	La Mesa	New Mexico	United States
Signature Cycles	$2,236,033.80	Coronado	California	United States
Electronic Bike Repair & Supplies	$2,154,773.37	Tacoma	Washington	United States
Vista Road Bikes	$2,090,857.52	Salem	Oregon	United States
Victory Bikes	$2,052,173.62	Issaquah	Washington	United States
Bicycle Specialists	$1,952,375.30	Lake Oswego	Oregon	United States

The HAVING Clause to Filter Aggregates

The HAVING clause is similar to the WHERE clause filtering but applies to GROUP BY aggregates.

```
USE AdventureWorks;
SELECT
                V.Name                                      AS Vendor,
                FORMAT(SUM(TotalDue), 'c', 'en-US')         AS TotalPurchase,
                A.City,
                SP.Name                                     AS State,
                CR.Name                                     AS Country
FROM Purchasing.Vendor AS V
   INNER JOIN Purchasing.VendorAddress AS VA
                ON VA.VendorID = V.VendorID
   INNER JOIN Person.Address AS A
                ON A.AddressID = VA.AddressID
   INNER JOIN Person.StateProvince AS SP
                ON SP.StateProvinceID =   A.StateProvinceID
   INNER JOIN Person.CountryRegion AS CR
                ON CR.CountryRegionCode = SP.CountryRegionCode
   INNER JOIN Purchasing.PurchaseOrderHeader POH
                ON POH.VendorID = V.VendorID
GROUP BY  V.Name, A.City, SP.Name, CR.Name
HAVING SUM(TotalDue) < $26000   -- HAVING clause predicate
ORDER BY SUM(TotalDue) DESC,  Vendor;
```

Vendor	TotalPurchase	City	State	Country
Speed Corporation	$25,732.84	Anacortes	Washington	United States
Gardner Touring Cycles	$25,633.64	Altadena	California	United States
National Bike Association	$25,513.90	Sedro Woolley	Washington	United States
Australia Bike Retailer	$25,060.04	Bellingham	Washington	United States
WestAmerica Bicycle Co.	$25,060.04	Houston	Texas	United States
Ready Rentals	$23,635.06	Kirkland	Washington	United States
Morgan Bike Accessories	$23,146.99	Albany	New York	United States
Continental Pro Cycles	$22,960.07	Long Beach	California	United States
American Bicycles and Wheels	$9,641.01	West Covina	California	United States
Litware, Inc.	$8,553.32	Santa Cruz	California	United States
Business Equipment Center	$8,497.80	Everett	Montana	United States
Bloomington Multisport	$8,243.95	West Covina	California	United States
International	$8,061.10	Salt Lake City	Utah	United States
Wide World Importers	$8,025.60	Concord	California	United States
Midwest Sport, Inc.	$7,328.72	Detroit	Michigan	United States
Wood Fitness	$6,947.58	Philadelphia	Pennsylvania	United States
Metro Sport Equipment	$6,324.53	Lebanon	Oregon	United States
Burnett Road Warriors	$5,779.99	Corvallis	Oregon	United States
Lindell	$5,412.57	Lebanon	Oregon	United States
Consumer Cycles	$3,378.17	Torrance	California	United States
Northern Bike Travel	$2,048.42	Anacortes	Washington	United States

The ORDER BY Clause to Sort Results

The ORDER BY clause sorts the result set. It guarantees ordering according to the columns or expressions listed from major to minor keys. Unique ordering requires a set of keys which generate unique data rows. The major key, YEAR(HireDate), in the first example is not sufficient for uniqueness.

```
USE AdventureWorks2012;
-- Sort on 2 keys
SELECT BusinessEntityID AS EmployeeID, JobTitle, HireDate
FROM HumanResources.Employee  ORDER BY YEAR(HireDate) DESC, EmployeeID;
-- (290 row(s) affected) - Partial results.
```

EmployeeID	JobTitle	HireDate
285	Pacific Sales Manager	2007-04-15
286	Sales Representative	2007-07-01
288	Sales Representative	2007-07-01
284	Sales Representative	2006-11-01
287	European Sales Manager	2006-05-18
289	Sales Representative	2006-07-01
290	Sales Representative	2006-07-01
11	Senior Tool Designer	2005-01-05
13	Tool Designer	2005-01-23
14	Senior Design Engineer	2005-01-30

```
-- Sort on CASE conditional expression
SELECT   BusinessEntityID AS SalesStaffID, CONCAT(LastName, ', ', FirstName) AS FullName,
         CASE CountryRegionName WHEN 'United States' THEN TerritoryName
              ELSE '' END AS TerritoryName, CountryRegionName
FROM Sales.vSalesPerson   WHERE TerritoryName IS NOT NULL        -- view
ORDER BY CASE WHEN CountryRegionName != 'United States' THEN  CountryRegionName
              ELSE TerritoryName  END;
```

SalesStaffID	FullName	TerritoryName	CountryRegionName
286	Tsoflias, Lynn		Australia
278	Vargas, Garrett		Canada
282	Saraiva, José		Canada
277	Carson, Jillian	Central	United States
290	Varkey Chudukatil, Ranjit		France
288	Valdez, Rachel		Germany
275	Blythe, Michael	Northeast	United States
283	Campbell, David	Northwest	United States
284	Mensa-Annan, Tete	Northwest	United States
280	Ansman-Wolfe, Pamela	Northwest	United States
279	Reiter, Tsvi	Southeast	United States
276	Mitchell, Linda	Southwest	United States
281	Ito, Shu	Southwest	United States
289	Pak, Jae		United Kingdom

CTE - Common Table Expression

CTE helps with structured programming by the definition of named subqueries at the beginning of the query. It supports nesting and recursion.

```
USE AdventureWorks;
-- Testing CTE
WITH CTE (SalesPersonID, NumberOfOrders, MostRecentOrderDate)
    AS (        SELECT SalesPersonID, COUNT(*), CONVERT(date, MAX(OrderDate))
            FROM Sales.SalesOrderHeader
            GROUP BY SalesPersonID   )
SELECT * FROM CTE;
-- (18 row(s) affected) - Partial results.
```

SalesPersonID	NumberOfOrders	MostRecentOrderDate
284	39	2004-05-01
278	234	2004-06-01
281	242	2004-06-01

```
-- Using CTE in a query
;WITH CTE (SalesPersonID, NumberOfOrders, MostRecentOrderDate)
    AS ( SELECT SalesPersonID, COUNT(*), CONVERT(date, MAX(OrderDate))
        FROM Sales.SalesOrderHeader   GROUP BY SalesPersonID       )
-- Start of outer (main) query
 SELECT E.EmployeeID,
                OE.NumberOfOrders                    AS EmpOrders,
                OE.MostRecentOrderDate               AS EmpLastOrder,
                E.ManagerID,
                OM.NumberOfOrders                    AS MgrOrders,
                OM.MostRecentOrderDate               AS MgrLastOrder
 FROM   HumanResources.Employee AS E
        INNER JOIN CTE AS OE                 ON E.EmployeeID = OE.SalesPersonID
        LEFT OUTER JOIN CTE AS OM            ON E.ManagerID = OM.SalesPersonID
ORDER BY EmployeeID;
-- (17 row(s) affected) - Partial results.
```

EmployeeID	EmpOrders	EmpLastOrder	ManagerID	MgrOrders	MgrLastOrder
268	48	2004-06-01	273	NULL	NULL
275	450	2004-06-01	268	48	2004-06-01
276	418	2004-06-01	268	48	2004-06-01
277	473	2004-06-01	268	48	2004-06-01
278	234	2004-06-01	268	48	2004-06-01

Combining Results of Multiple Queries with UNION

UNION and UNION ALL (no duplicates elimination) operators can be used to **stack result sets from two or more queries into a single result set**.

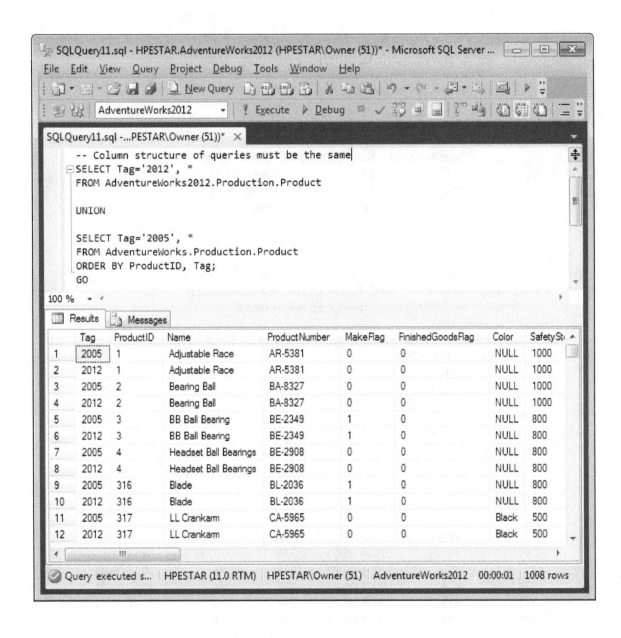

TOP n by Group Query with OVER PARTITION BY

OVER PARTITION BY method is very convenient for TOP n by group selection. List of top 3 orders placed by resellers (customers of AdventureWorks Cycles).

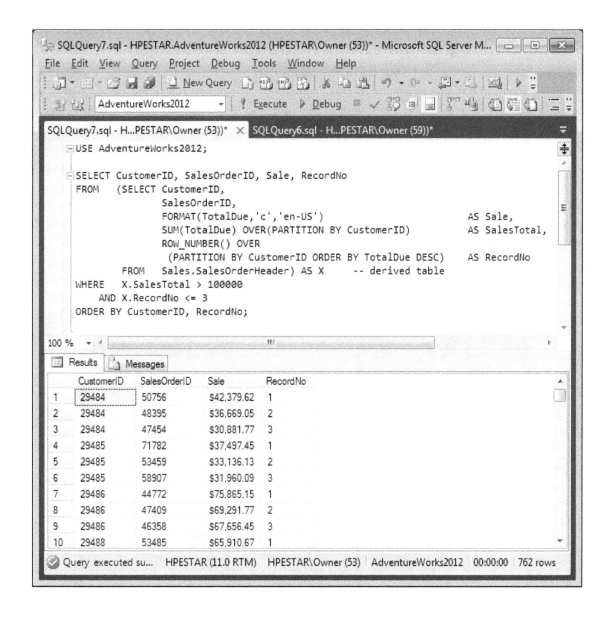

CHAPTER 4: SQL Server Management Studio

SQL Server Programming, Administration & Management Tool

SQL Server Management Studio (SSMS) is a GUI (Graphical User Interface) tool for accessing, configuring, managing, administering, and developing all major components of SQL Server with the exception of Business Intelligence components: SSAS (Analysis Services), SSRS (Reporting Services) & SSIS (Integration Services). The two main environments in SSMS: Object Explorer and Query Editor. Object Explorer is used to access servers, databases and db objects. Query Editor is to develop and execute queries. SSMS is used by a DBA (Data Base Administrator) for administrative and programming functions. SSMS can also be used by a database developer to develop application related db objects such as stored procedures, functions and triggers. Some developers prefer to stay in Visual Studio environment which has features to support database development albeit not as extensive as Management Studio. A typical screen display of Management Studio.

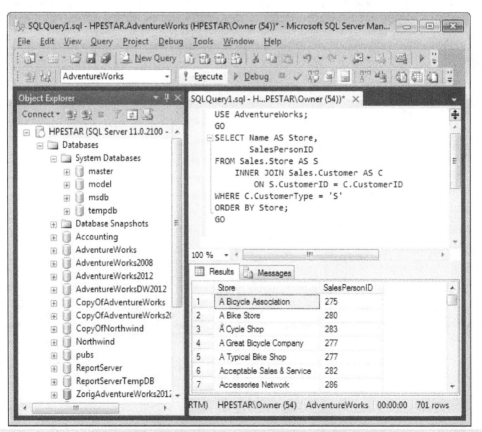

CHAPTER 4: SQL Server Management Studio

Query Editor

The Query Editor is used to type in queries, edit them and submit them for execution by the server. Queries can also be loaded from a disk file, typically with .sql extension. In addition to textual query development, a number of special tools available such as graphical query designer, debugger, execution plan display and query analysis in the Database Engine Tuning Advisor.

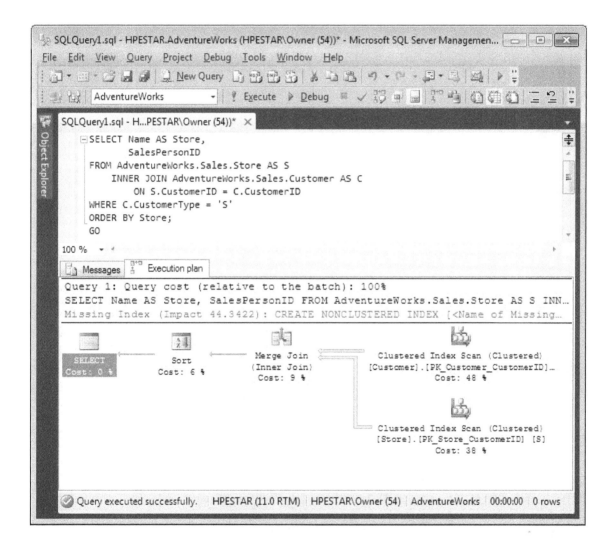

Execute All Batches in Query Editor

The entire content of the Query Editor is executed when we click on the Execute button. Batches typically separated by "GO" on a separate line.

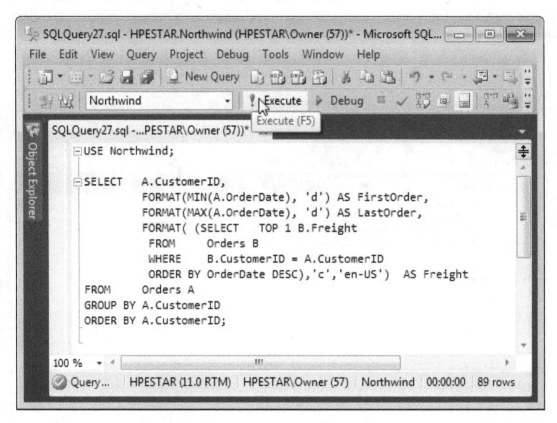

The Significance of GO in T-SQL Scripts

"GO" is not transmitted to SQL Server. "GO" indicates the end of batch to the client software such as SSMS. "GO" also indicates the end of a logical unit to the human reader. Certain statements must be the first line, or have "GO" preceding them.

```
USE AdventureWorks2012;
CREATE FUNCTION Z () RETURNS TABLE AS
RETURN  SELECT * FROM Production.ProductSubcategory;
GO
/* Msg 111, Level 15, State 1, Line 2   'CREATE FUNCTION' must be the first statement in a query batch. */
```

```
USE AdventureWorks2012;
GO
CREATE FUNCTION Z () RETURNS TABLE AS RETURN SELECT * FROM Production.ProductSubcategory;
GO
-- Command(s) completed successfully.
```

The Results Pane contains the result rows of the query. It is currently set to Grid format.

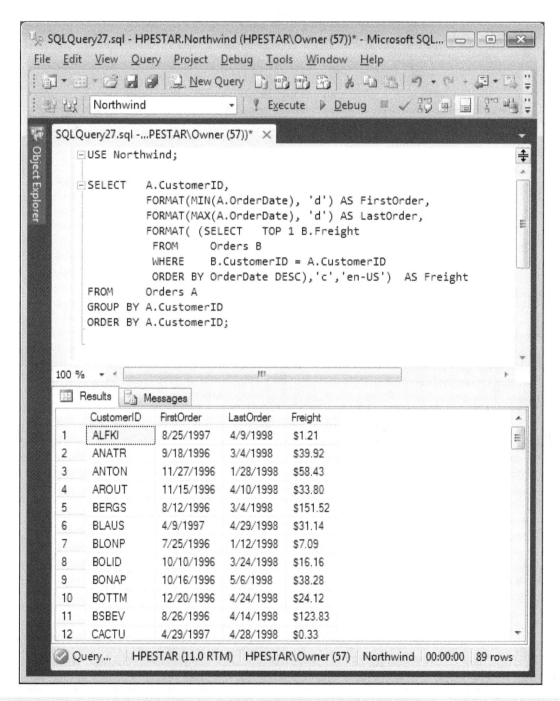

The Messages Pane gets the row count values, warning & error messages as well as the output of the PRINT & RAISERROR statements if any.

The client software also gets the same messages following query execution.

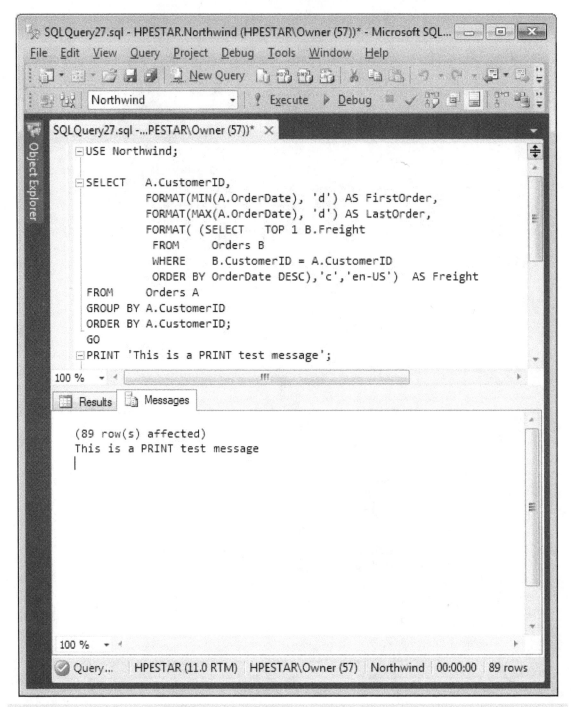

Routing Results to Grid, Text or File

Results can be routed to Grid, Text or File from the right-click menu or the Query drop-down menu.

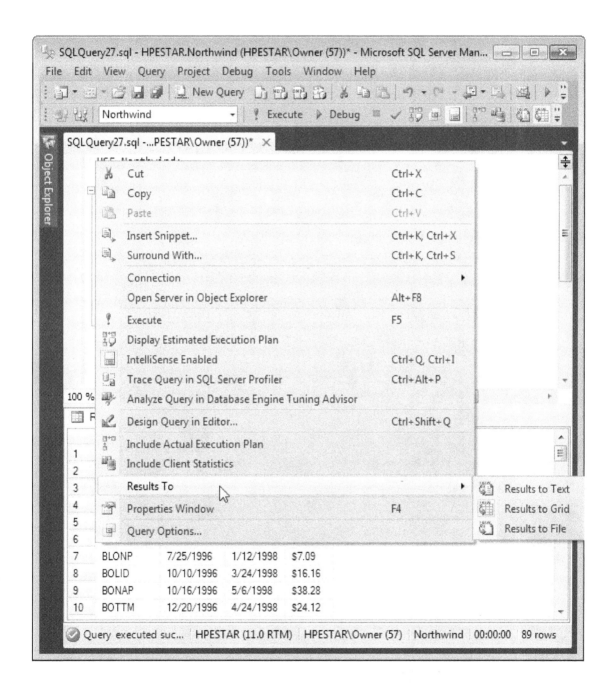

Routing Results to Text

The following screen window image displays results in text format. Messages also come to the Results window, following the results rows.

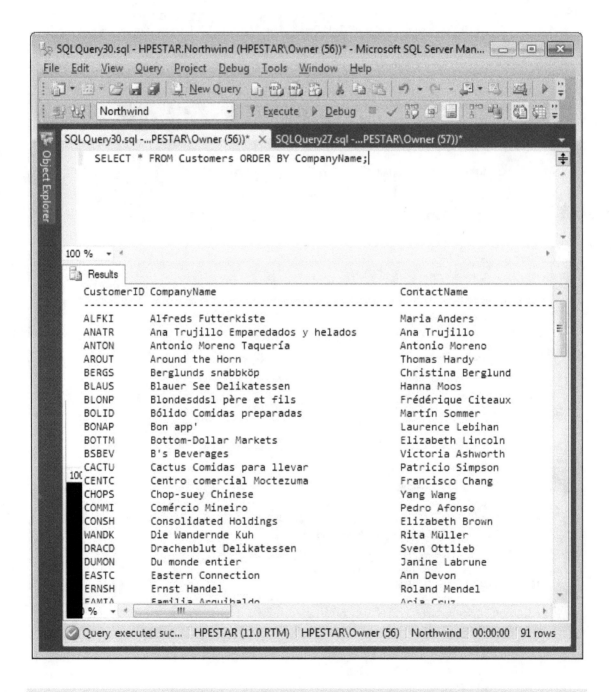

Routing Results to File

When the routing option is file, the file save window pops up upon query execution.

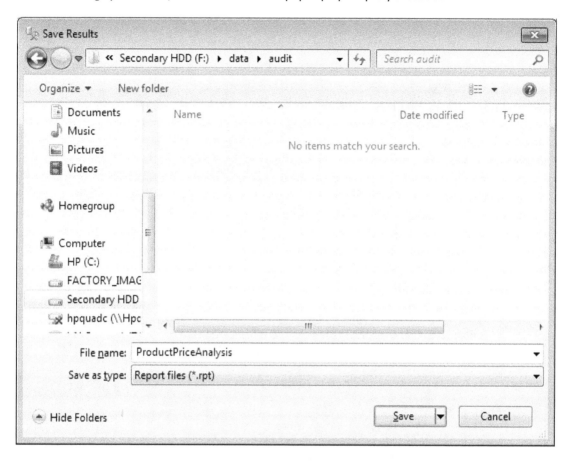

Part of the file in Notepad.

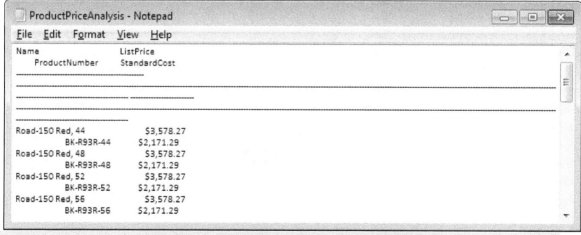

Saving Results in CSV Flat File Format

Results can also be saved in CSV (comma separated values) format which can be read by Excel and other software.

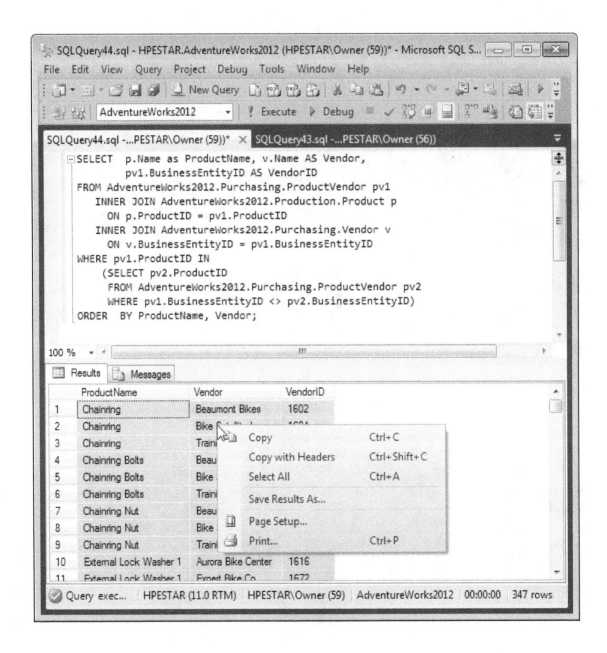

The saving file dialog box is configured automatically to csv saving.

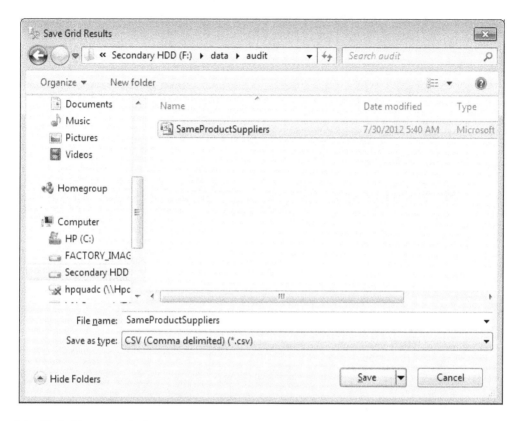

Part of the file in Notepad window.

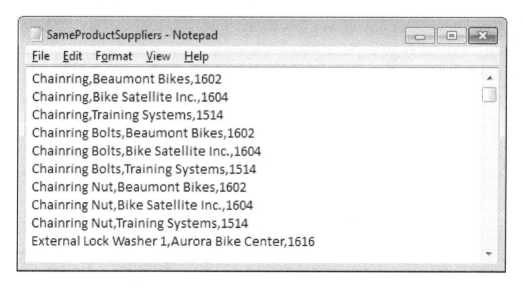

Copy & Paste Results to Excel

Using the copy / copy with headers option in SSMS result window, the query results can simply be pasted into an Excel worksheet. Excel may do implicit conversions on some columns.

After pasting into an Excel worksheet some formatting may be necessary such as for datetime columns.

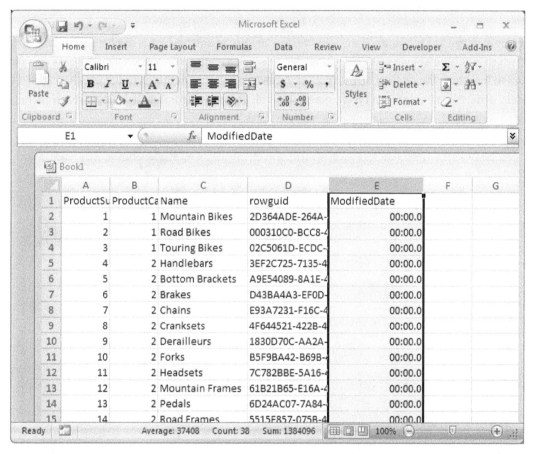

CHAPTER 4: SQL Server Management Studio

Error Handling & Debugging

Error handling and debugging is a major part of database development work. When there is an error, it is displayed in the Messages area (or returned to the application client software) which automatically becomes active. In the following example, we introduced an invalid column name which resulted in error. The error message line reference starts with the top line of the batch which is the first line after the first "GO" which indicates a new batch. The red wave-underlining comes from optional IntelliSense and not related to the execution attempt error message. IntelliSense gives warning ahead of time if it detects a potential error. Simple errors can be corrected with help from the error message. Complex errors may required web search and/or examining the query in parts.

Locating the Error Line in a Query

Position the cursor on the error and double click. The error line will be highlighted. This method does not work for all errors.

Error Message Pointing to the Wrong Line

For some errors, the first line of the query (3) is returned by the database engine not the actual error line (13). The error message is still very helpful though in this instance.

Parsing a Query for Syntax Errors

A query (or one or more batches) can be parsed for syntax errors. Parsing catches syntax errors such as
using "ORDER" instead of "ORDER BY" for sorting.

Deferred Name Resolution Process

Deferred Name Resolution Process: Only syntax errors are caught when parsed, not execution (runtime) errors as shown in the following demo which has an invalid table reference (EmployeePayHistoryx). Similarly, **stored procedures can be compiled without errors with invalid table references**. A table need not exist for stored procedure compilation, only for execution.

Executing Single Batch Only

A single batch can be executed by selecting (highlighting) it and clicking on Execute.

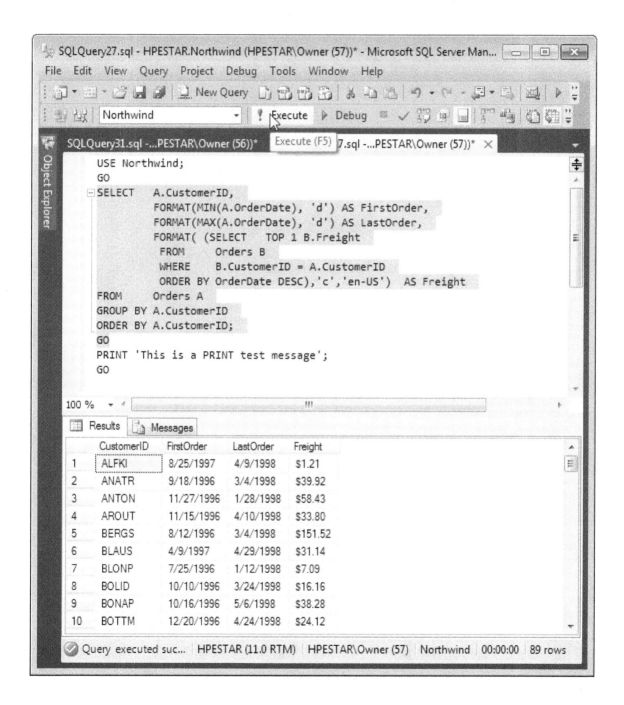

Executing Part of a Query

A part of a query can be executed as long as it is a valid query, otherwise error results. The query part has to be selected (highlighted) and the Execute button has to be pushed. The selected part of the query is considered a batch which is sent to the server. In this example, we executed the subquery (inner query) in the WHERE clause predicate.

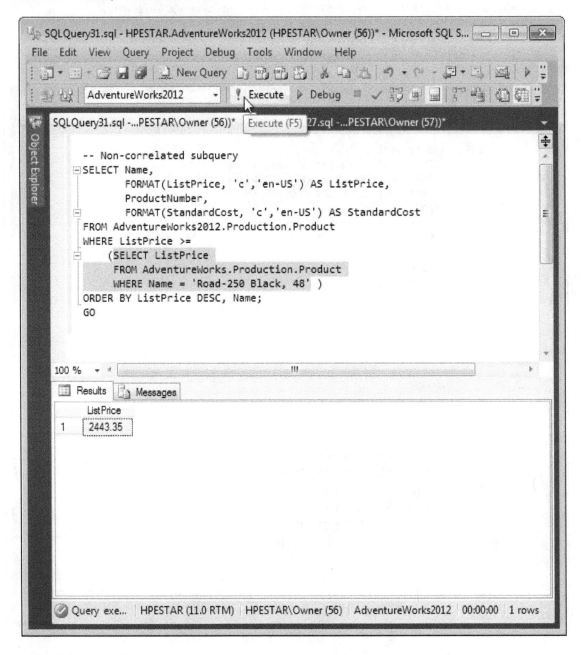

Object Explorer

SSMS Object Explorer functions as:

- ➢ A tree-based directory of all database objects
- ➢ A launching base for graphical user-interface tools
- ➢ An access way to object properties

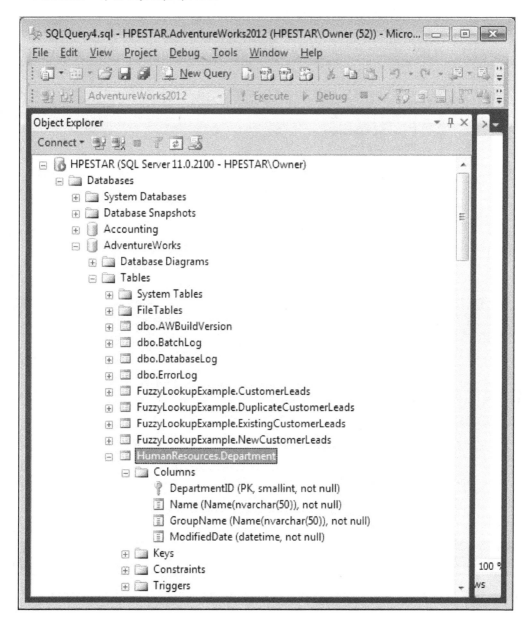

Context-Sensitive Right-Click Menu

Based on what object the cursor is on, right-click menu changes accordingly, it is context-sensitive. In the following demo the cursor is on table object when we right click on the mouse.

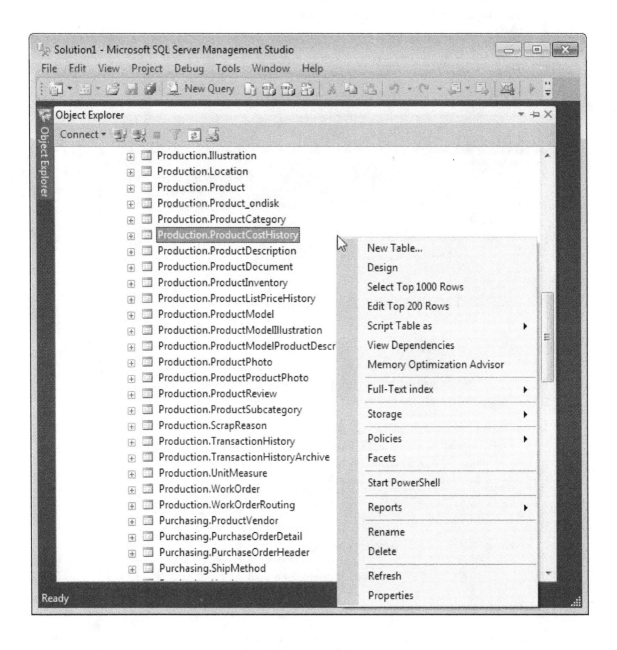

Server Administration & Management Tools

All the available SQL Server administration and management tools can be accessed from the Object Explorer. Usually the Database Administrator (DBA) uses these tools.

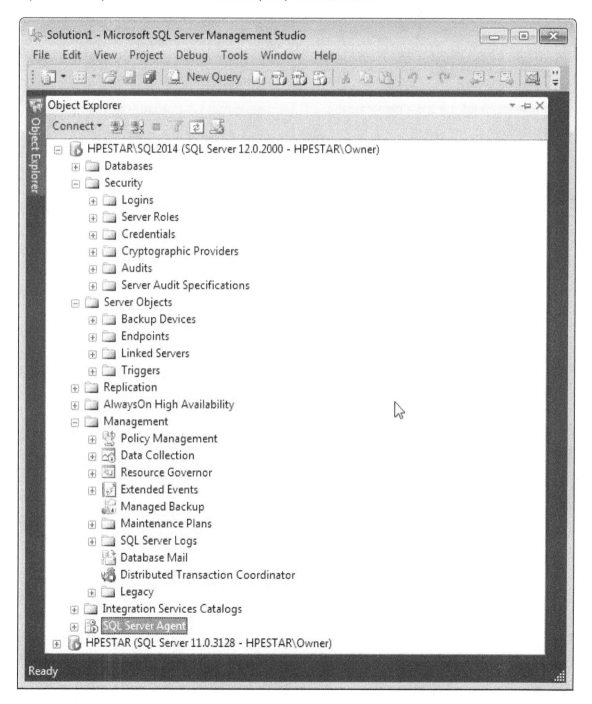

SQL Server Agent Jobs to Automate Administration Tasks

SQL Server Agent is a job creation and scheduling facility with notification features. For example, database backup job can be scheduled to execute 2:15AM every night as shown on the following dialog box. Stored procedure execution can also be setup as a job and scheduled for periodic execution.

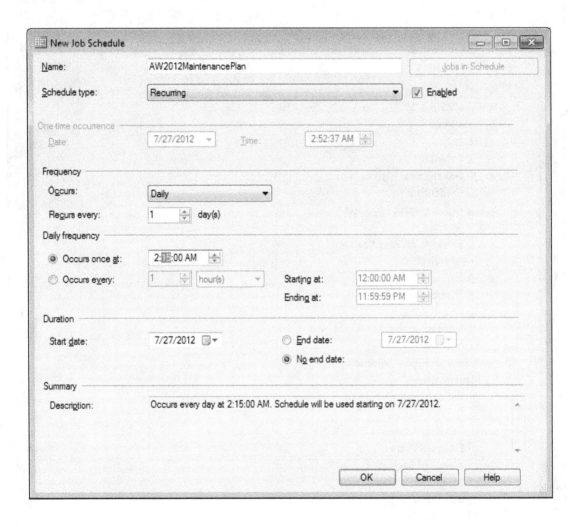

Job properties panel can be used to create and manage jobs with multiple job steps and multiple schedules.

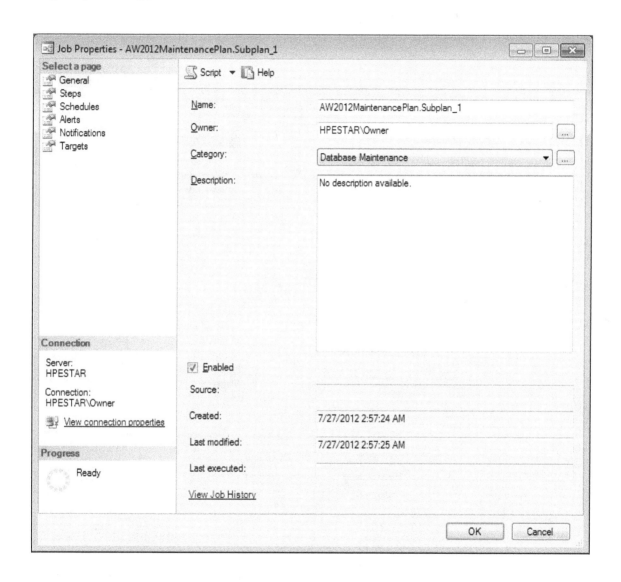

Graphical Query Designer

The Design Query in Editor entry on the Query drop-down menu launches the graphical Query Designer which can be used to design the query with GUI method and the T-SQL SELECT code will be generated automatically upon completion.

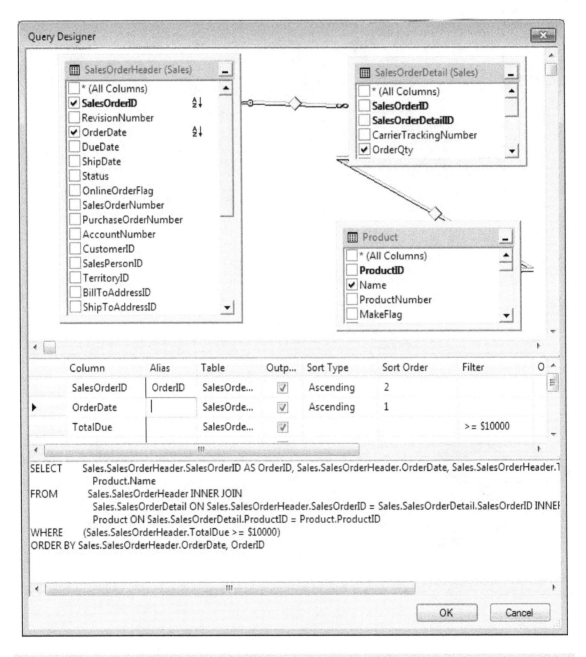

Designing a GROUP BY Query in Query Designer

Query Designer can be used to design from simple to complex queries. It can also serve as a starter query for a more complex query. It is really easy to get the tables JOINs graphically.

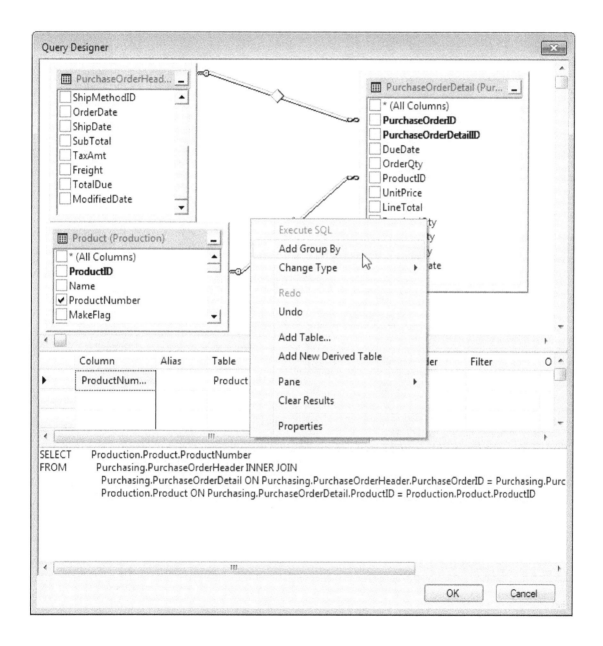

The Production.Product.Name column will also be configured as GROUP BY (drop-down default).

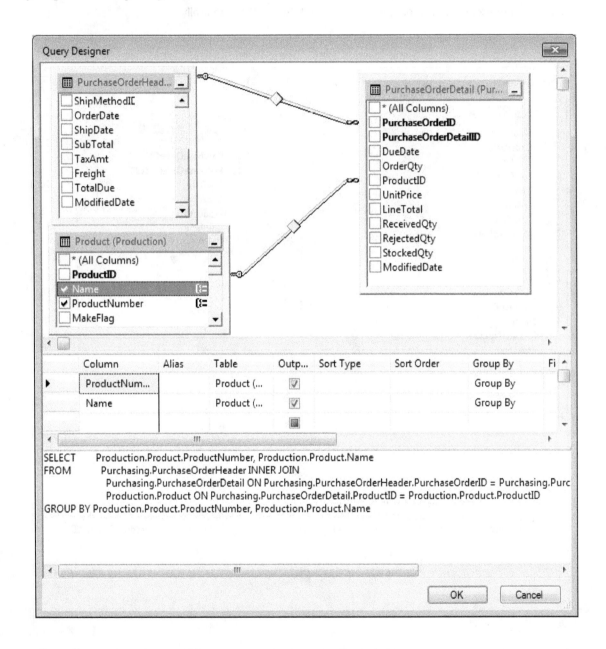

We add the TotalDue column and change the summary function to "SUM" from "Group by" and configure sorting on the first column.

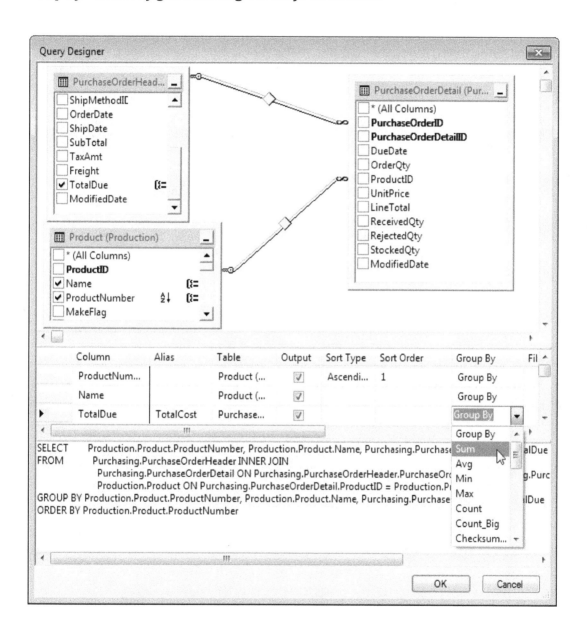

After pressing OK, the query is moved into the Query Editor window. Frequently it requires reformatting.

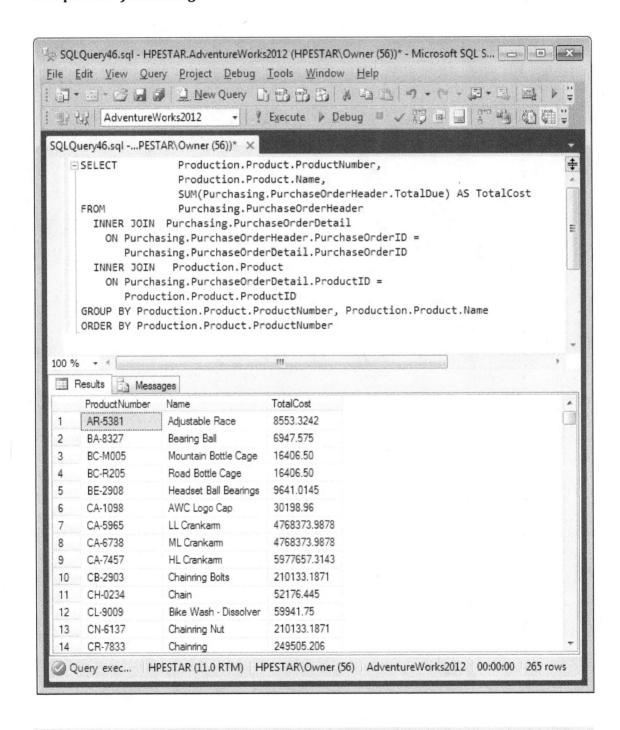

The only remaining issue with the query is the 3-part column references which is hard to read. We can change the query for readability improvement by using table aliases.

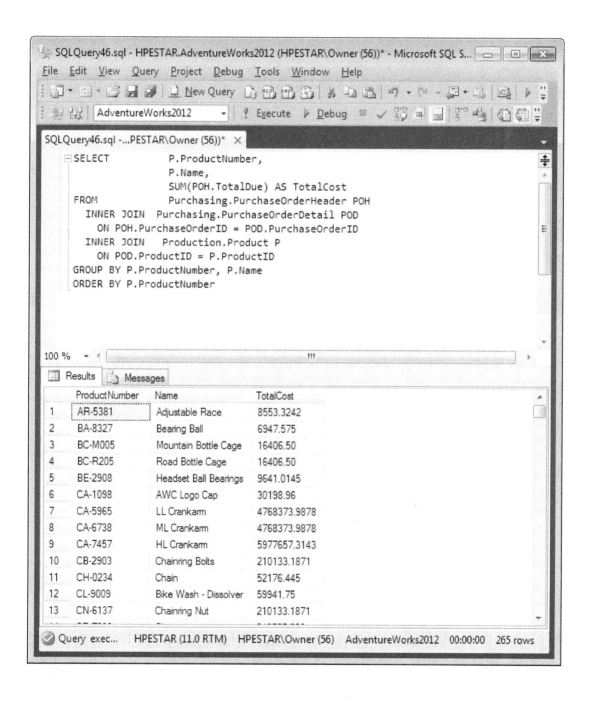

Graphically Editing of an Existing Query

An existing query, exception certain complex queries, can be uploaded into the Graphical Query Designer the following way: select (highlight) the query and right-click for the drop-down menu; click on Design Query in Editor.

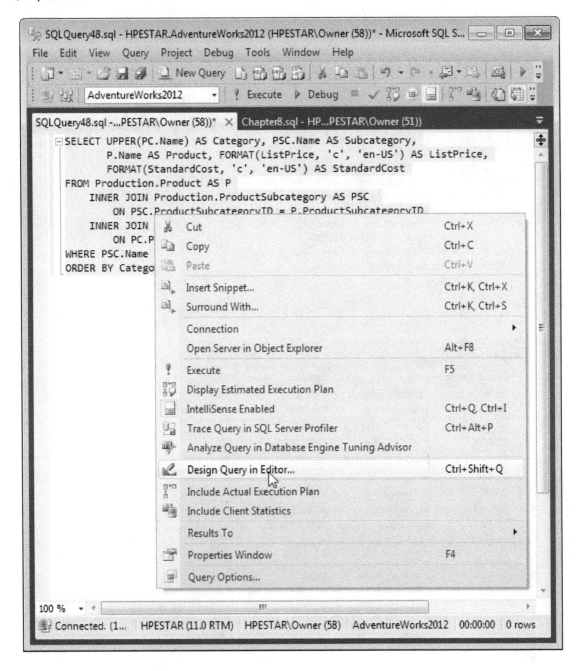

Following screen image shows the query in the Graphical Query Designer after some manual beautifying such as moving the tables for better display.

The query can be edited graphically and upon clicking on "OK", the query text is updated in the Query Editor window.

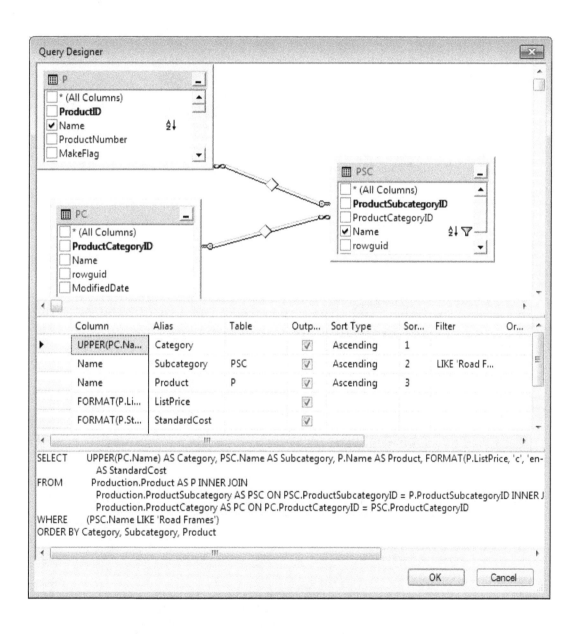

Configuring Line Numbers in Query Editor

Line numbering is an option which is off by default. Line numbers are helpful to find errors in large queries or T-SQL scripts (a sequence of T-SQL statements) when the error references a line number. Following is an example an error which includes the line number.

The Display Line Numbers option in the query editor can be activated from Options.

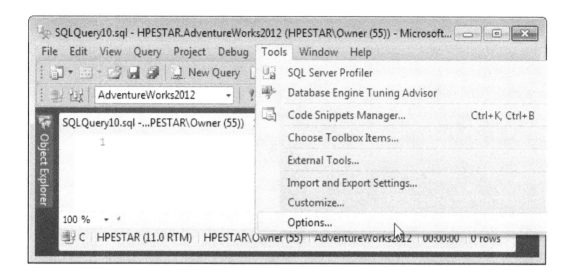

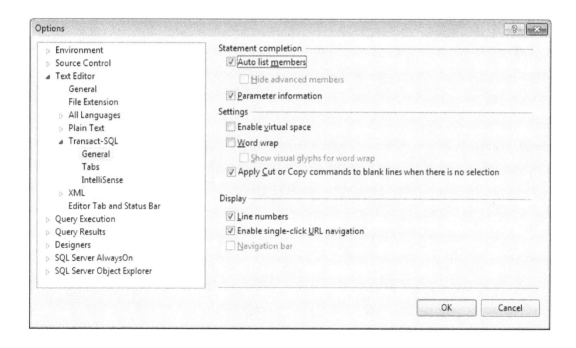

IntelliSense - Your Smart Assistant

IntelliSense is a smart agent in Query Editor. It helps completing long object names and pointing out potential errors by red wave-lining them.

The Options configuration screen for IntelliSense.

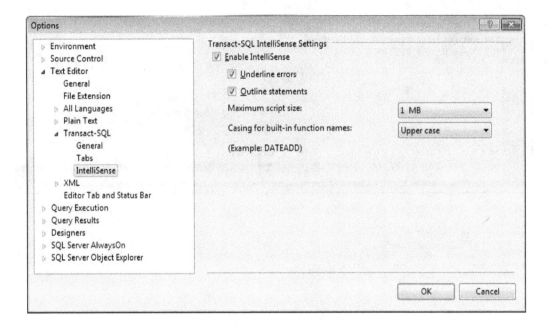

Underlining with red wave-line potential errors such as misspelling of a column name.

```
⊟SELECT TOP 1000 [BillOfMaterialsID]
       ,[ProductAssemblyID]
       ,[ComponentID]
       ,[StartDate]
       ,[EndDate]
       ,[UnitMeasureCodex]
       ,[BOMLevel]
       ,[PerAssemblyQty]
       ,[ModifiedDate]
  FROM [AdventureWorks2012].[Production].[BillOfMaterials]
```

IntelliSense Guessing and Completing Object Names

Screenshots show IntelliSense in action when typing queries.

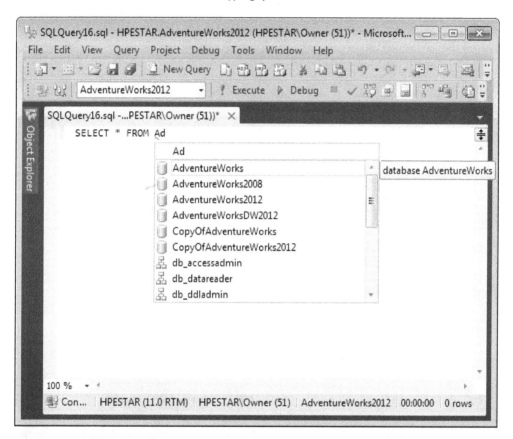

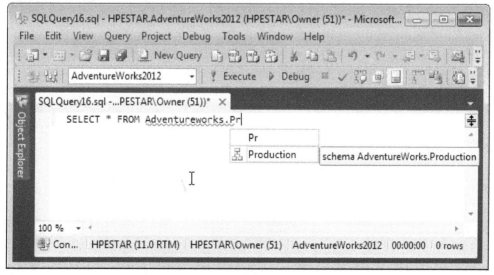

CHAPTER 4: SQL Server Management Studio

IntelliSense drop-down menu for "Prod".

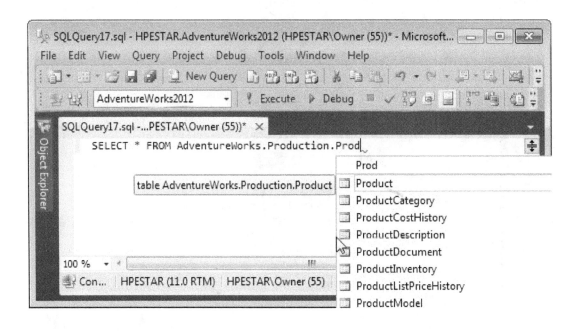

IntelliSense drop-down menu for "ProductS".

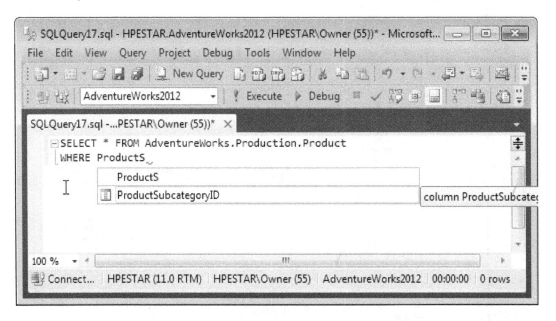

IntelliSense completion assistance for "ProductN"

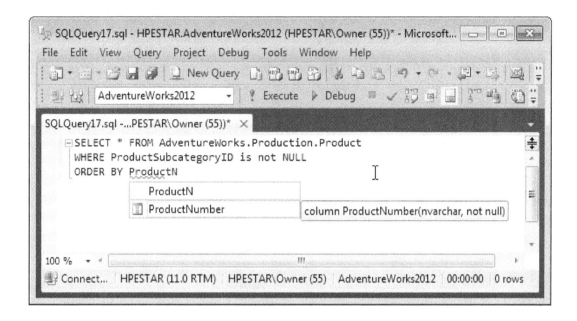

IntelliSense completion assistance for "Produ"

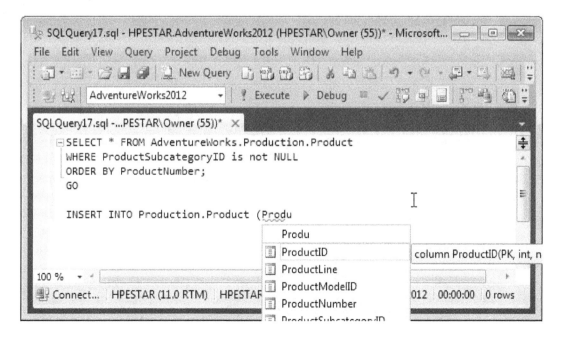

CHAPTER 4: SQL Server Management Studio

IntelliSense Assisting with User-Defined Objects

IntelliSense helps out with a user-defined stored procedure execution.

```
USE AdventureWorks2012;
GO
CREATE PROCEDURE sprocProductPaging
(
    @PageNumber int,
    @RowsPerPage int
)
AS
BEGIN
SELECT  ProductNumber,
        Name                AS ProductName,
        ListPrice,
        Color
    FROM Production.Product p
    WHERE ProductSubcategoryID is not NULL
    ORDER BY ProductNumber
    OFFSET (@PageNumber-1) * @RowsPerPage ROWS
    FETCH NEXT @RowsPerPage ROWS ONLY;
END;
GO
-- Command(s) completed successfully.

EXEC sprocProductPaging 10
```

AdventureWorks2012.dbo.sprocProductPaging **@PageNumber int**, @RowsPerPage int
Stored procedures always return INT.

IntelliSense Smart Guessing Partial Word in Middle of Object Names

You don't have to remember how an object name starts. You just have to remember some part of the name. Looking for the system view associated with "waits".

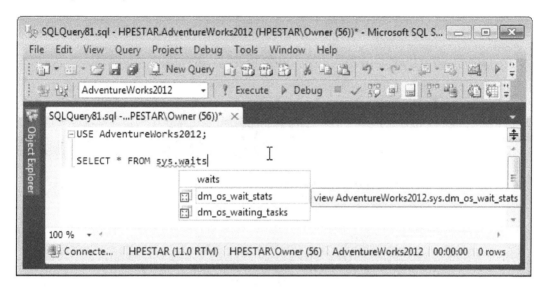

Looking for the SalesOrderHeader table but only remembering "head".

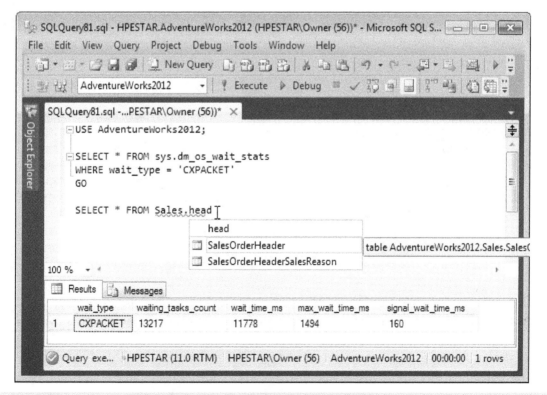

CHAPTER 4: SQL Server Management Studio

Hovering over Red Squiggly Underline Errors for Explanation

IntelliSense red wave (squiggly) underlining of errors which is caused, actually, by a single invalid table reference.

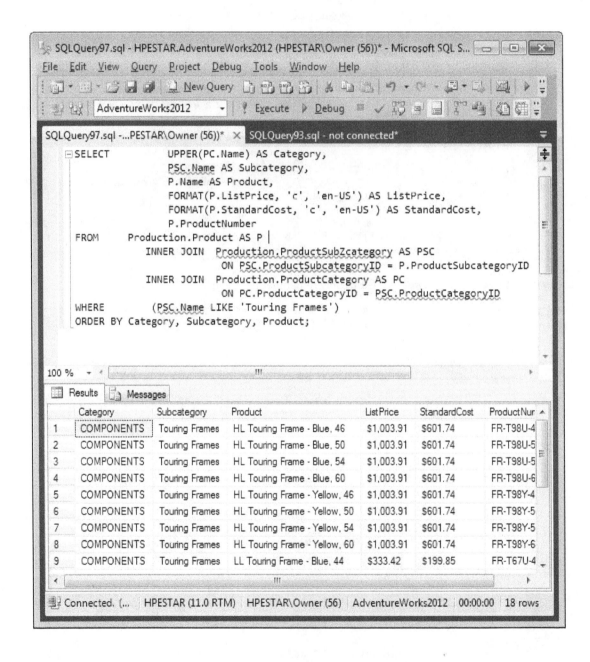

Common Error: The multi-part identifier "abc" could not be bound.

Hovering over the first error results in an explanation pop-up. This is a distant error, the kind usually the hardest to solve, because, actually, it is a secondary error caused by the primary error which is located on a different line. In this instance, there are few lines difference only, but in a large stored procedure the difference can be 200 lines as an example.

```
PSC.Name AS Subcategory,
    The multi-part identifier "PSC.Name" could not be bound.
```

Hovering over the second error yields the cause of all errors: "ProductSubZcategory".

```
Production.ProductSubZcategory AS PSC
    Invalid object name 'Production.ProductSubZcategory'.
```

The remaining error messages are all "multi-part..." caused by the solitary invalid table reference.

```
PSC.ProductSubcategoryID = P.ProductSubcategoryID
    The multi-part identifier "PSC.ProductSubcategoryID" could not be bound.
```

After fixing the table name, all errors are gone.

```
SELECT      UPPER(PC.Name)                          AS Category,
            PSC.Name                                AS Subcategory,
            P.Name                                  AS Product,
            FORMAT(P.ListPrice, 'c', 'en-US')       AS ListPrice,
            FORMAT(P.StandardCost, 'c', 'en-US')    AS StandardCost,
            P.ProductNumber
FROM      Production.Product AS P
          INNER JOIN  Production.ProductSubcategory AS PSC
                  ON PSC.ProductSubcategoryID = P.ProductSubcategoryID
          INNER JOIN  Production.ProductCategory AS PC
                  ON PC.ProductCategoryID = PSC.ProductCategoryID
WHERE       (PSC.Name LIKE 'Touring Frames')
ORDER BY Category, Subcategory, Product;
```

Refreshing IntelliSense Cache for New DB Objects

IntelliSense cache is not updated real-time. If new objects are created in another connection (session), they will not be seen until exit SSMS/reenter or IntelliSense cache is updated. No red-wave underline for the **newly created object SOD** in the same connection.

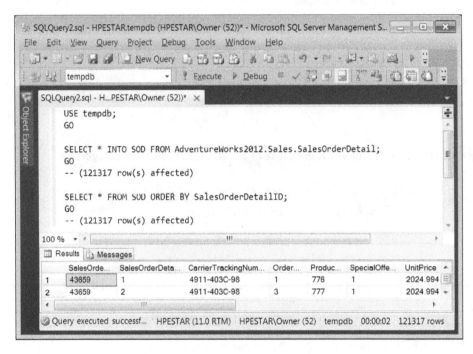

In another connection, the query works, but there are red squiggly underlining for the new table & column.

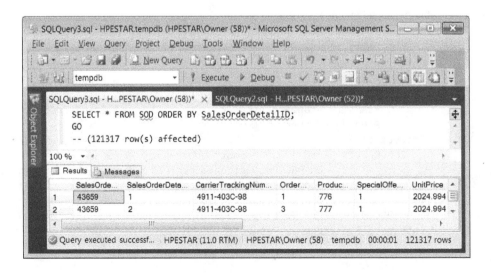

Refreshing IntelliSense Local Cache

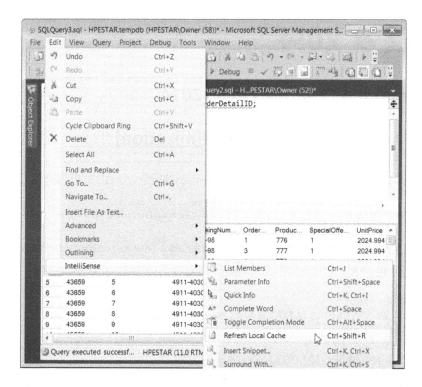

Squiggly red line goes away in all connections for the new database objects.

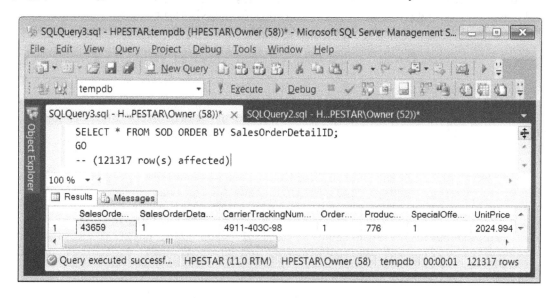

CHAPTER 5: New Programming Features in SS 2012 & 2014

New Programming Features in SS 2014

In-Memory OLTP (In-Memory Optimization)

BOL reference page: http://msdn.microsoft.com/en-us/library/dn133186(v=sql.120).aspx

Sample download: http://msftdbprodsamples.codeplex.com/releases/view/114491

SQL Server 2014 RTM In-Memory OLTP Sample creates a few in-memory tables with the _inmem suffix in AdventureWorks2012. Following is a performance comparison.

```
DBCC DROPCLEANBUFFERS;
SET STATISTICS IO ON; SET STATISTICS TIME ON;
SELECT OrderQty, Freq=count(*) from Sales.SalesOrderDetail_inmem GROUP BY OrderQty
ORDER BY Freq DESC;
SET STATISTICS TIME OFF; SET STATISTICS IO OFF;

/* Table 'Worktable'. Scan count 0, logical reads 0, physical reads 0, read-ahead
reads 0, lob logical reads 0, lob physical reads 0, lob read-ahead reads 0.
Table 'Workfile'. Scan count 0, logical reads 0, physical reads 0, read-ahead
reads 0, lob logical reads 0, lob physical reads 0, lob read-ahead reads 0.

SQL Server Execution Times:   CPU time = 47 ms,  elapsed time = 54 ms.  */

DBCC DROPCLEANBUFFERS;
SET STATISTICS IO ON; SET STATISTICS TIME ON;
SELECT OrderQty, Freq=count(*) from Sales.SalesOrderDetail GROUP BY OrderQty
ORDER BY Freq DESC;
SET STATISTICS TIME OFF; SET STATISTICS IO OFF;

/* Table 'Worktable'. Scan count 0, logical reads 0, physical reads 0, read-ahead
reads 0, lob logical reads 0, lob physical reads 0, lob read-ahead reads 0.
Table 'Workfile'. Scan count 0, logical reads 0, physical reads 0, read-ahead
reads 0, lob logical reads 0, lob physical reads 0, lob read-ahead reads 0.
Table 'SalesOrderDetail'. Scan count 1, logical reads 1246, physical reads 3,
read-ahead reads 1277, lob logical reads 0, lob physical reads 0, lob read-ahead
reads 0.

 SQL Server Execution Times:   CPU time = 78 ms,  elapsed time = 204 ms. */
```

Inline Specification Of Indexes For Disk-Based Tables

The default index for PRIMARY KEY is CLUSTERED, for UNIQUE KEY NONCLUSTERED. In the example below, we place the CLUSTERED index inline on a non-key column.

```
CREATE TABLE Celebrity (
        CelebrityID INT IDENTITY(1,1) PRIMARY KEY NONCLUSTERED,
        Name varchar(70) NOT NULL UNIQUE NONCLUSTERED,
        BirthDate DATE NOT NULL INDEX idxName CLUSTERED,
        ModifiedDate datetime2 default (sysdatetime())
);
-- Command(s) completed successfully.
```

Improved SELECT … INTO Statement

Comparing SQL Server 2014 vs. SQL Server 2012 we notice performance improvement in the new version.

```
USE tempdb;
GO
DBCC DROPCLEANBUFFERS;
SET STATISTICS IO ON; SET STATISTICS TIME ON;
SELECT * INTO SOD
FROM AdventureWorks2012.Sales.SalesOrderDetail;
SET STATISTICS TIME OFF; SET STATISTICS IO OFF;
GO
DROP TABLE SOD;
/*
SQL Server 2014

Table 'SalesOrderDetail'. Scan count 5, logical reads 1371, physical reads 3, read-ahead reads 1277, lob logical reads 0, lob physical reads 0, lob read-ahead reads 0.

SQL Server Execution Times:  CPU time = 218 ms,  elapsed time = 169 ms.

(121317 row(s) affected)

SQL Server 2012

SQL Server Execution Times:  CPU time = 265 ms,  elapsed time = 378 ms.

*/
```

New Programming Features in SS 2012

PARSE() Function

T-SQL script to demonstrate the use of the PARSE() function. The culture parameter provides support for various languages. It extends the CONVERT function which was available in T-SQL so far.

```
-- PARSE() returns the result of expression translated to requested data type - String to datetime
SELECT PARSE('SAT, 13 December 2014' AS datetime USING 'en-US') AS [Date&Time];
-- 2014-12-13 00:00:00.000
```

```
SELECT PARSE('Saturday, 13 December 2014' AS datetime USING 'en-US') AS [Date&Time];
-- 2014-12-13 00:00:00.000
```

```
SELECT PARSE('Saturday 13 December 2014' AS datetime USING 'en-US') AS [Date&Time];
-- 2014-12-13 00:00:00.000
```

```
SELECT PARSE('Saturday December 13 2014' AS datetime USING 'en-US') AS [Date&Time];
-- 2014-12-13 00:00:00.000
```

```
SELECT PARSE('Saturday December 13, 2014' AS datetime USING 'en-US') AS [Date&Time];
-- 2014-12-13 00:00:00.000
```

```
-- Inconsistent string date
SELECT PARSE('Monday, 13 December 2014' AS datetime USING 'en-US') AS [Date&Time];
/*Msg 9819, Level 16, State 1, Line 1
Error converting string value 'Monday, 13 December 2014' into data type datetime using culture 'en-US'*/
```

```
-- German culture
SELECT PARSE('Samstag December 13, 2014' AS datetime USING 'DE') AS [Date&Time];
-- 2014-12-13 00:00:00.000
```

```
-- Spanish
SELECT PARSE('Sábado December 13, 2014' AS datetime USING 'ES') AS [Date&Time];
-- 2014-12-13 00:00:00.000
```

```
-- Hungarian
SELECT PARSE('Szombat December 13, 2014' AS datetime USING 'HU') AS [Date&Time];
-- 2014-12-13 00:00:00.000
```

```
SELECT PARSE('Cumartesi December 13, 2014' AS datetime USING 'TR') AS [Date&Time];  -- Turkish
```

PARSE() Function Usage for Currency Conversion

```
-- German culture - Euro currency conversion
SELECT PARSE('€9999,95' AS money USING 'DE') AS Currency;
-- 9999.95


SELECT PARSE('€9999,95' AS money USING 'de-DE') AS Currency;
-- 9999.95


-- Italian culture - Euro currency conversion
SELECT PARSE('€9999,95' AS money USING 'IT') AS Currency;
-- 9999.95


-- Netherland culture - Euro currency conversion
SELECT PARSE('€9999,95' AS money USING 'NL') AS Currency;
-- 9999.95


-- Slovakian culture - Euro currency conversion
SELECT PARSE('€9999,95' AS money USING 'SK') AS Currency;
-- 9999.95


-- United States - Euro is not US currency
SELECT PARSE('€9999,95' AS money USING 'US') AS Currency;
/*  Msg 9818, Level 16, State 1, Line 1
The culture parameter 'US' provided in the function call is not supported.
*/


-- Italian
SELECT CONVERT(DECIMAL (12,0), PARSE('€99999,95' AS money USING 'IT')) AS DecimalValue;
-- 100000


-- PARSE with variable parameters
DECLARE @AMOUNT AS VARCHAR(12) = '$9999.00';   DECLARE @CULTURE AS CHAR(5) = 'EN-US';
SELECT DOLLAR = PARSE(@AMOUNT AS MONEY USING @CULTURE) ;
GO
-- 9999.00


-- PARSE invalid data
DECLARE @AMOUNT AS VARCHAR(12) = '$9999A.00';   DECLARE @CULTURE AS CHAR(5) = 'EN-US';
SELECT DOLLAR = PARSE(@AMOUNT AS MONEY USING @CULTURE);
GO
/*Msg 9819, Level 16, State 1, Line 4
Error converting string value '$9999A.00' into data type money using culture 'EN-US'.  */
```

TRY_CONVERT() Function

The TRY_CONVERT() function augments the CONVERT function to handle invalid data without giving an error. **It is a revolutionary new feature which makes invalid data handling significantly easier in T-SQL.**

```
-- CONVERT returns error on invalid data
SELECT [City]
        ,[PostalCode]
        ,CONVERT(INT, PostalCode)
 FROM AdventureWorks2012.Person.Address
 ORDER BY PostalCode;
/* Msg 245, Level 16, State 1, Line 1
Conversion failed when converting the nvarchar value '7L' to data type int.
*/
```

```
--  TRY_CONVERT() returns NULL for invalid data
SELECT DISTINCT [City]
        ,[PostalCode]
        ,TRY_CONVERT(INT, PostalCode) AS INTValue
 FROM AdventureWorks2012.Person.Address
 ORDER BY PostalCode;
```

City	PostalCode	INTValue
Union Gap	98903	98903
Ellensburg	98926	98926
Spokane	99202	99202
Kennewick	99337	99337
Walla Walla	99362	99362
Stoke-on-Trent	AS23	NULL
Birmingham	B29 6SL	NULL
Cambridge	BA5 3HX	NULL
W. York	BD1 4SJ	NULL
London	C2H 7AU	NULL
Cambridge	CB4 4BZ	NULL
Billericay	CM11	NULL

```
-- String date conversion to date data type
SET DATEFORMAT dmy;  -- US date format
SELECT TRY_CONVERT(date, '31/12/2016') AS Result;
-- 2016-12-31
```

```
-- Invalid date
SELECT TRY_CONVERT(date, '12/31/2016') AS Result;
-- NULL
GO
```

TRY_CONVERT() Usage in Adding Column to Table

Add new column as sequential row number (rowid) to table using the identity(int,1,1) function.

NOTE: **The IDENTITY values usually follow the ORDER BY specifications sequentially, but there is no guarantee**. If ordering is important, create an empty table first with IDENTITY column and populate it with INSERT SELECT ORDER BY.

```
USE tempdb;

SELECT TRY_CONVERT(int, [SalesOrderID]) AS [NewSalesOrderID],   -- disable IDENTITY inheritance
   *
INTO   SOH
FROM   AdventureWorks.Sales.SalesOrderHeader  ORDER  BY OrderDate,  CustomerID;
GO
-- (31465 row(s) affected)


-- Take out duplicate SalesOrderID with the IDENTITY property
ALTER TABLE SOH DROP COLUMN SalesOrderID;
GO


-- Rename NewSalesOrderID to SalesOrderID
EXEC sp_rename 'dbo.SOH.NewSalesOrderID', 'SalesOrderID';
GO


-- Add IDENTITY function as new first column  for sequence generation - sequential ID
SELECT RowNumber = IDENTITY(INT, 1, 1),     *
INTO  #SOH  FROM  SOH  ORDER  BY OrderDate, CustomerID;
GO


SELECT * INTO  SalesOrderHeader  FROM  #SOH ;  -- Create a permanent table
GO
SELECT TOP (5) *  FROM  SalesOrderHeader  ORDER  BY RowNumber ;
GO
```

RowNumber	SalesOrderID	RevisionNumber	OrderDate	DueDate	ShipDate
1	43676	1	2001-07-01 00:00:00.000	2001-07-13 00:00:00.000	2001-07-08 00:00:00.000
2	43695	1	2001-07-01 00:00:00.000	2001-07-13 00:00:00.000	2001-07-08 00:00:00.000
3	43674	1	2001-07-01 00:00:00.000	2001-07-13 00:00:00.000	2001-07-08 00:00:00.000
4	43660	1	2001-07-01 00:00:00.000	2001-07-13 00:00:00.000	2001-07-08 00:00:00.000
5	43672	1	2001-07-01 00:00:00.000	2001-07-13 00:00:00.000	2001-07-08 00:00:00.000

```
DROP TABLE SOH ;
DROP TABLE #SOH ;
DROP TABLE tempdb.dbo.SalesOrderHeader ;
```

TRY_PARSE() Function

The TRY_PARSE() function returns NULL instead of error in case of invalid data. T-SQL script to demonstrate the various uses of TRY_PARSE.

```
--  TRY_PARSE() parses or returns NULL if cast fails
SELECT TRY_PARSE('Monday, 13 December 2014' AS datetime USING 'en-US') AS [Date&Time];
-- NULL
```

```
SELECT TRY_PARSE('SAT, 13 December 2014' AS datetime USING 'en-US') AS [Date&Time];
-- 2014-12-13 00:00:00.000
```

```
-- Using the new feature with CASE Conditional.
SELECT CASE WHEN TRY_PARSE('Monday, 13 December 2014' AS datetime USING 'en-US') is NULL
        THEN (SELECT CONVERT(datetime, '19000101'))
    ELSE  (SELECT PARSE('Monday, 13 December 2014' AS datetime USING 'en-US')) END;
-- 1900-01-01 00:00:00.000
```

```
-- TRY_PARSE with variable parameters and IIF conditional
DECLARE @AMOUNT AS VARCHAR(12) = '$9999.00', @CULTURE AS CHAR(5) = 'EN-US';

SELECT RESULT = IIF(TRY_PARSE(@AMOUNT AS MONEY USING @CULTURE) IS NOT NULL
                        ,PARSE(@AMOUNT AS MONEY USING @CULTURE) ,-1.0);
-- 9999.0000
```

```
DECLARE @AMOUNT AS VARCHAR(12) = '$9999A.00'; DECLARE @CULTURE AS CHAR(5) = 'EN-US';

SELECT RESULT = IIF(TRY_PARSE(@AMOUNT AS MONEY USING @CULTURE) IS NOT NULL
                        ,PARSE(@AMOUNT AS MONEY USING @CULTURE) ,-1.0);
-- -1.0000
```

```
DECLARE @AMOUNT AS VARCHAR(12) = '$9999A.00', @CULTURE AS CHAR(5) = 'EN-US';

SELECT RESULT = IIF(TRY_PARSE(@AMOUNT AS MONEY USING @CULTURE) IS NOT NULL
                        ,PARSE(@AMOUNT AS MONEY USING @CULTURE) ,NULL);
GO
-- NULL
```

```
-- Note the multiplication by 100 using the German culture
DECLARE @AMOUNT AS VARCHAR(12) = '€77777.00'; DECLARE @CULTURE AS CHAR(5) = 'de-DE';

SELECT RESULT = IIF(TRY_PARSE(@AMOUNT AS MONEY USING @CULTURE) IS NOT NULL
                        ,PARSE(@AMOUNT AS MONEY USING @CULTURE) ,NULL);
GO
-- 7777700.00
```

FORMAT() Function

FORMAT() function is borrowed from the .NET languages. It augments the CONVERT function. T-SQL scripts to demonstrate some of the functionalities.

SELECT FORMAT(1111.22,'c','en-us');	$1,111.22
SELECT FORMAT(1111.22,'c','en-gb');	£1,111.22
SELECT FORMAT(1111.22,'c','de');	1.111,22 €
SELECT FORMAT(1111.22,'c','it');	€ 1.111,22
SELECT FORMAT(1111.22,'c','hu');	1 111,22 Ft
SELECT FORMAT(1111.22,'c','tr');	1.111,22 TL
SELECT FORMAT(1111.22,'c','es');	1.111,22 €
SELECT FORMAT(1111.22,'c','nl');	1.111,22 €
SELECT FORMAT(1111.22,'c','pl');	1 111,22 zł
SELECT FORMAT(1111.22,'c','ru');	1 111,22p.
SELECT FORMAT(1111.22,'c','se');	kr 1 111,22

```
DECLARE @culture char(2)='fr' ; SELECT FORMAT(1111.22, 'c', @culture); -- 1 111,22 €

SELECT FORMAT(1111.22,'c','gr');   /* Msg 9818, Level 16, State 1, Line 1
The culture parameter 'gr' provided in the function call is not supported.  */

SELECT FORMAT ( getdate(), 'yyyy/MM/dd hh:mm:ss tt', 'en-US' )';     -- 2016/06/03 09:56:44 AM
SELECT FORMAT ( getdate(), 'MMM dd, yyyy hh:mm:ss tt', 'en-US' );    -- Jun 03, 2016 09:57:45 AM
SELECT FORMAT(getdate(), 'MMMM d yyyy dddd','en-US'); -- April 28 2020 Monday

SELECT FORMAT ( getdate(), 'y', 'en-US' ) ;           -- July, 2016
SELECT FORMAT ( getdate(), 'M', 'en-US' ) ;           -- July 10
SELECT FORMAT ( getdate(), 'd', 'en-US' ) ;           -- 7/10/2016

-- Percent formatting
SELECT TOP (4) ProductNumber, ListPrice, StandardCost, Markup = FORMAT(ListPrice / StandardCost, 'p', 'en-us')
FROM AdventureWorks2012.Production.Product  WHERE ListPrice > 0.0  ORDER BY ProductNumber;
```

ProductNumber	ListPrice	StandardCost	Markup
BB-7421	53.99	23.9716	225.22 %
BB-8107	101.24	44.9506	225.22 %
BB-9108	121.49	53.9416	225.22 %
BC-M005	9.99	3.7363	267.37 %

CONCAT() Function

The CONCAT() function concatenates two or more strings. Previously the + operator was the only available way to concatenate. **NOTE: CONCAT treats NULL as an empty string, this is different from the + operator concatenation.** T-SQL scripts to demonstrate usage.

```
-- Using + string concatenation operator
SELECT  'New'+SPACE(1)+'York'+SPACE(1)+'City' ;        -- New York City
```

```
-- Using the new CONCAT() function
SELECT  CONCAT('New', SPACE(1),'York', SPACE(1), 'City'); -- New York City
```

```
-- Concatenating string columns with CONCAT()
SELECT CONCAT(FirstName, ' ',  LastName) AS FullName
FROM AdventureWorks2012.Person.Person
ORDER by FullName;
/* FullName
...
Blake Wright
Blake Young
Bob Alan
Bob Chapman
Bob Fernandez ... /
```

CHOOSE() Function

The CHOOSE() function returns an item from a list of values as specified by an index. T-SQL scripts to demonstrate usage.

```
SELECT CHOOSE ( 3, 'NYC', 'LA', 'Chicago', 'Houston' ) AS City;
-- Chicago
```

```
SELECT CHOOSE ( 3, 'one', 'two', 'three', 'four', 'five' ) AS Number;
-- three
```

```
DECLARE @weekday as tinyint=6;
SELECT CHOOSE(@weekday, 'Sunday', 'Monday', 'Tuesday', 'Wednesday', 'Thursday', 'Friday', 'Saturday');
-- Friday
```

```
-- Random weekday selection using newid() and rand() functions
DECLARE @weekday as tinyint=Round(Rand(Cast(Newid() AS VARBINARY)) * 6+1,0);
SELECT CHOOSE(@weekday, 'Sunday', 'Monday', 'Tuesday', 'Wednesday', 'Thursday', 'Friday', 'Saturday');
GO 10
-- Friday   Sunday  Tuesday  .....
```

CHAPTER 5: New Programming Features in SS 2012 & 2014

THROW Statement

The THROW statement passes the error incurred in TRY - CATCH to the application. Demonstration T-SQL script follows.

```
CREATE TABLE Alpha
(
        ID INT PRIMARY KEY
);
GO


BEGIN TRY
   INSERT Alpha(ID) VALUES(7);
   INSERT Alpha(ID) VALUES(7); -- Force error by attempting duplicate insert
END TRY
BEGIN CATCH
   PRINT 'In CATCH';
  -- The error message encountered will be passed down to the client software application
   THROW;
END CATCH;
/*
In CATCH

Msg 2627, Level 14, State 1, Line 7
Violation of PRIMARY KEY constraint 'PK__Alpha__3214EC272A076B44'. Cannot insert
duplicate key in object 'dbo.Alpha'. The duplicate key value is (1).
*/


-- No THROW catch  - Error message not materialized
BEGIN TRY
   INSERT Alpha(ID) VALUES(7);
END TRY
BEGIN CATCH
   PRINT 'In CATCH';
END CATCH;
/*
(0 row(s) affected)
In CATCH.
*/


-- Cleanup
DROP TABLE Alpha
GO
```

CHAPTER 5: New Programming Features in SS 2012 & 2014

IIF() Function

The IIF() function returns one of two values based on a condition. Here is a T-SQL demonstration script.

```
SELECT TOP 10    ProductID, ListPrice,
                 IIF ( Color is not null, Color, 'N/A' ) AS [Color]
FROM AdventureWorks2012.Production.Product
ORDER BY ProductID DESC;
GO
```

ProductID	ListPrice	Color
999	539.99	Black
998	539.99	Black
997	539.99	Black
996	121.49	N/A
995	101.24	N/A
994	53.99	N/A
993	539.99	Black
992	539.99	Black
991	539.99	Black
990	539.99	Black

DATEFROMPARTS() & DATETIMEFROMPARTS() Functions

The DATEFROMPARTS() & DATETIMEFROMPARTS() functions generate date / datetime value from date parts. Demonstration T-SQL script.

```
SELECT DATEFROMPARTS ( 2016, 10, 23 ) AS RealDate;
GO
-- 2016-10-23
```

```
SELECT DATETIMEFROMPARTS ( 2016, 10, 23, 10, 10, 10, 500 ) AS RealDateTime;
GO
-- 2016-10-23 10:10:10.500
```

```
DECLARE @Year smallint = 2016, @Month tinyint = 10, @Day tinyint = 23;
SELECT DATEFROMPARTS(@Year, @Month, @Day);
GO
-- 2016-10-23
```

EOMONTH() Function

The EOMONTH() function returns the last day of the month for the given input date parameter. T-SQL script to demonstrate usage.

```
SELECT EOMONTH('20140201') -- 2014-02-28

SELECT EOMONTH('20160201') -- 2016-02-29
GO

-- Future/past months optional parameter
DECLARE    @anydate DATE = '20161023';
SELECT
        CurrentMonthEnd         = EOMONTH(@anydate),
        NextMonthEnd            = EOMONTH(@anydate, 1),
        PrevMonthEnd            = EOMONTH(@anydate, -1);
GO
```

CurrentMonthEnd	NextMonthEnd	PrevMonthEnd
2016-10-31	2016-11-30	2016-09-30

```
-- Span 12 months of last day of month by using the sequence from spt_values
DECLARE    @anydate DATE = '20161023';
SELECT  TOP 12   LastDayOfMonth= EOMONTH(@anydate, number)
FROM master.dbo.spt_values WHERE type = 'P'  ORDER BY number;
GO
```

LastDayOfMonth
2016-10-31
2016-11-30
2016-12-31
2017-01-31
2017-02-28
2017-03-31
2017-04-30
2017-05-31
2017-06-30
2017-07-31
2017-08-31
2017-09-30

Result Set Paging with OFFSET & FETCH NEXT

Frequently a query produces a large results set. On the client side usually it has to be presented in small segments such as 20 lines at a time.

```
USE AdventureWorks2012;

SELECT ProductNumber, Name, ListPrice, Color
FROM Production.Product  ORDER BY ProductNumber
        OFFSET 0 ROWS    FETCH NEXT 10 ROWS ONLY;
-- (10 row(s) affected)
```

ProductNumber	Name	ListPrice	Color
AR-5381	Adjustable Race	0.00	NULL
BA-8327	Bearing Ball	0.00	NULL
BB-7421	LL Bottom Bracket	53.99	NULL
BB-8107	ML Bottom Bracket	101.24	NULL
BB-9108	HL Bottom Bracket	121.49	NULL
BC-M005	Mountain Bottle Cage	9.99	NULL
BC-R205	Road Bottle Cage	8.99	NULL
BE-2349	BB Ball Bearing	0.00	NULL
BE-2908	Headset Ball Bearings	0.00	NULL
BK-M18B-40	Mountain-500 Black, 40	539.99	Black

```
SELECT ProductNumber, Name, ListPrice, Color
FROM Production.Product  ORDER BY ProductNumber
        OFFSET 10 ROWS    FETCH NEXT 10 ROWS ONLY;
-- (10 row(s) affected)
```

ProductNumber	Name	ListPrice	Color
BK-M18B-42	Mountain-500 Black, 42	539.99	Black
BK-M18B-44	Mountain-500 Black, 44	539.99	Black
BK-M18B-48	Mountain-500 Black, 48	539.99	Black
BK-M18B-52	Mountain-500 Black, 52	539.99	Black
BK-M18S-40	Mountain-500 Silver, 40	564.99	Silver
BK-M18S-42	Mountain-500 Silver, 42	564.99	Silver
BK-M18S-44	Mountain-500 Silver, 44	564.99	Silver
BK-M18S-48	Mountain-500 Silver, 48	564.99	Silver
BK-M18S-52	Mountain-500 Silver, 52	564.99	Silver
BK-M38S-38	Mountain-400-W Silver, 38	769.49	Silver

```
SELECT ProductNumber, Name, ListPrice, Color
FROM Production.Product  ORDER BY ProductNumber OFFSET 500 ROWS    FETCH NEXT 10 ROWS ONLY;
-- (4 row(s) affected)
```

ProductNumber	Name	ListPrice	Color
VE-C304-L	Classic Vest, L	63.50	Blue
VE-C304-M	Classic Vest, M	63.50	Blue
VE-C304-S	Classic Vest, S	63.50	Blue
WB-H098	Water Bottle - 30 oz.	4.99	NULL

Result Paging Stored Procedure
The OFFSET FETCH functionality can be wrapped into a stored procedure.

```
USE AdventureWorks2012;
GO
CREATE PROCEDURE sprocProductPaging  (   @PageNumber int,   @RowsPerPage int  )   AS
BEGIN
SELECT          ProductNumber,
                Name AS ProductName,
                ListPrice,
                Color
  FROM Production.Product p
  WHERE ProductSubcategoryID is not NULL
  ORDER BY ProductNumber
  OFFSET (@PageNumber-1) * @RowsPerPage ROWS
  FETCH NEXT @RowsPerPage ROWS ONLY;
END;
 GO
-- Command(s) completed successfully.


EXEC sprocProductPaging 10, 20
GO
-- (20 row(s) affected)
```

ProductNumber	ProductName	ListPrice	Color
FR-T67Y-44	LL Touring Frame - Yellow, 44	333.42	Yellow
FR-T67Y-50	LL Touring Frame - Yellow, 50	333.42	Yellow
FR-T67Y-54	LL Touring Frame - Yellow, 54	333.42	Yellow
FR-T67Y-58	LL Touring Frame - Yellow, 58	333.42	Yellow
FR-T67Y-62	LL Touring Frame - Yellow, 62	333.42	Yellow
FR-T98U-46	HL Touring Frame - Blue, 46	1003.91	Blue
FR-T98U-50	HL Touring Frame - Blue, 50	1003.91	Blue
FR-T98U-54	HL Touring Frame - Blue, 54	1003.91	Blue
FR-T98U-60	HL Touring Frame - Blue, 60	1003.91	Blue
FR-T98Y-46	HL Touring Frame - Yellow, 46	1003.91	Yellow
FR-T98Y-50	HL Touring Frame - Yellow, 50	1003.91	Yellow
FR-T98Y-54	HL Touring Frame - Yellow, 54	1003.91	Yellow
FR-T98Y-60	HL Touring Frame - Yellow, 60	1003.91	Yellow
FW-M423	LL Mountain Front Wheel	60.745	Black
FW-M762	ML Mountain Front Wheel	209.025	Black
FW-M928	HL Mountain Front Wheel	300.215	Black
FW-R623	LL Road Front Wheel	85.565	Black
FW-R762	ML Road Front Wheel	248.385	Black
FW-R820	HL Road Front Wheel	330.06	Black
FW-T905	Touring Front Wheel	218.01	Black

LEAD() & LAG() Functions

THE LEAD() & LAG() analytical functions belong to the OVER family of functions.

```
USE AdventureWorks2012;
GO
 SELECT
        SalesOrderID,
        OrderQty,
        FORMAT(LineTotal, 'c', 'en-US')                                    AS LineTotal,
        LEAD(SalesOrderDetailID) OVER (ORDER BY SalesOrderDetailID )        AS [LEAD],
        SalesOrderDetailID                                                 AS SODID,
        LAG(SalesOrderDetailID) OVER (ORDER BY SalesOrderDetailID  )        AS [LAG]
FROM Sales.SalesOrderDetail sod
WHERE SalesOrderID IN    (SELECT SalesOrderID FROM Sales.SalesOrderHeader
                    WHERE TotalDue >= 180000)
ORDER BY SalesOrderDetailID;
--(111 row(s) affected) - Partial results.
```

SalesOrderID	OrderQty	LineTotal	LEAD	SODID	LAG
51131	11	$337.57	36817	36816	NULL
51131	12	$368.25	36818	36817	36816
51131	9	$5,421.11	36819	36818	36817
51131	2	$400.10	36820	36819	36818
51131	15	$200.76	36821	36820	36819
51131	2	$567.90	36822	36821	36820
51131	6	$8,582.65	36823	36822	36821
51131	4	$1,135.80	36824	36823	36822
51131	16	$12,206.44	36825	36824	36823
51131	8	$4,818.77	36826	36825	36824

.....

SalesOrderID	OrderQty	LineTotal	LEAD	SODID	LAG
55282	2	$76.20	55443	55442	55441
55282	4	$1,781.64	55444	55443	55442
55282	10	$146.94	55445	55444	55443
55282	3	$600.16	55446	55445	55444
55282	3	$1,807.04	55447	55446	55445
55282	28	$800.10	55448	55447	55446
55282	15	$18,685.15	55449	55448	55447
55282	8	$239.95	55450	55449	55448
55282	3	$1,336.23	55451	55450	55449
55282	7	$33.39	NULL	55451	55450

FIRST_VALUE() & LAST_VALUE() Analytic Functions

The FIRST_VALUE() and LAST_VALUE() analytic functions can be applied in conjunction with the OVER clause.

```
USE AdventureWorks2012;
GO
;WITH CTE AS
        (SELECT   PSC.Name AS Subcategory,
FIRST_VALUE(P.Name) OVER (PARTITION BY PSC.Name ORDER BY ListPrice ASC) AS LeastExpensive,
        MIN(ListPrice) OVER (PARTITION BY PSC.Name ORDER BY ListPrice ASC)        AS LowPrice,
LAST_VALUE(P.Name)  OVER (PARTITION BY PSC.Name ORDER BY ListPrice ASC) AS MostExpensive,
        MAX(ListPrice) OVER (PARTITION BY PSC.Name ORDER BY ListPrice ASC)        AS HighPrice,
        ROW_NUMBER() OVER (PARTITION BY PSC.Name ORDER BY ListPrice DESC)        AS RN
        FROM Production.Product P
        INNER JOIN Production.ProductSubcategory PSC
            ON P.ProductSubcategoryID = PSC.ProductSubcategoryID)
SELECT * FROM CTE WHERE RN = 1 ORDER BY Subcategory;
```

Subcategory	LeastExpensive	LowPrice	MostExpensive	HighPrice	RN
Bib-Shorts	Men's Bib-Shorts, S	89.99	Men's Bib-Shorts, L	89.99	1
Bike Racks	Hitch Rack - 4-Bike	120.00	Hitch Rack - 4-Bike	120.00	1
Bike Stands	All-Purpose Bike Stand	159.00	All-Purpose Bike Stand	159.00	1
Bottles and Cages	Water Bottle - 30 oz.	4.99	Mountain Bottle Cage	9.99	1
Bottom Brackets	LL Bottom Bracket	53.99	HL Bottom Bracket	121.49	1
Brakes	Rear Brakes	106.50	Front Brakes	106.50	1
Caps	AWC Logo Cap	8.99	AWC Logo Cap	8.99	1
Chains	Chain	20.24	Chain	20.24	1
Cleaners	Bike Wash - Dissolver	7.95	Bike Wash - Dissolver	7.95	1
Cranksets	LL Crankset	175.49	HL Crankset	404.99	1
Derailleurs	Front Derailleur	91.49	Rear Derailleur	121.46	1
Fenders	Fender Set - Mountain	21.98	Fender Set - Mountain	21.98	1
Forks	LL Fork	148.22	HL Fork	229.49	1
Gloves	Half-Finger Gloves, S	24.49	Full-Finger Gloves, L	37.99	1
Handlebars	LL Road Handlebars	44.54	HL Mountain Handlebars	120.27	1
Headsets	LL Headset	34.20	HL Headset	124.73	1
Helmets	Sport-100 Helmet, Blue	34.99	Sport-100 Helmet, Black	34.99	1
Hydration Packs	Hydration Pack - 70 oz.	54.99	Hydration Pack - 70 oz.	54.99	1
Jerseys	Long-Sleeve Logo Jersey, S	49.99	Short-Sleeve Classic Jersey, XL	53.99	1
Lights	Taillights - Battery-Powered	13.99	Headlights - Weatherproof	44.99	1
Locks	Cable Lock	25.00	Cable Lock	25.00	1
Mountain Bikes	Mountain-500 Black, 40	539.99	Mountain-100 Silver, 48	3399.99	1
Mountain Frames	LL Mountain Frame - Black, 40	249.79	HL Mountain Frame - Silver, 46	1364.50	1
Panniers	Touring-Panniers, Large	125.00	Touring-Panniers, Large	125.00	1
Pedals	LL Mountain Pedal	40.49	Touring Pedal	80.99	1
Pumps	Minipump	19.99	Mountain Pump	24.99	1
Road Bikes	Road-750 Black, 44	539.99	Road-150 Red, 56	3578.27	1
Road Frames	LL Road Frame - Black, 44	337.22	HL Road Frame - Red, 58	1431.50	1
Saddles	LL Mountain Seat/Saddle	27.12	HL Touring Seat/Saddle	52.64	1
Shorts	Men's Sports Shorts, S	59.99	Women's Mountain Shorts, L	69.99	1
Socks	Racing Socks, M	8.99	Mountain Bike Socks, L	9.50	1
Tights	Women's Tights, S	74.99	Women's Tights, L	74.99	1
Tires and Tubes	Patch Kit/8 Patches	2.29	HL Mountain Tire	35.00	1
Touring Bikes	Touring-3000 Blue, 44	742.35	Touring-1000 Blue, 60	2384.07	1
Touring Frames	LL Touring Frame - Blue, 50	333.42	HL Touring Frame - Yellow, 60	1003.91	1
Vests	Classic Vest, S	63.50	Classic Vest, L	63.50	1
Wheels	LL Mountain Front Wheel	60.745	HL Road Rear Wheel	357.06	1

CUME_DIST() & PERCENT_RANK() Analytic Functions

CUME_DIST() and PERCENT_RANK() analytic functions work in conjunction with the OVER clause.

```
SELECT   Department,
         CONCAT(LastName,', ', FirstName)                                AS FullName,
         Rate,
         FORMAT(CUME_DIST () OVER (PARTITION BY Department ORDER BY Rate),'p')   AS CumuDist,
         FORMAT(PERCENT_RANK()  OVER (PARTITION BY Department ORDER BY Rate ),'p') AS PctRnk
FROM HumanResources.vEmployeeDepartmentHistory AS edh  -- view
   INNER JOIN HumanResources.EmployeePayHistory AS e
            ON e.BusinessEntityID = edh.BusinessEntityID
ORDER BY Department, Rate DESC;
-- (334 row(s) affected) - Partial results.
```

Department	FullName	Rate	CumuDist	PctRnk
Facilities and Maintenance	Altman, Gary	24.0385	100.00 %	100.00 %
Facilities and Maintenance	Kleinerman, Christian	20.4327	85.71 %	83.33 %
Facilities and Maintenance	Hedlund, Magnus	9.75	71.43 %	66.67 %
Facilities and Maintenance	Penor, Lori	9.25	57.14 %	0.00 %
Facilities and Maintenance	Macrae, Stuart	9.25	57.14 %	0.00 %
Facilities and Maintenance	Berry, Jo	9.25	57.14 %	0.00 %
Facilities and Maintenance	Coleman, Pat	9.25	57.14 %	0.00 %
Finance	Norman, Laura	60.0962	100.00 %	100.00 %
Finance	Norman, Laura	48.5577	92.31 %	91.67 %
Finance	Kahn, Wendy	43.2692	84.62 %	83.33 %
Finance	Norman, Laura	39.06	76.92 %	75.00 %
Finance	Liu, David	34.7356	69.23 %	66.67 %
Finance	Moreland, Barbara	26.4423	61.54 %	50.00 %
Finance	Seamans, Mike	26.4423	61.54 %	50.00 %
Finance	Tomic, Dragan	19.00	46.15 %	8.33 %
Finance	Sheperdigian, Janet	19.00	46.15 %	8.33 %
Finance	Poe, Deborah	19.00	46.15 %	8.33 %
Finance	Spoon, Candy	19.00	46.15 %	8.33 %
Finance	Walton, Bryan	19.00	46.15 %	8.33 %
Finance	Barber, David	13.4615	7.69 %	0.00 %
Human Resources	Barreto de Mattos, Paula	27.1394	100.00 %	100.00 %
Human Resources	Johnson, Willis	18.2692	83.33 %	60.00 %
Human Resources	Luthra, Vidur	18.2692	83.33 %	60.00 %
Human Resources	Martin, Mindy	16.5865	50.00 %	40.00 %
Human Resources	Culbertson, Grant	13.9423	33.33 %	0.00 %
Human Resources	Chen, Hao	13.9423	33.33 %	0.00 %

EXEC New Option: WITH RESULT SETS

The WITH RESULT SETS clause can be used to remap the result set of a stored procedure or system procedure execution.

```
EXEC sp_who;
GO
-- (145 row(s) affected) - Partial results.
```

spid	ecid	status	loginame	hostname	blk	dbname	cmd	request_id
1	0	background	sa		0	NULL	LOG WRITER	0
2	0	background	sa		0	NULL	RECOVERY WRITER	0
3	0	background	sa		0	NULL	LAZY WRITER	0
4	0	background	sa		0	master	SIGNAL HANDLER	0
5	0	background	sa		0	NULL	LOCK MONITOR	0

```
EXEC sp_who
 WITH RESULT SETS
 (
 (
 SPID INT,
 ECID INT,
 STATUS VARCHAR(32),
 LOGINAME SYSNAME,
 HOSTNAME SYSNAME,
 BLK TINYINT,
 DBNAME SYSNAME,
 CMD VARCHAR(64),
 REQUESTID INT
 )
);
-- (145 row(s) affected) - Partial results.
```

SPID	ECID	STATUS	LOGINAME	HOSTNAME	BLK	DBNAME	CMD	REQUESTID
1	0	background	sa		0	NULL	LOG WRITER	0
2	0	background	sa		0	NULL	RECOVERY WRITER	0
3	0	background	sa		0	NULL	LAZY WRITER	0
4	0	background	sa		0	master	SIGNAL HANDLER	0
5	0	background	sa		0	NULL	LOCK MONITOR	0

CHAPTER 6: JOINing Tables with INNER & OUTER JOINs

SELECT with INNER JOIN

The SELECT statement is used to retrieve data from table(s). An INNER JOIN is a join in which the values in the columns being joined are compared using a comparison operator. Inner join also known as equi-join when equality condition is applied. Equi-join: PRIMARY KEY (table a) = FOREIGN KEY (table b).

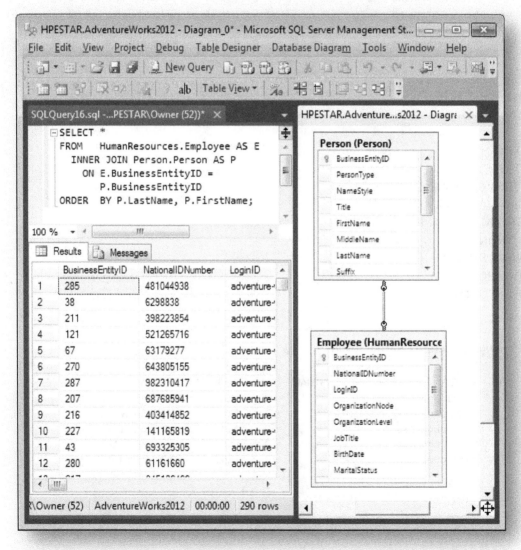

FOREIGN KEY Constraint as Base for INNER JOIN

The INNER JOIN is based on HumanResources.Employee.BusinessEntityID (PRIMARY KEY) is a FOREIGN KEY to Person.Person.BusinessEntityID. The Employee table is in one-to-one relationship with a subset of the Person table.

Diagram of Person.Person and Related Tables

The population of Person.Person includes all employees, contacts, and customers, therefore a key table in the database.

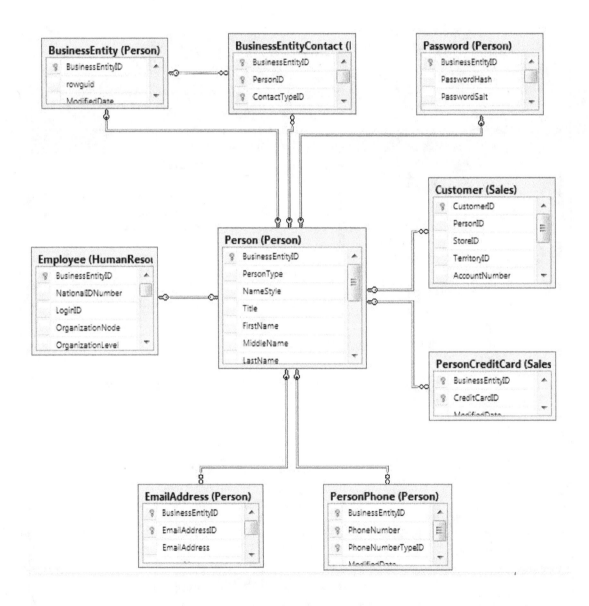

EQUI-JOIN BETWEEN FOREIGN KEY & PRIMARY KEY

EQUI JOIN means the equality operator is used to match the left and right keys. The reason for the popularity: the goal of most query is to gather information from related tables records (rows). Query to demonstrate why are 3 tables necessary to get a meaningful business report with just a few columns.

```
USE AdventureWorks;
GO

SELECT          CONCAT(LastName, ', ', FirstName)          AS Consumer,
                EmailAddress,
                Phone,
                CU.AccountNumber,
                C.ContactID,
                I.CustomerID
FROM Person.Contact AS C
   INNER JOIN Sales.Individual AS I
     ON C.ContactID = I.ContactID
   INNER JOIN Sales.Customer AS CU
     ON I.CustomerID = CU.CustomerID
WHERE CU.CustomerType = 'I'
ORDER BY LastName, FirstName ;
GO
-- (18484 row(s) affected) - Partial results.
```

Consumer	EmailAddress	Phone	AccountNumber	ContactID	CustomerID
Pal, Yolanda	yolanda11@adventure-works.com	1 (11) 500 555-0110	AW00023748	2837	23748
Palit, Punya	punya0@adventure-works.com	164-555-0118	AW00017574	14759	17574
Parker, Adam	adam29@adventure-works.com	808-555-0157	AW00018228	14771	18228
Parker, Alex	alex26@adventure-works.com	613-555-0123	AW00029252	14783	29252
Parker, Alexandra	alexandra50@adventure-works.com	974-555-0142	AW00016866	8977	16866
Parker, Allison	allison30@adventure-works.com	750-555-0124	AW00026501	9021	26501
Parker, Amanda	amanda51@adventure-works.com	978-555-0167	AW00018081	8985	18081
Parker, Amber	amber7@adventure-works.com	1 (11) 500 555-0198	AW00023959	8999	23959
Parker, Andrea	andrea23@adventure-works.com	612-555-0113	AW00020091	8461	20091
Parker, Angel	angel21@adventure-works.com	815-555-0120	AW00014273	14779	14273
Parker, Bailey	bailey28@adventure-works.com	604-555-0112	AW00019529	9007	19529
Parker, Blake	blake44@adventure-works.com	432-555-0151	AW00015008	3413	15008
Parker, Caleb	caleb28@adventure-works.com	593-555-0116	AW00026318	14760	26318
Parker, Carlos	carlos25@adventure-works.com	937-555-0143	AW00020676	14778	20676
Parker, Charles	charles43@adventure-works.com	266-555-0118	AW00021267	4105	21267
Parker, Chloe	chloe5@adventure-works.com	360-555-0121	AW00027480	8965	27480
Parker, Connor	connor28@adventure-works.com	936-555-0177	AW00028839	14763	28839
Parker, Courtney	courtney5@adventure-works.com	266-555-0176	AW00017612	9002	17612
Parker, Dalton	dalton42@adventure-works.com	535-555-0190	AW00013064	3722	13064
Parker, Devin	devin40@adventure-works.com	897-555-0155	AW00011684	4192	11684
Parker, Eduardo	eduardo41@adventure-works.com	131-555-0192	AW00012939	4269	12939

Diagram of Sales.Customer and Related Tables

Customer is the source of revenue for any business. Therefore, proper table design is paramount.

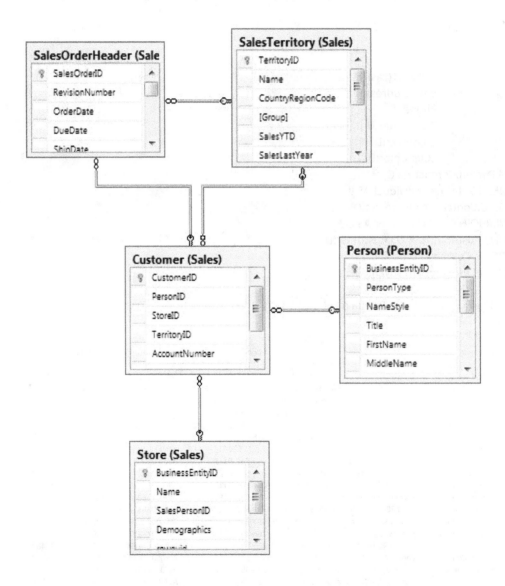

Extracting All or Partial Data from JOINed Tables

T-SQL scripts to demonstrate how to JOIN two tables and extract all or subset of the information.

```
USE AdventureWorks2012;
```

```
-- SELECT all columns from the JOINed tables
SELECT *
FROM   HumanResources.Employee          AS E      -- E is a table alias
    INNER JOIN Person.Person            AS P      -- P is a table alias
        ON E.BusinessEntityID = P.BusinessEntityID
ORDER  BY P.LastName;
-- (290 row(s) affected) - Partial results.
```

FirstName	MiddleName	LastName
Syed	E	Abbas
Kim	B	Abercrombie
Hazem	E	Abolrous
Pilar	G	Ackerman
Jay	G	Adams

```
SELECT E.*                      -- SELECT Employee columns from the JOINed tables
FROM   HumanResources.Employee AS E
    INNER JOIN Person.Person AS P    ON E.BusinessEntityID = P.BusinessEntityID
ORDER  BY P.LastName;
-- Partial results.
```

JobTitle	BirthDate	MaritalStatus	Gender
Pacific Sales Manager	1969-02-11	M	M
Production Technician - WC60	1961-01-14	M	F
Quality Assurance Manager	1971-11-27	S	M
Shipping and Receiving Supervisor	1966-10-11	S	M

```
-- SELECT Person columns from the JOINed tables
SELECT P.* FROM   HumanResources.Employee AS E
                INNER JOIN Person.Person AS P     ON E.BusinessEntityID = P.BusinessEntityID
ORDER  BY P.LastName;
-- Partial results.
```

BusinessEntityID	PersonType
285	SP
38	EM
211	EM

SELECT All Columns From The Joined Tables Using Table Alias And Wildcard

```
SELECT E.*, P.*
FROM   HumanResources.Employee              AS E    -- E is a table alias
    INNER JOIN Person.Person                AS P    -- P is a table alias
        ON E.BusinessEntityID = P.BusinessEntityID
ORDER  BY P.LastName;
-- Same results as SELECT * FROM
```

```
-- Count JOINed rows
SELECT count(*)
FROM   HumanResources.Employee AS E
    INNER JOIN Person.Person AS P
        ON E.BusinessEntityID = P.BusinessEntityID
-- 290
```

```
-- Vertically output reduction: eliminate columns from the available pool
SELECT   E.BusinessEntityID              AS EmployeeID,   -- column alias
         E.JobTitle,
         P.FirstName,
         P.LastName
FROM   HumanResources.Employee AS E
    INNER JOIN Person.Person AS P    ON E.BusinessEntityID = P.BusinessEntityID
ORDER  BY P.LastName;
-- (290 row(s) affected) - Partial results.
```

EmployeeID	JobTitle	FirstName	LastName
285	Pacific Sales Manager	Syed	Abbas
38	Production Technician - WC60	Kim	Abercrombie
211	Quality Assurance Manager	Hazem	Abolrous
121	Shipping and Receiving Supervisor	Pilar	Ackerman

```
-- Create a new output column from the available pool of columns
SELECT   E.BusinessEntityID                  AS EmployeeID,
         E.JobTitle,
         CONCAT(P.FirstName, ' ', P.LastName)      AS NAME
FROM   HumanResources.Employee AS E
    INNER JOIN Person.Person AS P     ON E.BusinessEntityID = P.BusinessEntityID
ORDER  BY P.LastName;
-- (290 row(s) affected) - Partial results.
```

EmployeeID	JobTitle	NAME
285	Pacific Sales Manager	Syed Abbas
38	Production Technician - WC60	Kim Abercrombie
211	Quality Assurance Manager	Hazem Abolrous
121	Shipping and Receiving Supervisor	Pilar Ackerman

CHAPTER 6: JOINing Tables with INNER & OUTER JOINs

Table Aliases for Readability

The table alias serves as shorthand for table name to improve the **readability of queries**. It should be as short as possible and as meaningful as possible when we have to use a few letters. The next T-SQL query applies four table aliases: c, soh, sod, p.

```
USE AdventureWorks;
SELECT DISTINCT SalesPerson = CONCAT(c.FirstName,SPACE(1), c.LastName)
FROM   Person.Contact c
    INNER JOIN Sales.SalesOrderHeader soh
    ON soh.SalesPersonId = c.ContactID
    INNER JOIN Sales.SalesOrderDetail sod
    ON soh.SalesOrderId = sod.SalesOrderId
    INNER JOIN Production.Product p
    ON sod.ProductID = p.ProductID    AND p.Name LIKE ('%Touring Frame%');
GO
/*      SalesPerson
        Carla Eldridge
        Carol Elliott
        Gail Erickson  ....*/
```

Column Aliases for Readability & Presentation

The column alias serves as a meaningful column name either replacing a column name or filling in when there is no column name. In the previous example the = sign was used to establish the column alias. Alternate setting follows applying "AS" (it can be skipped) after the column. If the alias has spaces it has to be included in square brackets like [Bond Sales] or double quotes.

```
USE AdventureWorks;
SELECT DISTINCT  CONCAT(c.FirstName,' ', c.LastName)                      AS SalesPerson
FROM   Person.Contact c
    INNER JOIN Sales.SalesOrderHeader soh
    ON soh.SalesPersonId = c.ContactID
    INNER JOIN Sales.SalesOrderDetail sod
    ON soh.SalesOrderId = sod.SalesOrderId
    INNER JOIN Production.Product p
    ON sod.ProductID = p.ProductID   AND p.Name LIKE ('%Touring Frame%');
-- (17 row(s) affected) - Partial results.
```

SalesPerson
Carla Eldridge
Carol Elliott
Gail Erickson
Gary Drury
Janeth Esteves
Jauna Elson
John Emory

CHAPTER 6: JOINing Tables with INNER & OUTER JOINs

Derived Table Alias with a List of Column Aliases

Optionally column alias list can be specified for derived tables just like in CTE definition. T-SQL query demonstrates nested derived tables with table-column aliases (P & J).

```
SELECT DISTINCT ProdID, ProdName, ProdPrice, OrderQuantity
FROM    (
             SELECT   ID, ProductName, Price,          -- Derived table columns
                      OrderQty                         -- SOD column
             FROM AdventureWorks2012.Sales.SalesOrderDetail SOD
             INNER JOIN
                  (SELECT ProductID, Name, ListPrice
                   FROM AdventureWorks2012.Production.Product
                  ) P(ID, ProductName, Price)          -- inner derived table
             ON SOD.ProductID = P.ID
        ) J (ProdID, ProdName, ProdPrice, OrderQuantity)       -- outer derived table
ORDER BY ProdPrice DESC, ProdName;
-- (2667 row(s) affected) - Partial results.
```

ProdID	ProdName	ProdPrice	OrderQuantity
750	Road-150 Red, 44	3578.27	3
750	Road-150 Red, 44	3578.27	6
750	Road-150 Red, 44	3578.27	1
750	Road-150 Red, 44	3578.27	4
750	Road-150 Red, 44	3578.27	2
750	Road-150 Red, 44	3578.27	5
751	Road-150 Red, 48	3578.27	6
751	Road-150 Red, 48	3578.27	3
751	Road-150 Red, 48	3578.27	2
751	Road-150 Red, 48	3578.27	5
751	Road-150 Red, 48	3578.27	4
751	Road-150 Red, 48	3578.27	1
752	Road-150 Red, 52	3578.27	5
752	Road-150 Red, 52	3578.27	3
752	Road-150 Red, 52	3578.27	6
752	Road-150 Red, 52	3578.27	1
752	Road-150 Red, 52	3578.27	4
752	Road-150 Red, 52	3578.27	2
753	Road-150 Red, 56	3578.27	6
753	Road-150 Red, 56	3578.27	3

INNER JOIN with Additional Conditions

The ON clause of a JOIN can include additional conditions as the following demonstration shows. The INNER JOIN is still based on FOREIGN KEY relationship, but only a subset of records (rows) returned due to the additional conditions, or JOIN predicates. The first query returns the distinct set of cases where the Selling Price was below the ListPrice for ProductID 800 which is a yellow road bike. The second query covers the remaining range where the Selling Price was equal or above the ListPrice

```
USE AdventureWorks2012;
SELECT DISTINCT( P.ProductID ),
        ProductName = P.Name,           -- column alias
        P.ListPrice,
        SOD.UnitPrice AS 'Selling Price'   -- column alias
FROM   Sales.SalesOrderDetail AS SOD       -- table alias
   INNER JOIN  Production.Product AS P     -- table alias
   ON SOD.ProductID = P.ProductID
     AND SOD.UnitPrice < P.ListPrice               -- JOIN predicate
     AND  P.ProductID = 800;                       -- JOIN predicate
```

ProductID	ProductName	ListPrice	Selling Price
800	Road-550-W Yellow, 44	1120.49	600.2625
800	Road-550-W Yellow, 44	1120.49	672.294
800	Road-550-W Yellow, 44	1120.49	1000.4375

```
SELECT DISTINCT( P.ProductID ),
        ProductName = P.Name,
        P.ListPrice,
        SOD.UnitPrice AS 'Selling Price'
FROM   Sales.SalesOrderDetail AS SOD
   INNER JOIN  Production.Product AS P
   ON SOD.ProductID = P.ProductID
     AND SOD.UnitPrice >= P.ListPrice
     AND  P.ProductID BETWEEN 800 AND 900
ORDER BY ProductName;
-- (26 row(s) affected) - Partial results.
```

ProductID	ProductName	ListPrice	Selling Price
879	All-Purpose Bike Stand	159.00	159.00
877	Bike Wash - Dissolver	7.95	7.95
866	Classic Vest, L	63.50	63.50
865	Classic Vest, M	63.50	63.50
864	Classic Vest, S	63.50	63.50
878	Fender Set - Mountain	21.98	21.98
860	Half-Finger Gloves, L	24.49	24.49
859	Half-Finger Gloves, M	24.49	24.49
858	Half-Finger Gloves, S	24.49	24.49
876	Hitch Rack - 4-Bike	120.00	120.00

Counting Rows in JOINs

As the T-SQL script following shows, the basic FOREIGN KEY based JOIN returns 121,317 rows which is all the rows in Sales.SalesOrderDetail table. The additional condition P.ProductID = 800 selects a subset of 495 rows which is then divided between the < and >= conditions.

```
USE AdventureWorks2012;
SELECT Rows = count(*)
FROM   Sales.SalesOrderDetail AS SOD
    INNER JOIN  Production.Product AS P     ON SOD.ProductID = P.ProductID
-- 121317
```

```
SELECT Rows = count(*)
FROM   Sales.SalesOrderDetail AS SOD
    INNER JOIN  Production.Product AS P   ON SOD.ProductID = P.ProductID   AND P.ProductID = 800;
-- 495
```

```
SELECT Rows = count(*)
FROM   Sales.SalesOrderDetail AS SOD
    INNER JOIN  Production.Product AS P
    ON SOD.ProductID = P.ProductID
        AND SOD.UnitPrice < P.ListPrice
        AND P.ProductID = 800;
-- 285
```

```
SELECT Rows = count(*)
FROM   Sales.SalesOrderDetail AS SOD
    INNER JOIN  Production.Product AS P
    ON SOD.ProductID = P.ProductID
        AND SOD.UnitPrice >= P.ListPrice
        AND P.ProductID = 800;
-- 210
```

```
SELECT COUNT(P.ProductID)
FROM   Sales.SalesOrderDetail AS SOD
    INNER JOIN  Production.Product AS P
    ON SOD.ProductID = P.ProductID
        AND SOD.UnitPrice >= P.ListPrice
        AND  P.ProductID BETWEEN 800 AND 900;
-- 21085
```

```
SELECT COUNT(DISTINCT P.ProductID)
FROM   Sales.SalesOrderDetail AS SOD
    INNER JOIN  Production.Product AS P
    ON SOD.ProductID = P.ProductID   AND SOD.UnitPrice >= P.ListPrice
        AND  P.ProductID BETWEEN 800 AND 900;
```

INNER JOIN with 3 Tables

T-SQL query to demonstrate JOINing three tables. Due to the application of the FORMAT function, column name is lost. Therefore we have to alias the formatted column with the original column name or something else. Both INNER JOINs are based on FOREIGN KEY relationships. PV.ProductID is an FK to the Production.Product table, and the PV.VendorID is an FK to the Purchasing.Vendor table. The Purchasing.ProductVendor table is a junction table representing many-to-many relationships between products and vendors: a vendor may supply many products (see Beaumont Bikes in results) and a product may be supplied by many vendors (see Chainring in results).

```
USE AdventureWorks;
GO
SELECT          P.ProductNumber,
                P.Name                          AS Product,
                V.Name                          AS Vendor,
                FORMAT (PV.LastReceiptCost, 'c', 'en-US')    AS LastReceiptCost
FROM Production.Product AS P
  INNER JOIN Purchasing.ProductVendor AS PV
        ON P.ProductID = PV.ProductID
  INNER JOIN Purchasing.Vendor AS V
        ON V.VendorID = PV.VendorID
ORDER BY Product;
GO
-- (406 row(s) affected) - Partial results.
```

ProductNumber	Product	Vendor	LastReceiptCost
AR-5381	Adjustable Race	Litware, Inc.	$50.26
BA-8327	Bearing Ball	Wood Fitness	$41.92
CH-0234	Chain	Varsity Sport Co.	$15.74
CR-7833	Chainring	Beaumont Bikes	$25.42
CR-7833	Chainring	Bike Satellite Inc.	$26.37
CR-7833	Chainring	Training Systems	$28.70
CB-2903	Chainring Bolts	Beaumont Bikes	$47.47
CB-2903	Chainring Bolts	Bike Satellite Inc.	$45.37
CB-2903	Chainring Bolts	Training Systems	$49.64
CN-6137	Chainring Nut	Beaumont Bikes	$42.80
CN-6137	Chainring Nut	Bike Satellite Inc.	$40.49
CN-6137	Chainring Nut	Training Systems	$44.32
RA-7490	Cone-Shaped Race	Midwest Sport, Inc.	$44.22
CR-9981	Crown Race	Business Equipment Center	$50.26
RA-2345	Cup-Shaped Race	Bloomington Multisport	$48.76
DC-8732	Decal 1	SUPERSALES INC.	$0.21
DC-9824	Decal 2	SUPERSALES INC.	$0.21
LE-6000	External Lock Washer 1	Pro Sport Industries	$41.24
LE-6000	External Lock Washer 1	Aurora Bike Center	$43.27
LE-6000	External Lock Washer 1	Expert Bike Co	$41.17

T-SQL Query To Return All Road Frames Offered For Sale By AdventureWorks Cycles

```
USE AdventureWorks2012;
SELECT          UPPER(PC.Name)          AS Category,   PSC.Name                    AS Subcategory,
                P.Name          AS Product,   FORMAT(ListPrice, 'c', 'en-US')      AS ListPrice,
                FORMAT(StandardCost, 'c', 'en-US')                                 AS StandardCost
FROM Production.Product AS P
   INNER JOIN Production.ProductSubcategory AS PSC
          ON PSC.ProductSubcategoryID = P.ProductSubcategoryID
   INNER JOIN Production.ProductCategory AS PC
          ON PC.ProductCategoryID = PSC.ProductCategoryID
WHERE PSC.Name like 'Road Frames'  ORDER BY Category, Subcategory, Product;
```

Category	Subcategory	Product	ListPrice	StandardCost
COMPONENTS	Road Frames	HL Road Frame - Black, 44	$1,431.50	$868.63
COMPONENTS	Road Frames	HL Road Frame - Black, 48	$1,431.50	$868.63
COMPONENTS	Road Frames	HL Road Frame - Black, 52	$1,431.50	$868.63
COMPONENTS	Road Frames	HL Road Frame - Black, 58	$1,431.50	$1,059.31
COMPONENTS	Road Frames	HL Road Frame - Black, 62	$1,431.50	$868.63
COMPONENTS	Road Frames	HL Road Frame - Red, 44	$1,431.50	$868.63
COMPONENTS	Road Frames	HL Road Frame - Red, 48	$1,431.50	$868.63
COMPONENTS	Road Frames	HL Road Frame - Red, 52	$1,431.50	$868.63
COMPONENTS	Road Frames	HL Road Frame - Red, 56	$1,431.50	$868.63
COMPONENTS	Road Frames	HL Road Frame - Red, 58	$1,431.50	$1,059.31
COMPONENTS	Road Frames	HL Road Frame - Red, 62	$1,431.50	$868.63
COMPONENTS	Road Frames	LL Road Frame - Black, 44	$337.22	$204.63
COMPONENTS	Road Frames	LL Road Frame - Black, 48	$337.22	$204.63
COMPONENTS	Road Frames	LL Road Frame - Black, 52	$337.22	$204.63
COMPONENTS	Road Frames	LL Road Frame - Black, 58	$337.22	$204.63
COMPONENTS	Road Frames	LL Road Frame - Black, 60	$337.22	$204.63
COMPONENTS	Road Frames	LL Road Frame - Black, 62	$337.22	$204.63
COMPONENTS	Road Frames	LL Road Frame - Red, 44	$337.22	$187.16
COMPONENTS	Road Frames	LL Road Frame - Red, 48	$337.22	$187.16
COMPONENTS	Road Frames	LL Road Frame - Red, 52	$337.22	$187.16
COMPONENTS	Road Frames	LL Road Frame - Red, 58	$337.22	$187.16
COMPONENTS	Road Frames	LL Road Frame - Red, 60	$337.22	$187.16
COMPONENTS	Road Frames	LL Road Frame - Red, 62	$337.22	$187.16
COMPONENTS	Road Frames	ML Road Frame - Red, 44	$594.83	$352.14
COMPONENTS	Road Frames	ML Road Frame - Red, 48	$594.83	$352.14
COMPONENTS	Road Frames	ML Road Frame - Red, 52	$594.83	$352.14
COMPONENTS	Road Frames	ML Road Frame - Red, 58	$594.83	$352.14
COMPONENTS	Road Frames	ML Road Frame - Red, 60	$594.83	$352.14
COMPONENTS	Road Frames	ML Road Frame-W - Yellow, 38	$594.83	$360.94
COMPONENTS	Road Frames	ML Road Frame-W - Yellow, 40	$594.83	$360.94
COMPONENTS	Road Frames	ML Road Frame-W - Yellow, 42	$594.83	$360.94
COMPONENTS	Road Frames	ML Road Frame-W - Yellow, 44	$594.83	$360.94
COMPONENTS	Road Frames	ML Road Frame-W - Yellow, 48	$594.83	$360.94

INNER JOIN with Junction Table

Three tables INNER JOIN includes the titleauthor junction table which represent many-to-many relationship. All JOINs are EQUI-JOINs with FOREIGN KEYs and PRIMARY KEYs.

```
USE pubs;

SELECT          FORMAT(ytd_sales, 'c', 'en-US')                          AS YTDSales,
                CONCAT(au.au_fname, ' ', au.au_lname)                    AS Author,
                FORMAT((ytd_sales * royalty) / 100,'c','en-US')          AS AuthorRev,
                FORMAT((ytd_sales - (ytd_sales * royalty) / 100),'c','en-US')   AS PublisherRev
FROM titles t
        INNER JOIN titleauthor ta
            ON t.title_id = ta.title_id
        INNER JOIN authors au
            ON ta.au_id = au.au_id
ORDER BY        YTDSales DESC,          -- Major sort key
                Author ASC;             -- Minor sort key
GO
```

YTDSales	Author	AuthorRev	PublisherRev
$8,780.00	Cheryl Carson	$1,404.00	$7,376.00
$4,095.00	Abraham Bennet	$409.00	$3,686.00
$4,095.00	Akiko Yokomoto	$409.00	$3,686.00
$4,095.00	Ann Dull	$409.00	$3,686.00
$4,095.00	Burt Gringlesby	$409.00	$3,686.00
$4,095.00	Dean Straight	$409.00	$3,686.00
$4,095.00	Marjorie Green	$409.00	$3,686.00
$4,095.00	Michael O'Leary	$409.00	$3,686.00
$4,095.00	Sheryl Hunter	$409.00	$3,686.00
$4,072.00	Johnson White	$407.00	$3,665.00
$375.00	Livia Karsen	$37.00	$338.00
$375.00	Stearns MacFeather	$37.00	$338.00
$375.00	Sylvia Panteley	$37.00	$338.00
$3,876.00	Michael O'Leary	$387.00	$3,489.00
$3,876.00	Stearns MacFeather	$387.00	$3,489.00
$3,336.00	Charlene Locksley	$333.00	$3,003.00
$22,246.00	Anne Ringer	$5,339.00	$16,907.00
$22,246.00	Michel DeFrance	$5,339.00	$16,907.00
$2,045.00	Albert Ringer	$245.00	$1,800.00
$2,045.00	Anne Ringer	$245.00	$1,800.00
$2,032.00	Innes del Castillo	$243.00	$1,789.00
$18,722.00	Marjorie Green	$4,493.00	$14,229.00
$15,096.00	Reginald Blotchet-Halls	$2,113.00	$12,983.00
$111.00	Albert Ringer	$11.00	$100.00
NULL	Charlene Locksley	NULL	NULL

NON-EQUI JOINs for Data Analytics

We can use not equal operators in JOIN predicates as demonstrated in the next query. The second predicate in the JOIN is less than JOIN.

```
USE AdventureWorks2012;
GO
-- List of "red" products sold at a discount
SELECT DISTINCT         p.ProductNumber,
                        p.Name                              AS ProductName,
                        FORMAT(p.ListPrice,'c','en-US')     AS ListPrice,
                        FORMAT(sod.UnitPrice,'c','en-US')   AS SellPrice
FROM Sales.SalesOrderDetail AS sod
   INNER JOIN Production.Product AS p
        ON sod.ProductID = p.ProductID
        AND sod.UnitPrice < p.ListPrice
WHERE Color = 'Red'
ORDER BY p.ProductNumber;
--(86 row(s) affected) - Partial results.
```

ProductNumber	ProductName	ListPrice	SellPrice
BK-R50R-44	Road-650 Red, 44	$782.99	$234.90
BK-R50R-44	Road-650 Red, 44	$782.99	$419.46
BK-R50R-44	Road-650 Red, 44	$782.99	$430.64
BK-R50R-44	Road-650 Red, 44	$782.99	$454.13
BK-R50R-44	Road-650 Red, 44	$782.99	$469.79
BK-R50R-44	Road-650 Red, 44	$782.99	$563.75
BK-R50R-44	Road-650 Red, 44	$782.99	$699.10
BK-R50R-48	Road-650 Red, 48	$782.99	$419.46
BK-R50R-48	Road-650 Red, 48	$782.99	$430.64
BK-R50R-48	Road-650 Red, 48	$782.99	$454.13
BK-R50R-48	Road-650 Red, 48	$782.99	$469.79
BK-R50R-48	Road-650 Red, 48	$782.99	$563.75

To resolve the duplicate issue which makes DISTINCT usage necessary, we have to include the SalesOrderID column.

```
SELECT                  p.ProductNumber,
                        p.Name                              AS ProductName,
                        FORMAT(p.ListPrice,'c','en-US')     AS ListPrice,
                        FORMAT(sod.UnitPrice,'c','en-US')   AS SellPrice,
                        sod.SalesOrderID
FROM Sales.SalesOrderDetail AS sod
   INNER JOIN Production.Product AS p
        ON sod.ProductID = p.ProductID
        AND sod.UnitPrice < p.ListPrice
WHERE Color = 'Red'   ORDER BY p.ProductNumber;
-- (8408 row(s) affected)
```

Interchangeability of ON & WHERE Predicates in INNER JOINs

We can freely place the predicates to either the ON clause or the WHERE clause in an INNER JOIN. This is not true for OUTER JOINs such as LEFT JOINs.

```
USE AdventureWorks2012;
-- List of "blue" products sold at a discount
SELECT DISTINCT p.ProductNumber, p.Name              AS ProductName,
                FORMAT(p.ListPrice,'c','en-US')      AS ListPrice,
                FORMAT(sod.UnitPrice,'c','en-US')    AS SellPrice
FROM Sales.SalesOrderDetail AS sod
  INNER JOIN Production.Product AS p
      ON sod.ProductID = p.ProductID
      AND sod.UnitPrice < p.ListPrice
WHERE Color = 'Blue'  ORDER BY p.ProductNumber;
--(57 row(s) affected)


SELECT DISTINCT  p.ProductNumber, p.Name             AS ProductName,
                FORMAT(p.ListPrice,'c','en-US')      AS ListPrice,
                FORMAT(sod.UnitPrice,'c','en-US')    AS SellPrice
FROM Sales.SalesOrderDetail AS sod
  INNER JOIN Production.Product AS p
       ON sod.ProductID = p.ProductID
       AND sod.UnitPrice < p.ListPrice
       AND Color = 'Blue'
ORDER BY p.ProductNumber;
--(57 row(s) affected)


SELECT DISTINCT  p.ProductNumber, p.Name             AS ProductName,
                FORMAT(p.ListPrice,'c','en-US')      AS ListPrice,
                FORMAT(sod.UnitPrice,'c','en-US')    AS SellPrice
FROM Sales.SalesOrderDetail AS sod
  INNER JOIN Production.Product AS p
  ON sod.ProductID = p.ProductID
WHERE sod.UnitPrice < p.ListPrice   AND Color = 'Blue'  ORDER BY p.ProductNumber;
--(57 row(s) affected)


-- Old-style INNER JOIN with table list and WHERE clause
SELECT DISTINCT p.ProductNumber, p.Name              AS ProductName,
                FORMAT(p.ListPrice,'c','en-US')      AS ListPrice,
                FORMAT(sod.UnitPrice,'c','en-US')    AS SellPrice
FROM Sales.SalesOrderDetail AS sod,  Production.Product AS p
WHERE sod.ProductID = p.ProductID
       AND sod.UnitPrice < p.ListPrice
       AND Color = 'Blue'
ORDER BY p.ProductNumber;         --(57 row(s) affected)
```

SELF-JOIN for Analytics Within a Table

When a table is JOINed to itself, it is a called a self-join. The purpose of such a JOIN is to examine data relations within the table. The Production.Product table is self-joined to itself on the ProductSubcategoryID FOREIGN KEY(not on a PRIMARY KEY), a many-to-many JOIN. Subsequently, we made the query "friendlier" by using subcategory names as opposed to ID-s.

```
SELECT DISTINCT  P1.ProductSubcategoryID,
                 P1.ListPrice            AS ListPrice1,
                 P2.ListPrice            AS ListPrice2
FROM   Production.Product P1
 INNER JOIN Production.Product P2
   ON P1.ProductSubcategoryID = P2.ProductSubcategoryID
   AND P1.ListPrice < P2.ListPrice
   AND P1.ListPrice < $15
   AND P2.ListPrice < $15;
```

ProductSubcategoryID	ListPrice1	ListPrice2
23	8.99	9.50
28	4.99	8.99
28	4.99	9.99
28	8.99	9.99
37	2.29	3.99
37	2.29	4.99
37	3.99	4.99

```
SELECT DISTINCT  PS.Name AS Subcategory,
                 P1.ListPrice     AS ListPrice1,
                 P2.ListPrice     AS ListPrice2
FROM   Production.ProductSubcategory PS
   INNER JOIN Production.Product P1
       ON PS.ProductSubcategoryID = P1.ProductSubcategoryID
   INNER JOIN Production.Product P2
       ON P1.ProductSubcategoryID = P2.ProductSubcategoryID
       AND P1.ListPrice < P2.ListPrice            -- To prevent duplicate processing
       AND P1.ListPrice < $15
       AND P2.ListPrice < $15;
```

Subcategory	ListPrice1	ListPrice2
Bottles and Cages	4.99	8.99
Bottles and Cages	4.99	9.99
Bottles and Cages	8.99	9.99
Socks	8.99	9.50
Tires and Tubes	2.29	3.99
Tires and Tubes	2.29	4.99
Tires and Tubes	3.99	4.99

T-SQL SELF-JOIN Query Lists The Competing Suppliers For Each Product Purchased From Vendor

Since the ProductID in the ProductVendor table is part of a composite PRIMARY KEY, we can conclude that it is a many-to-many JOIN.

```
SELECT DISTINCT
            Vendor = V.[Name],
            P1.BusinessEntityID,
            Product = P.[Name],
            P1.ProductID
FROM   Production.Product P
    INNER JOIN Purchasing.ProductVendor P1
        ON P.ProductID = P1.ProductID
    INNER JOIN Purchasing.Vendor V
        ON P1.BusinessEntityID = V.BusinessEntityID
    INNER JOIN Purchasing.ProductVendor P2
        ON P1.ProductID = P2.ProductID
WHERE  P1.BusinessEntityID <> P2.BusinessEntityID
ORDER  BY Product, Vendor
-- (347 row(s) affected) - Partial results.
```

Vendor	BusinessEntityID	Product	ProductID
Beaumont Bikes	1602	Chainring	322
Bike Satellite Inc.	1604	Chainring	322
Training Systems	1514	Chainring	322
Beaumont Bikes	1602	Chainring Bolts	320
Bike Satellite Inc.	1604	Chainring Bolts	320
Training Systems	1514	Chainring Bolts	320
Beaumont Bikes	1602	Chainring Nut	321
Bike Satellite Inc.	1604	Chainring Nut	321
Training Systems	1514	Chainring Nut	321
Aurora Bike Center	1616	External Lock Washer 1	409
Expert Bike Co	1672	External Lock Washer 1	409
Pro Sport Industries	1686	External Lock Washer 1	409
Aurora Bike Center	1616	External Lock Washer 2	411
Pro Sport Industries	1686	External Lock Washer 2	411
Aurora Bike Center	1616	External Lock Washer 3	403
Expert Bike Co	1672	External Lock Washer 3	403
Pro Sport Industries	1686	External Lock Washer 3	403
Aurora Bike Center	1616	External Lock Washer 4	404
Expert Bike Co	1672	External Lock Washer 4	404
Pro Sport Industries	1686	External Lock Washer 4	404
Aurora Bike Center	1616	External Lock Washer 5	406
Expert Bike Co	1672	External Lock Washer 5	406
Pro Sport Industries	1686	External Lock Washer 5	406
Aurora Bike Center	1616	External Lock Washer 6	408
Expert Bike Co	1672	External Lock Washer 6	408

Applying SELF-JOIN for Numbering Result Lines

T-SQL script to demonstrate how SELF-JOIN can be used for numbering lines in query results. Note that in these days we would use **ROW_NUMBER()** function which has been introduced with SQL Server 2005.

```
USE Northwind ;
GO


SELECT   OD.OrderID,
                SeqNo                              AS LineItem,
                OD.ProductID,
                FORMAT(UnitPrice,'c','en-US')      AS UnitPrice,
                Quantity,
                FORMAT(Discount, 'p')              AS Discount
FROM    [Order Details] OD
   INNER JOIN (SELECT   count(* )  AS SeqNo,
                a.OrderID,
                a.ProductID
        FROM    [Order Details] A
                INNER JOIN [Order Details] B
                ON A.ProductID >= B.ProductID              -- Prevent duplicates
                AND A.OrderID = B.OrderID
        GROUP BY A.OrderID,   A.ProductID) a
     ON OD.OrderID = a.OrderID
        AND OD.ProductID = a.ProductID
WHERE   OD.OrderID < 10400
ORDER BY        OD.OrderID,
                LineItem
-- (405 row(s) affected) - Partial results.
```

Vendor	AddressLine1	AddressLine2	City	State	Country
A. Datum Corporation	2596 Big Canyon Road		New York	New York	United States
Advanced Bicycles	7995 Edwards Ave.		Lynnwood	Washington	United States
Allenson Cycles	4659 Montoya		Altadena	California	United States
American Bicycles and Wheels	1667 Warren Street		West Covina	California	United States
American Bikes	7179 Montana		Torrance	California	United States
Anderson's Custom Bikes	9 Guadalupe Dr.		Burbank	California	United States
Aurora Bike Center	65 Park Glen Court		Port Orchard	Washington	United States
Australia Bike Retailer	28 San Marino Ct.		Bellingham	Washington	United States
Beaumont Bikes	2472 Alexander Place		West Covina	Idaho	United States
Bergeron Off-Roads	9830 May Way		Mill Valley	Montana	United States
Bicycle Specialists	1286 Cincerto Circle		Lake Oswego	Oregon	United States
Bike Satellite Inc.	2141 Delaware Ct.		Downey	Tennessee	United States
Bloomington Multisport	218 Fall Creek Road		West Covina	California	United States
Burnett Road Warriors	5807 Churchill Dr.		Corvallis	Oregon	United States
Business Equipment Center	6061 St. Paul Way		Everett	Montana	United States
Capital Road Cycles	628 Muir Road		Los Angeles	California	United States
Carlson Specialties	2313 B Southampton Rd		Missoula	Montana	United States
Chicago City Saddles	3 Gehringer Drive		Daly City	California	United States
Chicago Rent-All	15 Pear Dr.		Newport Beach	California	United States
Circuit Cycles	1 Mt. Dell Drive		Portland	Oregon	United States

INNER JOIN with 5 Tables

It takes accessing five tables to get the vendor name & address information in AdventureWorks. In fact this is the main complaint against 3NF relational database design: too many JOINs required to extract data. True, but the benefits of 3NF design are overwhelming. A way to overcome the "too many JOINs" issue is creating views which are pre-canned SELECT queries.

```
USE AdventureWorks;
GO

SELECT V.Name                    AS Vendor,
    A.AddressLine1,
    isnull(A.AddressLine2, '')    AS AddressLine2,
    A.City,
    SP.Name                      AS State,
    CR.Name           AS Country
FROM   Purchasing.Vendor AS V
    INNER JOIN Purchasing.VendorAddress AS VA
        ON VA.VendorID = V.VendorID
    INNER JOIN Person.Address AS A
        ON A.AddressID = VA.AddressID
    INNER JOIN Person.StateProvince AS SP
        ON SP.StateProvinceID = A.StateProvinceID
    INNER JOIN Person.CountryRegion AS CR
        ON CR.CountryRegionCode = SP.CountryRegionCode
ORDER  BY Vendor;
GO
-- (104 row(s) affected) - Partial results.
```

Vendor	AddressLine1	AddressLine2	City	State	Country
A. Datum Corporation	2596 Big Canyon Road		New York	New York	United States
Advanced Bicycles	7995 Edwards Ave.		Lynnwood	Washington	United States
Allenson Cycles	4659 Montoya		Altadena	California	United States
American Bicycles and Wheels	1667 Warren Street		West Covina	California	United States
American Bikes	7179 Montana		Torrance	California	United States
Anderson's Custom Bikes	9 Guadalupe Dr.		Burbank	California	United States
Aurora Bike Center	65 Park Glen Court		Port Orchard	Washington	United States
Australia Bike Retailer	28 San Marino Ct.		Bellingham	Washington	United States
Beaumont Bikes	2472 Alexander Place		West Covina	Idaho	United States
Bergeron Off-Roads	9830 May Way		Mill Valley	Montana	United States
Bicycle Specialists	1286 Cincerto Circle		Lake Oswego	Oregon	United States
Bike Satellite Inc.	2141 Delaware Ct.		Downey	Tennessee	United States

Creating View as Workaround for "Too Many JOINs"

It is so simple to create a view, that sinful if not done for queries which are used again and again.

```sql
-- No implicit ORDER BY can be included in a view - no trick around it either
CREATE VIEW vVendorAddress  AS
SELECT V.Name                   AS Vendor,
    A.AddressLine1,
    isnull(A.AddressLine2, '')        AS AddressLine2,
    A.City,
    SP.Name                     AS State,
    CR.Name              AS Country
FROM   Purchasing.Vendor AS V
    INNER JOIN Purchasing.VendorAddress AS VA        ON VA.VendorID = V.VendorID
    INNER JOIN Person.Address AS A                   ON A.AddressID = VA.AddressID
    INNER JOIN Person.StateProvince AS SP            ON SP.StateProvinceID = A.StateProvinceID
    INNER JOIN Person.CountryRegion AS CR            ON CR.CountryRegionCode =
SP.CountryRegionCode
ORDER  BY Vendor;
GO
/* Msg 1033, Level 15, State 1, Procedure vVendorAddress, Line 18
The ORDER BY clause is invalid in views, inline functions, derived tables, subqueries, and common table
expressions, unless TOP, OFFSET or FOR XML is also specified.  */
```

```sql
CREATE VIEW vVendorAddress  AS
SELECT V.Name                   AS Vendor,
    A.AddressLine1,
    isnull(A.AddressLine2, '')        AS AddressLine2,
    A.City,
    SP.Name                     AS State,
    CR.Name              AS Country
FROM   Purchasing.Vendor AS V
    INNER JOIN Purchasing.VendorAddress AS VA        ON VA.VendorID = V.VendorID
    INNER JOIN Person.Address AS A                   ON A.AddressID = VA.AddressID
    INNER JOIN Person.StateProvince AS SP            ON SP.StateProvinceID = A.StateProvinceID
    INNER JOIN Person.CountryRegion AS CR            ON CR.CountryRegionCode =
SP.CountryRegionCode
GO
```

```sql
SELECT TOP 5 * FROM vVendorAddress ORDER BY Vendor;
```

Vendor	AddressLine1	AddressLine2	City	State	Country
A. Datum Corporation	2596 Big Canyon Road		New York	New York	United States
Advanced Bicycles	7995 Edwards Ave.		Lynnwood	Washington	United States
Allenson Cycles	4659 Montoya		Altadena	California	United States
American Bicycles and Wheels	1667 Warren Street		West Covina	California	United States
American Bikes	7179 Montana		Torrance	California	United States

Non-Key INNER JOIN for Analytics

So far we have seen INNER JOINs based on FOREIGN KEY to PRIMARY equality relationships. The next INNER JOIN is based on the equality of the first 5 letters of last names. It is also a SELF-JOIN. In addition to the last name part equality, two more conditions are reducing the result set. The < condition is intended to reduce duplicates and the first letter of last name is 'S' limits the query results further. This is a many-to-many JOIN.

```
USE AdventureWorks2012;

SELECT  DISTINCT
    CONCAT( A.FirstName, space(1), A.LastName)      AS Person,
    CONCAT( B.FirstName, space(1), B.LastName)      AS LastNameNeighbor
FROM   Person.Person A
    INNER JOIN  Person.Person B
     ON LEFT(A.LastName, 5) = LEFT(B.LastName, 5)
       AND A.LastName < B.LastName
       AND LEFT(A.LastName, 1) = 'S'
ORDER  BY        Person,
                 LastNameNeighbor;
-- (169 row(s) affected) - Partial results.
```

Person	LastNameNeighbor
Abigail Smith	Lorrin Smith-Bates
Adriana Smith	Lorrin Smith-Bates
Alexander Smith	Lorrin Smith-Bates
Alexandra Smith	Lorrin Smith-Bates
Alexis Smith	Lorrin Smith-Bates
Allen Smith	Lorrin Smith-Bates
Alyssa Smith	Lorrin Smith-Bates
Andre Smith	Lorrin Smith-Bates
Andrew Smith	Lorrin Smith-Bates
Arthur Smith	Lorrin Smith-Bates
Ashley Smith	Lorrin Smith-Bates
Austin Smith	Lorrin Smith-Bates
Barry Srini	Sethu Srinivasan
Ben Smith	Lorrin Smith-Bates
Benjamin Smith	Lorrin Smith-Bates
Beth Srini	Sethu Srinivasan
Brandon Smith	Lorrin Smith-Bates
Brandy Srini	Sethu Srinivasan
Brett Srini	Sethu Srinivasan
Brianna Smith	Lorrin Smith-Bates

JOINing Tables without Relationship for Combinatorics

While it is not commonly done, SQL Server will execute such a JOIN as demonstrated by the next T-SQL query. Note this is only a demo, there is no business meaning to it unless the combinatorial results are useful for some application.

```
USE Northwind;
-- Cross database JOIN query
SELECT  P.ProductID,
         P.ProductName            AS NorthwindProduct,
         PP.Name                  AS AWProduct
FROM dbo.Products P
         INNER JOIN AdventureWorks2008.Production.Product PP      ON P.ProductID = PP.ProductID
ORDER BY P.ProductID;
```

ProductID	NorthwindProduct	AWProduct
1	Chai	Adjustable Race
2	Chang	Bearing Ball
3	Aniseed Syrup	BB Ball Bearing
4	Chef Anton's Cajun Seasoning	Headset Ball Bearings

Cartesian Product

When all rows in one table combined with all rows of another table it is called a Cartesian product. The cardinality of such a JOIN is (Table 1 Rows) x (Table 2 Rows).

```
-- Old-fashioned no JOIN predicate 2-table query - Cardinality 4x4 = 16
SELECT Category1 = A.Name, Category2 = B.Name
FROM Production.ProductCategory A, Production.ProductCategory B ORDER BY Category1, Category2;
```

```
-- Equivalent CROSS JOIN
SELECT Category1 = A.Name, Category2 = B.Name
FROM Production.ProductCategory A  CROSS JOIN Production.ProductCategory B
ORDER BY Category1, Category2;
```

Category1	Category2
Accessories	Accessories
Accessories	Bikes
Accessories	Clothing
Accessories	Components
Bikes	Accessories
Bikes	Bikes
Bikes	Clothing
Bikes	Components
Clothing	Accessories
Clothing	Bikes
Clothing	Clothing
Clothing	Components
Components	Accessories
Components	Bikes
Components	Clothing
Components	Components

SQL OUTER JOIN for Inclusion of Unmatched Rows

We have seen that INNER JOINs return rows only when there is at least one row from both tables that satisfies the join condition or conditions such as FOREIGN KEY matching the referenced PRIMARY KEY. Inner join queries do not return the rows that do not meet the ON condition with a row from the other table.

OUTER JOINs, however, return all rows from one or both tables in the JOIN. All rows are returned from the left table in a LEFT OUTER JOIN (including non-matching rows), and all rows are returned from the right table in a RIGHT OUTER JOIN. All rows from both tables are returned in a FULL OUTER JOIN. LEFT OUTER JOIN is totally equivalent to RIGHT OUTER JOIN. LEFT OUTER JOIN is mostly used by programmers in countries where the writing is left to right. **RIGHT OUTER JOIN is typically used by developers in countries where the writing is right to left**. **The non-matching rows in an OUTER JOIN are returned with NULL value fields**, therefore, they can be distinquished from the matching rows with a null test.

The following are synonyms:

LEFT JOIN - LEFT OUTER JOIN

RIGHT JOIN - RIGHT OUTER JOIN

FULL JOIN - FULL OUTER JOIN

The legacy syntax for outer joins *= (left join) or =* (right join) is not supported anymore.

T-SQL example script lists products (left table) even if they are not being sold such as assembly parts.

```
USE AdventureWorks2012;

SELECT        P.Name,        SOD.SalesOrderID,
              CASE    WHEN SalesOrderID is null THEN 'Non-matching'
                      ELSE 'Matching' END              AS JoinInfo
FROM   Production.Product P
    LEFT OUTER JOIN Sales.SalesOrderDetail SOD      ON P.ProductID = SOD.ProductID
ORDER  BY P.Name;
-- (121555 row(s) affected) - Partial results.
```

Name	SalesOrderID	JoinInfo
Adjustable Race	NULL	Non-matching
All-Purpose Bike Stand	51179	Matching
All-Purpose Bike Stand	51488	Matching
All-Purpose Bike Stand	51520	Matching
All-Purpose Bike Stand	51558	Matching
All-Purpose Bike Stand	51882	Matching
All-Purpose Bike Stand	51903	Matching
All-Purpose Bike Stand	51970	Matching
All-Purpose Bike Stand	52010	Matching
All-Purpose Bike Stand	52032	Matching

LEFT JOIN: Include Unmatched Rows from Left Table

In the LEFT JOIN example, the Vendor table is LEFT JOINed to the PurchaseOrderHeader table to find out which vendors did not supply anything. The LEFT JOIN is based on FOREIGN KEY relationship.

```
USE AdventureWorks2012;

SELECT Vendor = V.Name
FROM   Purchasing.Vendor V
    LEFT JOIN Purchasing.PurchaseOrderHeader POH
    ON V.BusinessEntityID = POH.VendorID
WHERE  POH.VendorID IS NULL           -- Test if POH columns are null
ORDER by Vendor;
-- (18 row(s) affected) - Partial results.
```

Vendor
A. Datum Corporation
Cycling Master
Electronic Bike Co.
GMA Ski & Bike
Holiday Skate & Cycle
Illinois Trek & Clothing

T-SQL query to check which pedal products for sale were reviewed and which ones not.

```
SELECT  p.Name            AS ProductName,
        ProductNumber,
        pr.ProductReviewID,
        pr.ReviewerName,
        pr.Rating
FROM Production.Product p
   LEFT JOIN Production.ProductReview pr
     ON p.ProductID = pr.ProductID
WHERE p.ProductSubcategoryID is not null   AND p.Name like '%pedal%'  ORDER BY ProductNumber;
-- (8 row(s) affected)
```

ProductName	ProductNumber	ProductReviewID	ReviewerName	Rating
LL Mountain Pedal	PD-M282	NULL	NULL	NULL
ML Mountain Pedal	PD-M340	NULL	NULL	NULL
HL Mountain Pedal	PD-M562	2	David	4
HL Mountain Pedal	PD-M562	3	Jill	2
LL Road Pedal	PD-R347	NULL	NULL	NULL
ML Road Pedal	PD-R563	NULL	NULL	NULL
HL Road Pedal	PD-R853	NULL	NULL	NULL
Touring Pedal	PD-T852	NULL	NULL	NULL

RIGHT JOIN - Same as LEFT with Tables Switched

The RIGHT JOIN is totally equivalent, including performance, to the corresponding LEFT JOIN.

```
USE AdventureWorks2012;

SELECT Vendor = V.Name
FROM   Purchasing.PurchaseOrderHeader POH
    RIGHT JOIN Purchasing.Vendor V
      ON V.BusinessEntityID = POH.VendorID
WHERE  POH.VendorID IS NULL
ORDER by Vendor;
-- (18 row(s) affected) - Partial results.
```

Vendor
A. Datum Corporation
Cycling Master
Electronic Bike Co.
GMA Ski & Bike
Holiday Skate & Cycle

T-SQL RIGHT JOIN examples progress toward a query to provide users with a good report.

```
USE AdventureWorks2012;

SELECT ST.Name AS  Territory,
    SP.BusinessEntityID
FROM   Sales.SalesTerritory ST
    RIGHT OUTER JOIN Sales.SalesPerson SP
      ON ST.TerritoryID = SP.TerritoryID;
-- (17 row(s) affected)
```

```
SELECT   isnull(ST.Name, ' ')                    AS Territory,
        SP.BusinessEntityID,
        CONCAT (C.FirstName, ' ', C.LastName)    AS Name
FROM   Sales.SalesTerritory ST
    RIGHT OUTER JOIN Sales.SalesPerson SP
      ON ST.TerritoryID = SP.TerritoryID
    INNER JOIN Person.Person C
      ON SP.BusinessEntityID = C.BusinessEntityID;
-- (17 row(s) affected)
```

Add a WHERE condition filter on Sales.SalesPerson SalesYTD column

The NULLs indicate the no match rows in the RIGHT OUTER JOIN.

```
SELECT   ST.CountryRegionCode,
         ST.Name                                    AS Territory,
         SP.BusinessEntityID                        AS EmployeeID,
         CONCAT(C.FirstName, ' ', C.LastName )      AS Name
FROM   Sales.SalesTerritory ST
    RIGHT OUTER JOIN Sales.SalesPerson SP
    ON ST.TerritoryID = SP.TerritoryID
    INNER JOIN Person.Person C
    ON SP.BusinessEntityID = C.BusinessEntityID
WHERE SP.SalesYTD > 1000.0
ORDER BY        CountryRegionCode,
                Territory;
GO
-- (17 row(s) affected)
```

CountryRegionCode	Territory	EmployeeID	Name
NULL	NULL	274	Stephen Jiang
NULL	NULL	285	Syed Abbas
NULL	NULL	287	Amy Alberts
AU	Australia	286	Lynn Tsoflias
CA	Canada	278	Garrett Vargas
CA	Canada	282	José Saraiva
DE	Germany	288	Rachel Valdez
FR	France	290	Ranjit Varkey Chudukatil
GB	United Kingdom	289	Jae Pak
US	Central	277	Jillian Carson
US	Northeast	275	Michael Blythe
US	Northwest	283	David Campbell
US	Northwest	284	Tete Mensa-Annan
US	Northwest	280	Pamela Ansman-Wolfe
US	Southeast	279	Tsvi Reiter
US	Southwest	276	Linda Mitchell
US	Southwest	281	Shu Ito

Cardinality of OUTER JOINs

The number of rows returned in an OUTER JOIN is equal to the matching rows plus the non-matching rows from either or both tables. **To identify the non-matching rows (the ones with the NULLs) in an outer join we have to choose a not-nullable column like the PRIMARY KEY column.**

T-SQL script demonstrates the cardinality involved with a LEFT JOIN.

```
USE AdventureWorks2012;
```

```
-- Rows in LEFT JOIN
SELECT Rows = count(*)
FROM   Production.Product P
    LEFT OUTER JOIN Sales.SalesOrderDetail SOD
        ON P.ProductID = SOD.ProductID
-- 121555
```

```
-- Rows in right table
SELECT Rows = count(*)
FROM Sales.SalesOrderDetail
-- 121317
```

```
-- Non-matching rows in left table
SELECT Rows = count(*)
FROM   Production.Product P
    LEFT OUTER JOIN Sales.SalesOrderDetail SOD
        ON P.ProductID = SOD.ProductID
WHERE SalesOrderID is NULL
-- 238
```

```
-- Right table rows + non-matching left table rows = rows returned by left join
SELECT 121317 + 238
-- 121555
```

Since the count queries are single valued, we can do the following summation.

```
SELECT (SELECT Rows = count(*)  FROM Sales.SalesOrderDetail )
+
(SELECT Rows = count(*)
FROM   Production.Product P
    LEFT OUTER JOIN Sales.SalesOrderDetail SOD
        ON P.ProductID = SOD.ProductID
WHERE SalesOrderID is NULL);
GO
-- 121555
```

CHAPTER 6: JOINing Tables with INNER & OUTER JOINs

LEFT JOIN & RIGHT JOIN on the Same Table

LEFT JOIN & RIGHT JOIN can be combined on the same table to keep all rows from that table even if they don't match the other two tables. The Production.Product table has a FOREIGN KEY referencing the ProductSubcategory table and another FOREIGN KEY referencing the UnitMeasure table.

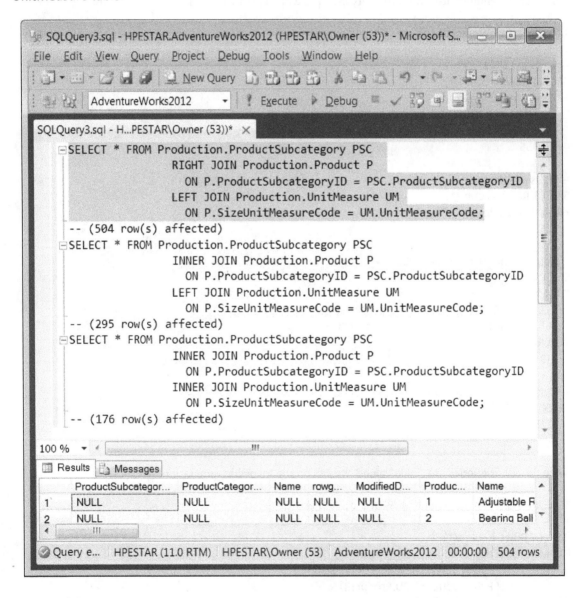

FULL JOIN to Include All Unmatched Rows

The operation FULL JOIN combines LEFT JOIN and RIGHT JOIN, therefore it does not matter which is the left table or right table, it is a fully symmetrical set operation. T-SQL script demonstrates FULL OUTER JOIN.

```
USE tempdb;
-- Create tables for demo
SELECT distinct Color INTO Color
FROM AdventureWorks2012.Production.Product
WHERE Color is not null;
GO
```

```
SELECT ID=IDENTITY(int, 1, 1), * INTO NormalColor
FROM Color;
SELECT ID=IDENTITY(int, 1, 1), Color=CONCAT('Light', Color)  INTO LightColor
FROM Color;
```

```
DELETE NormalColor WHERE Color = 'Red';
```

```
DELETE LightColor WHERE Color = 'LightBlue';
```

```
-- Demo tables ready - full join query
SELECT   NormalColor      = n.Color,
         LightColor       = l.Color
FROM   NormalColor n      FULL OUTER JOIN LightColor l    ON n.ID = l.ID
ORDER BY NormalColor;
```

NormalColor	LightColor
NULL	LightRed
Black	LightBlack
Blue	NULL
Grey	LightGrey
Multi	LightMulti
Silver	LightSilver
Silver/Black	LightSilver/Black
White	LightWhite
Yellow	LightYellow

```
DROP TABLE  tempdb.dbo.Color;  DROP TABLE tempdb.dbo.NormalColor;
DROP TABLE tempdb.dbo.LightColor;
GO
```

CROSS JOIN for Cartesian Product

A CROSS JOIN with no connecting columns for joining produces a Cartesian product: combines all rows of the left table with all rows of the right tables. If the left table has x rows and the right table y rows, the CROSS JOIN is going to have x*y rows. That is called Cartesian explosion as it happens sometimes unintentionally in database development. In fact, a huge CROSS JOIN can bring SQL Server "to its knees", overwhelming CPU and disk resources. On the same note, no matter how powerful is the hardware platform, a bad runaway query can make SQL Server unresponsive to normal queries from other connections. T-SQL script to demonstrate CROSS JOIN.

USE AdventureWorks2012;

```
-- Cardinality of CROSS JOIN
SELECT count(*) from HumanResources.Employee;        -- 290
SELECT count(*) from HumanResources.Department;      -- 16
SELECT 16 * 290;                                     -- 4640
```

```
SELECT          E.BusinessEntityID              AS EMPLOYEEID,
                D.Name                          AS DEPARTMENT
FROM   HumanResources.Employee E   CROSS JOIN HumanResources.Department D
ORDER  BY       EMPLOYEEID,      DEPARTMENT;
-- (4640 row(s) affected) - Partial results.
```

EMPLOYEEID	DEPARTMENT
1	Production Control
1	Purchasing
1	Quality Assurance
1	Research and Development
1	Sales
1	Shipping and Receiving
1	Tool Design
2	Document Control
2	Engineering
2	Executive
2	Facilities and Maintenance
2	Finance
2	Human Resources
2	Information Services
2	Marketing
2	Production

CROSS JOIN Generated Multiplication Table

A CROSS JOIN can be used to create combinatorical results. In the next example, a multiplication table is created using a CROSS JOIN which is also a SELF-JOIN. CTE stands for Common Table Expression, which can be used as a table in SELECT and other queries. The master database spt_values table is used to get a sequence of numbers. The ".." in the table reference means: use the default schema which is "dbo".

```
; WITH cteNumber                          -- cte for numbers 1 to 10
    AS (SELECT NUMBER
        FROM   master..spt_values
        WHERE  TYPE = 'P'
            AND NUMBER BETWEEN 1 AND 10)
SELECT MULTIPLICATION=CONCAT( ltrim(str(B.NUMBER)) , ' * '
            , ltrim(str(A.NUMBER)) , ' = '
            , ltrim(str(A.NUMBER * B.NUMBER)) )
FROM   cteNumber A   CROSS JOIN cteNumber B;
-- (100 row(s) affected) - Partial results.
```

MULTIPLICATION
1 * 1 = 1
1 * 2 = 2
1 * 3 = 3
1 * 4 = 4
1 * 5 = 5
1 * 6 = 6
1 * 7 = 7
1 * 8 = 8
1 * 9 = 9
1 * 10 = 10
2 * 1 = 2
2 * 2 = 4
2 * 3 = 6
2 * 4 = 8
2 * 5 = 10
2 * 6 = 12
2 * 7 = 14
2 * 8 = 16
2 * 9 = 18
2 * 10 = 20
3 * 1 = 3
3 * 2 = 6
3 * 3 = 9
3 * 4 = 12
3 * 5 = 15

INNER JOIN with 7 Tables

T-SQL query lists AdventureWorks Cycles retail (web) customers with total purchase amount and order dates. The name & address displays multiple times if a customer did multiple purchases. Generally, that is undesirable, and requires end-user report design considerations how to resolve it. The sorting uses Sales.SalesOrderHeader OrderDate which is datetime data type, instead of the mdy format string report date. mdy string format dates do not sort in chronological order.

```
USE AdventureWorks;
GO
```

```
SELECT CONCAT(C.LastName, ', ', C.FirstName)          AS CustomerName,
       A.City,
       SP.Name                                         AS State,
       CR.Name                                         AS Country,
       A.PostalCode,
       FORMAT(SOH.TotalDue, 'c','en-US')               AS SalesAmount,
       FORMAT(SOH.OrderDate,'d')                       AS OrderDate
FROM Person.Contact AS C
   INNER JOIN Sales.Individual AS I
        ON C.ContactID = I.ContactID
   INNER JOIN Sales.CustomerAddress AS CA
        ON CA.CustomerID = I.CustomerID
   INNER JOIN Person.Address AS A
        ON A.AddressID = CA.AddressID
   INNER JOIN Person.StateProvince SP
        ON SP.StateProvinceID = A.StateProvinceID
   INNER JOIN Person.CountryRegion CR
        ON CR.CountryRegionCode = SP.CountryRegionCode
   INNER JOIN Sales.SalesOrderHeader SOH
        ON C.ContactID = SOH.CustomerID
ORDER BY CustomerName, soh.OrderDate ;
-- (16493 row(s) affected)  - Partial results.
```

CustomerName	City	State	Country	PostalCode	SalesAmount	OrderDate
Adams, Aaron	Downey	California	United States	90241	$734.70	3/4/2004
Adams, Adam	Newport Beach	California	United States	92625	$2,566.12	4/16/2004
Adams, Alex	Lake Oswego	Oregon	United States	97034	$2,410.63	3/18/2003
Adams, Alex	Lake Oswego	Oregon	United States	97034	$1,293.38	12/9/2003
Adams, Alex	Lake Oswego	Oregon	United States	97034	$2,643.12	2/1/2004
Adams, Angel	Burlingame	California	United States	94010	$865.20	5/24/2003
Adams, Angel	Burlingame	California	United States	94010	$2,597.81	3/1/2004
Adams, Carlos	Langford	British Columbia	Canada	V9	$44.18	6/28/2004
Adams, Connor	Westminster	British Columbia	Canada	V3L 1H4	$183.74	4/14/2004
Adams, Elijah	Seattle	Washington	United States	98104	$8.04	11/2/2003

INNER JOIN with GROUP BY Subquery

We have to make the GROUP BY subquery into a derived table first. Subsequently, we can apply it just like any other table in a query.

```
USE AdventureWorks2012;
GO


SELECT  Subcategory = Name,
        Color,
        ColorCount,
        AvgListPrice
FROM  (
        SELECT ProductSubcategoryID,                    -- grouping column
         Color = COALESCE(Color, 'N/A'),               -- grouping column with transformation
         ColorCount = COUNT(*),                         -- aggregate function
         AvgListPrice = AVG(COALESCE(ListPrice, 0.0))   -- aggregate function
        FROM   AdventureWorks2008.Production.Product
        GROUP  BY        ProductSubcategoryID,
                         Color) x                       -- derived table (subquery)
    INNER JOIN Production.ProductSubcategory psc
        ON psc.ProductSubcategoryID = x.ProductSubcategoryID
ORDER  BY Subcategory,
        Color;
GO
-- (48 row(s) affected) - Partial results.
```

Subcategory	Color	ColorCount	AvgListPrice
Bib-Shorts	Multi	3	89.990000
Bike Racks	N/A	1	120.000000
Bike Stands	N/A	1	159.000000
Bottles and Cages	N/A	3	7.990000
Bottom Brackets	N/A	3	92.240000
Brakes	Silver	2	106.500000
Caps	Multi	1	8.990000
Chains	Silver	1	20.240000
Cleaners	N/A	1	7.950000
Cranksets	Black	3	278.990000
Derailleurs	Silver	2	106.475000
Fenders	N/A	1	21.980000

Making Queries Readable & Results Presentable

A database developer has to make a query readable for productivity gain in development and ease of maintenance. At the same time the results must be readable to the user. The next query with results demonstrates how to achieve both objectives.

```
USE AdventureWorks2012;
GO

SELECT  PC.Name                         AS Category,
        PSC.Name                        AS Subcategory,
        PM.Name                         AS Model,
        P.Name                          AS ProductName,
        FORMAT(ListPrice,'c','en-US')   AS Price
FROM Production.Product AS P
   INNER JOIN Production.ProductModel AS PM
        ON PM.ProductModelID = P.ProductModelID
   INNER JOIN Production.ProductSubcategory AS PSC
        ON PSC.ProductSubcategoryID = P.ProductSubcategoryID
   INNER JOIN Production.ProductCategory AS PC
        ON PC.ProductCategoryID = PSC.ProductCategoryID
ORDER BY Category, Subcategory, ProductName;
-- (295 row(s) affected) - Partial results.
```

The confusing 4 "Name" columns are clarified by well-chosen column aliases. The meaningful column aliases are used in the ORDER BY clause even though not required. To help the user, the list price is currency formatted.

Category	Subcategory	Model	ProductName	Price
Accessories	Bike Racks	Hitch Rack - 4-Bike	Hitch Rack - 4-Bike	$120.00
Accessories	Bike Stands	All-Purpose Bike Stand	All-Purpose Bike Stand	$159.00
Accessories	Bottles and Cages	Mountain Bottle Cage	Mountain Bottle Cage	$9.99
Accessories	Bottles and Cages	Road Bottle Cage	Road Bottle Cage	$8.99
Accessories	Bottles and Cages	Water Bottle	Water Bottle - 30 oz.	$4.99
Accessories	Cleaners	Bike Wash	Bike Wash - Dissolver	$7.95
Accessories	Fenders	Fender Set - Mountain	Fender Set - Mountain	$21.98
Accessories	Helmets	Sport-100	Sport-100 Helmet, Black	$34.99
Accessories	Helmets	Sport-100	Sport-100 Helmet, Blue	$34.99
Accessories	Helmets	Sport-100	Sport-100 Helmet, Red	$34.99

A 12 Tables JOIN Query

The next query JOINs 11 tables, some of the tables occur more than once in the query.

```
USE AdventureWorks;
```

```
DECLARE @Year  int,
        @Month int

SET @Year   = 2004;
SET @Month  = 1;

SELECT SOH.SalesOrderNumber              AS SON,
    SOH.PurchaseOrderNumber              AS PO,
    S.Name                               AS Store,
    CONVERT(VARCHAR, SOH.OrderDate, 110) AS OrderDate,
    CONVERT(VARCHAR, SOH.ShipDate, 110)  AS ShipDate,
    FORMAT(TotalDue,'c','en-US')         AS [Total Due],
    CONCAT(C.FirstName,' ',C.LastName)   AS SalesStaff,
    SM.Name                              AS ShpngMethod,
    BA.AddressLine1                      AS BlngAddress1,
    Isnull(BA.AddressLine2, '')          AS BlngAddress2,
    BA.City                              AS BlngCity,
    BSP.Name                             AS BlngStateProvince,
    BA.PostalCode                        AS BlngPostalCode,
    BCR.Name                             AS BlngCountryRegion,
    SA.AddressLine1                      AS ShpngAddress1,
    Isnull(SA.AddressLine2, '')          AS ShpngAddress2,
    SA.City                              AS ShpngCity,
    SSP.Name                             AS ShpngStateProvince,
    SA.PostalCode                        AS ShpngPostalCode,
    SCR.Name                             AS ShpngCountryRegion,
    CONCAT(CC.FirstName,' ',CC.LastName) AS CustomerContact,
    CC.Phone                             AS CustomerPhone,
    SOH.AccountNumber
FROM   Person.Address SA
    INNER JOIN Person.StateProvince SSP
        ON SA.StateProvinceID = SSP.StateProvinceID
    INNER JOIN Person.CountryRegion SCR
        ON SSP.CountryRegionCode = SCR.CountryRegionCode
    INNER JOIN Sales.SalesOrderHeader SOH
        INNER JOIN Person.Contact CC
            ON SOH.ContactID = CC.ContactID
        INNER JOIN Person.Address BA
            INNER JOIN Person.StateProvince BSP
                ON BA.StateProvinceID = BSP.StateProvinceID
            INNER JOIN Person.CountryRegion BCR
```

-- T-SQL query continued

```
                    ON BSP.CountryRegionCode =
                       BCR.CountryRegionCode
                  ON SOH.BillToAddressID = BA.AddressID
              ON SA.AddressID = SOH.ShipToAddressID
        INNER JOIN Person.Contact C
            INNER JOIN HumanResources.Employee E
                ON C.ContactID = E.ContactID
            ON SOH.SalesPersonID = E.EmployeeID
        INNER JOIN Purchasing.ShipMethod SM
            ON SOH.ShipMethodID = SM.ShipMethodID
        INNER JOIN Sales.Store S
            ON SOH.CustomerID = S.CustomerID
WHERE  SOH.OrderDate >= datefromparts(@Year, @month, 1)
    AND  SOH.OrderDate < dateadd(mm,1,datefromparts(@Year, @month, 1))
ORDER  BY Store,  OrderDate DESC;
-- (96 row(s) affected) - Partial results.
```

SON	PO	Store	OrderDate	ShipDate	Total Due	SalesStaff	ShpngMethod	BlngAddress1
SO61257	PO3741176337	Activity Center	01-01-2004	01-08-2004	$12,764.08	Tsvi Reiter	CARGO TRANSPORT 5	Factory Stores Of America
SO61256	PO1421187796	All Cycle Shop	01-01-2004	01-08-2004	$201.08	Tete Mensa-Annan	CARGO TRANSPORT 5	25111 228th St Sw
SO61251	PO6380165323	All Seasons Sports Supply	01-01-2004	01-08-2004	$2,863.30	Michael Blythe	CARGO TRANSPORT 5	Ohms Road
SO61263	PO5452121402	Amalgamated Parts Shop	01-01-2004	01-08-2004	$39,103.04	Rachel Valdez	CARGO TRANSPORT 5	Brunnenstr 422
SO61227	PO10730172247	Area Bike Accessories	01-01-2004	01-08-2004	$75,916.89	Shu Ito	CARGO TRANSPORT 5	6900 Sisk Road
SO61187	PO13978135025	Basic Bike Company	01-01-2004	01-08-2004	$72.92	David Campbell	CARGO TRANSPORT 5	15 East Main
SO61190	PO12441157171	Best Cycle Store	01-01-2004	01-08-2004	$49,337.61	Rachel Valdez	CARGO TRANSPORT 5	Berliner Platz 45
SO61221	PO15399128383	Best o' Bikes	01-01-2004	01-08-2004	$5,872.73	Michael Blythe	CARGO TRANSPORT 5	250880 Baur Blvd
SO61173	PO522171689	Better Bike Shop	01-01-2004	01-08-2004	$38,511.29	Tsvi Reiter	CARGO TRANSPORT 5	42525 Austell Road
SO61254	PO4872176154	Bicycle Exporters	01-01-2004	01-08-2004	$10,665.06	Rachel Valdez	CARGO TRANSPORT 5	Hellweg 4934
SO61243	PO7859152962	Bike Dealers Association	01-01-2004	01-08-2004	$18,976.48	Shu Ito	CARGO TRANSPORT 5	9952 E. Lohman Ave.
SO61250	PO4930183869	Bikes for Kids and Adults	01-01-2004	01-08-2004	$3,852.87	Jae Pak	CARGO TRANSPORT 5	9900 Ronson Drive
SO61209	PO11484136165	Casual Bicycle Store	01-01-2004	01-08-2004	$37,314.33	Jillian Carson	CARGO TRANSPORT 5	Westside Plaza
SO61204	PO15312134209	Citywide Service and Repair	01-01-2004	01-08-2004	$29,797.18	Jae Pak	CARGO TRANSPORT 5	Box 99354 300 Union Street
SO61192	PO10092119585	Classic Cycle Store	01-01-2004	01-08-2004	$3,691.57	Jillian Carson	CARGO TRANSPORT 5	630 Oldgate Lane

Order of Tables or Predicates Does Not Matter

A frequent question: does the order of tables matter in a JOIN? Should I put BETWEEN predicate before LIKE predicate? Valid syntax variations do not matter. The database engine translates the query to an internal form prior to creating an execution plan. Thus the different variations get translated to the same internal form. The only way we have some control over the database engine if we rewrite a single statement complex query to a multi-statements script.

Nondeterministic CTE

CTE is evaluated for every reference, therefore it may return different results if certain functions are used such as newid(), thus yielding a nondeterministic CTE.

```
;WITH CTE AS (SELECT Random = NEWID()),
CTE1 AS (SELECT * FROM CTE),
CTE2 AS (SELECT * FROM CTE),
CTE3 AS (SELECT * FROM CTE),
CTE4 AS (SELECT * FROM CTE),
CTE5 AS (SELECT * FROM CTE)
SELECT * FROM CTE1
UNION ALL
SELECT * FROM CTE2
UNION ALL
SELECT * FROM CTE3
UNION ALL
SELECT * FROM CTE4
UNION ALL
SELECT * FROM CTE5
UNION ALL
SELECT * FROM CTE
UNION ALL
SELECT * FROM CTE
UNION ALL
SELECT * FROM CTE;
```

Random
08D45FE2-52C6-4E15-83A3-0B2F27837887
D6A094E6-0C8A-43E4-B6C4-8821F6EE8E73
281A5852-3D9A-4F2A-99FA-F60EE28FD2E0
C327ED19-5C03-4D9B-A8E8-6ACABAA08F1C
80DDE508-A6AA-4F2B-AB2F-CEEF7EC5E163
5F611B03-46F4-4EED-A8E0-76020527899D
FF8DAE17-65F6-4D80-8AF5-29EBAEBD2FEB
CF342DC9-4CF9-46FD-87F0-3213106C447D

The CROSS APPLY Operator

The APPLY (CROSS APPLY & OUTER APPLY) operators were introduced with SQL Server 2005. The CROSS APPLY operator merges rows from tables (or views) with rows from table-valued function, a form of JOIN.

```
USE AdventureWorks2012;
SELECT
        q.last_execution_time              AS LastRun,
        t.TEXT                             AS QueryText,
        q.sql_handle                       AS SQLHandle
FROM    sys.dm_exec_query_stats AS q                     -- system view
            CROSS APPLY
            sys.dm_exec_sql_text(q.sql_handle) AS t      -- table-valued system function
WHERE LEFT(t.TEXT,8)='SELECT *'  ORDER BY LastRun DESC;
```

LastRun	QueryText
2016-08-01 14:46:12.537	SELECT * FROM Sales.SalesOrderHeader
2016-08-01 14:44:54.257	SELECT * FROM Production.Product
2016-08-01 13:29:25.213	SELECT * FROM sys.dm_os_wait_stats
2016-08-01 09:36:57.980	select * from sys.sysforeignkeys s
2016-08-01 09:36:39.077	select * from sysforeignkeys s

```
-- Return the top N purchase order by amount - inline table-valued function
CREATE FUNCTION dbo.ufnGetTopNPurchases(@VendorID AS INT, @N AS INT)
RETURNS TABLE  AS
RETURN
 SELECT TOP ( @N ) *   FROM Purchasing.PurchaseOrderHeader
 WHERE VendorID = @VendorID   ORDER BY TotalDue DESC;
GO
-- Command(s) completed successfully.
```

```
-- List the top 5 highest purchases from vendors
SELECT V.VendorID,
       P.PurchaseOrderID,
       FORMAT(P.TotalDue, 'c','en-US')    AS TotalDue
FROM   Purchasing.Vendor AS V  CROSS APPLY  dbo.ufnGetTopNPurchases(V.VendorID, 5) AS P
ORDER BY  V.VendorID, TotalDue DESC
-- (395 row(s) affected) - Partial results.
```

VendorID	PurchaseOrderID	TotalDue
74	325	$1,654.75
74	1727	$855.22
74	2517	$855.22
74	3307	$855.22
74	167	$785.61

Using CROSS APPLY with Columns Specified Table Alias

A regular table alias would result in error in the following delimited string list query. Table alias with column(s) specifications "o(list)" works, the table alias is "o", it has one column "list".

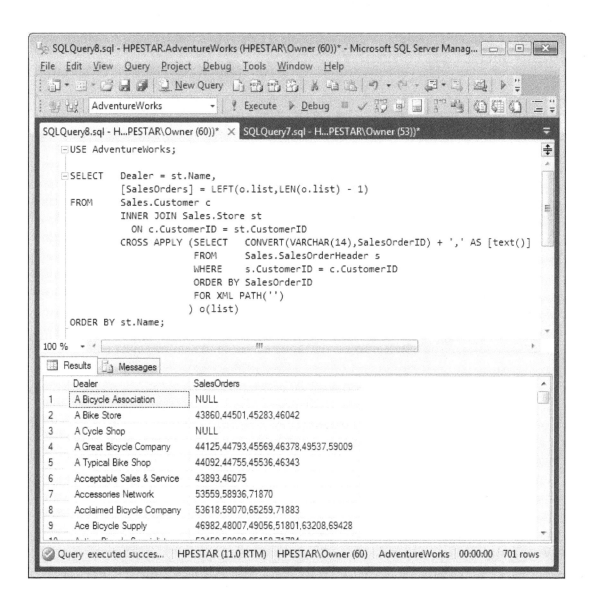

CHAPTER 7: Basic SELECT Statement Syntax & Examples

Simple SELECT Statement Variations

SELECT is the most famous statement in the SQL language. It is used to query tables, and generate reports for users. Although SQL Server Reporting Services and other 3rd party packages available for reporting purposes, frequently reports are generated straight from the database with SELECT queries. The next query returns all rows, all columns sorted on DepartmentID.

```
USE AdventureWorks2012;
```

```
SELECT * FROM  HumanResources.Department  ORDER BY DepartmentID;
-- (16 row(s) affected)
```

DepartmentID	Name	GroupName	ModifiedDate
1	Engineering	Research and Development	1998-06-01 00:00:00.000
2	Tool Design	Research and Development	1998-06-01 00:00:00.000
3	Sales	Sales and Marketing	1998-06-01 00:00:00.000
4	Marketing	Sales and Marketing	1998-06-01 00:00:00.000
5	Purchasing	Inventory Management	1998-06-01 00:00:00.000
6	Research and Development	Research and Development	1998-06-01 00:00:00.000
7	Production	Manufacturing	1998-06-01 00:00:00.000
8	Production Control	Manufacturing	1998-06-01 00:00:00.000
9	Human Resources	Executive General and Administration	1998-06-01 00:00:00.000
10	Finance	Executive General and Administration	1998-06-01 00:00:00.000
11	Information Services	Executive General and Administration	1998-06-01 00:00:00.000
12	Document Control	Quality Assurance	1998-06-01 00:00:00.000
13	Quality Assurance	Quality Assurance	1998-06-01 00:00:00.000
14	Facilities and Maintenance	Executive General and Administration	1998-06-01 00:00:00.000
15	Shipping and Receiving	Inventory Management	1998-06-01 00:00:00.000
16	Executive	Executive General and Administration	1998-06-01 00:00:00.000

Since the time part of ModifiedDate is not being used, and that makes business sense, we can format it just as date.

```
SELECT TOP (3) DepartmentID, Name, GroupName, CONVERT(DATE, ModifiedDate) AS ModifiedDate
FROM  HumanResources.Department  ORDER BY DepartmentID;
-- (16 row(s) affected)
```

DepartmentID	Name	GroupName	ModifiedDate
1	Engineering	Research and Development	1998-06-01
2	Tool Design	Research and Development	1998-06-01
3	Sales	Sales and Marketing	1998-06-01

SELECT query with sort on EnglishProductName in DESCending order
ASCending sort is the default.

```
USE AdventureWorksDW2012
GO


SELECT  *
FROM    DimProduct
ORDER BY EnglishProductName DESC
GO
-- (606 row(s) affected) - Partial results.
```

EnglishProductName	SpanishProductName	FrenchProductName	StandardCost
Women's Tights, S	Mallas para mujer, P	Collants pour femmes, taille S	30.9334
Women's Tights, M	Mallas para mujer, M	Collants pour femmes, taille M	30.9334
Women's Tights, L	Mallas para mujer, G	Collants pour femmes, taille L	30.9334
Women's Mountain Shorts, S			26.1763
Women's Mountain Shorts, M			26.1763
Women's Mountain Shorts, L			26.1763
Water Bottle - 30 oz.			1.8663
Touring-Panniers, Large	Cesta de paseo, grande	Sacoches de vélo de randonnée, grande capacité	51.5625
Touring-3000 Yellow, 62	Paseo: 3000, amarilla, 62	Vélo de randonnée 3000 jaune, 62	461.4448
Touring-3000 Yellow, 58	Paseo: 3000, amarilla, 58	Vélo de randonnée 3000 jaune, 58	461.4448

The next query sorts on the SpanishProductName column in ascending order.

```
SELECT  *
FROM    DimProduct
ORDER BY SpanishProductName ASC
GO
-- (606 row(s) affected) - Partial results.
```

EnglishProductName	SpanishProductName
HL Crankset	Bielas GA
LL Crankset	Bielas GB
ML Crankset	Bielas GM
Mountain Pump	Bomba de montaña
Cable Lock	Cable antirrobo
Chain	Cadena
Mountain Bike Socks,	Calcetines para bicicleta de montaña, G

Sorting on FrenchProductName, if empty, use EnglishProductName.

```
SELECT  * FROM    DimProduct ORDER BY FrenchProductName, EnglishProductName;
GO
```

Using the TOP Clause in SELECT Queries

The TOP clause limits the number of rows returned as specified in the TOP expression according the sorted order if any. In the following query, the sorting is based on a major key (LastName) and a minor key (FirstName).

```
USE AdventureWorks2012
GO
```

```
SELECT  TOP 100 *
FROM    Person.Person ORDER BY LastName, FirstName
-- (100 row(s) affected) - Partial results.
```

BusinessEntityID	PersonType	Title	FirstName	LastName	EmailPromotion
285	SP	Mr.	Syed	Abbas	0
293	SC	Ms.	Catherine	Abel	1
295	SC	Ms.	Kim	Abercrombie	0
2170	GC	NULL	Kim	Abercrombie	2
38	EM	NULL	Kim	Abercrombie	2
211	EM	NULL	Hazem	Abolrous	0
2357	GC	NULL	Sam	Abolrous	1
297	SC	Sr.	Humberto	Acevedo	2
291	SC	Mr.	Gustavo	Achong	2
299	SC	Sra.	Pilar	Ackerman	0

The total population of the Person.Person table is 19,972 rows.

```
SELECT  * FROM    Person.Person ORDER BY LastName, FirstName
-- (19972 row(s) affected)
```

We can also count the rows applying the COUNT function.

```
SELECT  RowsCount = count(*)  FROM    Person.Person
-- 19972
```

When counting, it is safe to count the PRIMARY KEY (ProductID) values.

```
SELECT  RowsCount = count(ProductID)   FROM    Production.Product;
-- 504
```

```
SELECT  RowsCount = count(Color)   FROM    Production.Product;      -- 256
```

Using the WHERE Clause in SELECT Queries

The WHERE clause filters the rows to be returned according the one or more predicates. The next T-SQL scripts demonstrate simple WHERE clause predicates, including multiple WHERE conditions.

```
-- Last name starts with S
SELECT *
FROM    Person.Person
WHERE   LEFT(LastName,1) = 'S'
ORDER BY LastName;
-- (2130 row(s) affected)
```

```
-- First name is Shelly
SELECT  *
FROM    Person.Person
WHERE   FirstName = 'Shelly'
ORDER BY LastName;
-- (1 row(s) affected)
```

```
-- First name is John
SELECT  *
FROM    Person.Person
WHERE   FirstName = 'John'
ORDER BY LastName;
-- (58 row(s) affected)
```

```
-- First name John, last name starts with S - Multiple WHERE conditions
SELECT  *
FROM    Person.Person
WHERE   FirstName = 'John'
    AND LEFT(LastName,1) = 'S'
ORDER BY LastName ;
-- (2 row(s) affected)
```

```
-- Last name starts with S OR first name starts with J
SELECT  *
FROM    Person.Person
WHERE   LEFT(FirstName,1) = 'J'  OR LEFT(LastName,1) = 'S'
ORDER BY LastName;
-- (4371 row(s) affected)
```

```
-- Last name starts with S AND first name starts with J
SELECT  *
FROM    Person.Person  WHERE   LEFT(FirstName,1) = 'J'    AND LEFT(LastName,1) = 'S'
ORDER BY LastName;
-- (221 row(s) affected)
```

Using Literals in SELECT Queries

Literals or constants are used commonly in T-SQL queries, also as defaults for columns, local variables, and parameters. The format of a literal depends on the data type of the value it represents. The database engine may perform implicit conversion to match data types. Explicit conversion of literals can be achieved with the CONVERT or CAST functions. T-SQL scripts demonstrate literal use in WHERE clause predicates.

```
USE AdventureWorks2012;
-- Integer literal  in WHERE clause predicate
SELECT * FROM Production.Product
WHERE ProductID = 800;
-- (1 row(s) affected)
```

```
-- String literal in WHERE clause predicate
SELECT * FROM Production.Product WHERE Color = 'Blue';
-- (26 row(s) affected)
```

```
USE AdventureWorksDW2012;
-- UNICODE (2 bytes per character) string literal
SELECT * FROM DimProduct
WHERE SpanishProductName = N'Jersey clásico de manga corta, G';
-- (1 row(s) affected)
```

```
-- UNICODE string literal
SELECT * FROM DimProduct
WHERE FrenchProductName = N'Roue arrière de vélo de randonnée';
-- (1 row(s) affected)
```

```
USE AdventureWorks2012;
-- Money literal in WHERE clause predicate
SELECT * FROM Production.Product
WHERE ListPrice > = $2000.0;
-- (35 row(s) affected)
```

```
-- Floating point literal with implicit conversion to MONEY
SELECT * FROM Production.Product  WHERE ListPrice > = 2.000E+3;
-- (35 row(s) affected)
```

```
-- Hex (binary) literal
SELECT * FROM Production.Product  WHERE rowguid >= 0x23D89CEE9F444F3EB28963DE6BA2B737
-- (302 row(s) affected)
```

```
-- The rest of the 504 products
SELECT * FROM Production.Product  WHERE rowguid < 0x23D89CEE9F444F3EB28963DE6BA2B737
-- (202 row(s) affected)
```

Date & Time Literals in SELECT Queries

Date and time literals appear to come from an infinite pool. Every country has tens of string date & time variations. Despite the many external string representation, **date, datetime, datetime, time, smalldatetime** and other temporal data types have unique, well-defined representation within the database engine.

ymd date literal format is the cleanest. There is eternal confusion about the North American mdy string date format and the European dmy string date format. The date and time format with "T" separator (last one) is the ISO date time format literal. ANSI Date literal - YYYYMMDD - the best choice since it work in any country.

CONVERT or CAST Date Time Literal	Result
SELECT [Date] = CAST('20160228' AS date)	2016-02-28
SELECT [Datetime] = CAST('20160228' AS datetime)	2016-02-28 00:00:00.000
SELECT [SmallDatetime] = CAST('20160228' AS smalldatetime)	2016-02-28 00:00:00
SELECT [Datetime] = CONVERT(datetime,'2016-02-28')	2016-02-28 00:00:00.000
SELECT [Datetime2] = CONVERT(datetime2,'2016-02-28')	2016-02-28 00:00:00.0000000
SELECT [Datetime] = CONVERT(datetime, '20160228')	2016-02-28 00:00:00.000
SELECT [Datetime2] = CONVERT(datetime2,'20160228')	2016-02-28 00:00:00.0000000
SELECT [Datetime] = CAST('Mar 15, 2016' AS datetime)	2016-03-15 00:00:00.000
SELECT [Datetime2] = CAST('Mar 15, 2016' AS datetime2)	2016-03-15 00:00:00.0000000
SELECT [Date] = CAST('Mar 15, 2016' AS date)	2016-03-15
SELECT CAST('16:40:31' AS datetime)	1900-01-01 16:40:31.000
SELECT CAST('16:40:31' AS time)	16:40:31.0000000
SELECT [Datetime] = CAST('Mar 15, 2016 12:07:34.444' AS datetime)	2016-03-15 12:07:34.443
SELECT [Datetime2] = CAST('Mar 15, 2016 12:07:34.4445555' AS datetime2)	2016-03-15 12:07:34.4445555
SELECT [Datetime] = CAST('2016-03-15T12:07:34.513' AS datetime)	2016-03-15 12:07:34.513

CHAPTER 7: Basic SELECT Statement Syntax & Examples

ymd, dmy & mdy String Date Format Literals

Date and time string literals are the least understood part of the T-SQL language by database developers. It is a constant source of confusion and frustration, in addition huge economic cost of lost programmer's productivity. ymd, dmy & mdy are the main string date formats. Some countries use ydm format. Setting dateformat overrides the implicit setting by language.

The basic principles:

> **There is only one DATETIME data type internal format**, independent where SQL Server is operated: New York, London, Amsterdam, Berlin, Moscow, Hong Kong, Singapore, Tokyo, Melbourne or Rio de Janeiro.
> There are hundreds of national string date & time formats which have nothing to do with SQL Server.
> String date must be properly converted to DATETIME format.

```
SET DATEFORMAT ymd
SELECT convert(datetime,'16/05/08')              -- 2016-05-08 00:00:00.000


-- Setting DATEFORMAT to UK-Style (European)
SET DATEFORMAT dmy
SELECT convert(datetime,'20/05/16')              -- 2016-05-20 00:00:00.000


-- Setting DATEFORMAT to US-Style
SET DATEFORMAT mdy
SELECT convert(datetime,'05/20/16')              -- 2016-05-20 00:00:00.000
SELECT convert(datetime,'05/20/2016')            -- 2016-05-20 00:00:00.000
```
Interestingly we can achieve the same implicit conversion action by setting language.

```
-- Setting DATEFORMAT ymd  via language
SET LANGUAGE Japanese;  SELECT convert(datetime,'16/05/08') ;          -- 2016-05-08
00:00:00.000


-- Setting DATEFORMAT to UK-Style (European) via language
SET LANGUAGE British;  SELECT convert(datetime,'20/05/16');              -- 2016-05-20
00:00:00.000
SELECT convert(datetime,'05/20/16');
/* Msg 242, Level 16, State 3, Line 3
The conversion of a varchar data type to a datetime data type resulted in an out-of-range value.  */


-- Setting DATEFORMAT to US-Style via language
SET LANGUAGE English;  SELECT convert(datetime,'05/20/16');          -- 2016-05-20 00:00:00.000
SELECT convert(datetime,'05/20/2016');                  -- 2016-05-20 00:00:00.000
SELECT convert(datetime,'20/05/2016');  /* Msg 242, Level 16, State 3, Line 4
The conversion of a varchar data type to a datetime data type resulted in an out-of-range value.  */
```

CHAPTER 7: Basic SELECT Statement Syntax & Examples

Setting DATEFIRST with Literal

DATEFIRST indicates the first day of the week which may vary by country, culture or business. The next T-SQL script demonstrates how it can be set by integer literal 1-7. It overrides the implicit setting by language. @@DATEFIRST is a system (SQL Server database engine) variable.

```
SET DATEFIRST 7  -- Sunday as first day of the week
SELECT DATEPART(dw, '20160315');              -- 3
SELECT DATENAME(dw, '20160315');              -- Tuesday
SELECT @@DATEFIRST                            -- 7


SET DATEFIRST 1  -- Monday as first day of the week
SELECT DATEPART(dw, '20160315');              -- 2
SELECT DATENAME(dw, '20160315');              -- Tuesday
SELECT @@DATEFIRST                            -- 1
```

Language Setting - SET LANGUAGE

DATEFIRST is tied to the language setting, just the like the date format (ymd, dmy, or mdy).

```
SET LANGUAGE us_english
SELECT DATEPART(dw, '20160315');              -- 3
SELECT DATENAME(dw, '20160315');              -- Tuesday
SELECT @@DATEFIRST                            -- 7


SET LANGUAGE german
SELECT DATEPART(dw, '20160315');              -- 2
SELECT DATENAME(dw, '20160315');              -- Dienstag
SELECT @@DATEFIRST                            -- 1


SET LANGUAGE british
SELECT DATEPART(dw, '20160315');              -- 2
SELECT DATENAME(dw, '20160315');              -- Tuesday
SELECT @@DATEFIRST                            -- 1


SET LANGUAGE hungarian
SELECT DATEPART(dw, '20160315');              -- 2
SELECT DATENAME(dw, '20160315');              -- kedd
SELECT @@DATEFIRST                            -- 1


SET LANGUAGE spanish
SELECT DATEPART(dw, '20160315');              -- 2
SELECT DATENAME(dw, '20160315');              -- Martes
SELECT @@DATEFIRST                            -- 1
```

The sys.syslanguages System View

The syslanguages table contains not only language related information, but date related settings as well.

```
SELECT   langid,
         dateformat,
         datefirst,
         name                              AS native_language,
         alias                             AS english,
         left(shortmonths, 15)             AS shortmonths,
          left(days,15)                    AS days
FROM AdventureWorks2012.sys.syslanguages
ORDER BY langid;
-- (34 row(s) affected)  -  Partial results.
```

langid	dateformat	datefirst	native_language	english	shortmonths	days
0	mdy	7	us_english	English	Jan,Feb,Mar,Apr	Monday,Tuesday,
1	dmy	1	Deutsch	German	Jan,Feb,Mär,Apr	Montag,Dienstag
2	dmy	1	Français	French	janv,févr,mars,	lundi,mardi,mer
3	ymd	7	日本語	Japanese	01,02,03,04,05,	月曜日,火曜日,水曜日,木曜日
4	dmy	1	Dansk	Danish	jan,feb,mar,apr	mandag,tirsdag,
5	dmy	1	Español	Spanish	Ene,Feb,Mar,Abr	Lunes,Martes,Mi
6	dmy	1	Italiano	Italian	gen,feb,mar,apr	lunedì,martedì,
7	dmy	1	Nederlands	Dutch	jan,feb,mrt,apr	maandag,dinsdag
8	dmy	1	Norsk	Norwegian	jan,feb,mar,apr	mandag,tirsdag,
9	dmy	7	Português	Portuguese	jan,fev,mar,abr	segunda-feira,t
10	dmy	1	Suomi	Finnish	tammi,helmi,maa	maanantai,tiist
11	ymd	1	Svenska	Swedish	jan,feb,mar,apr	måndag,tisdag,o
12	dmy	1	čeština	Czech	I,II,III,IV,V,V	pondělí,úterý,s
13	ymd	1	magyar	Hungarian	jan,febr,márc,á	hétfő,kedd,szer
14	dmy	1	polski	Polish	I,II,III,IV,V,V	poniedziałek,wt
15	dmy	1	română	Romanian	Ian,Feb,Mar,Apr	luni,marţi,mier
16	ymd	1	hrvatski	Croatian	sij,vel,ožu,tra	ponedjeljak,uto
17	dmy	1	slovenčina	Slovak	I,II,III,IV,V,V	pondelok,utorok
18	dmy	1	slovenski	Slovenian	jan,feb,mar,apr	ponedeljek,tore
19	dmy	1	ελληνικά	Greek	Ιαν,Φεβ,Μαρ,Απρ	Δευτέρα,Τρίτη,Τ
20	dmy	1	български	Bulgarian	януари,февруари	понеделник,втор
21	dmy	1	русский	Russian	янв,фев,мар,апр	понедельник,вто
22	dmy	1	Türkçe	Turkish	Oca,Şub,Mar,Nis	Pazartesi,Salı,
23	dmy	1	British	British English	Jan,Feb,Mar,Apr	Monday,Tuesday,
24	dmy	1	eesti	Estonian	jaan,veebr,märt	esmaspäev,teisi
25	ymd	1	latviešu	Latvian	jan,feb,mar,apr	pirmdiena,otrdi
26	ymd	1	lietuvių	Lithuanian	sau,vas,kov,bal	pirmadienis,ant
27	dmy	7	Português (Brasil)	Brazilian	Jan,Fev,Mar,Abr	Segunda-Feira,T
28	ymd	7	繁體中文	Traditional Chinese	01,02,03,04,05,	星期一,星期二,星期三,星期四
29	ymd	7	한국어	Korean	01,02,03,04,05,	월요일,화요일,수요일,목요일
30	ymd	7	简体中文	Simplified Chinese	01,02,03,04,05,	星期一,星期二,星期三,星期四
31	dmy	1	Arabic	Arabic	Jan,Feb,Mar,Apr	Monday,Tuesday,
32	dmy	7	ไทย	Thai	ม.ค.,ก.พ.,มี.ค.	จันทร์,อังคาร,พ
33	dmy	1	norsk (bokmål)	Bokmål	jan,feb,mar,apr	mandag,tirsdag,

DBCC USEROPTIONS

The DBCC USEROPTIONS command displays some of the connection (session) settings. As we have seen these settings play an important part on how date literals are interpreted by the system such as dateformat.

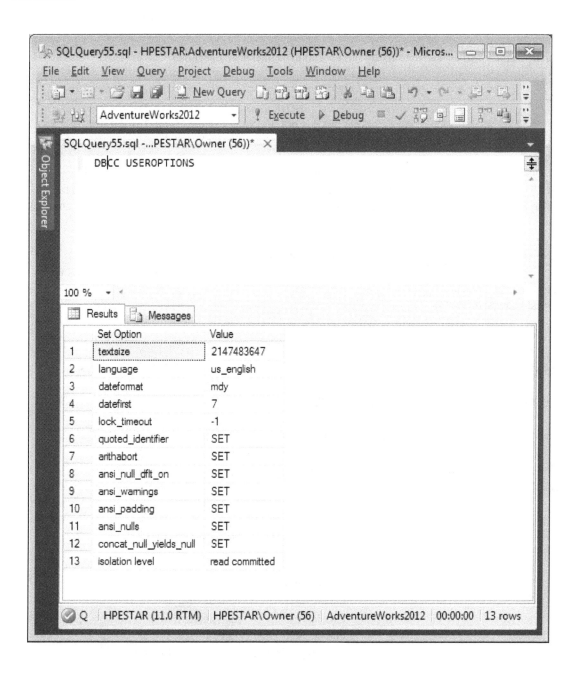

Easy SELECT Queries for Fun & Learning

T-SQL scripts to demonstrate simple, easy-to-read SELECT query variations. Important note: alias column names cannot be reused in successive computed columns by expressions or anywhere else in the query except the ORDER BY clause.

```
-- Datetime range with string literal date
SELECT  *  FROM    Person.Person
WHERE   ModifiedDate <= '2002-08-09 00:00:00.000'  ORDER BY LastName;
-- (38 row(s) affected)
```

```
                                    NOTE
The string literal above looks like datetime, but it is not. It is only a string literal. The database engine will
try to convert it to datetime data type at runtime (implicit conversion), and if successful the query will be
executed.
The syntax of the following query is OK, however, it will fail at execution time.
SELECT  *  FROM    Person.Person  WHERE   ModifiedDate <= 'New York City'  ORDER BY LastName;
/* Msg 241, Level 16, State 1, Line 1 Conversion failed when converting date and/or time from character
string. */
```

```
-- Complimentary (remaining) datetime range specified again with string literal
SELECT * FROM    Person.Person  WHERE   ModifiedDate > '2002-08-09 00:00:00.000'  ORDER BY
LastName;
-- (19934 row(s) affected)
```

```
-- Total rows in Person.Person
SELECT ( 38 + 19934 ) AS TotalRows;
-- 19972
```

```
SELECT count(* ) FROM   Person.Person -- 19972
```

```
SELECT TableRows = count(* ),  Calc = 38 + 19934  FROM   Person.Person;  -- 19972       19972
```

```
-- Get prefix left of comma or entire string if there is no comma present
SELECT TOP 4                                                              ProductNumber,
       LEFT(Name, COALESCE(NULLIF(CHARINDEX(',',Name)-1,-1),LEN(Name)))   AS NamePrefix,
       Name                                                               AS ProductName
FROM AdventureWorks2012.Production.Product   WHERE CHARINDEX(',',Name) > 0
ORDER BY ProductName;
```

ProductNumber	NamePrefix	ProductName
VE-C304-L	Classic Vest	Classic Vest, L
VE-C304-M	Classic Vest	Classic Vest, M
VE-C304-S	Classic Vest	Classic Vest, S
GL-F110-L	Full-Finger Gloves	Full-Finger Gloves, L

CHAPTER 7: Basic SELECT Statement Syntax & Examples

NULL refers to no information available. Note: "=" and "!=" operators are not used with NULL; "IS" or "IS NOT" operators are applicable.

```
SELECT *
FROM    Person.Person
WHERE   AdditionalContactInfo IS NOT NULL
ORDER BY LastName;
-- (10 row(s) affected)
```

```
SELECT *
FROM    Person.Person
WHERE   AdditionalContactInfo IS NULL
ORDER BY LastName;
-- (19962 row(s) affected)
```

```
SELECT   DISTINCT FirstName
FROM    Person.Person
ORDER BY FirstName;
-- (1018 row(s) affected)
```

```
-- Summary revenue by product, interesting sort
USE AdventureWorks2012;
GO
SELECT   TOP 10 p.Name                                      AS ProductName,
        FORMAT(SUM(((OrderQty * UnitPrice) * (1.0 - UnitPriceDiscount))),'c','en-US') AS SubTotal
FROM Production.Product AS p
INNER JOIN Sales.SalesOrderDetail AS sod
ON p.ProductID = sod.ProductID
GROUP BY p.Name
ORDER BY REVERSE(p.Name);
```

ProductName	SubTotal
Water Bottle - 30 oz.	$28,654.16
Hydration Pack - 70 oz.	$105,826.42
LL Mountain Frame - Black, 40	$1,198.99
ML Mountain Frame - Black, 40	$14,229.41
Mountain-300 Black, 40	$501,648.88
Mountain-500 Black, 40	$101,734.12
LL Mountain Frame - Silver, 40	$69,934.28
ML Mountain Frame-W - Silver, 40	$195,826.39
Mountain-500 Silver, 40	$145,089.43
Mountain-400-W Silver, 40	$323,703.82

DISTINCT & GROUP BY operations are generally "expensive".

```
SELECT  DISTINCT LastName FROM    Person.Person ORDER BY LastName;  -- (1206 row(s) affected)
```

```
-- LastName popularity descending
SELECT LastName,     Frequency = count(* )
FROM    Person.Person
GROUP BY LastName
ORDER BY Frequency DESC;
```

LastName	Frequency
Diaz	211
Hernandez	188
Sanchez	175
Martinez	173
Torres	172
Martin	171
Perez	170
Gonzalez	169
Lopez	168
Rodriguez	166

```
-- Sort on column not in SELECT list - Note: demo only, confusing to end user
SELECT   LastName
FROM    Person.Person
ORDER BY FirstName;
-- (19972 row(s) affected)
```

```
-- Sort on column not in SELECT list
SELECT   Name = CONCAT(LastName, ', ', FirstName )
FROM    Person.Person
ORDER BY LastName;
-- (19972 row(s) affected)
```

```
-- Sort on column alias
SELECT   Name = CONCAT(LastName, ', ', FirstName )
FROM    Person.Person
ORDER BY Name;
-- (19972 row(s) affected)
```

```
SELECT  CONCAT(LastName, ', ', FirstName ) AS FullName
FROM    Person.Person
WHERE   LastName >= 'K' ORDER BY LastName;
-- (12057 row(s) affected)
```

CHAPTER 7: Basic SELECT Statement Syntax & Examples

The NULLIF Function Actually Creates A NULL

```
SELECT  CONCAT(LastName, ', ', FirstName ) AS FullName
FROM    Person.Person  WHERE   LastName < 'K'  ORDER BY LastName;
-- (7915 row(s) affected)


-- Cardinality check
SELECT Difference= ((count(*)) - (12057 + 7915)) FROM  Person.Person; -- 0


-- Using the NULLIF function in counting
-- Count of all list prices - no NULLs in column
SELECT COUNT(ListPrice) FROM   AdventureWorks2012.Production.Product
-- 504


-- Counts only when ListPrice != 0 - does not count NULLs (ListPrice = 0.0)
SELECT COUNT(NULLIF(ListPrice,0.0)) FROM   AdventureWorks2012.Production.Product
-- 304


SELECT COUNT(ListPrice)  FROM  AdventureWorks2012.Production.Product   WHERE ListPrice = 0;
-- 200
```

Cardinality of DISTINCT & GROUP BY Clauses

The cardinality of DISTINCT and the cardinality of GROUP BY are the same with the same column(s).

```
-- FirstName by popularity descending
SELECT FirstName,
       Freq = count(* )
FROM    Person.Person
GROUP BY FirstName
ORDER BY Freq DESC;
-- (1018 row(s) affected)
```

FirstName	Freq
Richard	103
Katherine	99
Marcus	97
James	97
Jennifer	96
Dalton	93
Lucas	93
Alexandra	93
Morgan	92
Seth	92

```
SELECT  DISTINCT FirstName  FROM    Person.Person  ORDER BY FirstName;
-- (1018 row(s) affected)
```

Column Alias Can only Be Used in ORDER BY

Column aliases cannot be used in other computed columns (expressions), neither in the WHERE clause or GROUP BY clause.

```
SELECT   TableRows = count(* ),
         Calculated = 38 + 19934,
         Difference = (count(*) - 38 - 19934)
FROM   Person.Person;
```

TableRows	Calculated	Difference
19972	19972	0

Workaround for Column Alias Use Restriction

There is a simple workaround for recycling column aliases in other clauses than just the ORDER BY: make the query into a derived table (x) and include it in an outer query. Similarly, CTEs can be used instead of derived tables.

```
-- Derived table workaround
SELECT TableRows, Calculated, Difference = TableRows - Calculated
FROM (
        SELECT   TableRows = count(* ),      Calculated = 38 + 19934,
        FROM   Person.Person
        ) x ;   -- Derived table
GO
```

TableRows	Calculated	Difference
19972	19972	0

```
-- CTE workaround
;WITH CTE AS (
        SELECT   TableRows = count(* ),      Calculated = 38 + 19934
        FROM   Person.Person)
-- Outer query
SELECT TableRows, Calculated, Difference = TableRows - Calculated
FROM CTE;
```

TableRows	Calculated	Difference
19972	19972	0

When the Clock Strikes Midnight: datetime Behaviour

This is one of the most troublesome issues in T-SQL programming: the predicate YYYYMMDD (date string literal) = DatetimeColumn does not include the entire day, only records with time at midnight: 00:00:00.000 .

```
-- Note: only midnight 2003-08-09 included
-- Even a second after midnight is not included like 2003-08-09 00:00:01.000
SELECT  *
FROM    Person.Person
WHERE   ModifiedDate BETWEEN '2002-08-09 00:00:00.000'
            AND '2003-08-09 00:00:00.000'
ORDER BY LastName;
GO
-- (396 row(s) affected)
```

```
-- Entire day of 2003-08-09 included
-- The count same as before because no records after midnight 2003-08-09
SELECT  *
FROM    Person.Person
WHERE     ModifiedDate >= '2002-08-09 00:00:00.000'
    AND ModifiedDate < '2003-08-10 00:00:00.000'
ORDER BY LastName;
GO
-- (396 row(s) affected)
```

CHAPTER 7: Basic SELECT Statement Syntax & Examples

LEFT(), RIGHT() & SUBSTRING() String Functions

```
SELECT   FirstCharOfFirstName = LEFT(FirstName,1),              -- column alias
         FirstCharOfLastName  = LEFT(LastName,1),               -- column alias
         LastCharOfLastName  = RIGHT(LastName,1),               -- column alias
         FullName = CONCAT(FirstName, SPACE(1), LastName) ,     -- column alias
         *                                                      -- wild card, all columns
FROM    Person.Person
WHERE    SUBSTRING(FirstName,1,1) = 'J'
     AND SUBSTRING (LastName,1,1) = 'S'
     AND (RIGHT(LastName,1) = 'H' OR RIGHT(LastName,1) = 'Z')
ORDER BY LastName;
-- (59 row(s) affected) - Partial result.
```

FirstCharOfFirstName	FirstCharOfLastName	LastCharOfLastName	FullName	BusinessEntityID
J	S	z	Jacqueline Sanchez	8975
J	S	z	Jada Sanchez	9499
J	S	z	Jade Sanchez	9528
J	S	z	Janelle Sanchez	18590
J	S	z	Jared Sanchez	15266
J	S	z	Jarrod Sanchez	2948
J	S	z	Jay Sanchez	10298
J	S	z	Jennifer Sanchez	20440
J	S	z	Jeremiah Sanchez	15292
J	S	z	Jermaine Sanchez	8040

```
-- Sort on first column
SELECT BusinessEntityID, JobTitle, SUBSTRING(JobTitle, 5, 7)  AS MiddleOfJobTitle
FROM   HumanResources.Employee
WHERE  BirthDate <= '1960/12/31'    -- date literal (constant)
ORDER BY 1;
-- (27 row(s) affected) - Partial results.
```

BusinessEntityID	JobTitle	MiddleOfJobTitle
5	Design Engineer	gn Engi
6	Design Engineer	gn Engi
12	Tool Designer	Design
15	Design Engineer	gn Engi
23	Marketing Specialist	eting S
27	Production Supervisor - WC60	uction

```
-- String functions usage in formatting
DECLARE @SSN char(9) = '123456789';
SELECT SSN=CONCAT(LEFT(@SSN,3),'-', SUBSTRING(@SSN,4,2),'-', RIGHT(@SSN,4));
-- 123-45-6789
```

ASCII value range is 0-127. Extended ASCII: 128-255. Size is 8-bit, one byte.

```
SELECT TOP 5    ProductNumber,
                SUBSTRING(ProductNumber,9,1)          AS MiddleSubstring,
                ASCII(SUBSTRING(ProductNumber,9,1))   AS ASCIIValue
FROM AdventureWorks2008.Production.Product
WHERE LEN(ProductNumber) > 8
ORDER BY Name;                          - OK syntax, but does not make sense
```

ProductNumber	MiddleSubstring	ASCIIValue
VE-C304-L	L	76
VE-C304-M	M	77
VE-C304-S	S	83
GL-F110-L	L	76
GL-F110-M	M	77

NOTE
Table columns and columns by expressions (computed) can be mixed in a query at will.

```
-- Computed (expressions) & table columns
SELECT FirstCharOfFirstName = LEFT(FirstName,1),        -- string expression
       FirstCharOfLastName  = LEFT(LastName,1),         -- string expression
       FullName = CONCAT(LastName, ', ', FirstName ),   -- string expression
       SquareOfID = SQUARE(BusinessEntityID),           -- math expression
       *                                                -- wild card, all table columns
FROM    Person.Person
WHERE   LEFT(FirstName,1) = 'J'
    AND LEFT(LastName,2) = 'Sm'
ORDER BY FullName;
-- (14 row(s) affected)   - Partial results.
```

FirstCharOfFirstName	FirstCharOfLastName	FullName	SquareOfID	BusinessEntityID
J	S	Smith, Jacob	348680929	18673
J	S	Smith, James	308986084	17578
J	S	Smith, Jasmine	129572689	11383
J	S	Smith, Jeff	3139984	1772
J	S	Smith, Jennifer	122699929	11077
J	S	Smith, Jeremiah	20511841	4529
J	S	Smith, Jessica	145829776	12076
J	S	Smith, John	332041284	18222
J	S	Smith, Jonathan	312228900	17670
J	S	Smith, Jose	300710281	17341
J	S	Smith, Joseph	357474649	18907
J	S	Smith, Joshua	351825049	18757
J	S	Smith, Julia	121616784	11028
J	S	Smith, Justin	324900625	18025

CHAPTER 7: Basic SELECT Statement Syntax & Examples

Transact-SQL Reserved Keywords

List of reserved keywords in SQL Server 2012 Transact-SQL. Keywords can only be used as delimited identifiers such as [Inner] or "Order".

ADD	EXTERNAL	PROCEDURE
ALL	FETCH	PUBLIC
ALTER	FILE	RAISERROR
AND	FILLFACTOR	READ
ANY	FOR	READTEXT
AS	FOREIGN	RECONFIGURE
ASC	FREETEXT	REFERENCES
AUTHORIZATION	FREETEXTTABLE	REPLICATION
BACKUP	FROM	RESTORE
BEGIN	FULL	RESTRICT
BETWEEN	FUNCTION	RETURN
BREAK	GOTO	REVERT
BROWSE	GRANT	REVOKE
BULK	GROUP	RIGHT
BY	HAVING	ROLLBACK
CASCADE	HOLDLOCK	ROWCOUNT
CASE	IDENTITY	ROWGUIDCOL
CHECK	IDENTITY_INSERT	RULE
CHECKPOINT	IDENTITYCOL	SAVE
CLOSE	IF	SCHEMA
CLUSTERED	IN	SECURITYAUDIT
COALESCE	INDEX	SELECT
COLLATE	INNER	SEMANTICKEYPHRASETABLE
COLUMN	INSERT	SEMANTICSIMILARITYDETAILSTABLE
COMMIT	INTERSECT	SEMANTICSIMILARITYTABLE
COMPUTE	INTO	SESSION_USER
CONSTRAINT	IS	SET
CONTAINS	JOIN	SETUSER
CONTAINSTABLE	KEY	SHUTDOWN
CONTINUE	KILL	SOME
CONVERT	LEFT	STATISTICS
CREATE	LIKE	SYSTEM_USER
CROSS	LINENO	TABLE
CURRENT	LOAD	TABLESAMPLE
CURRENT_DATE	MERGE	TEXTSIZE
CURRENT_TIME	NATIONAL	THEN
CURRENT_TIMESTAMP	NOCHECK	TO
CURRENT_USER	NONCLUSTERED	TOP
CURSOR	NOT	TRAN
DATABASE	NULL	TRANSACTION
DBCC	NULLIF	TRIGGER
DEALLOCATE	OF	TRUNCATE
DECLARE	OFF	TRY_CONVERT
DEFAULT	OFFSETS	TSEQUAL
DELETE	ON	UNION
DENY	OPEN	UNIQUE
DESC	OPENDATASOURCE	UNPIVOT
DISK	OPENQUERY	UPDATE
DISTINCT	OPENROWSET	UPDATETEXT
DISTRIBUTED	OPENXML	USE
DOUBLE	OPTION	USER
DROP	OR	VALUES
DUMP	ORDER	VARYING
ELSE	OUTER	VIEW
END	OVER	WAITFOR
ERRLVL	PERCENT	WHEN
ESCAPE	PIVOT	WHERE
EXCEPT	PLAN	WHILE
EXEC	PRECISION	WITH
EXECUTE	PRIMARY	WITHIN GROUP
EXISTS	PRINT	WRITETEXT
EXIT	PROC	

Case Sensitive Sort with Latin1_General_CS_AI

For case sensitive sort on a column with case insensitive collation, we have use a case sensitive (CS) collation such as Latin1_General_CS_AI.

```
-- CASE INSENSITIVE sort using default collation
SELECT lname FROM
        (SELECT TOP 5 UPPER (LastName) AS lname FROM Person.Person ORDER BY FirstName) x
UNION ALL   SELECT lname FROM
        (SELECT TOP 5 LOWER (LastName) AS lname FROM Person.Person ORDER BY FirstName) y
ORDER BY lname;
-- ADAMS, adams, alexander, ALEXANDER, leonetti, LEONETTI, WRIGHT, WRIGHT, wright, wright
```

```
-- CASE SENSITIVE sort using %CS% collation
SELECT lname FROM ( SELECT lname FROM
  (SELECT TOP 5 UPPER (LastName) AS lname FROM Person.Person ORDER BY FirstName) x
  UNION ALL  SELECT lname FROM
  (SELECT TOP 5 LOWER (LastName) AS lname FROM Person.Person ORDER BY FirstName) y  ) z
ORDER BY lname COLLATE Latin1_General_CS_AI;
-- adams,ADAMS,alexander,ALEXANDER,leonetti,LEONETTI,wright,wright,WRIGHT,WRIGHT
```

CHAPTER 7: Basic SELECT Statement Syntax & Examples

The ORDER BY Clause for Sorting Query Results

The ORDER BY clause is located at the very end of the query. In fact the sorting itself takes place after the query executed and generated **an unordered result set**. Although frequently, especially for small sets, the results appear to be sorted, **only an ORDER BY clause can guarantee proper sorting**. INSERT, UPDATE, DELETE & MERGE statement do not support sorting, **the database engine performs all set operations unordered**. T-SQL scripts demonstrate the many variations of the ORDER BY clause.

```
USE AdventureWorks2012;
GO
```

```
-- A column can be used for sorting even though not explicitly used in the SELECT list
SELECT *
FROM   Production.Product
ORDER  BY Name ASC;
GO
```

```
-- Sort on the second column, whatever it may be
SELECT *
FROM   Production.Product
ORDER  BY 2 DESC;
GO
```

```
-- ASCending is the default sort order, it is not necessary to use
SELECT  Name AS ProductName,
        *
FROM   Production.Product
ORDER  BY ProductName ASC;
GO
```

```
SELECT  TOP (10) Name AS ProductName,            *
FROM   Production.Product  ORDER  BY 1 ASC;
```

ProductName	ProductID	Name	ProductNumber	MakeFlag	FinishedGoodsFlag	Color	SafetyStockLevel
Adjustable Race	1	Adjustable Race	AR-5381	0	0	NULL	1000
All-Purpose Bike Stand	879	All-Purpose Bike Stand	ST-1401	0	1	NULL	4
AWC Logo Cap	712	AWC Logo Cap	CA-1098	0	1	Multi	4
BB Ball Bearing	3	BB Ball Bearing	BE-2349	1	0	NULL	800
Bearing Ball	2	Bearing Ball	BA-8327	0	0	NULL	1000
Bike Wash - Dissolver	877	Bike Wash - Dissolver	CL-9009	0	1	NULL	4
Blade	316	Blade	BL-2036	1	0	NULL	800
Cable Lock	843	Cable Lock	LO-C100	0	1	NULL	4
Chain	952	Chain	CH-0234	0	1	Silver	500
Chain Stays	324	Chain Stays	CS-2812	1	0	NULL	1000

Using Column Alias in the ORDER BY Clause

Column alias can be used in an ORDER BY clause. In fact, it should be used to make the query more readable.

```
-- ProductName is a column alias, it can only be used in the ORDER BY clause, not anywhere before
SELECT ProductName = Name, *
FROM Production.Product
WHERE ProductName like '%glove%'
ORDER BY ProductName ASC ;
GO
/* ERROR
Msg 207, Level 16, State 1, Line 3
Invalid column name 'ProductName'.
*/
```

```
-- The TOP clause uses the ORDER BY sorting to select the 5 rows
SELECT TOP (5) ProductName = Name, *
FROM Production.Product
WHERE Name like '%glove%'
ORDER BY ProductName ASC ;
```

ProductName	ProductID	Name	ProductNumber	MakeFlag	FinishedGoodsFlag	Color	SafetyStockLevel
Full-Finger Gloves, L	863	Full-Finger Gloves, L	GL-F110-L	0	1	Black	4
Full-Finger Gloves, M	862	Full-Finger Gloves, M	GL-F110-M	0	1	Black	4
Full-Finger Gloves, S	861	Full-Finger Gloves, S	GL-F110-S	0	1	Black	4
Half-Finger Gloves, L	860	Half-Finger Gloves, L	GL-H102-L	0	1	Black	4
Half-Finger Gloves, M	859	Half-Finger Gloves, M	GL-H102-M	0	1	Black	4

```
-- Descending sort on name which is string data type
SELECT TOP (10) ProductName = Name, *
FROM Production.Product
WHERE Name like '%road%'
ORDER BY ProductName DESC ;
```
.

ProductName	ProductID	Name	ProductNumber	MakeFlag	FinishedGoodsFlag	Color	SafetyStockLevel
Road-750 Black, 58	977	Road-750 Black, 58	BK-R19B-58	1	1	Black	100
Road-750 Black, 52	999	Road-750 Black, 52	BK-R19B-52	1	1	Black	100
Road-750 Black, 48	998	Road-750 Black, 48	BK-R19B-48	1	1	Black	100
Road-750 Black, 44	997	Road-750 Black, 44	BK-R19B-44	1	1	Black	100
Road-650 Red, 62	761	Road-650 Red, 62	BK-R50R-62	1	1	Red	100
Road-650 Red, 60	760	Road-650 Red, 60	BK-R50R-60	1	1	Red	100
Road-650 Red, 58	759	Road-650 Red, 58	BK-R50R-58	1	1	Red	100
Road-650 Red, 52	764	Road-650 Red, 52	BK-R50R-52	1	1	Red	100
Road-650 Red, 48	763	Road-650 Red, 48	BK-R50R-48	1	1	Red	100
Road-650 Red, 44	762	Road-650 Red, 44	BK-R50R-44	1	1	Red	100

Using Table Alias in the ORDER BY Clause

Unlike the column alias, table alias can be used anywhere in the query within the scope of the alias.

```
-- Using table alias in ORDER BY
SELECT P.*
FROM   Production.Product P
ORDER  BY P.Name ASC;
GO
```

ProductID	Name	ProductNumber	MakeFlag	FinishedGoodsFlag	Color	SafetyStockLevel
958	Touring-3000 Blue, 54	BK-T18U-54	1	1	Blue	100
959	Touring-3000 Blue, 58	BK-T18U-58	1	1	Blue	100
960	Touring-3000 Blue, 62	BK-T18U-62	1	1	Blue	100
961	Touring-3000 Yellow, 44	BK-T18Y-44	1	1	Yellow	100
962	Touring-3000 Yellow, 50	BK-T18Y-50	1	1	Yellow	100
963	Touring-3000 Yellow, 54	BK-T18Y-54	1	1	Yellow	100
964	Touring-3000 Yellow, 58	BK-T18Y-58	1	1	Yellow	100
965	Touring-3000 Yellow, 62	BK-T18Y-62	1	1	Yellow	100
842	Touring-Panniers, Large	PA-T100	0	1	Grey	4
870	Water Bottle - 30 oz.	WB-H098	0	1	NULL	4
869	Women's Mountain Shorts, L	SH-W890-L	0	1	Black	4
868	Women's Mountain Shorts, M	SH-W890-M	0	1	Black	4
867	Women's Mountain Shorts, S	SH-W890-S	0	1	Black	4
854	Women's Tights, L	TG-W091-L	0	1	Black	4
853	Women's Tights, M	TG-W091-M	0	1	Black	4
852	Women's Tights, S	TG-W091-S	0	1	Black	4

```
-- Specific column list instead of all (*)
SELECT   Name,
         ProductNumber,
         ListPrice AS PRICE
FROM   Production.Product  P
ORDER  BY P.Name ASC;
GO
```

```
SELECT          Name,
                ProductNumber,
                ListPrice AS PRICE
FROM   Production.Product  P
ORDER  BY P.ListPrice DESC;
```

```
-- Equivalent to above with column alias usage
SELECT          Name,
                ProductNumber,
                ListPrice AS PRICE
FROM   Production.Product  P ORDER  BY PRICE DESC;
```

Easy ORDER BY Queries for Exercises

T-SQL scripts demonstrate easily readable queries with sorted result sets.

```
USE pubs ;
GO
```

```
SELECT TYPE,  AvgPrice=FORMAT(AVG(price) , 'c', 'en-US')
FROM   titles WHERE  royalty = 10 GROUP  BY TYPE ORDER  BY TYPE ;
```

TYPE	AvgPrice
business	$17.31
popular_comp	$20.00
psychology	$14.14
trad_cook	$17.97

```
SELECT          type = type,
                AvgPrice = FORMAT(AVG(price),'c', 'en-US')
FROM   titles
WHERE  royalty = 10
GROUP  BY type
ORDER  BY AvgPrice;
```

type	AvgPrice
psychology	$14.14
business	$17.31
trad_cook	$17.97
popular_comp	$20.00

```
SELECT  type                            AS [type],
        FORMAT(AVG(price),'c', 'en-US')    AS AvgPrice
FROM   titles  GROUP  BY [type]  ORDER  BY [type] desc;
```

type	AvgPrice
UNDECIDED	NULL
trad_cook	$15.96
psychology	$13.50
popular_comp	$21.48
mod_cook	$11.49
business	$13.73

CHAPTER 7: Basic SELECT Statement Syntax & Examples

Eliminate NULL in result with COALESCE or ISNULL functions

```
SELECT [type] = type,
       AvgPrice = COALESCE(FORMAT(AVG(price),'c', 'en-US') ,'')
FROM  titles  GROUP  BY [type]  ORDER  BY [type] desc;
```

type	AvgPrice
UNDECIDED	
trad_cook	$15.96
psychology	$13.50
popular_comp	$21.48
mod_cook	$11.49
business	$13.73

```
SELECT           pub_name                              Publisher,
                 FORMAT(AVG(price),'c', 'en-US')    AvgPrice
FROM  titles
    INNER JOIN publishers
    ON  titles.pub_id = publishers.pub_id
GROUP  BY pub_name
ORDER  BY pub_name;
```

Publisher	AvgPrice
Algodata Infosystems	$18.98
Binnet & Hardley	$15.41
New Moon Books	$9.78

```
SELECT TOP(3) * FROM  titles ORDER  BY title;
```

title_id	title	type	pub_id	price	advance	royalty	ytd_sales	notes	pubdate
PC1035	But Is It User Friendly?	popular_comp	1389	22.95	7000.00	16	8780	A survey of software for the naive user, focusing on the 'friendliness' of each.	1991-06-30 00:00:00.000
PS1372	Computer Phobic AND Non-Phobic Individuals: Behavior Variations	psychology	0877	21.59	7000.00	10	375	A must for the specialist, this book examines the difference between those who hate and fear computers and those who don't.	1991-10-21 00:00:00.000
BU1111	Cooking with Computers: Surreptitious Balance Sheets	business	1389	11.95	5000.00	10	3876	Helpful hints on how to use your electronic resources to the best advantage.	1991-06-09 00:00:00.000

```
SELECT TOP(3) * FROM  publishers ORDER  BY pub_name;
```

pub_id	pub_name	city	state	country
1389	Algodata Infosystems	Berkeley	CA	USA
0877	Binnet & Hardley	Washington	DC	USA
1622	Five Lakes Publishing	Chicago	IL	USA

CHAPTER 7: Basic SELECT Statement Syntax & Examples

Sorting Products by Attributes

```
USE Northwind;
GO

SELECT          UnitsInStock,
                ProductID,
                ProductName,
                QuantityPerUnit,
                FORMAT( UnitPrice, 'c', 'en-US')          AS UnitPrice  -- Column alias is same as
column
FROM   Northwind.dbo.Products WHERE  UnitsInStock BETWEEN 15 AND 25  ORDER  BY UnitsInStock;
```

UnitsInStock	ProductID	ProductName	QuantityPerUnit	UnitPrice
15	7	Uncle Bob's Organic Dried Pears	12 - 1 lb pkgs.	$30.00
15	26	Gumbär Gummibärchen	100 - 250 g bags	$31.23
15	48	Chocolade	10 pkgs.	$12.75
15	70	Outback Lager	24 - 355 ml bottles	$15.00
17	38	Côte de Blaye	12 - 75 cl bottles	$263.50
17	43	Ipoh Coffee	16 - 500 g tins	$46.00
17	62	Tarte au sucre	48 pies	$49.30
17	2	Chang	24 - 12 oz bottles	$19.00
19	60	Camembert Pierrot	15 - 300 g rounds	$34.00
20	24	Guaraná Fantástica	12 - 355 ml cans	$4.50
20	35	Steeleye Stout	24 - 12 oz bottles	$18.00
20	51	Manjimup Dried Apples	50 - 300 g pkgs.	$53.00
21	54	Tourtière	16 pies	$7.45
21	56	Gnocchi di nonna Alice	24 - 250 g pkgs.	$38.00
22	11	Queso Cabrales	1 kg pkg.	$21.00
22	64	Wimmers gute Semmelknödel	20 bags x 4 pieces	$33.25
24	13	Konbu	2 kg box	$6.00
24	63	Vegie-spread	15 - 625 g jars	$43.90
25	19	Teatime Chocolate Biscuits	10 boxes x 12 pieces	$9.20

```
-- A second key is necessary for unique ordering
SELECT   TOP(8)  UnitsInStock,
                 ProductID,
                 ProductName,
                 QuantityPerUnit,
                 FORMAT( UnitPrice, 'c', 'en-US') AS UnitPrice
FROM   Northwind.dbo.Products
WHERE  UnitsInStock BETWEEN 15 AND 25 ORDER  BY UnitsInStock, ProductName;
```

UnitsInStock	ProductID	ProductName	QuantityPerUnit	UnitPrice
15	48	Chocolade	10 pkgs.	$12.75
15	26	Gumbär Gummibärchen	100 - 250 g bags	$31.23
15	70	Outback Lager	24 - 355 ml bottles	$15.00
15	7	Uncle Bob's Organic Dried Pears	12 - 1 lb pkgs.	$30.00
17	2	Chang	24 - 12 oz bottles	$19.00
17	38	Côte de Blaye	12 - 75 cl bottles	$263.50
17	43	Ipoh Coffee	16 - 500 g tins	$46.00
17	62	Tarte au sucre	48 pies	$49.30

Changing WHERE condition changes the cardinality of result set

```
SELECT          UnitsInStock,
                ProductID,
                ProductName,
                QuantityPerUnit,
                FORMAT( UnitPrice, 'c', 'en-US')           AS UnitPrice
FROM   Northwind.dbo.Products
WHERE  UnitsInStock = 15 or UnitsInStock =  25  -- same as UnitsInStock IN (15, 25)
ORDER  BY UnitsInStock, ProductName;
```

UnitsInStock	ProductID	ProductName	QuantityPerUnit	UnitPrice
15	48	Chocolade	10 pkgs.	$12.75
15	26	Gumbär Gummibärchen	100 - 250 g bags	$31.23
15	70	Outback Lager	24 - 355 ml bottles	$15.00
15	7	Uncle Bob's Organic Dried Pears	12 - 1 lb pkgs.	$30.00
25	19	Teatime Chocolate Biscuits	10 boxes x 12 pieces	$9.20

```
SELECT  TOP(7)  UnitsInStock,
                ProductID,
                ProductName,
                QuantityPerUnit,
                FORMAT( UnitPrice, 'c', 'en-US')           AS UnitPrice
FROM   Northwind.dbo.Products  ORDER  BY UnitsInStock DESC, ProductName ASC;
```

UnitsInStock	ProductID	ProductName	QuantityPerUnit	UnitPrice
125	75	Rhönbräu Klosterbier	24 - 0.5 l bottles	$7.75
123	40	Boston Crab Meat	24 - 4 oz tins	$18.40
120	6	Grandma's Boysenberry Spread	12 - 8 oz jars	$25.00
115	55	Pâté chinois	24 boxes x 2 pies	$24.00
113	61	Sirop d'érable	24 - 500 ml bottles	$28.50
112	33	Geitost	500 g	$2.50
112	36	Inlagd Sill	24 - 250 g jars	$19.00

```
SELECT  TOP(5)  UnitsInStock, ProductID, ProductName,        QuantityPerUnit,
                FORMAT( UnitPrice, 'c', 'en-US') AS UnitPrice
FROM   Northwind.dbo.Products
WHERE  UnitsInStock > 15  AND UnitsInStock < 25  ORDER  BY UnitsInStock DESC, ProductName ASC;
```

UnitsInStock	ProductID	ProductName	QuantityPerUnit	UnitPrice
24	13	Konbu	2 kg box	$6.00
24	63	Vegie-spread	15 - 625 g jars	$43.90
22	11	Queso Cabrales	1 kg pkg.	$21.00
22	64	Wimmers gute Semmelknödel	20 bags x 4 pieces	$33.25
21	56	Gnocchi di nonna Alice	24 - 250 g pkgs.	$38.00

The "Tricky" BETWEEN & NOT BETWEEN Operators
They are very English-like, but results should be verified to make sure they work as intended.

```
SELECT  TOP(5)  UnitsInStock, ProductID, ProductName,      QuantityPerUnit,
                FORMAT( UnitPrice, 'c', 'en-US') AS UnitPrice
FROM  Northwind.dbo.Products
WHERE  UnitsInStock BETWEEN 15 AND 25  ORDER  BY UnitsInStock DESC, ProductName ASC;
```

UnitsInStock	ProductID	ProductName	QuantityPerUnit	UnitPrice
25	19	Teatime Chocolate Biscuits	10 boxes x 12 pieces	$9.20
24	13	Konbu	2 kg box	$6.00
24	63	Vegie-spread	15 - 625 g jars	$43.90
22	11	Queso Cabrales	1 kg pkg.	$21.00
22	64	Wimmers gute Semmelknödel	20 bags x 4 pieces	$33.25

```
SELECT  TOP(5)  UnitsInStock, ProductID, ProductName,      QuantityPerUnit,
                FORMAT( UnitPrice, 'c', 'en-US') AS UnitPrice
FROM  Northwind.dbo.Products
WHERE  UnitsInStock NOT BETWEEN 15 AND 25
ORDER  BY UnitsInStock DESC, ProductName ASC;
```

UnitsInStock	ProductID	ProductName	QuantityPerUnit	UnitPrice
125	75	Rhönbräu Klosterbier	24 - 0.5 l bottles	$7.75
123	40	Boston Crab Meat	24 - 4 oz tins	$18.40
120	6	Grandma's Boysenberry Spread	12 - 8 oz jars	$25.00
115	55	Pâté chinois	24 boxes x 2 pies	$24.00
113	61	Sirop d'érable	24 - 500 ml bottles	$28.50

```
SELECT          Orders.OrderID,
                Shippers.*
FROM  Shippers
    INNER JOIN Orders
      ON ( Shippers.ShipperID = Orders.ShipVia )
ORDER  BY Orders.OrderID;
GO
-- (830 row(s) affected) - Partial results.
```

OrderID	ShipperID	CompanyName	Phone
10248	3	Federal Shipping	(503) 555-9931
10249	1	Speedy Express	(503) 555-9831
10250	2	United Package	(503) 555-3199
10251	1	Speedy Express	(503) 555-9831
10252	2	United Package	(503) 555-3199
10253	2	United Package	(503) 555-3199

A second key is frequently required in sorting exception is PRIMARY KEY column.

```
SELECT  OrderID,
        ProductID,
        FORMAT( UnitPrice, 'c', 'en-US')          AS UnitPrice,
        Quantity,
        Discount
FROM  [Order Details]  ORDER  BY OrderID ASC, ProductID ASC;
-- (2155 row(s) affected) - Partial results.
```

OrderID	ProductID	UnitPrice	Quantity	Discount
10248	11	$14.00	12	0
10248	42	$9.80	10	0
10248	72	$34.80	5	0
10249	14	$18.60	9	0
10249	51	$42.40	40	0
10250	41	$7.70	10	0
10250	51	$42.40	35	0.15
10250	65	$16.80	15	0.15

```
-- Sort keys are different from expression column EmployeeName
SELECT  CONCAT(LastName,', ', FirstName)  AS EmployeeName ,
        Title, City, Country
FROM   Northwind.dbo.Employees ORDER  BY LastName,  FirstName ASC;
```

EmployeeName	Title	City	Country
Buchanan, Steven	Sales Manager	London	UK
Callahan, Laura	Inside Sales Coordinator	Seattle	USA
Davolio, Nancy	Sales Representative	Seattle	USA
Dodsworth, Anne	Sales Representative	London	UK
Fuller, Andrew	Vice President, Sales	Tacoma	USA
King, Robert	Sales Representative	London	UK
Leverling, Janet	Sales Representative	Kirkland	USA
Peacock, Margaret	Sales Representative	Redmond	USA
Suyama, Michael	Sales Representative	London	UK

```
-- Equivalent sort
SELECT TOP(3)     CONCAT(LastName,', ', FirstName) AS EmployeeName ,    Title, City, Country
FROM   Northwind.dbo.Employees  ORDER  BY EmployeeName ASC;
```

EmployeeName	Title	City	Country
Buchanan, Steven	Sales Manager	London	UK
Callahan, Laura	Inside Sales Coordinator	Seattle	USA
Davolio, Nancy	Sales Representative	Seattle	USA

Using Multiple Keys in the ORDER BY Clause

If a single sort key does not result in unique ordering, multiple keys can be used. In the next example the Price (major) key is based on a column which is not unique. If we add Name as a second (minor) key, unique ordering will be guaranteed since Name is a unique column, it has a unique index and not null. It's worth noting if Name would allow nulls, we would need a third key for unique ordering.

```
-- Single key sort
SELECT  P.Name,
        P.ProductNumber,
        P.ListPrice            AS PRICE
FROM   Production.Product P
WHERE  P.ProductLine = 'R'   AND P.DaysToManufacture < 4    ORDER  BY P. ListPrice DESC;
```

Name	ProductNumber	PRICE
HL Road Frame - Black, 58	FR-R92B-58	1431.50
HL Road Frame - Red, 58	FR-R92R-58	1431.50
HL Road Frame - Red, 62	FR-R92R-62	1431.50
HL Road Frame - Red, 44	FR-R92R-44	1431.50
HL Road Frame - Red, 48	FR-R92R-48	1431.50
HL Road Frame - Red, 52	FR-R92R-52	1431.50
HL Road Frame - Red, 56	FR-R92R-56	1431.50
HL Road Frame - Black, 62	FR-R92B-62	1431.50
HL Road Frame - Black, 44	FR-R92B-44	1431.50
HL Road Frame - Black, 48	FR-R92B-48	1431.50
HL Road Frame - Black, 52	FR-R92B-52	1431.50
ML Road Frame-W - Yellow, 40	FR-R72Y-40	594.83

```
-- Double key sort - PRICE is the major key, Name is the minor key
SELECT  P.Name,
        P.ProductNumber,
        P.ListPrice            AS PRICE
FROM   Production.Product P
WHERE  P.ProductLine = 'R'  AND P.DaysToManufacture < 4  ORDER  BY  PRICE DESC, Name;
```

Name	ProductNumber	PRICE
HL Road Frame - Black, 44	FR-R92B-44	1431.50
HL Road Frame - Black, 48	FR-R92B-48	1431.50
HL Road Frame - Black, 52	FR-R92B-52	1431.50
HL Road Frame - Black, 58	FR-R92B-58	1431.50
HL Road Frame - Black, 62	FR-R92B-62	1431.50
HL Road Frame - Red, 44	FR-R92R-44	1431.50
HL Road Frame - Red, 48	FR-R92R-48	1431.50
HL Road Frame - Red, 52	FR-R92R-52	1431.50
HL Road Frame - Red, 56	FR-R92R-56	1431.50
HL Road Frame - Red, 58	FR-R92R-58	1431.50
HL Road Frame - Red, 62	FR-R92R-62	1431.50
ML Road Frame - Red, 44	FR-R72R-44	594.83

ORDER BY in Complex Queries

An ORDER BY can be in a complex query and/or ORDER BY can be complex itself. T-SQL scripts demonstrate complex ORDER BY usage.

```
-- We cannot tell just by query inspection if the second key is sufficient for unique ordering or not
-- If we inspect the result set it becomes obvious that we need a third key at least (SalesOrderID unsorted)
SELECT   ProductName            = P.Name,
         NonDiscountSales        = ( OrderQty * UnitPrice ),
         Discounts               = ( ( OrderQty * UnitPrice ) * UnitPriceDiscount ) ,
         SalesOrderID
FROM   Production.Product P
    INNER JOIN Sales.SalesOrderDetail SOD
        ON P.ProductID = SOD.ProductID
ORDER  BY       ProductName DESC,
                NonDiscountSales DESC;
GO
```

ProductName	NonDiscountSales	Discounts	SalesOrderID
Women's Tights, S	1049.86	104.986	47355
Women's Tights, S	824.89	41.2445	46987
Women's Tights, S	783.6455	39.1823	47400
Women's Tights, S	742.401	37.1201	50206
Women's Tights, S	701.1565	35.0578	46993
Women's Tights, S	701.1565	35.0578	46671
Women's Tights, S	701.1565	35.0578	50688
Women's Tights, S	701.1565	35.0578	49481
Women's Tights, S	659.912	32.9956	48295
Women's Tights, S	659.912	32.9956	46967
Women's Tights, S	618.6675	30.9334	46652
Women's Tights, S	608.9188	12.1784	46672
Women's Tights, S	608.9188	12.1784	47365
Women's Tights, S	565.4246	11.3085	47004
Women's Tights, S	565.4246	11.3085	50663

NOTE

Even though SELECT DISTINCT results may appear to be sorted, **only ORDER BY clause can guarantee sort**. This holds true for any kind of SELECT statement, simple or complex.

```
SELECT DISTINCT JobTitle  FROM  HumanResources.Employee ;
```

```
SELECT DISTINCT JobTitle  FROM  HumanResources.Employee ORDER  BY JobTitle;
```

ORDER BY with ROW_NUMBER()

T-SQL queries demonstrate sorting with not matching and matching ROW_NUMBER() sequence number.

```
SELECT
  ROW_NUMBER() OVER( PARTITION BY CountryRegionName  ORDER BY SalesYTD ASC) AS SeqNo,
  CountryRegionName AS Country,  FirstName, LastName,  JobTitle,
  FORMAT(SalesYTD, 'c', 'en-US') AS SalesYTD,
  FORMAT(SalesLastYear, 'c', 'en-US') AS SalesLastYear
FROM  Sales.vSalesPerson          ORDER BY JobTitle,  SalesYTD DESC;
```

SeqNo	Country	FirstName	LastName	JobTitle	SalesYTD	SalesLastYear
2	United States	Amy	Alberts	European Sales Manager	$519,905.93	$0.00
3	United States	Stephen	Jiang	North American Sales Manager	$559,697.56	$0.00
1	United States	Syed	Abbas	Pacific Sales Manager	$172,524.45	$0.00
11	United States	Linda	Mitchell	Sales Representative	$4,251,368.55	$1,439,156.03
1	United Kingdom	Jae	Pak	Sales Representative	$4,116,871.23	$1,635,823.40
10	United States	Michael	Blythe	Sales Representative	$3,763,178.18	$1,750,406.48
9	United States	Jillian	Carson	Sales Representative	$3,189,418.37	$1,997,186.20
1	France	Ranjit	Varkey Chudukatil	Sales Representative	$3,121,616.32	$2,396,539.76
2	Canada	José	Saraiva	Sales Representative	$2,604,540.72	$2,038,234.65
8	United States	Shu	Ito	Sales Representative	$2,458,535.62	$2,073,506.00
7	United States	Tsvi	Reiter	Sales Representative	$2,315,185.61	$1,849,640.94
1	Germany	Rachel	Valdez	Sales Representative	$1,827,066.71	$1,307,949.79
6	United States	Tete	Mensa-Annan	Sales Representative	$1,576,562.20	$0.00
5	United States	David	Campbell	Sales Representative	$1,573,012.94	$1,371,635.32
1	Canada	Garrett	Vargas	Sales Representative	$1,453,719.47	$1,620,276.90
1	Australia	Lynn	Tsoflias	Sales Representative	$1,421,810.92	$2,278,548.98
4	United States	Pamela	Ansman-Wolfe	Sales Representative	$1,352,577.13	$1,927,059.18

```
-- ROW_NUMBER() ORDER BY in synch with sort ORDER BY
SELECT  ROW_NUMBER() OVER( ORDER BY JobTitle, SalesYTD DESC) AS SeqNo,
    CountryRegionName AS Country,  FirstName, LastName,  JobTitle,
    FORMAT(SalesYTD, 'c', 'en-US') AS SalesYTD,  FORMAT(SalesLastYear, 'c', 'en-US') AS SalesLastYear
FROM  Sales.vSalesPerson  ORDER BY      SeqNo;
```

SeqNo	Country	FirstName	LastName	JobTitle	SalesYTD	SalesLastYear
1	United States	Amy	Alberts	European Sales Manager	$519,905.93	$0.00
2	United States	Stephen	Jiang	North American Sales Manager	$559,697.56	$0.00
3	United States	Syed	Abbas	Pacific Sales Manager	$172,524.45	$0.00
4	United States	Linda	Mitchell	Sales Representative	$4,251,368.55	$1,439,156.03
5	United Kingdom	Jae	Pak	Sales Representative	$4,116,871.23	$1,635,823.40
6	United States	Michael	Blythe	Sales Representative	$3,763,178.18	$1,750,406.48
7	United States	Jillian	Carson	Sales Representative	$3,189,418.37	$1,997,186.20
8	France	Ranjit	Varkey Chudukatil	Sales Representative	$3,121,616.32	$2,396,539.76
9	Canada	José	Saraiva	Sales Representative	$2,604,540.72	$2,038,234.65
10	United States	Shu	Ito	Sales Representative	$2,458,535.62	$2,073,506.00
11	United States	Tsvi	Reiter	Sales Representative	$2,315,185.61	$1,849,640.94
12	Germany	Rachel	Valdez	Sales Representative	$1,827,066.71	$1,307,949.79
13	United States	Tete	Mensa-Annan	Sales Representative	$1,576,562.20	$0.00
14	United States	David	Campbell	Sales Representative	$1,573,012.94	$1,371,635.32
15	Canada	Garrett	Vargas	Sales Representative	$1,453,719.47	$1,620,276.90
16	Australia	Lynn	Tsoflias	Sales Representative	$1,421,810.92	$2,278,548.98
17	United States	Pamela	Ansman-Wolfe	Sales Representative	$1,352,577.13	$1,927,059.18

ORDER BY Clause with CASE Conditional Expression
Sort by LastName, MiddleName if exists else FirstName, and FirstName in case MiddleName is used.

```
USE AdventureWorks;

SELECT          FirstName,
                COALESCE(MiddleName, '')          AS MName,  -- ISNULL can also be used
                LastName,
                AddressLine1,
                COALESCE(AddressLine2, '')        AS Addr2,
                City,
                SP.Name                           AS [State],
                CR.Name                           AS Country,
                I.CustomerID
FROM   Person.Contact AS C
    INNER JOIN Sales.Individual AS I
        ON C.ContactID = I.ContactID
    INNER JOIN Sales.CustomerAddress AS CA
        ON CA.CustomerID = I.CustomerID
    INNER JOIN Person.[Address] AS A
        ON A.AddressID = CA.AddressID
    INNER JOIN Person.StateProvince SP
        ON SP.StateProvinceID = A.StateProvinceID
    INNER JOIN Person.CountryRegion CR
        ON CR.CountryRegionCode = SP.CountryRegionCode
ORDER  BY LastName,
       CASE
         WHEN MiddleName != '' THEN MiddleName
         ELSE FirstName
       END,
       FirstName;
-- (18508 row(s) affected) -Partial results.
```

FirstName	MName	LastName	AddressLine1	Addr2	City	State	Country	CustomerID
Chloe	A	Adams	3001 N. 48th Street		Marysville	Washington	United States	19410
Eduardo	A	Adams	4283 Meaham Drive		San Diego	California	United States	25292
Kaitlyn	A	Adams	3815 Berry Dr.		Westminster	British Columbia	Canada	11869
Mackenzie	A	Adams	9639 Ida Drive		Langford	British Columbia	Canada	14640
Sara	A	Adams	7503 Hill Drive		Milwaukie	Oregon	United States	16986
Adam		Adams	9381 Bayside Way		Newport Beach	California	United States	13323
Amber		Adams	9720 Morning Glory Dr.		Brisbane	Queensland	Australia	26746
Angel		Adams	9556 Lyman Rd.		Burlingame	California	United States	18504
Aaron	B	Adams	4116 Stanbridge Ct.		Downey	California	United States	28866
Noah	B	Adams	6738 Wallace Dr.		El Cajon	California	United States	16977
Bailey		Adams	1817 Adobe Drive		Kirkland	Washington	United States	13280
Ben		Adams	1534 Land Ave		Bremerton	Washington	United States	28678
Alex	C	Adams	237 Bellwood Dr.		Lake Oswego	Oregon	United States	21139
Courtney	C	Adams	6089 Santa Fe Dr.		Torrance	California	United States	18075
Ian	C	Adams	7963 Elk Dr	#4	Versailles	Yveline	France	29422

Special Sorting, Like United States On Top Of The Country Pop-Up List
It requires CASE or IIF conditional expression.

```
-- Major sort key is Color if not null, else product name
-- Minor sort on ProductNumber
SELECT ProductID,
    ProductNumber,
    Name AS ProductName,
    FORMAT(ListPrice, 'c', 'en-US')  AS ListPrice,
    Color
FROM   Production.Product
WHERE  Name LIKE ( '%Road%' )
ORDER  BY       CASE
                    WHEN Color IS NULL THEN Name
                    ELSE Color
                END,
                ProductNumber DESC;
-- (103 row(s) affected) - Partial results.
```

ProductID	ProductNumber	ProductName	ListPrice	Color
768	BK-R50B-44	Road-650 Black, 44	$782.99	Black
977	BK-R19B-58	Road-750 Black, 58	$539.99	Black
999	BK-R19B-52	Road-750 Black, 52	$539.99	Black
998	BK-R19B-48	Road-750 Black, 48	$539.99	Black
997	BK-R19B-44	Road-750 Black, 44	$539.99	Black
813	HB-R956	HL Road Handlebars	$120.27	NULL
512	RM-R800	HL Road Rim	$0.00	NULL
519	SA-R522	HL Road Seat Assembly	$196.92	NULL
913	SE-R995	HL Road Seat/Saddle	$52.64	NULL
933	TI-R982	HL Road Tire	$32.60	NULL
811	HB-R504	LL Road Handlebars	$44.54	NULL
510	RM-R436	LL Road Rim	$0.00	NULL
517	SA-R127	LL Road Seat Assembly	$133.34	NULL
911	SE-R581	LL Road Seat/Saddle	$27.12	NULL
931	TI-R092	LL Road Tire	$21.49	NULL
812	HB-R720	ML Road Handlebars	$61.92	NULL
511	RM-R600	ML Road Rim	$0.00	NULL
518	SA-R430	ML Road Seat Assembly	$147.14	NULL
912	SE-R908	ML Road Seat/Saddle	$39.14	NULL
932	TI-R628	ML Road Tire	$24.99	NULL
717	FR-R92R-62	HL Road Frame - Red, 62	$1,431.50	Red
706	FR-R92R-58	HL Road Frame - Red, 58	$1,431.50	Red
721	FR-R92R-56	HL Road Frame - Red, 56	$1,431.50	Red

T-SQL queries demonstrate complex sorting with the CASE expression usage.
CASE expression returns a SINGLE SCALAR VALUE of the same data type.

```
SELECT   SellStartDate,
         SellEndDate,
         *
FROM   Production.Product
WHERE  Name LIKE ( '%mountain%' )
ORDER  BY CASE
                 WHEN SellEndDate IS NULL THEN SellStartDate
                 ELSE SellEndDate
         END DESC, Name;
GO
-- (94 row(s) affected) -Partial results.
```

SellStartDate	SellEndDate	ProductID	Name	ProductNumber
2007-07-01 00:00:00.000	NULL	986	Mountain-500 Silver, 44	BK-M18S-44
2007-07-01 00:00:00.000	NULL	987	Mountain-500 Silver, 48	BK-M18S-48
2007-07-01 00:00:00.000	NULL	988	Mountain-500 Silver, 52	BK-M18S-52
2007-07-01 00:00:00.000	NULL	869	Women's Mountain Shorts, L	SH-W890-L
2007-07-01 00:00:00.000	NULL	868	Women's Mountain Shorts, M	SH-W890-M
2007-07-01 00:00:00.000	NULL	867	Women's Mountain Shorts, S	SH-W890-S
2006-07-01 00:00:00.000	2007-06-30 00:00:00.000	817	HL Mountain Front Wheel	FW-M928
2006-07-01 00:00:00.000	2007-06-30 00:00:00.000	825	HL Mountain Rear Wheel	RW-M928
2006-07-01 00:00:00.000	2007-06-30 00:00:00.000	815	LL Mountain Front Wheel	FW-M423
2006-07-01 00:00:00.000	2007-06-30 00:00:00.000	823	LL Mountain Rear Wheel	RW-M423
2006-07-01 00:00:00.000	2007-06-30 00:00:00.000	814	ML Mountain Frame - Black, 38	FR-M63B-38
2006-07-01 00:00:00.000	2007-06-30 00:00:00.000	830	ML Mountain Frame - Black, 40	FR-M63B-40

```
-- 2 keys descending sort
SELECT         PRODUCTNAME   = P.Name,
               SALETOTAL     = ( OrderQty * UnitPrice ),
               NETSALETOTAL  = ( ( OrderQty - RejectedQty ) * UnitPrice )
FROM   Production.Product P
    INNER JOIN Purchasing.PurchaseOrderDetail SOD
        ON P.ProductID = SOD.ProductID
ORDER  BY PRODUCTNAME  DESC,  SALETOTAL DESC;

-- Column alias sorting of GROUP BY aggregation results
SELECT [YEAR]=YEAR(OrderDate), Orders = COUNT(*)
FROM AdventureWorks2012.Sales.SalesOrderHeader
GROUP BY YEAR(OrderDate)  ORDER BY [YEAR];
```

YEAR	Orders
2005	1379
2006	3692
2007	12443
2008	13951

ORDER BY Clause with IIF Conditional Function

Sort by LastName, MiddleName if exists else FirstName, and FirstName in case MiddleName is used.

```
USE AdventureWorks;

SELECT          FirstName,
                COALESCE(MiddleName, '')        AS MName,  -- ISNULL can also be used
                LastName,
                AddressLine1,
                COALESCE(AddressLine2, '')      AS Addr2,
                City,
                SP.Name                         AS [State],
                CR.Name                         AS Country,
                I.CustomerID
FROM   Person.Contact AS C
    INNER JOIN Sales.Individual AS I
        ON C.ContactID = I.ContactID
    INNER JOIN Sales.CustomerAddress AS CA
        ON CA.CustomerID = I.CustomerID
    INNER JOIN Person.[Address] AS A
        ON A.AddressID = CA.AddressID
    INNER JOIN Person.StateProvince SP
        ON SP.StateProvinceID = A.StateProvinceID
    INNER JOIN Person.CountryRegion CR
        ON CR.CountryRegionCode = SP.CountryRegionCode
ORDER  BY       LastName,
                IIF( MiddleName != '', MiddleName, FirstName),
                FirstName;
-- (18508 row(s) affected) -Partial results.
```

FirstName	MName	LastName	AddressLine1	Addr2	City	State	Country	CustomerID
Chloe	A	Adams	3001 N. 48th Street		Marysville	Washington	United States	19410
Eduardo	A	Adams	4283 Meaham Drive		San Diego	California	United States	25292
Kaitlyn	A	Adams	3815 Berry Dr.		Westminster	British Columbia	Canada	11869
Mackenzie	A	Adams	9639 Ida Drive		Langford	British Columbia	Canada	14640
Sara	A	Adams	7503 Hill Drive		Milwaukie	Oregon	United States	16986
Adam		Adams	9381 Bayside Way		Newport Beach	California	United States	13323
Amber		Adams	9720 Morning Glory Dr.		Brisbane	Queensland	Australia	26746
Angel		Adams	9556 Lyman Rd.		Burlingame	California	United States	18504
Aaron	B	Adams	4116 Stanbridge Ct.		Downey	California	United States	28866
Noah	B	Adams	6738 Wallace Dr.		El Cajon	California	United States	16977
Bailey		Adams	1817 Adobe Drive		Kirkland	Washington	United States	13280
Ben		Adams	1534 Land Ave		Bremerton	Washington	United States	28678
Alex	C	Adams	237 Bellwood Dr.		Lake Oswego	Oregon	United States	21139
Courtney	C	Adams	6089 Santa Fe Dr.		Torrance	California	United States	18075
Ian	C	Adams	7963 Elk Dr	#4	Versailles	Yveline	France	29422

ORDER BY Clause with the RANK() Function

T-SQL query demonstrates the combination of CASE expression and RANK() function in an ORDER BY clause. Note that while such a complex sort is technically impressive, ultimately it has to make sense to the user, the Business Intelligence consumer.

```
-- SQL complex sorting
USE AdventureWorks;

SELECT          ContactID,
                FirstName,
                LastName,
                COALESCE(Title, '')  AS Title
FROM   Person.Contact
WHERE  LEFT(FirstName, 1) = 'M'
ORDER  BY CASE
                WHEN LEFT(LastName, 1) = 'A' THEN RANK()
                        OVER( ORDER BY CONCAT(FirstName, SPACE(1), LastName))
                WHEN LEFT(LastName, 1) = 'M' THEN RANK()
                        OVER( ORDER BY CONCAT(LastName,', ', FirstName), Title)
                WHEN LEFT(LastName, 1) = 'U' THEN RANK()
                        OVER( ORDER BY CONCAT(LastName,', ', FirstName)  DESC)
                ELSE RANK()
                        OVER( ORDER BY LastName ASC, FirstName DESC)
        END;
```

ContactID	FirstName	LastName	Title
9500	Mackenzie	Adams	
10144	Mackenzie	Allen	
10128	Madeline	Allen	
11708	Madison	Alexander	
11527	Madison	Anderson	
19872	Morgan	Bailey	
8059	Michelle	Bailey	
8080	Melissa	Bailey	
18291	Megan	Bailey	
8070	Mariah	Bailey	
2432	Maria	Bailey	
14378	Marcus	Bailey	
8063	Makayla	Bailey	
8032	Mackenzie	Bailey	
9521	Morgan	Baker	
3320	Miguel	Baker	
15437	Mason	Baker	
9546	Mary	Baker	
1082	Mary	Baker	
9539	Maria	Baker	

ORDER BY Clause with Custom Mapped Sort Sequence

Typically we rely on alphabets or numbers for sorting. What if, for example, we don't want United States way down on a website drop-down menu, rather than on the top with Canada and United Kingdom just above "lucky" Australia? We have to do custom mapping for such a sort in the ORDER BY clause.

```
USE AdventureWorks;
GO

SELECT          AddressLine1,
                City,
                SP.StateProvinceCode            AS State,
                PostalCode,
                CR.Name                         AS  Country
FROM   Person.[Address] A
    INNER JOIN Person.StateProvince SP          ON A.StateProvinceID = SP.StateProvinceID
    INNER JOIN Person.CountryRegion CR          ON SP.CountryRegionCode = CR.CountryRegionCode
ORDER  BY (     CASE
                    WHEN CR.Name = 'United States' THEN 0
                    WHEN CR.Name = 'Canada' THEN 1
                    WHEN CR.Name = 'United Kingdom' THEN 2
                    ELSE 3
                END ),
                Country,
                City
                AddressLine1;
-- (19614 row(s) affected) - Partial results.
```

AddressLine1	City	State	PostalCode	Country
9355 Armstrong Road	York	ENG	YO15	United Kingdom
939 Vista Del Diablo	York	ENG	YO15	United Kingdom
9458 Flame Drive	York	ENG	YO15	United Kingdom
9557 Steven Circle	York	ENG	Y03 4TN	United Kingdom
9589 Rae Anne Dr	York	ENG	Y03 4TN	United Kingdom
9643 Willow Pass Road	York	ENG	YO15	United Kingdom
9700 Terra Grand	York	ENG	Y024 1GF	United Kingdom
9790 Deer Creek Lane	York	ENG	Y024 1GF	United Kingdom
9896 Ida Ave	York	ENG	Y024 1GF	United Kingdom
9903 Mt. Washington Way	York	ENG	Y024 1GF	United Kingdom
9907 Via Appia	York	ENG	Y03 4TN	United Kingdom
P. O. Box 5413	York	ENG	Y024 1GF	United Kingdom
2565-175 Mitchell Road	Alexandria	NSW	2015	Australia
Level 59	Alexandria	NSW	2015	Australia
1058 Kirker Pass Road	Bendigo	VIC	3550	Australia
1153 Loma Linda	Bendigo	VIC	3550	Australia
1218 Trasher Road	Bendigo	VIC	3550	Australia
1277 Argenta Dr.	Bendigo	VIC	3550	Australia
1286 Cincerto Circle	Bendigo	VIC	3550	Australia
1589 Mt. Tamalpais Place	Bendigo	VIC	3550	Australia
1688 Sudan Loop	Bendigo	VIC	3550	Australia
1729 Panorama Drive	Bendigo	VIC	3550	Australia

ORDER BY Clause with Custom Alphanumeric Sort Sequence

A frequent requirement is custom sorting on alphanumeric field (column). The next T-SQL query demonstrates special alphanumeric sorting.

```
USE AdventureWorks;

SELECT AddressLine1,
                isnull(AddressLine2, '')      AS Addressline2,
                City,
                SP.StateProvinceCode      AS State,
                PostalCode,
                CR.Name                   AS Country
FROM   Person.[Address] A
    INNER JOIN Person.StateProvince SP
     ON A.StateProvinceID = SP.StateProvinceID
    INNER JOIN Person.CountryRegion CR
     ON SP.CountryRegionCode = CR.CountryRegionCode
ORDER  BY (      CASE
                      WHEN Ascii([AddressLine1]) BETWEEN 65 AND 90 THEN 0 -- Upper case alpha
                      WHEN Ascii([AddressLine1]) BETWEEN 48 AND 57 THEN 1 -- Digits
                      ELSE 2
                END ),
            AddressLine1,
            City;
-- (19614 row(s) affected) - Partial results.
```

AddressLine1	Addressline2	City	State	PostalCode	Country
Zur Lindung 46		Leipzig	NW	04139	Germany
Zur Lindung 6		Saarlouis	SL	66740	Germany
Zur Lindung 6		Solingen	NW	42651	Germany
Zur Lindung 609		Sulzbach Taunus	SL	66272	Germany
Zur Lindung 7		Berlin	HE	14129	Germany
Zur Lindung 7		Neunkirchen	SL	66578	Germany
Zur Lindung 764		Paderborn	HH	33041	Germany
Zur Lindung 78		Berlin	HH	10791	Germany
Zur Lindung 787		München	NW	80074	Germany
00, rue Saint-Lazare		Dunkerque	59	59140	France
02, place de Fontenoy		Verrieres Le Buisson	91	91370	France
035, boulevard du Montparnasse		Verrieres Le Buisson	91	91370	France
081, boulevard du Montparnasse		Saint-Denis	93	93400	France
081, boulevard du Montparnasse		Seattle	WA	98104	United States
084, boulevard du Montparnasse		Les Ulis	91	91940	France
1 Corporate Center Drive		Miami	FL	33127	United States
1 Mt. Dell Drive		Portland	OR	97205	United States
1 Smiling Tree Court	Space 55	Los Angeles	CA	90012	United States
1, allée des Princes		Courbevoie	92	92400	France

T-SQL Script Demonstrates Unusual Sorting Techniques

```
/**************************************************
*    SORTING ON THE LAST WORD OF A STRING
**************************************************/
USE tempdb;

-- SELECT INTO table create sorted on BusinessEntityID
SELECT BusinessEntityID,
        FULLNAME = CONCAT(FirstName , SPACE(1), LastName )
INTO   People
FROM   AdventureWorks2012.Person.Person
ORDER  BY BusinessEntityID

SELECT TOP 2 * FROM   People;
```

BusinessEntityID	FULLNAME
285	Syed Abbas
293	Catherine Abel

```
-- Sorting on the Last Name given the Full Name string
SELECT *
FROM   People
ORDER  BY REVERSE(LEFT(REVERSE(FullName), charindex(' ', REVERSE(FullName) + ' ' ) - 1)),
        FullName ;
GO
-- (19972 row(s) affected) - Partial results.
```

BusinessEntityID	FULLNAME
285	Syed Abbas
293	Catherine Abel
295	Kim Abercrombie
2170	Kim Abercrombie
38	Kim Abercrombie
211	Hazem Abolrous

```
DROP TABLE People
GO
```

Date & Time Conversion To / From String

While there are only a few internal representation of date and time, string representations are many, even not deterministic since they may change from one country to another such as weekday and month names.   T-SQL scripts demonstrate the myriad of date and time conversion possibilities.

The CONVERT() Function with Style Number Parameter

```
-- String source  format: mon dd yyyy hh:mmAM (or PM)
-- 100 is the style number parameter for CONVERT
SELECT [Date&Time] = convert(datetime, 'Oct 23 2020 11:01AM', 100)
```

Date&Time
2020-10-23 11:01:00.000

```
-- Default without style number
SELECT convert(datetime, 'Oct 23 2020 11:01AM')                  -- 2020-10-23 11:01:00.000
```

```
-- Without century (yy) string date conversion with style number 0
-- Input format: mon dd yy hh:mmAM (or PM)
SELECT [Date&Time] = convert(datetime, 'Oct 23 20 11:01AM', 0)
```

Date&Time
2020-10-23 11:01:00.000

```
-- Default without style number
SELECT convert(datetime, 'Oct 23 20 11:01AM')                  -- 2020-10-23
11:01:00.000
```

 Convert string date & time to datetime (8-bytes internal representation) data type.

```
SELECT convert(datetime, '10/23/2016', 101)        -- mm/dd/yyyy
```

```
SELECT convert(datetime, '2016.10.23', 102)        -- yyyy.mm.dd ANSI date with century
```

```
SELECT convert(datetime, '23/10/2016', 103)        -- dd/mm/yyyy
```

```
SELECT convert(datetime, '23.10.2016', 104)-- dd.mm.yyyy
```

```
SELECT convert(datetime, '23-10-2016', 105)        -- dd-mm-yyyy
```

```
-- mon (month) types are nondeterministic conversions, dependent on language setting.
SELECT convert(datetime, '23 OCT 2016', 106)        -- dd mon yyyy
```

String Datetime Formats With "Mon" Are Nondeterministic, Language Dependent

SELECT [Date&Time] = convert(datetime, 'Oct 23, 2016', 107) -- mon dd, yyyy

> | Date&Time |
> |---|
> | 2016-10-23 00:00:00.000 |

SELECT [Date&Time]=convert(datetime, '20:10:44', 108)   -- hh:mm:ss

> | Date&Time |
> |---|
> | 1900-01-01 20:10:44.000 |

SELECT [Date&Time]=convert(datetime, 'Oct 23 2016 11:02:44:013AM', 109) -- mon dd yyyy hh:mm:ss:mmmAM (or PM)

> | Date&Time |
> |---|
> | 2016-10-23 11:02:44.013 |

SELECT convert(datetime, '10-23-2016', 110)   -- mm-dd-yyyy
SELECT convert(datetime, '2016/10/23', 111)   -- yyyy/mm/dd

-- YYYYMMDD ISO date format works at any language setting - international standard
SELECT [Date&Time]=convert(datetime, '20161023')

> | Date&Time |
> |---|
> | 2016-10-23 00:00:00.000 |

SELECT [Date&Time]=convert(datetime, '20161023', 112)   -- ISO yyyymmdd

> | Date&Time |
> |---|
> | 2016-10-23 00:00:00.000 |

SELECT [Date&Time]=convert(datetime, '23 Oct 2016 11:02:07:577', 113) -- dd mon yyyy hh:mm:ss:mmm

> | Date&Time |
> |---|
> | 2016-10-23 11:02:07.577 |

SELECT [Date&Time]=convert(datetime, '20:10:25:300', 114)   -- hh:mm:ss:mmm(24h)

> | Date&Time |
> |---|
> | 1900-01-01 20:10:25.300 |

SELECT [Date&Time]=convert(datetime, '2016-10-23 20:44:11', 120)   -- yyyy-mm-dd hh:mm:ss(24h)

> | Date&Time |
> |---|
> | 2016-10-23 20:44:11.000 |

Style 126 Is ISO 8601 Format: International Standard; Works With Any Language Setting

```
SELECT [Date&Time ]=convert(datetime, '2018-10-23T18:52:47.513', 126) -- yyyy-mm-
ddThh:mm:ss(.mmm)
```

Date&Time
2018-10-23 18:52:47.513

```
SELECT [Date&Time ]=convert(datetime, '2016-10-23 20:44:11.500', 121)        -- yyyy-mm-dd
hh:mm:ss.mmm
```

Date&Time
2016-10-23 20:44:11.500

```
-- Islamic / Hijri date conversion

SELECT CONVERT(nvarchar(32), convert(datetime,'2016-10-23'), 130);
-- 22 محرم 1438 12:00:00:000AM

SELECT [Date&Time ]=convert(datetime, N'23 شوال 1441  6:52:47:513PM', 130)
```

Date&Time
2020-06-14 18:52:47.513

```
SELECT [Date&Time ]=convert(datetime, '23/10/1441  6:52:47:513PM',    131)
```

Date&Time
2020-06-14 18:52:47.513

```
-- Convert DDMMYYYY format to datetime with intermediate conversion using STUFF().

SELECT STUFF(STUFF('31012016',3,0,'-'),6,0,'-');
-- 31-01-2016

SELECT [Date&Time ]=convert(datetime, STUFF(STUFF('31012016',3,0,'-'),6,0,'-'), 105)
```

Date&Time
2016-01-31 00:00:00.000

```
-- Equivalent
SELECT STUFF(STUFF('31012016',3,0,'/'),6,0,'/');   -- 31/01/2016
SELECT [Date&Time ]=convert(datetime, STUFF(STUFF('31012016',3,0,'/'),6,0,'/'), 103)
```

CHAPTER 7: Basic SELECT Statement Syntax & Examples

String to Datetime Conversion Without Century

String to datetime conversion without century - some exceptions.   Nondeterministic means language setting dependent such as Mar/Mär/mars/márc .

SELECT [Date&Time]=convert(datetime, 'Oct 23 16 11:02:44AM')   -- Default

Date&Time
2016-10-23 11:02:44.000

SELECT convert(datetime, '10/23/16', 1)	mm/dd/yy	U.S.
SELECT convert(datetime, '16.10.23', 2)	yy.mm.dd	ANSI
SELECT convert(datetime, '23/10/16', 3)	dd/mm/yy	UK/FR
SELECT convert(datetime, '23.10.16', 4)	dd.mm.yy	German
SELECT convert(datetime, '23-10-16', 5)	dd-mm-yy	Italian
SELECT convert(datetime, '23 OCT 16', 6)	dd mon yy	non-det.
SELECT convert(datetime, 'Oct 23, 16', 7)	mon dd, yy	non-det.
SELECT convert(datetime, '20:10:44', 8)	hh:mm:ss	
SELECT convert(datetime, 'Oct 23 16 11:02:44:013AM', 9)	Default with msec	
SELECT convert(datetime, '10-23-16', 10)	mm-dd-yy	U.S.
SELECT convert(datetime, '16/10/23', 11)	yy/mm/dd	Japan
SELECT convert(datetime, '161023', 12)	yymmdd	ISO
SELECT convert(datetime, '23 Oct 16 11:02:07:577', 13)	dd mon yy hh:mm:ss:mmm EU dflt	
SELECT convert(datetime, '20:10:25:300', 14)	hh:mm:ss:mmm(24h)	
SELECT convert(datetime, '2016-10-23 20:44:11',20)	yyyy-mm-dd hh:mm:ss(24h) ODBC can.	
SELECT convert(datetime, '2016-10-23 20:44:11.500', 21)	yyyy-mm-dd hh:mm:ss.mmm ODBC	

Combine Date & Time String into Datetime

```
DECLARE @DateTimeValue varchar(32), @DateValue char(8), @TimeValue char(6)
 SELECT @DateValue = '20200718',          @TimeValue = '211920'
SELECT            @DateTimeValue =
                  CONCAT(
                  convert(varchar, convert(datetime, @DateValue), 111),
                     ' ', substring(@TimeValue, 1, 2) , ':', substring(@TimeValue, 3, 2) , ':',
substring(@TimeValue, 5, 2)  )

SELECT  DateInput = @DateValue, TimeInput = @TimeValue,  DateTimeOutput = @DateTimeValue;
GO
```

DateInput	TimeInput	DateTimeOutput
20200718	211920	2020/07/18 21:19:20

```
SELECT DATETIMEFROMPARTS (2020, 07, 1, 21, 01, 20, 700)          -- New in SQL Server 2012
```

Date and Time Internal Storage Format

DATETIME 8 bytes internal storage structure:

- ➢ 1st 4 bytes: number of days after the base date 1900-01-01
- ➢ 2nd 4 bytes: number of clock-ticks (3.33 milliseconds) since midnight

```
SELECT CONVERT(binary(8), CURRENT_TIMESTAMP);
```

Hex
0x0000A09C00F23CE1

DATE 3 bytes internal storage structure:

- ➢ 3 bytes integer: number of days after the first date 0001-01-01
- ➢ Note: hex byte order reversed

SMALLDATETIME 4 bytes internal storage structure

- ➢ 1st 2 bytes: number of days after the base date 1900-01-01
- ➢ 2nd 2 bytes: number of minutes since midnight

```
SELECT Hex=CONVERT(binary(4), convert(smalldatetime, getdate()));
```

Hex
0xA09C0375

Date & Time Operations Using System Operators & Functions

```
-- Conversion from hex (binary) to datetime value
DECLARE @dtHex binary(8)= 0x00009966002d3344;  DECLARE @dt datetime = @dtHex;
SELECT @dt;   -- 2007-07-09 02:44:34.147
```

```
-- SQL convert seconds to HH:MM:SS -
DECLARE  @Seconds INT;  SET @Seconds = 20000 ;
SELECT HH = @Seconds / 3600, MM = (@Seconds%3600) / 60, SS = (@Seconds%60) ;
```

HH	MM	SS
5	33	20

Extract Date Only from DATETIME Data Type

```
DECLARE @Now datetime = CURRENT_TIMESTAMP -- getdate()

SELECT  DateAndTime      = @Now     -- Date portion and Time portion
        ,DateString              = REPLACE(LEFT(CONVERT (varchar, @Now, 112),10),' ','-')
        ,[Date]                  = CONVERT(DATE, @Now)  -- SQL Server 2008 and on - date part
        ,Midnight1               = dateadd(day, datediff(day,0, @Now), 0)
        ,Midnight2               = CONVERT(DATETIME,CONVERT(int, @Now))
        ,Midnight3               = CONVERT(DATETIME,CONVERT(BIGINT,@Now) &
(POWER(Convert(bigint,2),32)-1));
```

DateAndTime	DateString	Date	Midnight1	Midnight2	Midnight3
2020-07-28 15:01:51.960	20200728	2020-07-28	2020-07-28 00:00:00.000	2020-07-29 00:00:00.000	2020-07-29 00:00:00.000

```
-- Compare today with database dates
SELECT          TOP (10)  OrderDate = CONVERT(date, OrderDate),
                Today = CONVERT(date, getdate()),
                DeltaDays = DATEDIFF(DD, OrderDate, getdate())
FROM AdventureWorks2012.Sales.SalesOrderHeader  ORDER BY NEWID(); -- random sort
```

OrderDate	Today	DeltaDays
2008-01-15	2012-08-10	1669
2006-07-14	2012-08-10	2219
2008-07-05	2012-08-10	1497
2008-03-01	2012-08-10	1623
2007-10-01	2012-08-10	1775
2007-01-15	2012-08-10	2034
2008-05-27	2012-08-10	1536
2008-04-18	2012-08-10	1575
2008-04-25	2012-08-10	1568
2006-12-17	2012-08-10	2063

CHAPTER 7: Basic SELECT Statement Syntax & Examples

String Date Formats Without Time

```
-- String date format yyyy/mm/dd from datetime
SELECT CONVERT(VARCHAR(10), GETDATE(), 111) AS [YYYY/MM/DD] ;
```

YYYY/MM/DD
2012/07/28

```
SELECT CONVERT(VARCHAR(10), GETDATE(), 112) AS [YYYYMMDD];
```

YYYYMMDD
20120728

```
SELECT REPLACE(CONVERT(VARCHAR(10), GETDATE(), 111),'/',' ') AS [YYYY MM DD];
```

YYYY MM DD
2020 07 28

```
-- Converting to special (non-standard) date formats: DD-MMM-YY
SELECT UPPER(REPLACE(CONVERT(VARCHAR,GETDATE(),6),' ','-')) AS CustomDate;
```

CustomDate
28-JUL-20

```
-- SQL convert date string to datetime - time set to 00:00:00.000 or 12:00AM

PRINT CONVERT(datetime,'07-10-2020',110) ;       -- Jul 10 2020 12:00AM
PRINT CONVERT(datetime,'2020/07/10',111) ;       -- Jul 10 2020 12:00AM
PRINT CONVERT(datetime,'20200710',  112);        -- Jul 10 2020 12:00AM
GO
```

```
-- SQL Server cast string to date / datetime
DECLARE @DateValue char(8) = '20200718'

SELECT [Date] = CAST (@DateValue AS datetime);
GO
```

Date
2020-07-18 00:00:00.000

String date to string date conversion with nested CONVERT

```
SELECT CONVERT(varchar, CONVERT(datetime, '20140508'), 100) AS StringDate;
GO
```

StringDate
May 8 2014 12:00AM

```
-- T-SQL convert date to integer

DECLARE @Date datetime;  SET @Date = getdate();
SELECT DateAsInteger = CAST (CONVERT(varchar,@Date,112) as INT);
GO
```

DateAsInteger
20120728

```
-- SQL Server convert integer to datetime

DECLARE @iDate int = 20151225;
SELECT IntegerToDatetime = CAST(convert(varchar,@iDate) as datetime)
GO
```

IntegerToDatetime
2015-12-25 00:00:00.000

```
-- Alternates: date-only datetime values

SELECT [DATE-ONLY]=CONVERT(DATETIME, FLOOR(CONVERT(FLOAT, GETDATE())));

SELECT [DATE-ONLY]=CONVERT(DATETIME, FLOOR(CONVERT(MONEY, GETDATE())));

SELECT [DATE-ONLY]=CONVERT(DATETIME, CONVERT(DATE, GETDATE()));

-- CAST string to datetime

-- String date preparation, length is 10 characters
SELECT CONVERT(varchar, GETDATE(), 101), LEN (CONVERT(varchar, GETDATE(), 101))
--         07/28/2018         10

SELECT [DATE-ONLY]=CAST(CONVERT(varchar, GETDATE(), 101) AS DATETIME);
```

DATE-ONLY
2018-07-28 00:00:00.000

CHAPTER 7: Basic SELECT Statement Syntax & Examples

DATEADD() and DATEDIFF() Functions

```
-- T-SQL strip time from date
SELECT getdate() AS [DateTime], dateadd(dd, datediff(dd, 0, getdate()), 0) [DateOnly];
```

DateTime	DateOnly
2012-07-28 17:24:07.300	2012-07-28 00:00:00.000

```
-- First day of current month
SELECT dateadd(month, datediff(month, 0, getdate()), 0)  AS FirstDayOfCurrentMonth;
SELECT dateadd(dd,1, EOMONTH(getdate(),-1)); -- New to SQL Server 2012
```

FirstDayOfCurrentMonth
2020-07-01 00:00:00.000

```
-- 15th day of current month
SELECT dateadd(day,14,dateadd(month, datediff(month,0,getdate()),0)) AS MiddleOfCurrentMonth;
SELECT dateadd(dd,15, EOMONTH(getdate(),-1));  -- New to SQL Server 2012
```

MiddleOfCurrentMonth
2012-07-15 00:00:00.000

```
-- First Monday of current month

SELECT   dateadd(day, (9-datepart(weekday,
         dateadd(month, datediff(month, 0, getdate()), 0)))%7,
         dateadd(month, datediff(month, 0, getdate()), 0))  AS [First Monday Of Current Month];
GO
```

First Monday Of Current Month
2012-07-02 00:00:00.000

```
-- Next Monday calculation from the reference date which was a Monday
DECLARE @Now datetime = GETDATE();
DECLARE @NextMonday datetime = dateadd(dd, ((datediff(dd, '19000101', @Now)
             / 7) * 7) + 7, '19000101');
SELECT [Now]=@Now, [Next Monday]=@NextMonday;
GO
```

Now	Next Monday
2012-07-28 17:35:29.657	2012-07-30 00:00:00.000

Last Date & First Date Calculations

-- Last Friday of current month

```
SELECT   dateadd(day, -7+(6-datepart(weekday,

         dateadd(month, datediff(month, 0, getdate())+1, 0)))%7,

         dateadd(month, datediff(month, 0, getdate())+1, 0)) ;
```

-- First day of next month

```
SELECT dateadd(month, datediff(month, 0, getdate())+1, 0) ;
```

-- 15th of next month

```
SELECT dateadd(day,14, dateadd(month, datediff(month, 0, getdate())+1, 0));
```

-- First Monday of next month

```
SELECT   dateadd(day, (9-datepart(weekday,
         dateadd(month, datediff(month, 0, getdate())+1, 0)))%7,
         dateadd(month, datediff(month, 0, getdate())+1, 0));
```

```
-- Next 12 months start & end - EOMONTH is new to SQL Server 2012
SELECT TOP 12
        DATEADD(DD,1, EOMONTH(getdate(),number-1))     AS Start,
        EOMONTH(getdate(),number)                      AS [End]
FROM master.dbo.spt_values   -- get integer sequence
WHERE type='P'  ORDER BY number;
```

Start	End
2016-08-01	2016-08-31
2016-09-01	2016-09-30
2016-10-01	2016-10-31
2016-11-01	2016-11-30
2016-12-01	2016-12-31
2017-01-01	2017-01-31
2017-02-01	2017-02-28
2017-03-01	2017-03-31
2017-04-01	2017-04-30
2017-05-01	2017-05-31
2017-06-01	2017-06-30
2017-07-01	2017-07-31

BETWEEN Operator for Date Range

Date time range SELECT using the using >= and < operators. Count Sales Orders for date range 2007 OCT-NOV.

```
DECLARE  @StartDate DATETIME,  @EndDate DATETIME
SET @StartDate = convert(DATETIME,'10/01/2007',101)
SET @EndDate  = convert(DATETIME,'11/30/2007',101)
SELECT @StartDate, @EndDate
-- 2007-10-01 00:00:00.000  2007-11-30 00:00:00.000
SELECT dateadd(DAY,1,@EndDate),    dateadd(ms,-3,dateadd(DAY,1,@EndDate))
-- 2007-12-01 00:00:00.000  2007-11-30 23:59:59.997

SELECT [Sales Orders for 2007 OCT-NOV] = COUNT(* )
FROM   AdventureWorks2012.Sales.SalesOrderHeader
WHERE  OrderDate >= @StartDate AND OrderDate < dateadd(DAY,1,@EndDate)
```

Sales Orders for 2007 OCT-NOV
3668

Equivalent date range query using BETWEEN comparison. It requires a bit of trick programming. 23.59.59.997 is the last available time in a day.

```
SELECT [Sales Orders for 2007 OCT-NOV] = COUNT(* )
FROM   AdventureWorks2012.Sales.SalesOrderHeader
WHERE  OrderDate BETWEEN @StartDate AND dateadd(ms,-3, dateadd(DAY, 1, @EndDate))
```

Sales Orders for 2007 OCT-NOV
3668

The BETWEEN operator can be used with string dates as well. Note: anything after midnight on 2004-02-10 is not included.

```
USE AdventureWorks;
SELECT POs=COUNT(*) FROM Purchasing.PurchaseOrderHeader
WHERE OrderDate BETWEEN '20040201' AND '20040210'
```

POs
108

BETWEEN Dates Without Time: Entire 2004-02-10 Day Included This Fashion

```
SELECT POs=COUNT(*) FROM Purchasing.PurchaseOrderHeader
WHERE datediff(dd,0,OrderDate)
        BETWEEN datediff(dd,0,'20040201 12:11:39') AND datediff(dd,0,'20040210 14:33:19')
```

POs
108

The datetime range BETWEEN is equivalent to >=...AND....<= operators.

```
SELECT POs=COUNT(*) FROM Purchasing.PurchaseOrderHeader
WHERE OrderDate  BETWEEN '2004-02-01 00:00:00.000' AND '2004-02-10  00:00:00.000'
```

POs
108

Orders with datetime OrderDate-s of

'2004-02-10 00:00:01.000'	1 second after midnight (start of day at 12:00AM)
'2004-02-10 00:01:00.000'	1 minute after midnight
'2004-02-10 01:00:00.000'	1 hour after midnight
'2004-02-10 23:00:00.000'	23 hours after midnight

would not included in the preceding two queries. Only datetime OrderDate of '2004-02-10 00:00:00.000' would be included. That would be OK if the time part is not used. But even in that case and order can be entered accidentally with a time part, that would throw off the count.

To include the entire day of 2004-02-10, move the day up by one and use the < operator:

```
SELECT POs=COUNT(*) FROM Purchasing.PurchaseOrderHeader
WHERE OrderDate >= '20040201' AND OrderDate < '20040211';
```

POs
108

The reason we cannot detect a difference is due to lack of data passed midnight on 2004-02-11.

```
SELECT  [PurchaseOrderID], [RevisionNumber], [Status],
        [EmployeeID], [VendorID], [ShipMethodID], [OrderDate]
FROM [AdventureWorks].[Purchasing].[PurchaseOrderHeader] WHERE PurchaseOrderID = 1665;
```

PurchaseOrderID	RevisionNumber	Status	EmployeeID	VendorID	ShipMethodID	OrderDate
1665	0	4	261	43	5	2004-02-10 00:00:00.000

CHAPTER 7: Basic SELECT Statement Syntax & Examples

Advance the datetime one second from midnight, the BETWEEN datetime query is not going to count it

```
UPDATE [AdventureWorks].[Purchasing].[PurchaseOrderHeader]
      SET OrderDate = '2004-02-10 00:00:01.000'
WHERE PurchaseOrderID = 1665;
-- (1 row(s) affected)
```

This is the current value for OrderDate datetime.

PurchaseOrderID	RevisionNumber	Status	EmployeeID	VendorID	ShipMethodID	OrderDate
1665	0	4	261	43	5	2004-02-10 00:00:01.000

The following queries are not going to count this passed midnight record any more.

```
SELECT POs=COUNT(*) FROM Purchasing.PurchaseOrderHeader
WHERE OrderDate BETWEEN '2004-02-01 00:00:00.000' AND '2004-02-10  00:00:00.000'
```

POs
107

```
USE AdventureWorks; SELECT POs=COUNT(*) FROM Purchasing.PurchaseOrderHeader
WHERE OrderDate BETWEEN '20040201' AND '20040210'
```

POs
107

While the query we designed specifically for a case like this will count it correctly.

```
SELECT POs=COUNT(*) FROM Purchasing.PurchaseOrderHeader
WHERE OrderDate >= '20040201' AND OrderDate < '20040211'
```

POs
108

We restore the data to its original value.

```
UPDATE [AdventureWorks].[Purchasing].[PurchaseOrderHeader]
      SET OrderDate = '2004-02-10 00:00:00.000'
WHERE PurchaseOrderID = 1665;    -- (1 row(s) affected)
```

CHAPTER 7: Basic SELECT Statement Syntax & Examples

Date Validation Function ISDATE()

```
DECLARE @StringDate varchar(32);
SET @StringDate = '2011-03-15 18:50';
IF EXISTS( SELECT * WHERE ISDATE(@StringDate) = 1)
   PRINT 'VALID DATE: ' + @StringDate
ELSE
   PRINT 'INVALID DATE: ' + @StringDate;
```

> VALID DATE: 2011-03-15 18:50

```
DECLARE @StringDate varchar(32) ;
SET @StringDate = '20112-03-15 18:50';
IF EXISTS( SELECT * WHERE ISDATE(@StringDate) = 1)
   PRINT 'VALID DATE: ' + @StringDate
ELSE  PRINT 'INVALID DATE: ' + @StringDate;
GO
```

> INVALID DATE: 20112-03-15 18:50

First and Last Day of Date Periods

Calculating date periods markers is a very important task in T-SQL programming, especially related to reporting queries.

```
DECLARE @Date DATE = '20161023'; SELECT ReferenceDate  = @Date;

SELECT FirstDayOfYear  = CONVERT(DATE, dateadd(yy, datediff(yy,0, @Date),0));

SELECT LastDayOfYear  = CONVERT(DATE, dateadd(yy, datediff(yy,0, @Date)+1,-1));

SELECT FDofSemester = CONVERT(DATE, dateadd(qq,((datediff(qq,0,@Date)/2)*2),0));

SELECT LastDayOfSemester  = CONVERT(DATE, dateadd(qq,((datediff(qq,0,@Date)/2)*2)+2,-1));

SELECT FirstDayOfQuarter  = CONVERT(DATE, dateadd(qq, datediff(qq,0, @Date),0));

SELECT LastDayOfQuarter = CONVERT(DATE, dateadd(qq, datediff(qq,0,@Date)+1,-1));
```

LastDayOfQuarter
2016-12-31

The brand-new EOMonth() function simplifies month end formulas

```
SELECT LastDayOfMonth = EOMonth (@Date);  -- New in SQL Server 2012

SELECT FirstDayOfMonth = CONVERT(DATE, dateadd(mm, datediff(mm,0, @Date),0));

SELECT LastDayOfMonth  = CONVERT(DATE, dateadd(mm, datediff(mm,0, @Date)+1,-1));

SELECT FirstDayOfWeek  = CONVERT(DATE, dateadd(wk, datediff(wk,0, @Date),0));

SELECT LastDayOfWeek   = CONVERT(DATE, dateadd(wk, datediff(wk,0, @Date)+1,-1));
GO
```

Month Sequence Generator

Sometimes date based data may have gaps missing months. For reporting purposes we may want to include all months from start date to end date. To do that we have to generate a continuous sequence of months, and use it to fill in the gaps. Calendar table can also be used for such a task.

```
DECLARE @Date date = '2000-01-01'
SELECT MonthStart=dateadd(MM, number, @Date)
FROM  master.dbo.spt_values
WHERE type='P' AND  dateadd(MM, number, @Date) <= CURRENT_TIMESTAMP
ORDER BY MonthStart;
-- (151 row(s) affected) - Partial results.
```

MonthStart
2000-01-01
2000-02-01
2000-03-01
2000-04-01
2000-05-01
2000-06-01
2000-07-01
2000-08-01
2000-09-01
2000-10-01
2000-11-01
2000-12-01
2001-01-01
2001-02-01
2001-03-01
2001-04-01

Selected U.S. & International Date Styles

The U.S. date style is m/d/y.

```
DECLARE @DateTimeValue varchar(32) = '10/23/2016';

SELECT StringDate=@DateTimeValue,  [SSMS-Style] = CONVERT(datetime, @DatetimeValue);

SELECT @DateTimeValue = '10/23/2016 23:01:05';

SELECT StringDate = @DateTimeValue,  [SSMS-Style] = CONVERT(datetime, @DatetimeValue);
GO
```

StringDate	SSMS-Style
10/23/2016	2016-10-23 00:00:00.000

StringDate	SSMS-Style
10/23/2016 23:01:05	2016-10-23 23:01:05.000

The UK or British/French style is dmy.

```
DECLARE @DateTimeValue varchar(32) = '23/10/16 23:01:05';

SELECT StringDate = @DateTimeValue,  [SSMS-Style] = CONVERT(datetime, @DatetimeValue, 3);

 SELECT @DateTimeValue = '23/10/2016 04:01 PM';

SELECT StringDate = @DateTimeValue,  [SSMS-Style] = CONVERT(datetime, @DatetimeValue, 103);
GO
```

The German style is dmy as well with a new twist to it: period instead of slash.

```
DECLARE @DateTimeValue varchar(32)  = '23.10.16 23:01:05';
SELECT StringDate = @DateTimeValue,  [SSMS -Style] = CONVERT(datetime, @DatetimeValue, 4);
 SELECT @DateTimeValue = '23.10.2016 04:01 PM';
SELECT StringDate = @DateTimeValue,  [SSMS -Style] = CONVERT(datetime, @DatetimeValue, 104);
GO
```

```
-- Nondeterministic month name (mon)
SET LANGUAGE Spanish; SELECT CONVERT(varchar, getdate(), 100);        -- Ago 10 2018  4:43PM
SET LANGUAGE Turkish; SELECT CONVERT(varchar, getdate(), 100);        -- Agu 10 2018  4:44PM
SET LANGUAGE Polish; SELECT CONVERT(varchar, getdate(), 100);         -- VIII 10 2018  4:46PM
SET LANGUAGE Hungarian; SELECT CONVERT(varchar, getdate(), 100);      -- aug 10 2018  4:46PM
SET LANGUAGE Russian; SELECT CONVERT(nvarchar, getdate(), 100);       -- авг 10 2018  4:47PM
```

The DATEPART() Function to Decompose a Date

The DATEPART() function returns a part of a date.

```
DECLARE @dt datetime = getdate();
SELECT DATEPART(YEAR, @dt)              AS YYYY,
       DATEPART(MONTH, @dt)             AS MM,
       DATEPART(DAY, @dt)               AS DD;
```

YYYY	MM	DD
2016	7	29

```
SELECT * FROM Northwind.dbo.Orders
WHERE DATEPART(YEAR, OrderDate)         = '1996' AND
      DATEPART(MONTH,OrderDate)         = '07'   AND
      DATEPART(DAY, OrderDate)          = '10'
```

```
/*OrderID      CustomerID     EmployeeID      OrderDate        RequiredDate      ShippedDate
      ShipVia Freight ShipName         Shipaddress      ShipCity ShipRegion       ShipPostalCode
      ShipCountry
10253  HANAR  3        1996-07-10 00:00:00.000 1996-07-24 00:00:00.000 1996-07-16 00:00:00.000
       2       58.17    Hanari Carnes    Rua do Paço, 67  Rio de Janeiro   RJ        05454-876
       Brazil */
```

Alternate syntax for DATEPART.

```
SELECT * FROM Northwind.dbo.Orders
WHERE        YEAR(OrderDate)    = 1996      AND
             MONTH(OrderDate)   = 07        AND
             DAY(OrderDate)     = 10
GO
```

```
-- Additional datepart parameters including Julian date
DECLARE @dt datetime = getdate();
SELECT DATEPART(DAY, @dt)                AS DD,
       DATEPART(WEEKDAY, @dt)            AS WD,
       DATEPART(DAYOFYEAR, @dt)          AS JulianDate,
       DATEPART(WEEK, @dt)               AS Week,
       DATEPART(ISO_WEEK, @dt)           AS ISOWeek,
       DATEPART(HOUR, @dt)               AS HH;
```

DD	WD	JulianDate	Week	ISOWeek	HH
10	5	223	33	32	17

The DATENAME() Function to Get Date Part Names

The DATENAME() function can be used to find out the words for months and weekdays.

```
SELECT DayName=DATENAME(weekday, OrderDate), SalesPerWeekDay = COUNT(*)
FROM AdventureWorks2008.Sales.SalesOrderHeader
GROUP BY DATENAME(weekday, OrderDate), DATEPART(weekday,OrderDate)
ORDER BY DATEPART(weekday,OrderDate);
```

DayName	SalesPerWeekDay
Sunday	4482
Monday	4591
Tuesday	4346
Wednesday	4244
Thursday	4483
Friday	4444
Saturday	4875

DATENAME application for month names

```
SELECT MonthName=DATENAME(month, OrderDate), SalesPerMonth = COUNT(*)
FROM AdventureWorks2008.Sales.SalesOrderHeader
GROUP BY DATENAME(month, OrderDate), MONTH(OrderDate) ORDER BY MONTH(OrderDate);
```

MonthName	SalesPerMonth
January	2483
February	2686
March	2750
April	2740
May	3154
June	3079
July	2094
August	2411
September	2298
October	2282
November	2474
December	3014

```
SELECT DATENAME(MM,dateadd(MM,7,-1))  -- July  - Month name from month number
```

Extract Date from Text with PATINDEX Pattern Matching

```
USE tempdb;
go

CREATE TABLE InsiderTransaction (
    InsiderTransactionID int identity primary key,
    TradeDate datetime,
    TradeMsg varchar(256),
    ModifiedDate datetime default (getdate())  );

-- Populate table with dummy data
INSERT InsiderTransaction (TradeMsg)
VALUES ('INSIDER TRAN QABC Hammer, Bruce D. CSO 09-02-08 Buy 2,000 6.10');
INSERT InsiderTransaction (TradeMsg)
VALUES ('INSIDER TRAN QABC Schmidt, Steven CFO 08-25-08 Buy 2,500 6.70') ;
INSERT InsiderTransaction (TradeMsg)
VALUES ('INSIDER TRAN QABC  Hammer, Bruce D. CSO  08-20-08 Buy 3,000 8.59');
INSERT InsiderTransaction (TradeMsg)
VALUES ('INSIDER TRAN QABC Walters,  Jeff CTO 08-15-08  Sell 5,648 8.49');
INSERT InsiderTransaction (TradeMsg)
VALUES  ('INSIDER TRAN  QABC  Walters, Jeff CTO   08-15-08 Option Exercise 5,648 2.15');
INSERT InsiderTransaction (TradeMsg)
VALUES('INSIDER TRAN QABC Hammer, Bruce D. CSO 07-31-08  Buy 5,000 8.05');
INSERT InsiderTransaction (TradeMsg)
VALUES('INSIDER TRAN QABC Lennot, Mark  Director  08-31-07 Buy 1,500 9.97');
INSERT InsiderTransaction (TradeMsg)
VALUES('INSIDER TRAN QABC  O''Neal, Linda COO  08-01-08 Sell 5,000 6.50');
```

Pattern match for MM-DD-YY using the PATINDEX string function to extract dates from stock trade message text.

```
SELECT   InsiderTransactionID ,       substring(TradeMsg,
        patindex('%[01][0-9]-[0123][0-9]-[0-9][0-9]%', TradeMsg),8) AS TradeDate
FROM InsiderTransaction  WHERE  patindex('%[01][0-9]-[0123][0-9]-[0-9][0-9]%', TradeMsg) > 0;
```

InsiderTransactionID	TradeDate
1	09-02-08
2	08-25-08
3	08-20-08
4	08-15-08
5	08-15-08
6	07-31-08
7	08-31-07
8	08-01-08

Valid Ranges for Date & Time Data Types

> ➢ DATE (3 bytes) date range:

> ➢ January 1, 1 through December 31, 9999 A.D.

> ➢ SMALLDATETIME (4 bytes) date range:

> ➢ January 1, 1900 through June 6, 2079

> ➢ DATETIME (8 bytes) date range:

> ➢ January 1, 1753 through December 31, 9999

> ➢ DATETIME2 (6-8 bytes) date range:

> ➢ January 1, 1 A.D. through December 31, 9999 A.D.

Smalldatetime has limited range. The statement below will give a date range error.

```
SELECT CONVERT(smalldatetime, '2110-01-01')
/* Msg 242, Level 16, State 3, Line 1
The conversion of a varchar data type to a smalldatetime data type
resulted in an out-of-range value. */
```

```
-- Date Columbus discovers America
SELECT CONVERT(datetime, '14921012');
/* Msg 242, Level 16, State 3, Line 2
The conversion of a varchar data type to a datetime data type resulted in an out-of-range value. */
```

```
SELECT CONVERT(datetime2, '14921012');   -- 1492-10-10 00:00:00.0000000
```

```
SELECT CONVERT(date, '14921012');                -- 1492-10-12
```

CHAPTER 7: Basic SELECT Statement Syntax & Examples

Last Week Calculations

```
-- SQL last Friday - Implied string to datetime conversions in dateadd & datediff
DECLARE @BaseFriday CHAR(8), @LastFriday datetime, @LastMonday datetime;
SET @BaseFriday = '19000105';
SELECT   @LastFriday = dateadd(dd,
         (datediff (dd, @BaseFriday, CURRENT_TIMESTAMP) / 7) * 7, @BaseFriday) ;
SELECT [Last Friday] = @LastFriday ;
```

Last Friday
2012-07-27 00:00:00.000

```
-- Last Monday (last week's Monday)
SELECT   @LastMonday=dateadd(dd,  (datediff (dd, @BaseFriday,
         CURRENT_TIMESTAMP) / 7) * 7 - 4, @BaseFriday)
SELECT [Last Monday]= @LastMonday;
```

Last Monday
2012-07-23 00:00:00.000

```
-- Last week - SUN - SAT
SELECT          [Last Week] = CONCAT(CONVERT(varchar,dateadd(day, -1, @LastMonday), 101), ' - ',
                CONVERT(varchar, dateadd(day, 1,  @LastFriday), 101))
```

Last Week
07/22/2012 - 07/28/2012

```
-- Next 10 weeks including this one; SUN - SAT
SELECT   TOP 10   [ Week] = CONCAT(CONVERT(varchar,dateadd(day, -1+number*7, @LastMonday), 101),
         ' - ',       CONVERT(varchar, dateadd(day, 1+number*7,  @LastFriday), 101))
FROM master.dbo.spt_values  WHERE type = 'P';
GO
```

Week
08/05/2012 - 08/11/2012
08/12/2012 - 08/18/2012
08/19/2012 - 08/25/2012
08/26/2012 - 09/01/2012
09/02/2012 - 09/08/2012
09/09/2012 - 09/15/2012
09/16/2012 - 09/22/2012
09/23/2012 - 09/29/2012
09/30/2012 - 10/06/2012
10/07/2012 - 10/13/2012

Specific Day Calculations

```
-- First day of current month
SELECT dateadd(month, datediff(month, 0, getdate()), 0);
```

```
-- 15th day of current month
SELECT dateadd(day,14,dateadd(month,datediff(month,0,getdate()),0));
```

```
-- First Monday of current month
SELECT   dateadd(day, (9-datepart(weekday,
         dateadd(month, datediff(month, 0, getdate()), 0)))%7,
         dateadd(month, datediff(month, 0, getdate()), 0)) ;
```

```
-- Next Monday calculation from the reference date which was a Monday
DECLARE @Now datetime = GETDATE();
DECLARE @NextMonday datetime = dateadd(dd, ((datediff(dd, '19000101', @Now)  / 7) * 7) + 7,
'19000101');
SELECT [Now]=@Now, [Next Monday]=@NextMonday;
```

```
-- Last Friday of current month
SELECT   dateadd(day, -7+(6-datepart(weekday,
         dateadd(month, datediff(month, 0, getdate())+1, 0)))%7,
         dateadd(month, datediff(month, 0, getdate())+1, 0)) ;
```

```
-- First day of next month
SELECT dateadd(month, datediff(month, 0, getdate())+1, 0);
```

```
-- 15th of next month
SELECT dateadd(day,14, dateadd(month, datediff(month, 0, getdate())+1, 0));
```

```
-- First Monday of next month
SELECT   dateadd(day, (9-datepart(weekday,
         dateadd(month, datediff(month, 0, getdate())+1, 0)))%7,
          dateadd(month, datediff(month, 0, getdate())+1, 0))  AS NextMonthMonday;
```

NextMonthMonday
2012-08-06 00:00:00.000

CHAPTER 7: Basic SELECT Statement Syntax & Examples

CHAPTER 8: Subqueries in SELECT Statements

Subqueries

Subquery ("Inner query") is query within a query which is called the "outer query".

When a subquery involves columns form the outer query, it is called correlated subquery.

When a subquery has a table alias, it is called a derived table.

With SQL Server 2005 a new kind of subquery was introduced: Common Table Expression (CTE). A query can have one or more CTEs. If they are related, they are called nested CTEs. CTEs support recursion.

Correlated subquery is used to retrieve the last freight cost for the customer.

```
-- Correlated subquery - it has reference to an outer query column: A.CustomerID
USE Northwind;

SELECT  A.CustomerID,
    FORMAT(MIN(A.OrderDate), 'd')                        AS FirstOrder,
    FORMAT(MAX(A.OrderDate), 'd')                        AS LastOrder,
    FORMAT( (SELECT  TOP 1 B.Freight
            FROM    Orders B
            WHERE   B.CustomerID = A.CustomerID
            ORDER BY OrderDate DESC),'c','en-US')        AS LastFreight
FROM    Orders A
GROUP BY A.CustomerID ORDER BY A.CustomerID;
-- (89 row(s) affected) - Partial results.
```

CustomerID	FirstOrder	LastOrder	LastFreight
ALFKI	8/25/1997	4/9/1998	$1.21
ANATR	9/18/1996	3/4/1998	$39.92
ANTON	11/27/1996	1/28/1998	$58.43
AROUT	11/15/1996	4/10/1998	$33.80
BERGS	8/12/1996	3/4/1998	$151.52
BLAUS	4/9/1997	4/29/1998	$31.14
BLONP	7/25/1996	1/12/1998	$7.09
BOLID	10/10/1996	3/24/1998	$16.16
BONAP	10/16/1996	5/6/1998	$38.28
BOTTM	12/20/1996	4/24/1998	$24.12
BSBEV	8/26/1996	4/14/1998	$123.83
CACTU	4/29/1997	4/28/1998	$0.33

Non-Correlated Subqueries

In the next query, the inner query is not linked to the outer query at all (no outer column is used in the inner query). The implication is that the inner query can be executed by itself. The inner query needs to return a single value in this instance due to the ">=" operator. If it were to return multiple values, error would result.

```
-- Non-correlated subquery
SELECT          Name,
                FORMAT(ListPrice, 'c','en-US')              AS ListPrice,
                ProductNumber,
                FORMAT(StandardCost, 'c','en-US')           AS StandardCost
FROM AdventureWorks2012.Production.Product
WHERE ListPrice >=
                (SELECT ListPrice
                 FROM AdventureWorks.Production.Product
                 WHERE Name = 'Road-250 Black, 48' )

ORDER BY ListPrice DESC, Name;
GO
```

Name	ListPrice	ProductNumber	StandardCost
Road-150 Red, 44	$3,578.27	BK-R93R-44	$2,171.29
Road-150 Red, 48	$3,578.27	BK-R93R-48	$2,171.29
Road-150 Red, 52	$3,578.27	BK-R93R-52	$2,171.29
Road-150 Red, 56	$3,578.27	BK-R93R-56	$2,171.29
Road-150 Red, 62	$3,578.27	BK-R93R-62	$2,171.29
Mountain-100 Silver, 38	$3,399.99	BK-M82S-38	$1,912.15
Mountain-100 Silver, 42	$3,399.99	BK-M82S-42	$1,912.15
Mountain-100 Silver, 44	$3,399.99	BK-M82S-44	$1,912.15
Mountain-100 Silver, 48	$3,399.99	BK-M82S-48	$1,912.15
Mountain-100 Black, 38	$3,374.99	BK-M82B-38	$1,898.09
Mountain-100 Black, 42	$3,374.99	BK-M82B-42	$1,898.09
Mountain-100 Black, 44	$3,374.99	BK-M82B-44	$1,898.09
Mountain-100 Black, 48	$3,374.99	BK-M82B-48	$1,898.09
Road-250 Black, 44	$2,443.35	BK-R89B-44	$1,554.95
Road-250 Black, 48	$2,443.35	BK-R89B-48	$1,554.95
Road-250 Black, 52	$2,443.35	BK-R89B-52	$1,554.95
Road-250 Black, 58	$2,443.35	BK-R89B-58	$1,554.95
Road-250 Red, 44	$2,443.35	BK-R89R-44	$1,518.79
Road-250 Red, 48	$2,443.35	BK-R89R-48	$1,518.79
Road-250 Red, 52	$2,443.35	BK-R89R-52	$1,518.79
Road-250 Red, 58	$2,443.35	BK-R89R-58	$1,554.95

Subquery returned more than 1 value Error

The following query fails. The reason: the ">=" requires a single value on the right side. The subquery returns 46 values.

```
-- Non-correlated subquery
SELECT          Name,
                FORMAT(ListPrice, 'c','en-US')              AS ListPrice,
                ProductNumber,
                FORMAT(StandardCost, 'c','en-US')           AS StandardCost
FROM AdventureWorks2012.Production.Product
WHERE ListPrice >=
  (SELECT ListPrice
   FROM AdventureWorks.Production.Product
   WHERE Name LIKE 'Road%' )
ORDER BY ListPrice DESC, Name;
GO
/*
Msg 512, Level 16, State 1, Line 3
Subquery returned more than 1 value. This is not permitted when the subquery follows =, !=, <, <= , >, >=
or when the subquery is used as an expression. */
```

If we change the WHERE clause predicate operator from ">=" to "IN" then the query will execute correctly since the IN operator works with a set of values on the right side.

```
-- Non-correlated subquery
SELECT   Name,
         FORMAT(ListPrice, 'c','en-US')              AS ListPrice,
         ProductNumber,
         FORMAT(StandardCost, 'c','en-US')           AS StandardCost
FROM AdventureWorks2012.Production.Product
WHERE ListPrice IN
         (SELECT ListPrice
          FROM AdventureWorks.Production.Product  WHERE Name LIKE 'Road%' )
ORDER BY ListPrice DESC, Name;
-- (253 row(s) affected) -- Partial results.
```

Name	ListPrice	ProductNumber	StandardCost
AWC Logo Cap	$8.99	CA-1098	$6.92
Racing Socks, L	$8.99	SO-R809-L	$3.36
Racing Socks, M	$8.99	SO-R809-M	$3.36
Road Bottle Cage	$8.99	BC-R205	$3.36
Road-650 Black, 44	$782.99	BK-R50B-44	$486.71
Road-650 Black, 48	$782.99	BK-R50B-48	$486.71
Road-650 Black, 52	$782.99	BK-R50B-52	$486.71

CHAPTER 8: Subqueries in SELECT Statements

Correlated Subqueries

In a correlated subquery there is a reference to an outer query column. In other words, the subquery by itself cannot be executed due to the correlation. In the next query, the inner query references soh.SalesOrderID column from the outer query in the WHERE clause predicate which is like an EQUI-JOIN.

```
SELECT      soh.SalesOrderID,
            FORMAT (soh.OrderDate, 'yyyy-MM-dd')                AS OrderDate,

            ( SELECT FORMAT(MAX(sod.UnitPrice),'c','en-US')
              FROM   AdventureWorks2012.Sales.SalesOrderDetail  AS sod
              WHERE  soh.SalesOrderID = sod.SalesOrderID )       AS MaxUnitPrice,

            FORMAT(TotalDue, 'c', 'en-US')                       AS TotalDue
FROM    AdventureWorks2012.Sales.SalesOrderHeader AS soh
ORDER BY MaxUnitPrice DESC, SalesOrderID;
-- (31465 row(s) affected) - Partial results.
```

SalesOrderID	OrderDate	MaxUnitPrice	TotalDue
51087	2007-07-01	$953.63	$2,721.27
51099	2007-07-01	$953.63	$5,276.64
51119	2007-07-01	$953.63	$2,040.14
51173	2007-07-01	$953.63	$1,457.54
51701	2007-08-01	$953.63	$2,634.93
51798	2007-08-01	$953.63	$907.09
51805	2007-08-01	$953.63	$907.09
51808	2007-08-01	$953.63	$1,827.45
51861	2007-08-01	$953.63	$11,762.43
53489	2007-09-01	$953.63	$1,814.18

The next query with correlated subquery list sales staff with 0.015 commission rate.

```
SELECT CONCAT(p.LastName,', ', p.FirstName) AS SalesPerson, e.BusinessEntityID AS EmployeeID
FROM AdventureWorks2012.Person.Person AS p
            INNER JOIN AdventureWorks2012.HumanResources.Employee AS e
            ON e.BusinessEntityID = p.BusinessEntityID
WHERE 0.015 IN  (SELECT CommissionPct   FROM AdventureWorks2012.Sales.SalesPerson sp
            WHERE e.BusinessEntityID = sp.BusinessEntityID)  ORDER BY SalesPerson;
```

SalesPerson	EmployeeID
Carson, Jillian	277
Mitchell, Linda	276
Saraiva, José	282

CHAPTER 8: Subqueries in SELECT Statements

Correlated Subqueries with Same Table

In a correlated subquery, we can use a table from the outer query. In such a case table alias usage is required. In the next query with correlated subquery which lists same part suppliers, the Purchasing.ProductVendor table is referenced by both the outer query and inner query, therefore table alias is required.

```
SELECT        p.Name                  AS ProductName,
              v.Name                  AS Vendor,
              pv1.BusinessEntItyID     AS VendorID
FROM AdventureWorks2012.Purchasing.ProductVendor pv1
   INNER JOIN AdventureWorks2012.Production.Product p
     ON p.ProductID = pv1.ProductID
   INNER JOIN AdventureWorks2012.Purchasing.Vendor v
     ON v.BusinessEntityID = pv1.BusinessEntityID
WHERE pv1.ProductID IN

  (SELECT pv2.ProductID
   FROM AdventureWorks2012.Purchasing.ProductVendor pv2
   WHERE pv1.BusinessEntityID <> pv2.BusinessEntityID)

ORDER  BY ProductName, Vendor;
-- (347 row(s) affected) - Partial results.
```

ProductName	Vendor	VendorID
Internal Lock Washer 7	Aurora Bike Center	1616
Internal Lock Washer 7	Pro Sport Industries	1686
Internal Lock Washer 8	Aurora Bike Center	1616
Internal Lock Washer 8	Pro Sport Industries	1686
Internal Lock Washer 9	Aurora Bike Center	1616
Internal Lock Washer 9	Pro Sport Industries	1686
LL Crankarm	Proseware, Inc.	1678
LL Crankarm	Vision Cycles, Inc.	1578
LL Grip Tape	Gardner Touring Cycles	1516
LL Grip Tape	National Bike Association	1572
LL Mountain Pedal	Crowley Sport	1658
LL Mountain Pedal	Greenwood Athletic Company	1506
LL Mountain Rim	Comfort Road Bicycles	1530
LL Mountain Rim	Competition Bike Training Systems	1624
LL Mountain Seat/Saddle	Chicago City Saddles	1696
LL Mountain Seat/Saddle	First Rate Bicycles	1570
LL Mountain Tire	Sport Fan Co.	1632
LL Mountain Tire	Vista Road Bikes	1538
LL Nipple	Lindell	1592
LL Nipple	Northern Bike Travel	1662
LL Road Pedal	Jackson Authority	1680
LL Road Pedal	Mitchell Sports	1586
LL Road Rim	Electronic Bike Repair & Supplies	1646
LL Road Rim	International Bicycles	1526

CROSS APPLY with Correlated Subquery

The CROSS APPLY operator can connect tables with correlated subqueries as demonstrated following, INNER JOIN would not work in this case.

```
USE AdventureWorks;
DECLARE        @Year  INT,
               @Month INT;
SET @Year      = 2003;
SET @Month     = 2;

SELECT   s.Name                                          AS Customer,
         FORMAT(SalesAmount.OrderTotal,'c','en-US')      AS [Total Sales]
FROM     Sales.Customer AS c
     INNER JOIN Sales.Store AS s
        ON s.CustomerID = c.CustomerID
     CROSS APPLY
               (        SELECT   soh.CustomerId,
                                 Sum(sod.LineTotal)       AS OrderTotal
                  FROM     Sales.SalesOrderHeader AS soh
               INNER JOIN Sales.SalesOrderDetail AS sod
                     ON sod.SalesOrderId = soh.SalesOrderId
                  WHERE soh.CustomerId = c.CustomerId
           AND OrderDate > = DATEFROMPARTS(@Year, @Month, 1)
           AND OrderDate <  DATEADD(mm, 1, DATEFROMPARTS(@Year, @Month, 1))
                  GROUP BY soh.CustomerId)                AS SalesAmount
ORDER BY Customer;
-- (132 row(s) affected) - Partial results.
```

Customer	Total Sales
Ace Bicycle Supply	$647.99
Affordable Sports Equipment	$50,953.32
Alpine Ski House	$939.59
Basic Sports Equipment	$159.56
Bicycle Lines Distributors	$22,243.33
Big-Time Bike Store	$20,078.26
Bike Boutique	$20,038.36
Bike Experts	$25,503.15
Bike Products and Accessories	$404.87
Bikes and Motorbikes	$17,060.91
Black Bicycle Company	$1,242.85
Bold Bike Accessories	$141.62
Brakes and Gears	$66,265.33
Brightwork Company	$7,736.05
Catalog Store	$17,259.86

Derived Tables: SELECT from SELECT

A non-correlated subquery can be made into a derived table by enclosing it in parenthesis and assigning a table alias, such as "CAT" in the following example. It can then be used like a regular table for example in JOINs.

```
USE Northwind;

SELECT   c.CategoryName  AS Category,
         p.ProductName,   p.UnitPrice,   CAT.NoOfProducts
FROM     Categories c
    INNER JOIN Products p
      ON c.CategoryID = p.CategoryID
    INNER JOIN
                     (SELECT  c.CategoryID,
                             NoOfProducts = count(* )
                     FROM     Categories c
                       INNER JOIN Products p1
                            ON c.CategoryID = p1.CategoryID
                     GROUP BY c.CategoryID)                         AS CAT

       ON c.CategoryID = CAT.CategoryID
ORDER BY Category;
-- (77 row(s) affected)  - Partial results.
```

Category	ProductName	UnitPrice
Dairy Products	Raclette Courdavault	55.00
Dairy Products	Camembert Pierrot	34.00
Dairy Products	Gudbrandsdalsost	36.00
Dairy Products	Flotemysost	21.50
Dairy Products	Mozzarella di Giovanni	34.80
Grains/Cereals	Gustaf's Knäckebröd	21.00
Grains/Cereals	Tunnbröd	9.00
Grains/Cereals	Singaporean Hokkien Fried Mee	14.00
Grains/Cereals	Filo Mix	7.00
Grains/Cereals	Gnocchi di nonna Alice	38.00
Grains/Cereals	Ravioli Angelo	19.50

Results from the subquery (derived table).

CategoryID	NoOfProducts
1	12
2	12
3	13
4	10
5	7
6	6
7	5
8	12

The UNION & UNION ALL Set Operators

UNION (distinct, duplicates eliminated) and UNION ALL (duplicates allowed) merge two or more sets of data into one set. Important points to remember about UNION:

> First SELECT column list establishes column names and data types; if INTO used it goes here
> Subsequent SELECTs must match the column structure; column names can be any; NULL if no data
> ORDER BY goes at the very end with the last SELECT

T-SQL UNION query merges data from different countries into a single result set.

```
USE NorthWind;
SELECT  ContactName,
        CompanyName,
        City,
        Country,
        Phone
FROM   Customers
WHERE  Country IN ( 'USA', 'Canada' )
-- (16 row(s) affected)
UNION
SELECT  ContactName,
        CompanyName          AS Company,
        City,    Country,
        Phone                AS Telephone
FROM   Customers
WHERE  Country IN ( 'Germany', 'France' )
-- (22 row(s) affected)
UNION
SELECT  ContactName          AS Contact,
        CompanyName,    City,   Country,
        Phone                AS Telephone
FROM   Customers
WHERE  Country IN ( 'Brazil', 'Spain' )
-- (14 row(s) affected)
ORDER  BY CompanyName,
     ContactName ASC;
-- (52 row(s) affected)   - Partial results.
```

ContactName	CompanyName	City	Country	Phone
Maria Anders	Alfreds Futterkiste	Berlin	Germany	030-0074321
Hanna Moos	Blauer See Delikatessen	Mannheim	Germany	0621-08460
Frédérique Citeaux	Blondesddsl père et fils	Strasbourg	France	88.60.15.31
Martín Sommer	Bólido Comidas preparadas	Madrid	Spain	(91) 555 22 82

CHAPTER 8: Subqueries in SELECT Statements

CTE: Common Table Expression for Structured Coding

Common Table Expression is new in SQL Server 2005. It is similar to derived tables in one aspect with a difference: it is defined at the very beginning of a the query, above the main(outer) query. In addition, CTEs can be nested and defined as recursive.

```
USE AdventureWorks;

WITH CTE(ManagerID, StaffCount)
AS
(
    SELECT ManagerID, COUNT(*)
    FROM HumanResources.Employee AS e
    GROUP BY ManagerID
)

SELECT          CONCAT(LEFT(FirstName,1), '. ', LastName)          AS Manager,
                e.Title, StaffCount
FROM CTE s
        INNER JOIN HumanResources.Employee e
    ON s.ManagerID = e.EmployeeID
        INNER JOIN Person.Contact c
    ON c.ContactID = e.ContactID
ORDER BY Manager;
-- (47 row(s) affected) - Partial results.
```

Manager	Title	StaffCount
A. Alberts	European Sales Manager	3
A. Hill	Production Supervisor - WC10	7
A. Wright	Master Scheduler	4
B. Diaz	Production Supervisor - WC40	12
B. Welcker	Vice President of Sales	3
C. Kleinerman	Maintenance Supervisor	4
C. Petculescu	Production Supervisor - WC10	5
C. Randall	Production Supervisor - WC30	6
D. Bradley	Marketing Manager	8
D. Hamilton	Production Supervisor - WC40	6
D. Liu	Accounts Manager	7
D. Miller	Research and Development Manager	3
E. Gubbels	Production Supervisor - WC20	10
G. Altman	Facilities Manager	2
H. Abolrous	Quality Assurance Manager	2

Multiple CTEs Query

A query can have multiple CTEs, they can even be nested (CTE has reference to previous CTE). The two CTEs in the following query are first name and last name frequencies.

```
USE AdventureWorks2012;

WITH cteLastNameFreq

    AS (SELECT    LastName      AS [LastNames],
                  count(* )     AS [LNFrequency]
        FROM    Person.Person
        GROUP BY LastName),

    cteFirstNameFreq
    AS (SELECT    FirstName     AS [FirstNames],
                  count(* )     AS [FNFrequency]
        FROM    Person.Person
        GROUP BY FirstName)

SELECT    CONCAT(rtrim(FirstName), ' ', rtrim(LastName))     AS [Name],
                  isnull(Title,'')                            AS [Title] ,
                  f.FNFrequency,
                  l.LNFrequency
FROM    Person.Person c
        INNER JOIN cteFirstNameFreq AS f
        ON c.FirstName = f.FirstNames
        INNER JOIN cteLastNameFreq AS l
        ON c.LastName = l.LastNames
WHERE    LastName LIKE 'P%' ORDER BY [Name];
-- (1187 row(s) affected) - Partial results;
```

Name	Title	FNFrequency	LNFrequency
Aaron Patterson		56	117
Aaron Perez		56	170
Aaron Perry		56	122
Aaron Phillips		56	80
Aaron Powell		56	116
Abby Patel		19	86
Abby Perez		19	170
Abigail Patterson		76	117
Abigail Patterson		76	117
Abigail Perry		76	122
Abigail Peterson		76	92
Abigail Powell		76	116

CHAPTER 8: Subqueries in SELECT Statements

Testing Common Table Expressions

A CTE can be tested independently of the main query if it does not have nesting (reference to a previous CTE). The following screen snapshot displays the execution of the first CTE SELECT query.

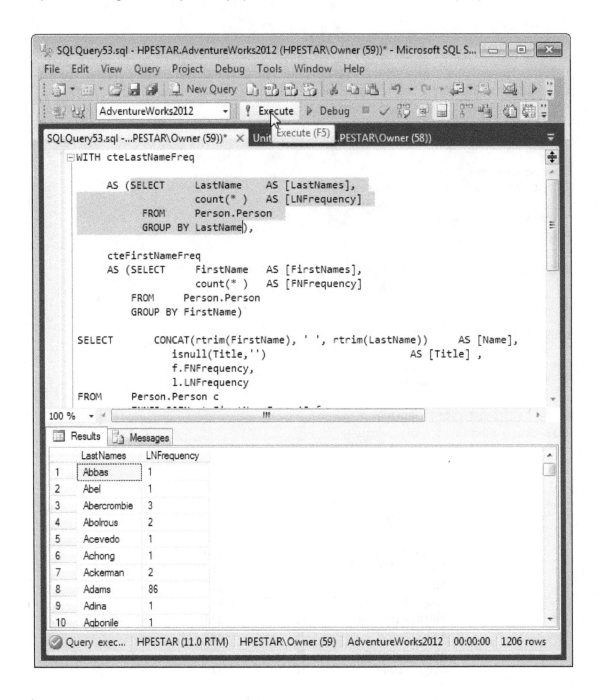

Nested CTEs Queries

CTEs can be nested by reference to a previous CTE like a table.

```
;WITH CTE1
   AS (SELECT 1 AS NUMBER
      UNION ALL
      SELECT 1),
   CTE2
   AS (SELECT 1 AS NUMBER
      FROM   CTE1 x,
          CTE1 y),
   CTE3
   AS (SELECT 1 AS NUMBER
      FROM   CTE2 x,
          CTE2 y),
   CTE4
   AS (SELECT 1 AS NUMBER
      FROM   CTE3 x,
          CTE3 y),
   CTE8BIT
   AS (SELECT ROW_NUMBER()
          OVER(ORDER BY NUMBER) AS INTSequence
      FROM   CTE4)
SELECT *
FROM   CTE8BIT
ORDER BY INTSequence;
-- (256 row(s) affected) - Partial results.
```

INTSequence
241
242
243
244
245
246
247
248
249
250
251
252
253
254
255
256

CTE nesting: cteLastSalary has a nested reference to cteLastSalaryChange

```
USE AdventureWorks2012;

WITH cteLastSalaryChange
    AS (SELECT      BusinessEntityID           AS EmployeeID,
                    Max(RateChangeDate)              AS ChangeDate
       FROM    HumanResources.EmployeePayHistory    GROUP BY BusinessEntityID),

    cteLastSalary
    AS (SELECT     eph.BusinessEntityID              AS EmployeeID,     Rate
       FROM   HumanResources.EmployeePayHistory eph
           INNER JOIN cteLastSalaryChange lsc
             ON lsc.EmployeeID = eph.BusinessEntityID
               AND lsc.ChangeDate = eph.RateChangeDate)

-- SELECT * FROM cteLastSalary  -- for testing & debugging

SELECT TOP 1 FORMAT( Rate, 'c', 'en-US') AS SecondHighestPayRate
FROM    (SELECT  TOP 2 Rate     FROM    cteLastSalary     ORDER BY Rate DESC) a    -- Derived table
ORDER BY Rate ASC;
```

SecondHighestPayRate
$84.13

Testing Nested CTEs

Nested CTEs can be tested independently of the main query the following way.

```
USE AdventureWorks2012;
WITH cteLastSalaryChange
    AS (SELECT      BusinessEntityID           AS EmployeeID,
                    Max(RateChangeDate)              AS ChangeDate
       FROM    HumanResources.EmployeePayHistory
       GROUP BY BusinessEntityID),
    cteLastSalary
    AS (SELECT     eph.BusinessEntityID              AS EmployeeID,
                    Rate
       FROM   HumanResources.EmployeePayHistory eph
           INNER JOIN cteLastSalaryChange lsc
             ON lsc.EmployeeID = eph.BusinessEntityID
               AND lsc.ChangeDate = eph.RateChangeDate)
SELECT * FROM cteLastSalary  -- for testing & debugging
```

CHAPTER 8: Subqueries in SELECT Statements

In Query Editor, uncomment the testing line, select (highlight) the top part of the query and execute it

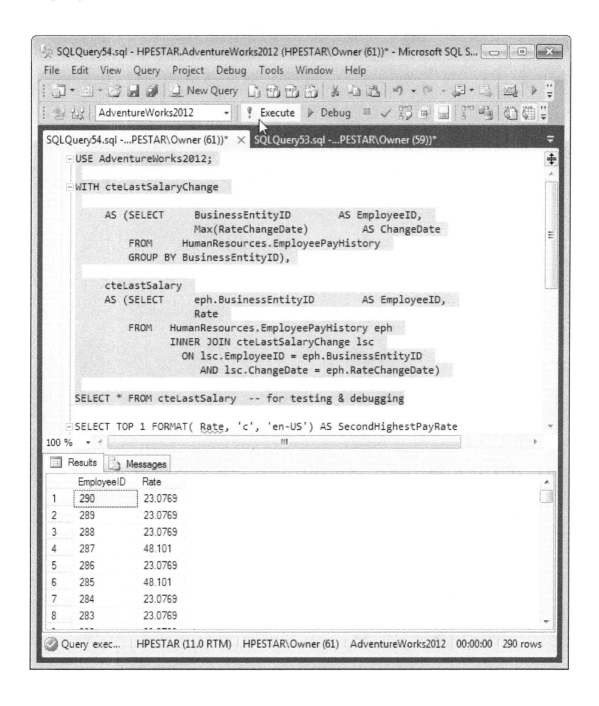

Recursive CTEs for Tree Hierarchy Processing

Recursive CTEs are one of the most exciting new features introduced with SQL Server 2005. They allow tree processing, such as organizational charts or bill of materials parts assembly, as well as generating sets of data without tables. The following recursive CTE generates 1 million integers all by itself. The query execution time is 10 seconds as it can be seen in the lower right.

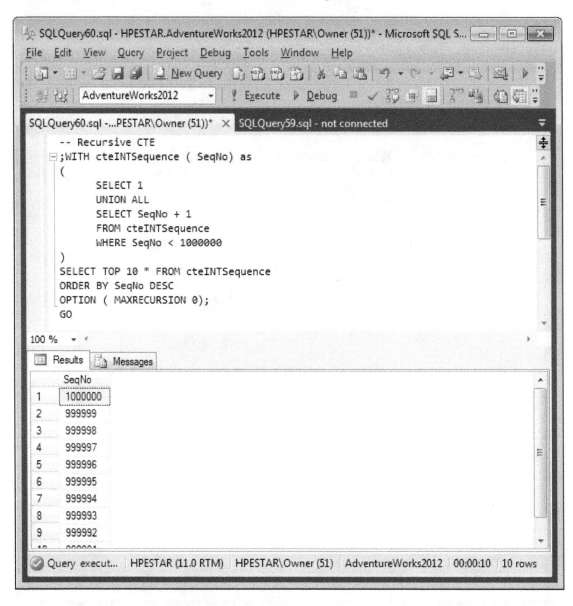

Recursive Generation of Date & Month Sequences

Date sequence can be generated without a calendar table (Note: generally it is helpful to have a calendar table in the database) using recursive CTE.

```
DECLARE @StartDate date = '20160701', @Range smallint = 1000;

WITH cteSEQ ( SeqNo) as
(
    SELECT 0                                      -- Anchor member
    UNION ALL                                     -- Assemble set
    SELECT SeqNo + 1                              -- Recursive member
    FROM cteSEQ
    WHERE SeqNo < @Range
)
SELECT TOP 10 [DATE]=DATEADD(day, SeqNo, @StartDate)
FROM cteSEQ
OPTION ( MAXRECURSION 0);
GO
```

DATE
2016-07-01
2016-07-02
2016-07-03
2016-07-04
2016-07-05
2016-07-06
2016-07-07
2016-07-08
2016-07-09
2016-07-10

```
-- Month sequence generation
DECLARE @StartDate date = '20160701', @Range smallint = 100;
WITH cteSEQ ( SeqNo) as
(
    SELECT 0                                      -- Anchor member
    UNION ALL                                     -- Assemble set
    SELECT SeqNo + 1                              -- Recursive member
    FROM cteSEQ
    WHERE SeqNo < @Range
)
SELECT TOP 3 [DATE]=DATEADD(month, SeqNo, @StartDate)
FROM cteSEQ  OPTION ( MAXRECURSION 0);
```

CHAPTER 8: Subqueries in SELECT Statements

Generate Month Names in Different Languages

The following query can be used to generate month names in any of the SQL Server 2012 supported languages.

```
SET language Spanish;  -- Se cambió la configuración de idioma a Español.
;WITH CTE AS
(   SELECT     1 MonthNo, CONVERT(DATE, '19000101') MonthFirst
    UNION ALL
    SELECT     MonthNo+1, DATEADD(Month, 1, MonthFirst)
    FROM  CTE
    WHERE Month(MonthFirst) < 12    )
SELECT  MonthNo AS MonthNumber,  DATENAME(MONTH, MonthFirst) AS MonthName
FROM  CTE
ORDER BY MonthNo;
SET language English; -- Changed language setting to us_english.
```

```
SET language Hungarian;  -- Nyelvi beállítás átállítva a következőre: magyar.
;WITH CTE AS
(   SELECT     1 MonthNo, CONVERT(DATE, '19000101') MonthFirst
    UNION ALL
    SELECT     MonthNo+1, DATEADD(Month, 1, MonthFirst)
    FROM  CTE
    WHERE Month(MonthFirst) < 12    )
SELECT  MonthNo AS MonthNumber,  DATENAME(MONTH, MonthFirst) AS MonthName
FROM  CTE
ORDER BY MonthNo;
SET language English; -- Changed language setting to us_english.
```

MonthNumber	MonthName	MonthNumber	MonthName
1	Enero	1	január
2	Febrero	2	február
3	Marzo	3	március
4	Abril	4	április
5	Mayo	5	május
6	Junio	6	június
7	Julio	7	július
8	Agosto	8	augusztus
9	Septiembre	9	szeptember
10	Octubre	10	október
11	Noviembre	11	november
12	Diciembre	12	december

Graphical Organizational Chart of AdventureWorks Cycles

T-SQL recursive CTE query generates the entire company chart of AdventureWorks Cycles. The anchor term is Ken Sanchez CEO with ManagerID as NULL. Everybody else in the company has a ManagerID which is not NULL.

```
USE AdventureWorks;

WITH cteEmployeeTree
   AS (SELECT     Root.EmployeeName,  Root.ManagerName,
                  Root.EmployeeId, Root.ManagerId,
                  CONVERT(VARCHAR(MAX),Root.PathSequence) AS PathLabel
      FROM   (SELECT EmployeeName = CONCAT(c.FirstName, SPACE(1), c.LastName),
             ManagerName = convert(VARCHAR(128),''),
             e.EmployeeId,
             e.ManagerId,
             char(64 + ROW_NUMBER()  OVER(ORDER BY e.EmployeeId)) AS PathSequence
         FROM   HumanResources.Employee e
            INNER JOIN Person.Contact c
            ON e.ContactID = c.ContactID
         WHERE  e.ManagerId IS NULL) Root          -- Anchor/root term (above)
      UNION ALL                                     -- Build a set
      SELECT     Branch.EmployeeName,               -- Recursive term (below)
                 Branch.ManagerName,
                 Branch.EmployeeId, Branch.ManagerId,
                 PathLabel = Branch.PathLabel + CONVERT(VARCHAR(MAX),  Branch.PathSequence)
      FROM   (SELECT EmployeeName = CONCAT(c.FirstName, SPACE(1), c.LastName),
             ManagerName = CONVERT(VARCHAR(128),CONCAT(cm.FirstName, SPACE(1), cm.LastName)),
             e.EmployeeId,
             e.ManagerId,
             cte.PathLabel,
             PathSequence = char(64 + ROW_NUMBER()  OVER(ORDER BY e.EmployeeId))
         FROM   cteEmployeeTree cte
            INNER JOIN HumanResources.Employee e
            ON e.ManagerId = cte.EmployeeId
            INNER JOIN Person.Contact c
            ON e.ContactID = c.ContactID
            INNER JOIN HumanResources.Employee em
            ON em.EmployeeID = e.ManagerID
            INNER JOIN Person.Contact cm
            ON em.ContactID = cm.ContactID) Branch)
-- Outer / main query
SELECT   CONCAT(REPLICATE(CHAR(9), LEN(PathLabel)-1),   -- tabs for indenting
                EmployeeName) AS EmployeeName
FROM   cteEmployeeTree  ORDER BY PathLabel;
```

The resulting organizational chart was generated by Word as tabs (CHAR(9)) were converted to table columns.

EmployeeName				
Ken Sánchez				
	David Bradley			
		Kevin Brown		
		Sariya Harnpadoungsataya		
		Mary Gibson		
		Jill Williams		
		Terry Eminhizer		
		Wanida Benshoof		
		John Wood		
		Mary Dempsey		
	Terri Duffy			
		Roberto Tamburello		
			Rob Walters	
			Gail Erickson	
			Jossef Goldberg	
			Dylan Miller	
				Diane Margheim
				Gigi Matthew
				Michael Raheem
			Ovidiu Cracium	
				Thierry D'Hers
				Janice Galvin
			Michael Sullivan	
			Sharon Salavaria	
	Jean Trenary			
		Janaina Bueno		
		Dan Bacon		
		François Ajenstat		
		Dan Wilson		
		Ramesh Meyyappan		
		Stephanie Conroy		
			Ashvini Sharma	
			Peter Connelly	
		Karen Berg		
	Laura Norman			
		Paula Barreto de Mattos		
			Willis Johnson	
			Mindy Martin	
			Vidur Luthra	
			Hao Chen	
			Grant Culbertson	

CHAPTER 8: Subqueries in SELECT Statements

	Wendy Kahn		
		Sheela Word	
			Mikael Sandberg
			Arvind Rao
			Linda Meisner
			Fukiko Ogisu
			Gordon Hee
			Frank Pellow
			Eric Kurjan
			Erin Hagens
			Ben Miller
			Annette Hill
			Reinout Hillmann
	David Barber		
	David Liu		
		Deborah Poe	
		Candy Spoon	
		Bryan Walton	
		Dragan Tomic	
		Barbara Moreland	
		Janet Sheperdigian	
		Mike Seamans	
James Hamilton			
	Peter Krebs		
		JoLynn Dobney	
			Simon Rapier
			James Kramer
			Nancy Anderson
			Bryan Baker
			Eugene Kogan
			Thomas Michaels
		Taylor Maxwell	
			Kendall Keil
			Bob Hohman
			Pete Male
			Diane Tibbott
			Denise Smith
			Frank Miller
		Jo Brown	
			Guy Gilbert
			Annik Stahl
			Rebecca Laszlo
			Margie Shoop
			Mark McArthur
			Britta Simon
			Brandon Heidepriem
			Jose Lugo
			Suchitra Mohan

CHAPTER 8: Subqueries in SELECT Statements

					Chris Okelberry
					Kim Abercrombie
					Ed Dudenhoefer
				John Campbell	
					David Ortiz
					Steve Masters
					Jay Adams
					Charles Fitzgerald
					Karan Khanna
					Maciej Dusza
					Michael Zwilling
					Randy Reeves
				Zheng Mu	
					Ebru Ersan
					Mary Baker
					Kevin Homer
					Christopher Hill
					John Kane
				Jinghao Liu	
					Alice Ciccu
					Jun Cao
					Suroor Fatima
					Linda Moschell
					John Evans
					Mindaugas Krapauskas
					Angela Barbariol
					Michael Patten
					Don Hall
					Chad Niswonger
					Michael Entin
					Kitti Lertpiriyasuwat
				Reuben D'sa	
					Ryan Cornelsen
					Brian Goldstein
					Mihail Frintu
					Sandeep Kaliyath
					Eric Brown
					Frank Martinez
					Patrick Cook
					Jack Creasey
				Cristian Petculescu	
					Betsy Stadick
					Kimberly Zimmerman
					Patrick Wedge
					Danielle Tiedt
					Tom Vande Velde
				Kok-Ho Loh	
					Russell Hunter
					Jim Scardelis

CHAPTER 8: Subqueries in SELECT Statements

				Nuan Yu
				Lolan Song
				Houman Pournasseh
				Mandar Samant
				Sameer Tejani
				Elizabeth Keyser
			Pilar Ackerman	
				Susan Eaton
				Vamsi Kuppa
				Kim Ralls
				Matthias Berndt
				Jimmy Bischoff
			David Hamilton	
				Paul Komosinski
				Gary Yukish
				Michael Rothkugel
				Rob Caron
				Baris Cetinok
				Nicole Holliday
			Eric Gubbels	
				Ivo Salmre
				Paul Singh
				Samantha Smith
				Anibal Sousa
				Sylvester Valdez
				Hung-Fu Ting
				Prasanna Samarawickrama
				Min Su
				Krishna Sunkammurali
				Olinda Turner
			Jeff Hay	
				Kirk Koenigsbauer
				Laura Steele
				Chris Preston
				Alex Nayberg
				Andrew Cencini
			Cynthia Randall	
				Jian Shuo Wang
				Sandra Reátegui Alayo
				Jason Watters
				Andy Ruth
				Rostislav Shabalin
				Michael Vanderhyde
			Yuhong Li	
				Hanying Feng
				Raymond Sam
				Fadi Fakhouri
				Lane Sacksteder

CHAPTER 8: Subqueries in SELECT Statements

				Linda Randall
				Terrence Earls
				Shelley Dyck
			Shane Kim	
				Yvonne McKay
				Douglas Hite
				Janeth Esteves
				Robert Rounthwaite
				Lionel Penuchot
			Michael Ray	
				Steven Selikoff
				Carole Poland
				Bjorn Rettig
				Michiko Osada
				Carol Philips
				Merav Netz
			Katie McAskill-White	
				Michael Hines
				Nitin Mirchandani
				Barbara Decker
				John Chen
				Stefen Hesse
			Jack Richins	
				David Johnson
				Garrett Young
				Susan Metters
				George Li
				David Yalovsky
				Marc Ingle
				Eugene Zabokritski
				Benjamin Martin
				Reed Koch
				David Lawrence
				Russell King
				John Frum
				Jan Miksovsky
			Andrew Hill	
				Ruth Ellerbrock
				Barry Johnson
				Sidney Higa
				Jeffrey Ford
				Doris Hartwig
				Diane Glimp
				Bonnie Kearney
			Lori Kane	
				Stuart Munson
				Greg Alderson
				Scott Gode

			Kathie Flood
			Belinda Newman
		Brenda Diaz	
			Alejandro McGuel
			Fred Northup
			Kevin Liu
			Shammi Mohamed
			Rajesh Patel
			Lorraine Nay
			Paula Nartker
			Frank Lee
			Brian Lloyd
			Tawana Nusbaum
			Ken Myer
			Gabe Mares
	A. Scott Wright		
		William Vong	
		Sairaj Uddin	
		Alan Brewer	
		Brian LaMee	
	Hazem Abolrous		
		Peng Wu	
			Sean Alexander
			Mark Harrington
			Andreas Berglund
			Sootha Charncherngkha
		Zainal Arifin	
			Tengiz Kharatishvili
			Sean Chai
			Karen Berge
			Chris Norred
	Gary Altman		
		Christian Kleinerman	
			Pat Coleman
			Lori Penor
			Stuart Macrae
			Jo Berry
		Magnus Hedlund	
Brian Welcker			
	Stephen Jiang		
		Michael Blythe	
		Linda Mitchell	
		Jillian Carson	
		Garrett Vargas	
		Tsvi Reiter	
		Pamela Ansman-Wolfe	

CHAPTER 8: Subqueries in SELECT Statements

			Shu Ito	
			José Saraiva	
			David Campbell	
			Tete Mensa-Annan	
		Amy Alberts		
			Jae Pak	
			Ranjit Varkey Chudukatil	
			Rachel Valdez	
		Syed Abbas		
			Lynn Tsoflias	

Graphical Bill of Materials for Mountain-100 Silver, 44 Bike

T-SQL query will generate bill of materials (assembly) listing for Mountain-100 Silver, 44 mountain bike. The AdventureWorks2012 database image for Mountain-100 Silver, 44 in Production.ProductPhoto table.

```
USE AdventureWorks2012;
DECLARE          @StartProductID int      = 773,              -- Mountain-100 Silver, 44
                 @CheckDate datetime      = '20080201';

   WITH cteBOM(ProductAssemblyID, ComponentID, ComponentName,  RecursionLevel)
   AS (
     SELECT b.ProductAssemblyID, b.ComponentID, p.Name,  0
           FROM Production.BillOfMaterials b
           INNER JOIN Production.Product p
         ON b.ComponentID = p.ProductID
     WHERE        b.ProductAssemblyID = @StartProductID
                  AND @CheckDate >= b.StartDate
                  AND @CheckDate <= ISNULL(b.EndDate, @CheckDate)          -- Anchor/root member
(above)
     UNION ALL                                                            -- Build a set
     SELECT       b.ProductAssemblyID, b.ComponentID, p.Name,      -- Recursive member (below)
                  RecursionLevel + 1
     FROM cteBOM c
       INNER JOIN Production.BillOfMaterials b
       ON b.ProductAssemblyID = c.ComponentID
       INNER JOIN Production.Product p
       ON b.ComponentID = p.ProductID
     WHERE        @CheckDate >= b.StartDate          AND @CheckDate <= ISNULL(b.EndDate, @CheckDate)
)
-- Outer/main query
   SELECT CONCAT(REPLICATE(CHAR(9), RecursionLevel), -- Generate indents with tab character
                (SELECT Name FROM Production.Product WHERE ProductID=ProductAssemblyID)) AS PartName,
                ComponentName
         FROM cteBOM    GROUP BY  RecursionLevel,ProductAssemblyID,ComponentName
   ORDER BY      RecursionLevel, ProductAssemblyID,ComponentName     OPTION (MAXRECURSION 10);
-- (87 row(s) affected)
```

The resulting graphical bill of materials for the mountain bike.

PartName	ComponentName			
Mountain-100 Silver, 44	Chain			
Mountain-100 Silver, 44	Front Brakes			
Mountain-100 Silver, 44	Front Derailleur			
Mountain-100 Silver, 44	HL Bottom Bracket			
Mountain-100 Silver, 44	HL Crankset			
Mountain-100 Silver, 44	HL Headset			
Mountain-100 Silver, 44	HL Mountain Frame - Silver, 44			
Mountain-100 Silver, 44	HL Mountain Front Wheel			
Mountain-100 Silver, 44	HL Mountain Handlebars			
Mountain-100 Silver, 44	HL Mountain Pedal			
Mountain-100 Silver, 44	HL Mountain Rear Wheel			
Mountain-100 Silver, 44	HL Mountain Seat Assembly			
Mountain-100 Silver, 44	Rear Brakes			
Mountain-100 Silver, 44	Rear Derailleur			
	HL Mountain Seat Assembly	HL Mountain Seat/Saddle		
	HL Mountain Seat Assembly	Pinch Bolt		
	HL Mountain Seat Assembly	Seat Lug		
	HL Mountain Seat Assembly	Seat Post		
	HL Mountain Frame - Silver, 44	Chain Stays		
	HL Mountain Frame - Silver, 44	Decal 1		
	HL Mountain Frame - Silver, 44	Decal 2		
	HL Mountain Frame - Silver, 44	Down Tube		
	HL Mountain Frame - Silver, 44	Head Tube		
	HL Mountain Frame - Silver, 44	HL Fork		
	HL Mountain Frame - Silver, 44	Paint - Silver		

HL Mountain Frame - Silver, 44	Seat Stays		
HL Mountain Frame - Silver, 44	Seat Tube		
HL Mountain Frame - Silver, 44	Top Tube		
HL Headset	Adjustable Race		
HL Headset	Crown Race		
HL Headset	Headset Ball Bearings		
HL Headset	Keyed Washer		
HL Headset	Lock Nut 19		
HL Headset	Lower Head Race		
HL Mountain Handlebars	Handlebar Tube		
HL Mountain Handlebars	HL Grip Tape		
HL Mountain Handlebars	Mountain End Caps		
HL Mountain Handlebars	Stem		
HL Mountain Front Wheel	HL Hub		
HL Mountain Front Wheel	HL Mountain Rim		
HL Mountain Front Wheel	HL Mountain Tire		
HL Mountain Front Wheel	HL Nipple		
HL Mountain Front Wheel	Mountain Tire Tube		
HL Mountain Front Wheel	Reflector		
HL Mountain Front Wheel	Spokes		
HL Mountain Rear Wheel	HL Hub		
HL Mountain Rear Wheel	HL Mountain Rim		
HL Mountain Rear Wheel	HL Mountain Tire		
HL Mountain Rear Wheel	HL Nipple		
HL Mountain Rear Wheel	Mountain Tire Tube		
HL Mountain Rear Wheel	Reflector		
HL Mountain Rear Wheel	Spokes		
Rear Derailleur	Guide Pulley		
Rear Derailleur	Rear Derailleur Cage		
Rear Derailleur	Tension Pulley		
Front Derailleur	Front Derailleur Cage		
Front Derailleur	Front Derailleur Linkage		
HL Crankset	Chainring		
HL Crankset	Chainring Bolts		
HL Crankset	Chainring Nut		
HL Crankset	Freewheel		
HL Crankset	HL Crankarm		
HL Bottom Bracket	BB Ball Bearing		
HL Bottom Bracket	HL Shell		
	BB Ball Bearing	Bearing Ball	
	BB Ball Bearing	Cone-Shaped Race	
	BB Ball Bearing	Cup-Shaped Race	
	BB Ball Bearing	Lock Ring	
	Chain Stays	Metal Sheet 5	
	Down Tube	Metal Sheet 3	

CHAPTER 8: Subqueries in SELECT Statements

		Mountain End Caps	Metal Sheet 2	
		Handlebar Tube	Metal Sheet 6	
		Head Tube	Metal Sheet 4	
		HL Hub	HL Shell	
		HL Hub	HL Spindle/Axle	
		Stem	Metal Bar 1	
		Seat Stays	Metal Sheet 7	
		Seat Tube	Metal Bar 2	
		Top Tube	Metal Sheet 2	
		HL Fork	Blade	
		HL Fork	Fork Crown	
		HL Fork	Fork End	
		HL Fork	Steerer	
			Blade	Metal Sheet 5
			Fork End	Metal Sheet 2
			Fork Crown	Metal Sheet 5
			Steerer	Metal Sheet 6

CHAPTER 8: Subqueries in SELECT Statements

PIVOT Operator to Transform Rows Into Columns

The PIVOT operator, new to SQL Server 2005, can be used to create pivot table also called cross tabulation (crosstab). The data to be PIVOTed is generated by a CTE.

```
USE AdventureWorks2012;
;WITH CTE    AS (SELECT  YEAR            = YEAR(orderDate),
                         QUARTER         = DatePart(qq,OrderDate),
                         Sales           = Sum(TotalDue)
     FROM    Sales.SalesOrderHeader  GROUP BY YEAR(OrderDate), DatePart(qq,OrderDate))
SELECT * FROM CTE;
```

YEAR	QUARTER	Sales
2007	4	14886562.6775
2006	3	11555907.1472
2007	1	7492396.3224
2007	2	9379298.7027
2006	1	6562121.6796
2006	4	9397824.1785
2008	3	56178.9223
2007	3	15413231.8434
2005	3	5203127.8807
2008	1	12744940.3554
2005	4	7490122.7457
2008	2	16087078.2305
2006	2	6947995.43

The PIVOT operator takes the data from the CTE source, aggregates it and transforms it to columns.

```
;WITH CTE    AS (SELECT  YEAR            = YEAR(orderDate),
                         QUARTER         = DatePart(qq,OrderDate),
                         Sales           = Sum(TotalDue)
     FROM    Sales.SalesOrderHeader  GROUP BY YEAR(OrderDate), DatePart(qq,OrderDate)   )
SELECT    YEAR
                ,FORMAT ([1], 'c','en-US') AS Q1
                ,FORMAT ([2], 'c','en-US') AS Q2
                ,FORMAT ([3], 'c','en-US') AS Q3
                ,FORMAT ([4], 'c','en-US') AS Q4
FROM    (SELECT * FROM CTE) AS PivotInput
     PIVOT    (SUM(Sales)  FOR QUARTER IN ( [1],[2],[3],[4] ) ) AS PivotOutput  ORDER BY YEAR;
```

YEAR	Q1	Q2	Q3	Q4
2005	NULL	NULL	$5,203,127.88	$7,490,122.75
2006	$6,562,121.68	$6,947,995.43	$11,555,907.15	$9,397,824.18
2007	$7,492,396.32	$9,379,298.70	$15,413,231.84	$14,886,562.68
2008	$12,744,940.36	$16,087,078.23	$56,178.92	NULL

UNPIVOT Crosstab View Results

The vSalesPersonSalesByFiscalYears view is a crosstab listing of sales person (rows) and sales by year (columns). The UNPIVOT operation transforms the year columns into rows.

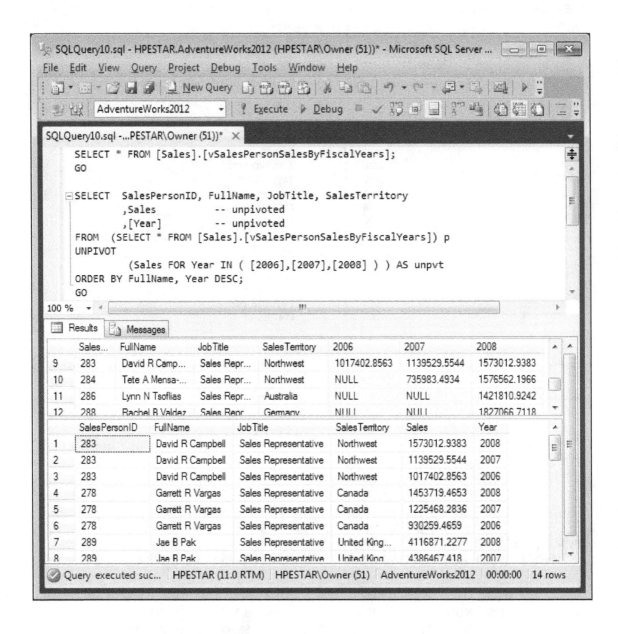

Using Subquery in Column List of SELECT

A subquery can be used in the column list of a SELECT statement.

```
USE Northwind;
GO
;WITH CTE AS
( SELECT ShipCity,
         CONVERT(DATE, OrderDate)                                  AS OrderDate,
         (SELECT CONVERT(DATE, MAX(OrderDate))   FROM dbo.Orders)   AS CurrentOrderDate,
         DATEDIFF(dd,OrderDate,(SELECT MAX(OrderDate) FROM dbo.Orders)) AS DeltaDays,
         ROW_NUMBER() OVER (PARTITION BY ShipCity
                           ORDER BY OrderDate DESC)                 AS RN
  FROM dbo.Orders
)
SELECT TOP 20 ShipCity, OrderDate, CurrentOrderDate, DeltaDays
FROM CTE
WHERE RN=1
ORDER BY DeltaDays DESC;
```

ShipCity	OrderDate	CurrentOrderDate	DeltaDays
Walla Walla	1997-05-22	1998-05-06	349
Elgin	1997-09-08	1998-05-06	240
Montréal	1997-10-30	1998-05-06	188
Reims	1997-11-12	1998-05-06	175
Caracas	1997-12-18	1998-05-06	139
Lille	1997-12-22	1998-05-06	135
Vancouver	1998-01-01	1998-05-06	125
Kirkland	1998-01-08	1998-05-06	118
Strasbourg	1998-01-12	1998-05-06	114
Lyon	1998-01-23	1998-05-06	103
San Francisco	1998-02-12	1998-05-06	83
Luleå	1998-03-04	1998-05-06	63
Barcelona	1998-03-05	1998-05-06	62
Cowes	1998-03-06	1998-05-06	61
Resende	1998-03-09	1998-05-06	58
Leipzig	1998-03-12	1998-05-06	55
Bergamo	1998-03-16	1998-05-06	51
Münster	1998-03-23	1998-05-06	44
Nantes	1998-03-24	1998-05-06	43
Versailles	1998-03-24	1998-05-06	43

CHAPTER 9: SELECT INTO Table Creation & Population

Simple SELECT INTO Statement Variations

SELECT INTO is an easy way to create a table for ad-hoc purposes in database development and administration. **An added benefit is minimal logging, therefore good performance**. INSERT SELECT is logged, although with special setup minimal logging can be achieved in some cases.

```
-- Create and populate copy of the product table in tempdb
SELECT *
INTO   tempdb.dbo.Product
FROM   AdventureWorks2012.Production.Product;
-- (504 row(s) affected)
```

```
SELECT TableRows = count(*)  FROM tempdb.dbo.Product;  -- 504
```

```
-- Copy all persons into new table with last name starting with 'A'
SELECT   BusinessEntityID              AS ID,
         CONCAT(FirstName, ' ', LastName)  AS FullName,
         PersonType
INTO   ListA
FROM   AdventureWorks2012.Person.Person
WHERE  LEFT(LastName, 1) = 'A'
ORDER BY LastName, FirstName;
-- (911 row(s) affected)
```

```
SELECT TOP (10) ID, FullName, PersonType FROM ListA ORDER BY ID;
```

ID	FullName	PersonType
38	Kim Abercrombie	EM
43	Nancy Anderson	EM
67	Jay Adams	EM
121	Pilar Ackerman	EM
207	Greg Alderson	EM
211	Hazem Abolrous	EM
216	Sean Alexander	EM
217	Zainal Arifin	EM
227	Gary Altman	EM
270	François Ajenstat	EM

```
USE AdventureWorks2012;

-- Create a copy of table in a different schema, same name
-- The WHERE clause predicate with >=, < comparison is better performing than the YEAR function
SELECT *
INTO   dbo.SalesOrderHeader
FROM   Sales.SalesOrderHeader
WHERE  OrderDate >= '20080101' AND OrderDate < '20090101';  -- YEAR(OrderDate)=2008
-- (13951 row(s) affected)

-- Create a table without population
SELECT TOP (0)   SalesOrderID,
         OrderDate
INTO   SOH
FROM   Sales.SalesOrderHeader;
-- (0 row(s) affected)

-- SELECT INTO cannot be used to target an existing table
SELECT * INTO  SOH FROM   Sales.SalesOrderHeader;
/* Msg 2714, Level 16, State 6, Line 1
There is already an object named 'SOH' in the database. */
```

NOTE

IDENTITY column is automatically populated. Direct insert into IDENTITY column requires using of SET IDENTITY_INSERT.

```
INSERT SOH (SalesOrderID, OrderDate)
SELECT SalesOrderID, OrderDate
FROM   Sales.SalesOrderHeader ORDER BY SalesOrderID;
GO
/* ERROR due to SalesOrderID in SOH inherited the IDENTITY property.
Msg 544, Level 16, State 1, Line 1
Cannot insert explicit value for identity column in table 'SOH' when IDENTITY_INSERT is set to OFF. */

-- Turn on forced IDENTITY insert
SET IDENTITY_INSERT dbo.SOH ON;
GO

INSERT SOH(SalesOrderID, OrderDate)
SELECT SalesOrderID, OrderDate
FROM   Sales.SalesOrderHeader ORDER BY SalesOrderID;
GO
-- (31465 row(s) affected)

SET IDENTITY_INSERT dbo.SOH OFF;
```

CHAPTER 9: SELECT INTO Table Creation & Population

```
-- Filter on date
SELECT *
INTO   SOH1
FROM   Sales.SalesOrderHeader
WHERE  OrderDate >= '20080101' AND OrderDate < '20090101';
-- (13951 row(s) affected)
```

```
-- Descending sort for population
SELECT *
INTO   SOH2
FROM   Sales.SalesOrderHeader
ORDER  BY SalesOrderID DESC
-- (31465 row(s) affected)
```

```
-- 3 columns only
SELECT   SalesOrderID,
         OrderDate,
         SubTotal
INTO   SOH3
FROM   Sales.SalesOrderHeader;
-- (31465 row(s) affected)
```

```
-- SELECT INTO with GROUP BY query source
SELECT   [Year]=YEAR(OrderDate),
         Orders=COUNT(*)
INTO   SOH4
FROM   Sales.SalesOrderHeader
GROUP  BY YEAR(OrderDate)
-- (4 row(s) affected)
```

```
SELECT * FROM SOH4 ORDER BY Year DESC;
```

Year	Orders
2008	13951
2007	12443
2006	3692
2005	1379

```
-- All source columns, and a new populated datetime column
SELECT   *,
         [CreateDate]=getdate()
INTO   SOH5
FROM   Sales.SalesOrderHeader ;
-- (31465 row(s) affected)
```

```
-- SELECT INTO temporary table
SELECT TotalOrders = COUNT(*)
INTO   #TotalOrders
FROM   Sales.SalesOrderHeader ;
-- (1 row(s) affected)
```

```
SELECT * FROM #TotalOrders;
```

TotalOrders
31465

```
-- Empty table create with one NULL row
SELECT   Name=CONVERT(VARCHAR(45), NULL),
         Age=CONVERT(INT, NULL)
INTO   tempdb.dbo.Person;
```

```
INSERT tempdb.dbo.Person (Name, Age)
SELECT 'Roger Bond', 45;
-- (1 row(s) affected)
```

```
SELECT * FROM tempdb.dbo.Person;
```

Name	Age
NULL	NULL
Roger Bond	45

```
DELETE tempdb.dbo.Person WHERE Name is NULL;
-- (1 row(s) affected)
```

```
SELECT * FROM tempdb.dbo.Person;
```

Name	Age
Roger Bond	45

```
-- Create gaps in ID sequence; increment by 2:  2, 4, 6, 8 instead of 1, 2, 3, 4
SELECT   2 * [BusinessEntityID]                AS BusinessEntityID
         ,[PhoneNumber]
         ,[PhoneNumberTypeID]
         ,[ModifiedDate]
 INTO dbo.Phone
 FROM [AdventureWorks2012].[Person].[PersonPhone] pp    ORDER BY pp.BusinessEntityID;
-- (19972 row(s) affected)
```

CHAPTER 9: SELECT INTO Table Creation & Population

```
-- Populate with 100 random rows
SELECT TOP (100) *
INTO   POH
FROM   Purchasing.PurchaseOrderHeader
ORDER  BY NEWID();
-- (100 row(s) affected)
```

```
SELECT        PurchaseOrderID,
              CONVERT(date, OrderDate)      AS OrderDate,
              FORMAT(SubTotal, 'c', 'en-US')    AS SubTotal
FROM POH;
```

PurchaseOrderID	OrderDate	SubTotal
3553	2008-08-03	$9,948.33
1637	2008-02-07	$25,531.28
2796	2008-05-31	$97.97
684	2007-09-26	$270.81
3478	2008-07-28	$28,072.28
1904	2008-03-09	$43,878.45
755	2007-10-01	$50,860.43
2660	2008-05-19	$944.37
2787	2008-05-31	$34,644.23
601	2007-09-19	$146.29

```
-- SELECT INTO with data transformation
SELECT   CultureID
       ,UPPER(Name)                  AS Name
        ,CONVERT(date,ModifiedDate)  AS ModifiedDate
INTO dbo.Culture
FROM [AdventureWorks2012].[Production].[Culture]
ORDER BY CultureID;
-- (8 row(s) affected)
```

```
SELECT * FROM dbo.Culture WHERE CultureID != '' ORDER BY CultureID;  -- exclude empty ID
```

CultureID	Name	ModifiedDate
ar	ARABIC	2002-06-01
en	ENGLISH	2002-06-01
es	SPANISH	2002-06-01
fr	FRENCH	2002-06-01
he	HEBREW	2002-06-01
th	THAI	2002-06-01
zh-cht	CHINESE	2002-06-01

CHAPTER 9: SELECT INTO Table Creation & Population

SELECT INTO with IDENTITY Column

The column data types are inherited in SELECT INTO table create. The IDENTITY property is also inherited in a SELECT INTO unless it is prevented with special coding. No other constraint is inherited.

```
-- IDENTITY property of ProductID is inherited
SELECT TOP (0) ProductID, ProductNumber, ListPrice, Color
INTO tempdb.dbo.Product
FROM AdventureWorks2012.Production.Product;
-- (0 row(s) affected)
```

```
INSERT tempdb.dbo.Product (ProductID, ProductNumber, ListPrice, Color)
SELECT 20001, 'FERRARI007RED', $400000, 'Red';
GO
/* Msg 544, Level 16, State 1, Line 1
Cannot insert explicit value for identity column in table 'Product'
when IDENTITY_INSERT is set to OFF. */
```

```
-- The following is one way to check for IDENTITY property
USE tempdb;
EXEC sp_help 'dbo.Product';
```

Identity	Seed	Increment	Not For Replication
ProductID	1	1	0

```
USE AdventureWorks2012;
```

```
DROP TABLE tempdb.dbo.Product;
GO
```

```
-- The following construct will prevent IDENTITY inheritance
SELECT TOP (0)    CAST(ProductID AS INT) AS ProductID,  -- Cast/Convert the identity column
                 ProductNumber,
                 ListPrice,
                 Color
INTO tempdb.dbo.Product  FROM AdventureWorks2012.Production.Product;
-- (0 row(s) affected)
```

```
INSERT tempdb.dbo.Product (ProductID, ProductNumber, ListPrice, Color)
SELECT 20001, 'FERRARI007RED', $400000, 'Firehouse Red';
GO
```

```
SELECT * FROM tempdb.dbo.Product;
```

ProductID	ProductNumber	ListPrice	Color
20001	FERRARI007RED	400000.00	Firehouse Red

CHAPTER 9: SELECT INTO Table Creation & Population

SELECT INTO From Multiple-Table Queries

SELECT INTO works with any query with some restrictions such as XML data type columns cannot be included.

```
SELECT   JobCandidateID
        ,BusinessEntityID
        ,Resume
        ,ModifiedDate
 INTO dbo.Resume
 FROM AdventureWorks2012.HumanResources.JobCandidate;
/* ERROR Msg 458, Level 16, State 0, Line 2
Cannot create the SELECT INTO target table "dbo.Resume" because the xml column "Resume"
is typed with a schema collection "HRResumeSchemaCollection" from database "AdventureWorks2012".
Xml columns cannot refer to schemata across databases. */
```

```
-- SELECT INTO from joined tables
 SELECT            soh.SalesOrderID,
                   OrderDate,
                   OrderQty,
                   ProductID
INTO   SalesOrder
FROM   Sales.SalesOrderHeader soh
     INNER JOIN Sales.SalesOrderDetail sod     ON soh.SalesOrderID = sod.SalesOrderID ;
-- (121317 row(s) affected)
```

```
SELECT TOP(5) * FROM SalesOrder ORDER BY SalesOrderID DESC;
```

SalesOrderID	OrderDate	OrderQty	ProductID
75123	2008-07-31 00:00:00.000	1	878
75123	2008-07-31 00:00:00.000	1	879
75123	2008-07-31 00:00:00.000	1	712
75122	2008-07-31 00:00:00.000	1	878
75122	2008-07-31 00:00:00.000	1	712

```
-- Check column types - partial results
EXEC sp_help SalesOrder;
```

Column_name	Type	Computed	Length	Prec	Scale
SalesOrderID	int	no	4	10	0
OrderDate	datetime	no	8		
OrderQty	smallint	no	2	5	0
ProductID	int	no	4	10	0

SELECT INTO with Sorted Table Population

We can create ordering in a new temporary table by using the IDENTITY function. **There is no guarantee though that the IDENTITY sequence will be the same as the ORDER BY clause specifications.** Unique identity values on the other hand are guaranteed.

```
SELECT  ID=IDENTITY(int, 1, 1),
        ProductNumber,
        ProductID=CAST(ProductID AS INT),
        ListPrice,
        COALESCE(Color, 'N/A') AS Color
INTO  #Product
FROM  Production.Product WHERE  ListPrice > 0.0 ORDER BY ProductNumber;
GO
-- (304 row(s) affected)
```

```
SELECT TOP 10 * FROM #Product  ORDER BY ID;
```

ID	ProductNumber	ProductID	ListPrice	Color
1	BB-7421	994	53.99	N/A
2	BB-8107	995	101.24	N/A
3	BB-9108	996	121.49	N/A
4	BC-M005	871	9.99	N/A
5	BC-R205	872	8.99	N/A
6	BK-M18B-40	989	539.99	Black
7	BK-M18B-42	990	539.99	Black
8	BK-M18B-44	991	539.99	Black
9	BK-M18B-48	992	539.99	Black
10	BK-M18B-52	993	539.99	Black

```
-- Permanent table create
SELECT * INTO ProductByProdNo FROM #Product ORDER BY ID;
GO -- (304 row(s) affected)
```

```
SELECT TOP (6) * FROM ProductByProdNo ORDER BY ID;
```

ID	ProductNumber	ProductID	ListPrice	Color
1	BB-7421	994	53.99	N/A
2	BB-8107	995	101.24	N/A
3	BB-9108	996	121.49	N/A
4	BC-M005	871	9.99	N/A
5	BC-R205	872	8.99	N/A
6	BK-M18B-40	989	539.99	Black

CHAPTER 9: SELECT INTO Table Creation & Population

SELECT INTO with Random Population

We can create a random population by sorting with the NEWID() function.

```
USE tempdb;

SELECT TOP(5)   ID              = ContactID,
                FullName        = CONCAT(FirstName, ' ', LastName),
                Email           = EmailAddress
INTO   dbo.Person
FROM   AdventureWorks.Person.Contact
WHERE  EmailPromotion = 2
ORDER  BY NEWID();
-- (5 row(s) affected)

SELECT * FROM  dbo.Person;
GO
```

ID	FullName	Email
1075	Diane Glimp	diane0@adventure-works.com
15739	Jesse Mitchell	jesse36@adventure-works.com
5405	Jose Patterson	jose33@adventure-works.com
1029	Wanida Benshoof	wanida0@adventure-works.com
8634	Andrea Collins	andrea26@adventure-works.com

```
-- Rerun the script again after dropping the table
DROP TABLE tempdb.dbo.Person;
GO
-- Command(s) completed successfully.

SELECT TOP(5) ID        = ContactID,
        FullName        = CONCAT(FirstName, ' ', LastName),
        Email           = EmailAddress
INTO   dbo.Person
FROM   AdventureWorks.Person.Contact
WHERE  EmailPromotion = 2 ORDER  BY NEWID();

SELECT * FROM  dbo.Person;
```

ID	FullName	Email
9984	Sydney Clark	sydney81@adventure-works.com
15448	Denise Raman	denise13@adventure-works.com
12442	Carson Jenkins	carson5@adventure-works.com
1082	Mary Baker	mary1@adventure-works.com
18728	Emma Kelly	emma46@adventure-works.com

Combining SELECT INTO with INSERT SELECT

First we create an empty table with identity property using SELECT INTO, then we populate it with INSERT SELECT.

```
-- Following will fail - only one IDENTITY column per table
SELECT TOP (0)    IDENTITY(int, 1, 1)              AS ID,
        ProductID,
        Name                              AS ProductName,
        ListPrice,
        COALESCE(Color, 'N/A')            AS Color
INTO  #Product  FROM  Production.Product;
GO
/* ERROR Msg 8108, Level 16, State 1, Line 1
Cannot add identity column, using the SELECT INTO statement, to table '#Product',
which already has column 'ProductID' that inherits the identity property.  */
```

```
SELECT TOP (0)    IDENTITY(int, 1, 1)      AS ID,
        CAST(ProductID AS INT)            AS ProductID, -- IDENTITY will not be inherited
        Name                              AS ProductName,
        ListPrice,
        COALESCE(Color, 'N/A')            AS Color
INTO  #Product  FROM  Production.Product;
GO
-- (0 row(s) affected)
```

```
DECLARE @Rows tinyint = 5;
INSERT INTO #Product    (ProductID, ProductName,  ListPrice,  Color)
SELECT TOP (@Rows)        ProductID,
                Name,
                ListPrice,
                Color
FROM   Production.Product
WHERE  ListPrice > 0.0    AND Color IS NOT NULL  ORDER BY ListPrice DESC;
-- (5 row(s) affected)
```

```
SELECT * FROM  #Product;
```

ID	ProductID	ProductName	ListPrice	Color
1	749	Road-150 Red, 62	3578.27	Red
2	750	Road-150 Red, 44	3578.27	Red
3	751	Road-150 Red, 48	3578.27	Red
4	752	Road-150 Red, 52	3578.27	Red
5	753	Road-150 Red, 56	3578.27	Red

Copy Table into Different Database with SELECT INTO

It requires 3-part name referencing to operate between databases (cross database). The current database requires only 2-part object name referencing.

```
USE tempdb;
SELECT *, CopyDate = CONVERT(DATE,GETDATE())
INTO Department
FROM AdventureWorks.HumanResources.Department  ORDER BY DepartmentID;
GO
```

```
SELECT TOP (5) DepartmentID, Department=Name, CopyDate  FROM Department ORDER BY DepartmentID;
```

DepartmentID	Department	CopyDate
1	Engineering	2016-07-19
2	Tool Design	2016-07-19
3	Sales	2016-07-19
4	Marketing	2016-07-19
5	Purchasing	2016-07-19

```
-- SQL drop table - full referencing of table for mistake reduction
DROP TABLE tempdb.dbo.Department;
```

Combining SELECT INTO with UPDATE

After creating a populated table with SELECT INTO, we perform UPDATE to change a column.

```
USE tempdb;
SELECT TOP 100 * INTO  PurchaseOrderHeader
FROM   AdventureWorks.Purchasing.PurchaseOrderHeader  ORDER  BY NEWID();
GO
```

```
-- The following logic updates dates to different values - multiple value assignment operator
DECLARE @OrderDate DATETIME = CURRENT_TIMESTAMP;
UPDATE PurchaseOrderHeader  SET    @OrderDate = OrderDate = dateadd(day, -1, @OrderDate);
GO
```

```
SELECT TOP (5) PurchaseOrderID,   VendorID,  OrderDate  FROM  PurchaseOrderHeader;
```

PurchaseOrderID	VendorID	OrderDate
631	39	2016-07-18 09:03:18.193
759	32	2016-07-17 09:03:18.193
2652	33	2016-07-16 09:03:18.193
769	80	2016-07-15 09:03:18.193
949	30	2016-07-14 09:03:18.193

```
DROP TABLE tempdb.dbo.PurchaseOrderHeader;
```

SELECT INTO Table Create from Complex Query

SELECT INTO table create works from simple to very complex queries.

```
USE AdventureWorks;

SELECT          SalesStaff      = CONCAT(C.LastName, ', ', C.FirstName),
                ZipCode         = A.PostalCode,
                TotalSales      = FORMAT(SUM(SOD.LineTotal),'c', 'en-US'),
                PercentOfTotal  = FORMAT( SUM(SOD.LineTotal) /
                                        SUM(SUM(SOD.LineTotal))
                                        OVER (PARTITION BY 1, 2 ),'p')
INTO   tempdb.dbo.SalesSummary
FROM   Person.Contact C
    INNER JOIN Person.[Address] A
        ON A.AddressID = C.ContactID
    INNER JOIN Sales.SalesOrderHeader SOH
        ON SOH.SalesPersonID = C.ContactID
    INNER JOIN Sales.SalesOrderDetail SOD
        ON SOD.SalesOrderID = SOH.SalesOrderID
WHERE  TerritoryID IS NOT NULL
GROUP  BY C.FirstName,    C.LastName,    A.PostalCode,    C.ContactID
ORDER  BY SalesStaff,    ZipCode;
-- (17 row(s) affected)

-- SELECT 10 rows random, then sort them by name (SalesStaff) - derived table construct
SELECT * FROM
(
        SELECT TOP (10) *
        FROM   tempdb.dbo.SalesSummary ORDER  BY NEWID()
) x        -- x is called a derived table; also dubbed SELECT FROM SELECT
ORDER BY SalesStaff;
```

SalesStaff	ZipCode	TotalSales	PercentOfTotal
Dusza, Maciej	98027	$9,293,903.00	11.55 %
Dyck, Shelley	98027	$10,367,007.43	12.88 %
Ecoffey, Linda	98027	$10,065,803.54	12.51 %
Eldridge, Carla	98027	$3,609,447.21	4.48 %
Elliott, Carol	98027	$7,171,012.75	8.91 %
Emanuel, Michael	98055	$5,926,418.36	7.36 %
Erickson, Gail	98055	$8,503,338.65	10.56 %
Estes, Julie	98055	$172,524.45	0.21 %
Esteves, Janeth	98055	$1,827,066.71	2.27 %
Evans, Twanna	98055	$1,421,810.92	1.77 %

```
DROP TABLE tempdb.dbo.SalesSummary ;
```

CHAPTER 9: SELECT INTO Table Creation & Population

SELECT INTO Table Create from System Procedure Execution

Using OPENROWSET and OPENQUERY, we can make the result sets of system procedures and user stored procedures table-like.

```
SELECT *
INTO  #spwho
FROM  OPENROWSET ( 'SQLOLEDB',
        'SERVER=.;Trusted_Connection=yes',
        'SET FMTONLY OFF EXEC sp_who');
GO  -- (64 row(s) affected) - it varies, depends on the number server connections
```

```
SELECT TOP (5) * FROM #spwho ORDER BY spid;
GO
```

spid	ecid	status	loginame	hostname	blk	dbname	cmd	request_id
1	0	background	sa		0	NULL	LOG WRITER	0
2	0	background	sa		0	NULL	RECOVERY WRITER	0
3	0	background	sa		0	NULL	LAZY WRITER	0
4	0	background	sa		0	NULL	LOCK MONITOR	0
5	0	background	sa		0	master	SIGNAL HANDLER	0

```
/* Requirement for OPENQUERY operation on current instance.

DATA ACCESS to current SQL Server named instance can be setup the following way:

exec sp_serveroption @server = 'PRODSVR\SQL2008'  -- computer name for default instance
   ,@optname = 'DATA ACCESS'
   ,@optvalue = 'TRUE' ;

This way, OPENQUERY can be used against current instance. Usually OPENQUERY is used to access linked
servers.
*/
```

```
SELECT  DB_NAME(dbid) AS DB, *
INTO  #splock
FROM  OPENQUERY(HPESTAR, 'EXEC sp_lock');
GO
-- (156 row(s) affected) - it varies, depends how busy is the system with OLTP activities
```

```
SELECT TOP(2) * FROM  #splock ;
```

DB	spid	dbid	ObjId	IndId	Type	Resource	Mode	Status
ReportServer	52	5	0	0	DB		S	GRANT
msdb	54	4	0	0	DB		S	GRANT

CHAPTER 9: SELECT INTO Table Creation & Population

SELECT INTO from OPENQUERY Stored Procedure Execution

The following is the only way to make stored procedure results table-like. The bill-of-materials stored procedure is recursive.

```
USE AdventureWorks2012;
GO
SELECT Name FROM Production.Product WHERE ProductID = 900;   -- LL Touring Frame - Yellow, 50

--  First we test the query execution
DECLARE @RC int;  DECLARE @StartProductID int; DECLARE @CheckDate datetime;

EXECUTE @RC = [dbo].[uspGetBillOfMaterials]     @StartProductID = 900 , @CheckDate = '20080216';
GO
-- 24 rows returned

-- Transform query into SELECT INTO table create  - Single quotes (around date literal) must be doubled
SELECT * INTO BOM900
FROM OPENQUERY(HPESTAR, 'EXECUTE [AdventureWorks2012].[dbo].[uspGetBillOfMaterials]
900,''20080216''');
GO
-- (1 row(s) affected)          -- create table
-- (24 row(s) affected)         -- inserts

SELECT * FROM BOM900;
```

ProductAssemblyID	ComponentID	ComponentDesc	TotalQuantity	StandardCost	ListPrice	BOMLevel	RecursionLevel
900	324	Chain Stays	2.00	0.00	0.00	2	0
900	325	Decal 1	2.00	0.00	0.00	2	0
900	326	Decal 2	1.00	0.00	0.00	2	0
900	327	Down Tube	1.00	0.00	0.00	2	0
900	399	Head Tube	1.00	0.00	0.00	2	0
900	496	Paint - Yellow	8.00	0.00	0.00	2	0
900	532	Seat Stays	4.00	0.00	0.00	2	0
900	533	Seat Tube	1.00	0.00	0.00	2	0
900	534	Top Tube	1.00	0.00	0.00	2	0
900	802	LL Fork	1.00	65.8097	148.22	2	0
324	486	Metal Sheet 5	1.00	0.00	0.00	3	1
327	483	Metal Sheet 3	1.00	0.00	0.00	3	1
399	485	Metal Sheet 4	1.00	0.00	0.00	3	1
532	484	Metal Sheet 7	1.00	0.00	0.00	3	1
533	478	Metal Bar 2	1.00	0.00	0.00	3	1
534	482	Metal Sheet 2	1.00	0.00	0.00	3	1
802	316	Blade	2.00	0.00	0.00	3	1
802	331	Fork End	2.00	0.00	0.00	3	1
802	350	Fork Crown	1.00	0.00	0.00	3	1
802	531	Steerer	1.00	0.00	0.00	3	1
316	486	Metal Sheet 5	1.00	0.00	0.00	4	2
331	482	Metal Sheet 2	1.00	0.00	0.00	4	2
350	486	Metal Sheet 5	1.00	0.00	0.00	4	2
531	487	Metal Sheet 6	1.00	0.00	0.00	4	2

Execution of SELECT INTO from Dynamic SQL

T-SQL script demonstrates SELECT INTO execution within a dynamic SQL. Biggest challenge is to get the single quotes right. CHAR(39) use is an option.

```
-- SQL Server 2008 new feature: instant assignment to a localvariable
DECLARE @DynamicQuery nvarchar(max) =
    'SELECT *
    INTO BOM400
    FROM OPENQUERY(' + QUOTENAME(CONVERT(sysname, @@SERVERNAME))+ ',
    ''EXECUTE [AdventureWorks2012].[dbo].[uspGetWhereUsedProductID] 400,
    ''''2007-11-21'''''')' ;
```

```
PRINT @DynamicQuery;      -- test query;  this is the static query which will be executed
/*
SELECT *
    INTO BOM400
    FROM OPENQUERY([HPESTAR],
    'EXECUTE [AdventureWorks2012].[dbo].[uspGetWhereUsedProductID] 400,
    ''2007-11-21''')
*/
```

```
EXEC sp_executeSQL @DynamicQuery;
GO
-- (64 row(s) affected)
```

```
SELECT TOP ( 5 ) *
FROM BOM400
ORDER BY NEWID() ;
```

ProductAssemblyID	ComponentID	ComponentDesc	TotalQuantity	StandardCost	ListPrice	BOMLevel	RecursionLevel
761	818	Road-650 Red, 62	1.00	486.7066	782.99	1	1
987	823	Mountain-500 Silver, 48	1.00	308.2179	564.99	1	1
990	823	Mountain-500 Black, 42	1.00	294.5797	539.99	1	1
765	826	Road-650 Black, 58	1.00	486.7066	782.99	1	1
770	818	Road-650 Black, 52	1.00	486.7066	782.99	1	1

```
-- Cleanup
DROP TABLE BOM400;
GO
```

SELECT INTO Table Create from View

Transact-SQL script demonstrates how to import view query results into a table.

```
SELECT [FullName],
    [SalesPersonID]                              AS StaffID,
    [SalesTerritory],
    COALESCE(FORMAT([2006], 'c','en-US'), '')    AS [2006],
    COALESCE(FORMAT([2007], 'c','en-US'), '')    AS [2007],
    COALESCE(FORMAT([2008], 'c','en-US'), '')    AS [2008]
INTO  #Sales
FROM   [AdventureWorks2012].[Sales].[vSalesPersonSalesByFiscalYears]
ORDER  BY SalesTerritory, FullName;
GO
```

```
SELECT *
FROM   #Sales
ORDER  BY SalesTerritory, FullName;
GO
```

FullName	StaffID	SalesTerritory	2006	2007	2008
Lynn N Tsoflias	286	Australia			$1,421,810.92
Garrett R Vargas	278	Canada	$930,259.47	$1,225,468.28	$1,453,719.47
José Edvaldo Saraiva	282	Canada	$2,088,491.17	$1,233,386.47	$2,604,540.72
Jillian Carson	277	Central	$2,737,537.88	$4,138,847.30	$3,189,418.37
Ranjit R Varkey Chudukatil	290	France		$1,388,272.61	$3,121,616.32
Rachel B Valdez	288	Germany			$1,827,066.71
Michael G Blythe	275	Northeast	$1,602,472.39	$3,928,252.44	$3,763,178.18
David R Campbell	283	Northwest	$1,017,402.86	$1,139,529.55	$1,573,012.94
Pamela O Ansman-Wolfe	280	Northwest	$1,226,461.83	$746,063.63	$1,352,577.13
Tete A Mensa-Annan	284	Northwest		$735,983.49	$1,576,562.20
Tsvi Michael Reiter	279	Southeast	$2,645,436.95	$2,210,390.19	$2,315,185.61
Linda C Mitchell	276	Southwest	$2,260,118.45	$3,855,520.42	$4,251,368.55
Shu K Ito	281	Southwest	$1,593,742.92	$2,374,727.02	$2,458,535.62
Jae B Pak	289	United Kingdom		$4,386,467.42	$4,116,871.23

SELECT INTO Data Import from Excel

T-SQL OPENROWSET query imports data into a temporary table from Excel. Your Excel library maybe different than the one in the example.

```
SELECT *  INTO ContactList  FROM OPENROWSET('Microsoft.Jet.OLEDB.4.0',
        'Excel 8.0;Database=D:\data\excel\Contact.xls', 'SELECT * FROM [Contact$]')
-- (19972 row(s) affected)
```

CHAPTER 10: Modify Data - INSERT, UPDATE, DELETE & MERGE

INSERT VALUES - Table Value Constructor

T-SQL scripts illustrate the use of INSERT VALUES with Table Value Constructor (a list of values). Because the text columns are defined as nvarchar the string literals are prefixed with "N" indicating UNICODE literal. Since only Latin letters used, the "N" can be omitted.

```
USE tempdb;
SELECT TOP 0 * INTO dbo.Department FROM AdventureWorks2012.HumanResources.Department;
-- This is necessary because IDENTITY property was inherited in the SELECT INTO
SET IDENTITY_INSERT dbo.Department ON;
GO
INSERT dbo.Department (DepartmentID, Name, GroupName, ModifiedDate) VALUES
(1, N'Engineering', N'Research and Development', getdate()),
(2, N'Tool Design', N'Research and Development', getdate()),
(3, N'Sales', N'Sales and Marketing', getdate()),
(4, N'Marketing', N'Sales and Marketing', getdate()),
(5, N'Purchasing', N'Inventory Management', getdate()),
(6, N'Research and Development', N'Research and Development', getdate()),
(7, N'Production', N'Manufacturing', getdate()),
(8, N'Production Control', N'Manufacturing', getdate()),
(9, N'Human Resources', N'Executive General and Administration', getdate()),
(10, N'Finance', N'Executive General and Administration', getdate()),
(11, N'Information Services', N'Executive General and Administration', getdate()),
(12, N'Document Control', N'Quality Assurance', getdate()),
(13, N'Quality Assurance', N'Quality Assurance', getdate()),
(14, N'Facilities and Maintenance', N'Executive General and Administration', getdate()),
(15, N'Shipping and Receiving', N'Inventory Management', getdate()),
(16, N'Executive', N'Executive General and Administration',getdate());
GO
SET IDENTITY_INSERT dbo.Department OFF;
GO
SELECT TOP 4 * FROM dbo.Department ORDER BY DepartmentID;
```

DepartmentID	Name	GroupName	ModifiedDate
1	Engineering	Research and Development	2016-08-02 06:35:44.623
2	Tool Design	Research and Development	2016-08-02 06:35:44.623
3	Sales	Sales and Marketing	2016-08-02 06:35:44.623
4	Marketing	Sales and Marketing	2016-08-02 06:35:44.623

```
DROP TABLE tempdb.dbo.Department;
```

INSERT VALUES - Ye Olde Way

T-SQL scripts illustrate the INSERT VALUES for single row insert, the only available method prior to SQL Server 2008.

```
USE AdventureWorks2012;
GO

CREATE TABLE Shift(
        ShiftID tinyint IDENTITY(1,1) NOT NULL,
        Name dbo.Name NOT NULL,
        StartTime time(7) NOT NULL,
        EndTime time(7) NOT NULL,
        ModifiedDate datetime NOT NULL,
        CONSTRAINT PK_Shift_ShiftID PRIMARY KEY CLUSTERED (ShiftID ASC) );
GO

SET IDENTITY_INSERT Shift ON;               -- To force insert into ShiftID

INSERT Shift (ShiftID, Name, StartTime, EndTime, ModifiedDate)
VALUES (1, N'Day', CAST(0x0700D85EAC3A0000 AS Time), CAST(0x07001882BA7D0000 AS Time),
CAST(0x0000921E00000000 AS DateTime))
INSERT Shift (ShiftID, Name, StartTime, EndTime, ModifiedDate)
VALUES (2, N'Evening', CAST(0x07001882BA7D0000 AS Time), CAST(0x070058A5C8C00000 AS Time),
getdate());
INSERT Shift (ShiftID, Name, StartTime, EndTime, ModifiedDate)
VALUES (3, N'Night', CAST(0x070058A5C8C00000 AS Time), CAST(0x0700D85EAC3A0000 AS Time),
CURRENT_TIMESTAMP);
GO

SET IDENTITY_INSERT Shift OFF;

ALTER TABLE Shift ADD  CONSTRAINT DF_Shift_ModifiedDate  DEFAULT (getdate()) FOR ModifiedDate
GO

SELECT * FROM Shift ORDER BY ShiftID;
GO
```

ShiftID	Name	StartTime	EndTime	ModifiedDate
1	Day	07:00:00.0000000	15:00:00.0000000	2002-06-01 00:00:00.000
2	Evening	15:00:00.0000000	23:00:00.0000000	2018-08-20 19:31:02.293
3	Night	23:00:00.0000000	07:00:00.0000000	2018-08-20 19:31:02.293

```
DROP TABLE Shift;
GO
```

CHAPTER 10: Modify Data - INSERT, UPDATE, DELETE & MERGE

INSERT SELECT

INSERT SELECT Literal List

T-SQL scripts demonstrate the insertion of literal records (rows) using INSERT SELECT.

```
USE tempdb;
GO
SELECT TOP 0 * INTO dbo.Department FROM AdventureWorks2012.HumanResources.Department;
GO
-- This is necessary because IDENTITY property was inherited in the SELECT INTO
SET IDENTITY_INSERT dbo.Department ON;
GO
INSERT dbo.Department (DepartmentID, Name, GroupName, ModifiedDate)
SELECT 1, N'Engineering', N'Research and Development', CURRENT_TIMESTAMP  UNION
SELECT 2, N'Tool Design', N'Research and Development', CURRENT_TIMESTAMP  UNION
SELECT 3, N'Sales', N'Sales and Marketing', CURRENT_TIMESTAMP  UNION
SELECT 4, N'Marketing', N'Sales and Marketing', CURRENT_TIMESTAMP  UNION
SELECT 5, N'Purchasing', N'Inventory Management', CURRENT_TIMESTAMP  UNION
SELECT 6, N'Research and Development', N'Research and Development', CURRENT_TIMESTAMP  UNION
SELECT 7, N'Production', N'Manufacturing', CURRENT_TIMESTAMP  UNION
SELECT 8, N'Production Control', N'Manufacturing', CURRENT_TIMESTAMP  UNION
SELECT 9, N'Human Resources', N'Executive General and Administration', CURRENT_TIMESTAMP  UNION
SELECT 10, N'Finance', N'Executive General and Administration', CURRENT_TIMESTAMP  UNION
SELECT 11, N'Information Services', N'Executive General and Administration', CURRENT_TIMESTAMP
UNION
SELECT 12, N'Document Control', N'Quality Assurance', CURRENT_TIMESTAMP  UNION
SELECT 13, N'Quality Assurance', N'Quality Assurance', CURRENT_TIMESTAMP  UNION
SELECT 14, N'Facilities and Maintenance', N'Executive General and Administration',
CURRENT_TIMESTAMP  UNION
SELECT 15, N'Shipping and Receiving', N'Inventory Management', CURRENT_TIMESTAMP  UNION
SELECT 16, N'Executive', N'Executive General and Administration', CURRENT_TIMESTAMP;
GO
SET IDENTITY_INSERT dbo.Department OFF;
GO
SELECT TOP 4 * FROM dbo.Department ORDER BY DepartmentID;
GO
```

DepartmentID	Name	GroupName	ModifiedDate
1	Engineering	Research and Development	2016-08-02 06:35:44.623
2	Tool Design	Research and Development	2016-08-02 06:35:44.623
3	Sales	Sales and Marketing	2016-08-02 06:35:44.623
4	Marketing	Sales and Marketing	2016-08-02 06:35:44.623

```
-- Cleanup
DROP TABLE tempdb.dbo.Department;
```

CHAPTER 10: Modify Data - INSERT, UPDATE, DELETE & MERGE

INSERT SELECT from Table

T-SQL script demonstrates table population with table SELECT.

```
USE tempdb;
SELECT TOP 0 * INTO dbo.Department FROM AdventureWorks2012.HumanResources.Department;
GO
-- This is necessary because IDENTITY property was inherited in the SELECT INTO
SET IDENTITY_INSERT dbo.Department ON;
GO
INSERT dbo.Department (DepartmentID, Name, GroupName, ModifiedDate)
SELECT TOP 15 DepartmentID, Name, GroupName, ModifiedDate
FROM AdventureWorks2012.HumanResources.Department  ORDER BY DepartmentID;
GO
-- (15 row(s) affected)
SELECT TOP 4 * FROM dbo.Department ORDER BY DepartmentID;
```

DepartmentID	Name	GroupName	ModifiedDate
1	Engineering	Research and Development	2016-08-02 06:35:44.623
2	Tool Design	Research and Development	2016-08-02 06:35:44.623
3	Sales	Sales and Marketing	2016-08-02 06:35:44.623
4	Marketing	Sales and Marketing	2016-08-02 06:35:44.623

SCOPE_IDENTITY() for Last-Inserted IDENTITY Value

The last inserted IDENTITY value can be returned with the SCOPE_IDENTITY() or @@IDENTITY system function (variable). SCOPE_IDENTITY() is better choice since it is within the current connection scope. @@IDENTITY is at server level.

```
INSERT dbo.Department (DepartmentID, Name, GroupName, ModifiedDate)
SELECT TOP 1 DepartmentID, Name, GroupName, ModifiedDate
FROM AdventureWorks2012.HumanResources.Department  ORDER BY DepartmentID DESC;
GO
-- (1 row(s) affected)
```

Alternate is SELECT @@IDENTITY; @@ variables are system variables.

```
DECLARE @LastID INT = SCOPE_IDENTITY();
SELECT @LastID;   -- 16
```

```
SET IDENTITY_INSERT dbo.Department OFF;
GO
```

```
-- Cleanup
DROP TABLE tempdb.dbo.Department;
```

INSERT with Subset of Columns

Only the required columns must be present in the INSERT column list. A column with default or NULL property can be omitted. In the next T-SQL script, ModifiedDate is filled by default with getdate().

```
USE tempdb;
SELECT TOP 0 * INTO dbo.Department FROM AdventureWorks2012.HumanResources.Department;
GO
ALTER TABLE dbo.Department ADD CONSTRAINT DF_Dept_ModDate DEFAULT getdate() FOR
ModifiedDate;
GO
SET IDENTITY_INSERT dbo.Department ON;
GO
INSERT dbo.Department (DepartmentID, Name, GroupName)
SELECT DepartmentID, Name, GroupName  FROM AdventureWorks2012.HumanResources.Department;
GO
-- (16 row(s) affected)
SELECT TOP 4 * FROM dbo.Department ORDER BY DepartmentID;
```

DepartmentID	Name	GroupName	ModifiedDate
1	Engineering	Research and Development	2016-08-02 06:35:44.623
2	Tool Design	Research and Development	2016-08-02 06:35:44.623
3	Sales	Sales and Marketing	2016-08-02 06:35:44.623
4	Marketing	Sales and Marketing	2016-08-02 06:35:44.623

Capturing Last-Inserted IDENTITY Set Values with OUTPUT

When more than one row is inserted with one statement, the OUTPUT clause can be used to capture the list of just inserted IDENTITY values.

```
DECLARE @LastInserted TABLE (ID INT);
INSERT dbo.Department (DepartmentID, Name, GroupName)
        OUTPUT inserted.DepartmentID INTO @LastInserted
SELECT DepartmentID+1000, Name, GroupName  FROM
AdventureWorks2012.HumanResources.Department;
SELECT TOP 5 * FROM @LastInserted ORDER BY ID;
GO
```

ID
1001
1002
1003
1004
1005

```
SET IDENTITY_INSERT dbo.Department OFF;
DROP TABLE tempdb.dbo.Department;
```

CHAPTER 10: Modify Data - INSERT, UPDATE, DELETE & MERGE

INSERT EXEC Stored Procedure

Data can be directly inserted from the execution of a user-defined stored procedure or system procedure. We create a table and a stored procedure, then perform INSERT EXEC.

```
USE AdventureWorks2012;
IF OBJECT_ID ('dbo.EmployeeSales', 'U') IS NOT NULL   DROP TABLE dbo.EmployeeSales;
IF OBJECT_ID ('dbo.uspGetEmployeeSales', 'P') IS NOT NULL   DROP PROCEDURE uspGetEmployeeSales;
CREATE TABLE dbo.EmployeeSales
 (
   BusinessEntityID        VARCHAR(11) NOT NULL PRIMARY KEY,
   LastName                VARCHAR(40) NOT NULL,
   SalesDollars            MONEY NOT NULL,
   DataSource              VARCHAR(20) NOT NULL
 );
GO


CREATE PROCEDURE dbo.uspGetEmployeeSales AS
 BEGIN
   SELECT        e.BusinessEntityID, c.LastName, sp.SalesYTD, 'PROCEDURE'
   FROM   HumanResources.Employee AS e
      INNER JOIN Sales.SalesPerson AS sp
          ON e.BusinessEntityID = sp.BusinessEntityID
      INNER JOIN Person.Person AS c
          ON e.BusinessEntityID = c.BusinessEntityID
   WHERE  e.BusinessEntityID > 280
   ORDER  BY      e.BusinessEntityID,  c.LastName;
 END;
GO


--INSERT...EXECUTE user-defined stored procedure
INSERT EmployeeSales EXECUTE uspGetEmployeeSales;

SELECT * FROM  EmployeeSales;
```

BusinessEntityID	LastName	SalesDollars	DataSource
281	Ito	2458535.6169	PROCEDURE
282	Saraiva	2604540.7172	PROCEDURE
283	Campbell	1573012.9383	PROCEDURE
284	Mensa-Annan	1576562.1966	PROCEDURE
285	Abbas	172524.4512	PROCEDURE
286	Tsoflias	1421810.9242	PROCEDURE
287	Alberts	519905.932	PROCEDURE
288	Valdez	1827066.7118	PROCEDURE
289	Pak	4116871.2277	PROCEDURE
290	Varkey Chudukatil	3121616.3202	PROCEDURE

Insert Into A Table Via The Direct Execution Of An SQL Query With The EXEC Command

```
SELECT Population = count(*)  FROM   dbo.EmployeeSales;
```

Population
10

```
--INSERT...EXECUTE('string') example
INSERT EmployeeSales
EXECUTE ('      SELECT e.BusinessEntityID, c.LastName,     sp.SalesYTD, "EXEC SQL STRING"
                FROM HumanResources.Employee AS e       INNER JOIN Sales.SalesPerson AS sp
                ON e.BusinessEntityID = sp.BusinessEntityID      INNER JOIN Person.Person AS c
                ON e.BusinessEntityID = c.BusinessEntityID
                WHERE e.BusinessEntityID BETWEEN 270 and 280
                ORDER BY e.BusinessEntityID, c.LastName ');
GO
-- (7 row(s) affected)
```

Inserted number of rows can be captured for later use. **Capture must be done immediately after the monitored statement.** Any following statement will change @@ROWCOUNT value.

```
DECLARE @InsertCount int = @@ROWCOUNT;
SELECT @InsertCount;   -- 7
GO
```

```
SELECT * FROM   dbo.EmployeeSales ORDER BY BusinessEntityID ;
```

BusinessEntityID	LastName	SalesDollars	DataSource
274	Jiang	559697.5639	EXEC SQL STRING
275	Blythe	3763178.1787	EXEC SQL STRING
276	Mitchell	4251368.5497	EXEC SQL STRING
277	Carson	3189418.3662	EXEC SQL STRING
278	Vargas	1453719.4653	EXEC SQL STRING
279	Reiter	2315185.611	EXEC SQL STRING
280	Ansman-Wolfe	1352577.1325	EXEC SQL STRING
281	Ito	2458535.6169	PROCEDURE
282	Saraiva	2604540.7172	PROCEDURE
283	Campbell	1573012.9383	PROCEDURE
284	Mensa-Annan	1576562.1966	PROCEDURE
285	Abbas	172524.4512	PROCEDURE
286	Tsoflias	1421810.9242	PROCEDURE
287	Alberts	519905.932	PROCEDURE
288	Valdez	1827066.7118	PROCEDURE
289	Pak	4116871.2277	PROCEDURE
290	Varkey Chudukatil	3121616.3202	PROCEDURE

CHAPTER 10: Modify Data - INSERT, UPDATE, DELETE & MERGE

INSERT EXEC System Procedure
Data can be inserted into a table by the execution of a system procedure. We create a test table with SELECT INTO FROM OPENQUERY. We can also create the table manually if we know the data type of columns.

```
-- DATA ACCESS must be turned on at YOURSERVER SQL Server instance
SELECT TOP(0) * INTO #SPWHO
FROM OPENQUERY(YOURSERVER, 'exec sp_who');          -- will not work with sp_who2 due to duplicate
column name
```

```
/*  Table created
CREATE TABLE [dbo].[#SPWHO](
        [spid] [smallint] NOT NULL,
        [ecid] [smallint] NOT NULL,
        [status] [nchar](30) NOT NULL,
        [loginame] [nvarchar](128) NULL,
        [hostname] [nchar](128) NOT NULL,
        [blk] [char](5) NULL,
        [dbname] [nvarchar](128) NULL,
        [cmd] [nchar](16) NOT NULL,
        [request_id] [int] NOT NULL
); */
```

```
INSERT #SPWHO   EXEC sp_who
```

The blk column contains blocking spid if any. A large update for example may block other queries until it completes. The spid of the current session is @@SPID.

```
SELECT * FROM  #SPWHO
GO
-- (42 row(s) affected) - Partial results.
```

spid	ecid	status	loginame	hostname	blk	dbname	cmd	request_id
21	0	background	sa		0	master	TASK MANAGER	0
22	0	background	sa		0	master	CHECKPOINT	0
23	0	sleeping	sa		0	master	TASK MANAGER	0
24	0	background	sa		0	master	BRKR TASK	0
25	0	sleeping	sa		0	master	TASK MANAGER	0
26	0	sleeping	sa		0	master	TASK MANAGER	0
27	0	sleeping	sa		0	master	TASK MANAGER	0
28	0	sleeping	sa		0	master	TASK MANAGER	0
29	0	sleeping	sa		0	master	TASK MANAGER	0
30	0	sleeping	sa		0	master	TASK MANAGER	0
40	0	background	sa		0	master	BRKR TASK	0
42	0	background	sa		0	master	BRKR TASK	0
43	0	background	sa		0	master	BRKR TASK	0
51	0	sleeping	YOURSERVER \Owner	YOURSERVER	0	AdventureWorks2012	AWAITING COMMAND	0
52	0	sleeping	NT SERVICE\SQLSERVERAGENT	YOURSERVER	0	msdb	AWAITING COMMAND	0

```
DROP TABLE #SPWHO
GO
```

CHAPTER 10: Modify Data - INSERT, UPDATE, DELETE & MERGE

INSERT Only New Rows Omit the Rest

INSERT only new records. If record exists, do nothing. Note: DELETE will not rollback IDENTITY current value. Therefore with repeated testing, the IDENTITY current value will roll ahead.

```
USE AdventureWorks2012;
SELECT COUNT(*) FROM HumanResources.Department;              -- 16


-- All rows exists, no new row insertion
INSERT HumanResources.Department (Name, GroupName)
SELECT Name, GroupName
FROM AdventureWorks2008.HumanResources.Department D
WHERE NOT EXISTS (      SELECT * FROM HumanResources.Department DD  -- Correlated subquery
                   WHERE D.Name = DD.Name
                      AND D.GroupName = DD.GroupName);
GO
-- (0 row(s) affected)


-- Prefix Name with "ZZZ", 16 successful new inserted rows
INSERT HumanResources.Department (Name, GroupName)
SELECT CONCAT('ZZZ', Name), GroupName
FROM AdventureWorks2008.HumanResources.Department D
WHERE NOT EXISTS (      SELECT * FROM HumanResources.Department DD
        WHERE DD.Name = CONCAT('ZZZ', D.Name)    AND DD.GroupName = D.GroupName);
GO
-- (16 row(s) affected)


DELETE TOP ( 7 ) HumanResources.Department WHERE Name LIKE ('ZZZ%');     -- (7 row(s) affected)
```

Only 7 rows will be inserted since the rest are duplicates.

```
INSERT HumanResources.Department (Name, GroupName)
SELECT CONCAT('ZZZ', Name), GroupName
FROM AdventureWorks2008.HumanResources.Department D
WHERE NOT EXISTS (      SELECT * FROM HumanResources.Department DD
                WHERE DD.Name = CONCAT('ZZZ', D.Name)    AND DD.GroupName = DD.GroupName);
GO
-- (7  row(s) affected)


SELECT * FROM HumanResources.Department;   -- (32 row(s) affected)  -- Partial results;
```

DepartmentID	Name	GroupName	ModifiedDate
16	Executive	Executive General and Administration	2002-06-01 00:00:00.000
65	ZZZEngineering	Research and Development	2018-08-13 08:32:43.133

```
DELETE HumanResources.Department WHERE Name LIKE ('ZZZ%');      -- (16 row(s) affected)
SELECT COUNT(*) FROM HumanResources.Department;              -- 16
```

CHAPTER 10: Modify Data - INSERT, UPDATE, DELETE & MERGE

DELETE - A Dangerous Operation

DELETE is a logged operation. DELETE may be slow from large table with indexes due to index reorganization. Warning: **DELETE is a dangerous operation since it removes data. Protection: regular database backup and/or creating a copy of the table prior to DELETE with SELECT INTO.**

```
USE [AdventureWorks2012]
GO
-- Create test table with SELECT INTO
SELECT [SalesOrderID]
    ,CONVERT(INT,[SalesOrderDetailID]) AS SalesOrderDetailID
    ,[CarrierTrackingNumber]
    ,[OrderQty]
    ,[ProductID]
    ,[SpecialOfferID]
    ,[UnitPrice]
    ,[UnitPriceDiscount]
    ,[LineTotal]
    ,[rowguid]
    ,[ModifiedDate]
INTO tempdb.dbo.SOD
FROM [Sales].[SalesOrderDetail];
GO
-- (121317 row(s) affected)
```

```
-- Increase table population 64 fold
INSERT  tempdb.dbo.SOD  SELECT * FROM tempdb.dbo.SOD;
GO 6
/* Beginning execution loop
(121317 row(s) affected)
(242634 row(s) affected)
(485268 row(s) affected)
(970536 row(s) affected)
(1941072 row(s) affected)
(3882144 row(s) affected)
Batch execution completed 6 times.
Execution time - 00:01.27  */
```

```
CREATE INDEX idxSOD on tempdb.dbo.SOD (SalesOrderID, ProductID);
-- Command(s) completed successfully. Time: 00:00:06
```

```
SELECT COUNT(*) FROM tempdb.dbo.SOD;  -- 7764288
```

```
-- Delete even SalesOrderID records
DELETE FROM tempdb.dbo.SOD WHERE SalesOrderID % 2 = 0;
-- (3925184 row(s) affected)  - Execution time - 00:01:30
```

TRUNCATE TABLE & DBCC CHECKIDENT

TRUNCATE TABLE command is very fast since it is minimally logged. It also resets IDENTITY column to (1,1). Warning: **TRUNCATE is a dangerous operation since it removes all the data in a table**. Protection: regular database backup and/or creating a copy of the table prior to TRUNCATE with SELECT INTO.

SELECT COUNT(*) FROM tempdb.dbo.SOD; -- 3839104

TRUNCATE TABLE tempdb.dbo.SOD;
-- Command(s) completed successfully. Execution time: 00:00:00

SELECT COUNT(*) FROM tempdb.dbo.SOD;   -- 0
GO

DROP TABLE tempdb.dbo.SOD;
GO
-- Command(s) completed successfully

-- Create new test table with SELECT INTO
USE tempdb;

SELECT * INTO SOD FROM AdventureWorks2012.Sales.SalesOrderDetail;
GO
-- (121317 row(s) affected)

-- Next IDENTITY value will be 121318.
DBCC CHECKIDENT ("dbo.SOD");
/* Checking identity information: current identity value '121317', current column value '121317'.
DBCC execution completed. If DBCC printed error messages, contact your system administrator. */

TRUNCATE TABLE SOD;
GO
-- Command(s) completed successfully.

-- IDENTITY is reset
DBCC CHECKIDENT ("dbo.SOD");
/* Checking identity information: current identity value 'NULL', current column value 'NULL'.
DBCC execution completed. If DBCC printed error messages, contact your system administrator. */

EXEC sp_help SOD;
GO
-- Partial results.

Identity	Seed	Increment	Not For Replication
SalesOrderDetailID	1	1	0

CHAPTER 10: Modify Data - INSERT, UPDATE, DELETE & MERGE

Reseeding IDENTITY

```
-- Without this command, it may not start at 1
DBCC CHECKIDENT ("SOD", RESEED, 1);


-- Populate the table with 5 rows
INSERT INTO SOD
      ([SalesOrderID]
      ,[CarrierTrackingNumber]
      ,[OrderQty]
      ,[ProductID]
      ,[SpecialOfferID]
      ,[UnitPrice]
      ,[UnitPriceDiscount]
      ,[LineTotal]
      ,[rowguid]
      ,[ModifiedDate])
SELECT  TOP (5)
      [SalesOrderID]
      ,[CarrierTrackingNumber]
      ,[OrderQty]
      ,[ProductID]
      ,[SpecialOfferID]
      ,[UnitPrice]
      ,[UnitPriceDiscount]
      ,[LineTotal]
      ,[rowguid]
      ,[ModifiedDate]
FROM AdventureWorks2012.Sales.SalesOrderDetail;
-- (5 row(s) affected)


-- Next value assigned is 6
DBCC CHECKIDENT ("dbo.SOD");
/*Checking identity information: current identity value '5', current column value '5'.
DBCC execution completed. If DBCC printed error messages, contact your system administrator. */


SELECT * FROM SOD;
-- (5 row(s) affected) - Partial results.
```

SalesOrderID	SalesOrderDetailID	CarrierTrackingNumber	OrderQty	ProductID	SpecialOfferID	UnitPrice	UnitPriceDiscount	LineTotal
43659	1	4911-403C-98	1	776	1	2024.994	0.00	2024.994000
43659	2	4911-403C-98	3	777	1	2024.994	0.00	6074.982000
43659	3	4911-403C-98	1	778	1	2024.994	0.00	2024.994000
43659	4	4911-403C-98	1	771	1	2039.994	0.00	2039.994000
43659	5	4911-403C-98	1	772	1	2039.994	0.00	2039.994000

UPDATE - A Complex Operation

UPDATE changes data content at a row and column level (cell). It is a logged operation: deleted row contains previous data, inserted row contains new data. Warning: UPDATE is a dangerous operation since it changes the data in a table. Protection: regular database backup and/or creating a copy of the table prior to UPDATE with SELECT INTO.

Some UPDATEs are reversible, such as some calculated UPDATE, others may be irreversible.

Checking Cardinality & Changes by UPDATE Prior to Execution

Since UPDATE is replaces previous data, it is very important to check prior to execution that is works correctly. It is quite simple to convert UPDATE into a checking SELECT. We intend to UPDATE the SalesYTD column with the last day sales for each salesperson.

```
USE AdventureWorks2012;
GO

SELECT   sp.BusinessEntityID, SalesYTD,
              [NewSalesYTD]=SalesYTD
         + (SELECT SUM(SODa.SubTotal)
           FROM   Sales.SalesOrderHeader AS SODa
           WHERE  CONVERT(date,SODa.OrderDate) = CONVERT(date,(SELECT MAX(OrderDate)
            FROM   Sales.SalesOrderHeader AS SODb
           WHERE
              SODb.SalesPersonID = SODa.SalesPersonID))
              AND sp.BusinessEntityID =  SODa.SalesPersonID
         GROUP  BY SODa.SalesPersonID)
FROM Sales.SalesPerson sp  ORDER BY sp.BusinessEntityID;
GO
```

BusinessEntityID	SalesYTD	NewSalesYTD
274	559697.5639	597350.4859
275	3763178.1787	4133185.161
276	4251368.5497	4534079.5941
277	3189418.3662	3527404.588
278	1453719.4653	1599132.4735
279	2315185.611	2548077.4756
280	1352577.1325	1503691.0098
281	2458535.6169	2678660.7921
282	2604540.7172	3030519.8258
283	1573012.9383	1714964.9067
284	1576562.1966	1719945.1917
285	172524.4512	176721.5652
286	1421810.9242	1649155.9058
287	519905.932	520578.226
288	1827066.7118	1962768.1658
289	4116871.2277	4556655.2802
290	3121616.3202	3240852.6195

ANSI Style UPDATE

T-SQL supports ANSI UPDATE, in addition T-SQL supports the FROM clause in UPDATE.

```
UPDATE Sales.SalesPerson
SET   SalesYTD = SalesYTD
         + (SELECT SUM(SODa.SubTotal)
           FROM  Sales.SalesOrderHeader AS SODa
           WHERE  CONVERT(date,SODa.OrderDate) =
                  CONVERT(date,(SELECT MAX(OrderDate)
             FROM  Sales.SalesOrderHeader AS SODb
             WHERE
               SODb.SalesPersonID = SODa.SalesPersonID))
               AND Sales.SalesPerson.BusinessEntityID =   SODa.SalesPersonID
           GROUP  BY SODa.SalesPersonID);
GO
-- (17 row(s) affected)
```

```
SELECT BusinessEntityID, SalesQuota, SalesYTD, SalesLastYear FROM Sales.SalesPerson
ORDER BY BusinessEntityID;
GO
```

BusinessEntityID	SalesQuota	SalesYTD	SalesLastYear
274	NULL	597350.4859	0.00
275	300000.00	4133185.161	1750406.4785
276	250000.00	4534079.5941	1439156.0291
277	250000.00	3527404.588	1997186.2037
278	250000.00	1599132.4735	1620276.8966
279	300000.00	2548077.4756	1849640.9418
280	250000.00	1503691.0098	1927059.178
281	250000.00	2678660.7921	2073505.9999
282	250000.00	3030519.8258	2038234.6549
283	250000.00	1714964.9067	1371635.3158
284	300000.00	1719945.1917	0.00
285	NULL	176721.5652	0.00
286	250000.00	1649155.9058	2278548.9776
287	NULL	520578.226	0.00
288	250000.00	1962768.1658	1307949.7917
289	250000.00	4556655.2802	1635823.3967
290	250000.00	3240852.6195	2396539.7601

UPDATE from Table in Another Database

UPDATE can be performed with data from a second database. ZorigAdventureWorks2012 is an original read-only copy of the AdventureWorks2012 database. The "Z" prefix is to force it to the end of alphabetical database list in SSMS Object Explorer.

```
UPDATE Sales.SalesPerson
       SET SalesYTD =   (
                          SELECT SalesYTD
                          FROM ZorigAdventureWorks2012.Sales.SalesPerson sp
                          WHERE sp.BusinessEntityID = Sales.SalesPerson.BusinessEntityID
                         );
GO
```

```
SELECT   BusinessEntityID,
         SalesQuota,
         SalesYTD,
         SalesLastYear
FROM Sales.SalesPerson
ORDER BY BusinessEntityID;
GO
```

BusinessEntityID	SalesQuota	SalesYTD	SalesLastYear
274	NULL	559697.5639	0.00
275	300000.00	3763178.1787	1750406.4785
276	250000.00	4251368.5497	1439156.0291
277	250000.00	3189418.3662	1997186.2037
278	250000.00	1453719.4653	1620276.8966
279	300000.00	2315185.611	1849640.9418
280	250000.00	1352577.1325	1927059.178
281	250000.00	2458535.6169	2073505.9999
282	250000.00	2604540.7172	2038234.6549
283	250000.00	1573012.9383	1371635.3158
284	300000.00	1576562.1966	0.00
285	NULL	172524.4512	0.00
286	250000.00	1421810.9242	2278548.9776
287	NULL	519905.932	0.00
288	250000.00	1827066.7118	1307949.7917
289	250000.00	4116871.2277	1635823.3967
290	250000.00	3121616.3202	2396539.7601

UPDATE Syntax Challenges

The UPDATE statement in SQL has perplexing and potentially confusing syntax. Typically mastered by expert DBA-s and SQL developers, and the rest of the database community uses it in an insecure manner: never sure if it works as intended. Simple T-SQL examples demonstrate some of the issues with the UPDATE syntax and offer solutions.

First we create a new table for experimentation from the AdventureWorks2012 database and perform a demo inner join UPDATE on the new table.

```
USE tempdb;

SELECT ProductID,
    ProductName = Name,
    StandardCost AS Cost,
    ListPrice,
    Color,
    CONVERT(date, ModifiedDate) AS ModifiedDate
INTO   Product
FROM   AdventureWorks2012.Production.Product
WHERE  ListPrice > 0.0
    AND Color IS NOT NULL;
GO
-- (245 row(s) affected)
```

```
SELECT TOP 5 * FROM Product  ORDER BY ProductID DESC;
GO
```

ProductID	ProductName	Cost	ListPrice	Color	ModifiedDate
999	Road-750 Black, 52	343.6496	539.99	Black	2008-03-11
998	Road-750 Black, 48	343.6496	539.99	Black	2008-03-11
997	Road-750 Black, 44	343.6496	539.99	Black	2008-03-11
993	Mountain-500 Black, 52	294.5797	539.99	Black	2008-03-11
992	Mountain-500 Black, 48	294.5797	539.99	Black	2008-03-11

We shall proceed and update ALL (no WHERE clause) the rows in the Product table. We increase the ListPrice by 5%.

```
UPDATE Product     SET ListPrice = ListPrice * 1.05;
-- (245 row(s) affected)
```

In this instance a reversible UPDATE. But not always.

```
UPDATE Product     SET ListPrice = ListPrice / 1.05;
-- (245 row(s) affected)
```

CHAPTER 10: Modify Data - INSERT, UPDATE, DELETE & MERGE

UPDATE with INNER JOIN
The UPDATE uses a table alias from the FROM clause.

```
SELECT TOP 2 * FROM Product  WHERE Color = 'Yellow' ORDER BY ProductID DESC;
```

ProductID	ProductName	Cost	ListPrice	Color	ModifiedDate
976	Road-350-W Yellow, 48	1082.51	1700.99	Yellow	2008-03-11
975	Road-350-W Yellow, 44	1082.51	1700.99	Yellow	2008-03-11

```
UPDATE p  SET   p.ModifiedDate = DATEADD(HH,1,awp.ModifiedDate)
FROM  Product p   INNER JOIN AdventureWorks2012.Production.Product awp
                ON p.ProductID = awp.ProductID  AND  p.Size LIKE '4%' ;
-- (91 row(s) affected)
```

Capturing Affected Rows with @@ROWCOUNT
When we have to know the number of updated rows, it is best to capture it into local variable and use it from there in the program logic.

```
DECLARE @UpdatedRows int;   -- capture @@ROWCOUNT for subsequent use in the program

UPDATE p
        SET   p.ModifiedDate = DATEADD(mm,1,awp.ModifiedDate)
FROM   Product p
    INNER JOIN AdventureWorks2012.Production.Product awp    ON p.ProductID = awp.ProductID
WHERE  p.Color = 'Yellow' ;
-- (36 row(s) affected)

SET @UpdatedRows = @@ROWCOUNT;

SELECT @@ROWCOUNT;           -- @@ROWCOUNT already changed
-- 1
SELECT TOP 5 * FROM Product  WHERE Color = 'Yellow' ORDER BY ProductID DESC;

SELECT @@ROWCOUNT;           -- @@ROWCOUNT changed again
-- 5
SELECT @UpdatedRows;         -- local variable kept the UPDATE count
-- 36
```

ProductID	ProductName	Cost	ListPrice	Color	ModifiedDate
976	Road-350-W Yellow, 48	1082.51	1700.99	Yellow	2008-04-11
975	Road-350-W Yellow, 44	1082.51	1700.99	Yellow	2008-04-11
974	Road-350-W Yellow, 42	1082.51	1700.99	Yellow	2008-04-11
973	Road-350-W Yellow, 40	1082.51	1700.99	Yellow	2008-04-11
965	Touring-3000 Yellow, 62	461.4448	742.35	Yellow	2008-04-11

UPDATE with Common Table Expression

UPDATE can be issued through a CTE to UPDATE the underlying table, Product in this case. Prices are increased 5% for products with over $1,000.00 list price.

```
SELECT TOP 5 * FROM Product  WHERE ListPrice > 1000.0 ORDER BY ProductID DESC;
GO
```

ProductID	ProductName	Cost	ListPrice	Color	ModifiedDate
976	Road-350-W Yellow, 48	1082.51	1700.99	Yellow	2008-04-11
975	Road-350-W Yellow, 44	1082.51	1700.99	Yellow	2008-04-11
974	Road-350-W Yellow, 42	1082.51	1700.99	Yellow	2008-04-11
973	Road-350-W Yellow, 40	1082.51	1700.99	Yellow	2008-04-11
972	Touring-2000 Blue, 54	755.1508	1214.85	Blue	2008-03-11

```
;WITH CTE
   AS (SELECT Price = ListPrice
     FROM   Product
     WHERE  ListPrice > 1000.0)
UPDATE CTE
SET    Price = Price * 1.05
GO
-- (86 row(s) affected)
```

```
SELECT TOP 5 * FROM Product  WHERE ListPrice > 1000.0 ORDER BY ProductID DESC;
```

ProductID	ProductName	Cost	ListPrice	Color	ModifiedDate
976	Road-350-W Yellow, 48	1082.51	1786.0395	Yellow	2008-04-11
975	Road-350-W Yellow, 44	1082.51	1786.0395	Yellow	2008-04-11
974	Road-350-W Yellow, 42	1082.51	1786.0395	Yellow	2008-04-11
973	Road-350-W Yellow, 40	1082.51	1786.0395	Yellow	2008-04-11
972	Touring-2000 Blue, 54	755.1508	1275.5925	Blue	2008-03-11

Similar data modification with ANSI SQL UPDATE.

```
UPDATE Product
SET   ListPrice = (SELECT p8.ListPrice * 1.05
         FROM  AdventureWorks2012.Production.Product p8   WHERE  Product.ProductID =
p8.ProductID)
WHERE  EXISTS (SELECT *  FROM  AdventureWorks2012.Production.Product p8
       WHERE  Product.ProductID = p8.ProductID   AND Product.ListPrice > 1000.0);
```

CHAPTER 10: Modify Data - INSERT, UPDATE, DELETE & MERGE

Four Methods of UPDATE with GROUP BY Query

UPDATE can be done a few ways with GROUP BY aggregates.

```
USE tempdb;
SELECT Color=ISNULL(Color,'N/A'), ItemCount=0 INTO ProductColor
FROM AdventureWorks2008.Production.Product
GROUP BY Color
GO
-- (10 row(s) affected)
```

```
SELECT * FROM ProductColor
GO
```

Color	ItemCount
N/A	0
Black	0
Blue	0
Grey	0
Multi	0
Red	0
Silver	0
Silver/Black	0
White	0
Yellow	0

ANSI UPDATE

```
UPDATE ProductColor
SET ItemCount = (SELECT ProductColorCount FROM  (SELECT Color=ISNULL(Color, 'N/A'),
                ProductColorCount=COUNT(*)
                FROM AdventureWorks2008.Production.Product
                GROUP BY Color) cg WHERE  ProductColor.Color = cg.Color)
GO
-- (10 row(s) affected)
```

FROM Clause UPDATE with Derived Table

```
UPDATE pc   SET pc.ItemCount = cg.ProductColorCount
FROM ProductColor pc
INNER JOIN (SELECT Color=ISNULL(Color, 'N/A'), ProductColorCount=COUNT(*)
      FROM AdventureWorks2008.Production.Product GROUP BY Color) cg
ON pc.Color = cg.Color;
-- (10 row(s) affected)
```

FROM Clause UPDATE with CTE

```
;WITH CTE AS (SELECT Color=ISNULL(Color, 'N/A'), ProductColorCount=COUNT(*)
      FROM AdventureWorks2008.Production.Product
      GROUP BY Color)
UPDATE pc
SET pc.ItemCount = CTE.ProductColorCount
FROM ProductColor pc
INNER JOIN CTE
ON pc.Color = CTE.Color;
GO
-- (10 row(s) affected)
```

CTE UPDATE

```
;WITH CTE AS (SELECT * FROM ProductColor pc
INNER JOIN (SELECT ColorPrd=ISNULL(Color, 'N/A'), ProductColorCount=COUNT(*)
      FROM AdventureWorks2008.Production.Product
      GROUP BY Color) cg
                  ON pc.Color = cg.ColorPrd)
UPDATE CTE SET CTE.ItemCount = CTE.ProductColorCount;
GO
-- (10 row(s) affected)
```

```
SELECT * FROM ProductColor
GO
```

Color	ItemCount
N/A	248
Black	93
Blue	26
Grey	1
Multi	8
Red	38
Silver	43
Silver/Black	7
White	4
Yellow	36

```
DROP TABLE tempdb.dbo.ProductColor;
GO
```

MERGE for Combination INSERT, UPDATE or DELETE

The MERGE statement can be used to INSERT, UPDATE and/or DELETE all in one statement.

```
USE tempdb;
go
```

```
-- Setup 2 test tables
SELECT TOP (5000) ResellerKey,
          OrderDateKey,
          ProductKey,
          OrderQuantity,
          SalesAmount
INTO   FactResellerSales
FROM   AdventureWorksDW2012.dbo.FactResellerSales ;
go
-- (5000 row(s) affected)
```

```
SELECT TOP (8000) ResellerKey,
          OrderDateKey,
          ProductKey,
          OrderQuantity,
          SalesAmount
INTO   ResellerSalesTransaction
FROM   AdventureWorksDW2012.dbo.FactResellerSales ;
go
-- (8000 row(s) affected)
```

```
DELETE rsc
FROM   ResellerSalesTransaction rsc
    JOIN (SELECT TOP 1000 *
       FROM   ResellerSalesTransaction
       ORDER  BY ResellerKey DESC) x
    ON x.ResellerKey = rsc.ResellerKey ;
go
-- (1010 row(s) affected)
```

```
UPDATE TOP (6000) ResellerSalesTransaction
SET   SalesAmount = SalesAmount * 1.1 ;
go
-- (6000 row(s) affected)
```

MERGE is a very powerful statement

```
SELECT TOP (10) *
FROM   FactResellerSales
ORDER  BY ResellerKey,        OrderDateKey,        ProductKey ;
go
```

ResellerKey	OrderDateKey	ProductKey	OrderQuantity	SalesAmount
1	20050801	270	1	183.9382
1	20050801	275	1	356.898
1	20050801	285	1	178.5808
1	20050801	314	2	4293.924
1	20050801	317	1	874.794
1	20050801	319	2	1749.588
1	20050801	324	2	838.9178
1	20050801	326	1	419.4589
1	20050801	328	1	419.4589
1	20050801	332	2	838.9178

```
SELECT BeforeFactCount=COUNT(*)
FROM   FactResellerSales ;
-- 5000

-- Ready for the MERGE (update if exists, insert otherwise)
MERGE FactResellerSales AS fact
USING (SELECT *
    FROM   ResellerSalesTransaction) AS feed
ON ( fact.ProductKey = feed.ProductKey
   AND fact.ResellerKey = feed.ResellerKey
   AND fact.OrderDateKey = feed.OrderDateKey )
WHEN MATCHED THEN
 UPDATE SET fact.OrderQuantity += feed.OrderQuantity,
       fact.SalesAmount += feed.SalesAmount
WHEN NOT MATCHED THEN
 INSERT (ResellerKey,
     OrderDateKey,
     ProductKey,
     OrderQuantity,
     SalesAmount)
 VALUES (feed.ResellerKey,
     feed.OrderDateKey,
     feed.ProductKey,
     feed.OrderQuantity,
     feed.SalesAmount);
go   -- (6990 row(s) affected)
```

Checking results after MERGE

```
SELECT TOP (10) *
FROM  FactResellerSales ORDER  BY        ResellerKey,    OrderDateKey,    ProductKey;
```

ResellerKey	OrderDateKey	ProductKey	OrderQuantity	SalesAmount
1	20050801	270	2	386.2702
1	20050801	275	2	749.4858
1	20050801	285	2	375.0197
1	20050801	314	4	9017.2404
1	20050801	317	2	1837.0674
1	20050801	319	4	3674.1348
1	20050801	324	4	1761.7274
1	20050801	326	2	880.8637
1	20050801	328	2	880.8637
1	20050801	332	4	1761.7274

```
SELECT AfterFactCount=COUNT(*)  FROM  FactResellerSales ;
go
-- 7658

DROP TABLE ResellerSalesTransaction;  DROP TABLE FactResellerSales;
go
```

Using MERGE Instead of UPDATE

MERGE statement can be used in the UPDATE only mode to replace UPDATE.

```
-- Prepare 2 test tables
USE tempdb;
SELECT TOP (5000) ResellerKey,  OrderDateKey, ProductKey, OrderQuantity, SalesAmount
INTO   FactResellerSales FROM   AdventureWorksDW2012.dbo.FactResellerSales;
GO -- (5000 row(s) affected)
SELECT TOP (8000) ResellerKey,  OrderDateKey, ProductKey, OrderQuantity, SalesAmount
INTO   ResellerSalesTransaction FROM   AdventureWorksDW2012.dbo.FactResellerSales;
GO -- (8000 row(s) affected)
```

```
-- Alter the test data
DELETE rsc
FROM   ResellerSalesTransaction rsc
    INNER JOIN (SELECT TOP 1000 * FROM   ResellerSalesTransaction
        ORDER  BY ResellerKey DESC) x   -- subquery inner join
    ON x.ResellerKey = rsc.ResellerKey;
GO --(1010 row(s) affected)
UPDATE TOP (6000) ResellerSalesTransaction SET SalesAmount = SalesAmount * 1.1;
GO -- (6000 row(s) affected)
```

```
SELECT BeforeFactCount=COUNT(*) FROM   FactResellerSales;
GO -- 5000
```

```
-- Ready for the MERGE UPDATE only mode
MERGE FactResellerSales AS fact
USING (SELECT * FROM   ResellerSalesTransaction) AS feed
ON ( fact.ProductKey = feed.ProductKey
    AND fact.ResellerKey = feed.ResellerKey
    AND fact.OrderDateKey = feed.OrderDateKey )
WHEN MATCHED THEN
 UPDATE SET fact.OrderQuantity = fact.OrderQuantity + feed.OrderQuantity,
        fact.SalesAmount = fact.SalesAmount + feed.SalesAmount;
GO -- 4332 row(s) affected)
```

```
SELECT AfterFactCount=COUNT(*) FROM   FactResellerSales;
GO -- 5000
```

```
DROP TABLE ResellerSalesTransaction;
DROP TABLE FactResellerSales;
```

CHAPTER 11: The Magic of Transact-SQL Programming

IF...ELSE Conditional

IF... ELSE is a step toward a bona fide programming language.

```
DECLARE @StringNumber varchar(32) ;
SET @StringNumber = '12,000,000';
IF EXISTS( SELECT * WHERE ISNUMERIC(@StringNumber) = 1)
        PRINT 'VALID NUMBER: ' + @StringNumber
ELSE    PRINT 'INVALID NUMBER: ' + @StringNumber;
GO
-- VALID NUMBER: 12,000,000
```

```
DECLARE @StringNumber varchar(32) = '12,000:000';

IF EXISTS( SELECT * WHERE ISNUMERIC(@StringNumber) = 1)
        PRINT CONCAT('VALID NUMBER: ' , @StringNumber)
ELSE    PRINT CONCAT('INVALID NUMBER: ', @StringNumber);
GO
-- INVALID NUMBER: 12,000:000
```

```
DECLARE @StringDate varchar(32);

SET @StringDate = '2017-03-15 18:50';

IF EXISTS( SELECT * WHERE ISDATE(@StringDate) = 1)
        PRINT 'VALID DATE: ' + @StringDate
ELSE    PRINT 'INVALID DATE: ' + @StringDate;
GO
-- Result: VALID DATE: 2017-03-15 18:50
```

```
DECLARE @StringDate varchar(32) = '20116-03-15 18:50';
IF EXISTS( SELECT * WHERE ISDATE(@StringDate) = 1)
        PRINT CONCAT('VALID DATE: ', @StringDate)
ELSE    PRINT CONCAT('INVALID DATE: ', @StringDate);
-- Result: INVALID DATE: 20116-03-15 18:50
```

WHILE Looping - UPDATE in Batches

WHILE looping can be used to break down large transaction to small batches. Executing in small batches is safer and does not block other OLTP transactions for a long time. Blocking can be seen by running sp_who system stored procedure

```
EXEC sp_who;
```

UPDATE of 121,317 rows is batched to 13 batches of 10,000 or less.

```
USE tempdb;
SELECT * INTO SOD
FROM AdventureWorks2012.Sales.SalesOrderDetail ORDER BY SalesOrderDetailID;
GO
--(121317 row(s) affected)
```

```
WHILE (2 > 1)   -- Infinite loop until BREAK is issued
 BEGIN
  UPDATE TOP ( 10000 ) SOD
  SET   UnitPriceDiscount = 0.08,  ModifiedDate = CONVERT(DATE, getdate())
  WHERE  ModifiedDate < CONVERT(DATE, getdate());

  IF @@ROWCOUNT = 0
   BEGIN
    BREAK;
   END
  -- 1 second delay - Very important for other OLTP transactions execution
  WAITFOR DELAY '00:00:01'
 END; -- WHILE
GO
```

```
(10000 row(s) affected)
(10000 row(s) affected)
(10000 row(s) affected)
(10000 row(s) affected)
(10000 row(s) affected)
(10000 row(s) affected)
(10000 row(s) affected)
(10000 row(s) affected)
(10000 row(s) affected)
(10000 row(s) affected)
(10000 row(s) affected)
(10000 row(s) affected)
(1317 row(s) affected)
(0 row(s) affected)
```

```
DROP TABLE tempdb.dbo.SOD
```

CHAPTER 11: The Magic of Transact-SQL Programming

WHILE Loop Usage in Cursors

Transact-SQL logic will visit all databases on the current SQL Server instance using a cursor. NOTE: **cursor solutions do not scale well, first choice is set-based logic if appropriate.**

```
DECLARE @CurrentDB sysname;
DECLARE AllDBCursor CURSOR  STATIC LOCAL FOR
         SELECT   name FROM    MASTER.dbo.sysdatabases
         WHERE    name NOT IN ('master','tempdb','model','msdb') ORDER BY name;
OPEN AllDBCursor;
FETCH  AllDBCursor INTO @CurrentDB;
WHILE (@@FETCH_STATUS = 0) -- loop through all db-s
  BEGIN
/***** PROCESSING (like BACKUP database)  *****/
         PRINT @CurrentDB;
         FETCH  AllDBCursor   INTO @CurrentDB;
  END; -- while
CLOSE AllDBCursor; DEALLOCATE AllDBCursor;
```

```
/*.... AdventureWorks
AdventureWorks2008
AdventureWorks2012
AdventureWorksDW2012 .... */
```

Transact-SQL script demonstrates a subcategory cursor.

```
USE AdventureWorks2012;
DECLARE curSubcategory CURSOR STATIC LOCAL  FOR          -- declare cursor
        SELECT ProductSubcategoryID, Subcategory=Name
        FROM Production.ProductSubcategory ORDER BY Subcategory;
DECLARE @Subcategory varchar(40), @PSID int
OPEN curSubcategory
FETCH NEXT FROM curSubcategory INTO @PSID, @Subcategory -- fetch cursor
WHILE (@@fetch_status = 0)             -- cursor fetch_status
BEGIN -- begin cursor loop
/***** USER DEFINED PROCESSING CODE HERE  *****/
         DECLARE @Msg varchar(128);
   SELECT @Msg = CONCAT('ProductSubcategory info: ', @Subcategory,' ',CONVERT(varchar, @PSID));
         PRINT @Msg;
FETCH NEXT FROM curSubcategory INTO @PSID, @Subcategory;   -- fetch cursor
END; -- end cursor loop
CLOSE curSubcategory;   DEALLOCATE curSubcategory;
```

```
/* ... ProductSubcategory info: Bike Stands 27
ProductSubcategory info: Bottles and Cages 28
ProductSubcategory info: Bottom Brackets 5  ... */
```

CHAPTER II: The Magic of Transact-SQL Programming

T-SQL Transaction

Transact-SQL language has been extended with features beyond ANSI SQL such as variables, IF... ELSE and WHILE. **"Transact" refers to the capability to execute business transactions which require the synchronized update of tables as one or none at all.**

DELETE from 2 Tables with TRANSACTION Control

DELETE PRIMARY KEY rows from PK table and related FOREIGN KEY rows from FK table in a single transaction. NOTE: Deleting lots of rows may interfere with online access in an ecommerce database.

Alternate method: define tables with CASCADE ON DELETE action.

```
BEGIN TRANSACTION


-- First delete from FOREIGN KEY table
DELETE OmegaFK
FROM Omega AS OmegaFK
 INNER JOIN Delta AS DeltaPK
  ON DeltaPK.ColApk = OmegaFK.ColBfk
WHERE DeltaPK.ColApk = {single value A} ;


IF @@ERROR <> 0
BEGIN
        ROLLBACK TRANSACTION;
        RAISERROR('FK delete failed.', 10, 1);
END
-- if no error, delete from PRIMARY KEY table
ELSE
        DELETE
        FROM Delta
        WHERE ColApk = = {single value A};


-- Commit transaction only if both DELETE-s succeeded
IF @@ERROR <> 0
BEGIN
        ROLLBACK TRANSACTION;
        RAISERROR('PK delete failed.', 10, 1);
ELSE
        COMMIT TRANSACTION;
```

Stored Procedure with Input & Output Parameters

A stored procedure usually returns a table-like result set from the SELECT(s) in the stored procedure. Scalar value can also be returned with the OUTPUT option.

```
USE AdventureWorks2012;
GO
CREATE PROCEDURE uspQuarterSales     @StartYear INT,     @TotalSales MONEY OUTPUT
AS
 BEGIN -- sproc definition
  SET NOCOUNT ON -- turn off rows affected messages
  SELECT @TotalSales = SUM(SubTotal)
  FROM  Sales.SalesOrderHeader   WHERE  OrderDate >= DATEADD(YY,@StartYear-1900,'19000101')

  SELECT  YEAR = YEAR(OrderDate),
      COALESCE(FORMAT(SUM(CASE
          WHEN DATEPART(QQ,OrderDate) = 1 THEN SubTotal
               END),'c','en-US'),'') AS 'Q1',
      COALESCE(FORMAT(SUM(CASE
          WHEN DATEPART(QQ,OrderDate) = 2 THEN SubTotal
               END),'c','en-US'),'') AS 'Q2',
      COALESCE(FORMAT(SUM(CASE
          WHEN DATEPART(QQ,OrderDate) = 3 THEN SubTotal
               END),'c','en-US'),'') AS 'Q3',
      COALESCE(FORMAT(SUM(CASE
          WHEN DATEPART(QQ,OrderDate) = 4 THEN SubTotal
               END),'c','en-US'),'') AS 'Q4'
   FROM    Sales.SalesOrderHeader soh   WHERE   OrderDate >= DATEADD(YY,@StartYear-
1900,'19000101')
   GROUP BY YEAR(OrderDate)    ORDER BY YEAR(OrderDate);
 END; -- sproc definition
GO
```

```
-- Execute stored procedure with INPUT/OUTPUT parameters
DECLARE @TotSales money
EXEC uspQuarterSales  2007, @TotSales OUTPUT;
SELECT TotalSales = @TotSales;
```

YEAR	Q1	Q2	Q3	Q4
2007	$6,679,873.80	$8,357,874.88	$13,681,907.05	$13,291,381.43
2008	$11,398,376.28	$14,379,545.19	$50,840.63	

TotalSales
67839799.2669

Dynamic SQL Stored Procedure to REBUILD Indexes

The following dynamic SQL stored procedure uses database metadata to loop through all tables in the database, assemble and execute the index REBUILD command.

```
USE AdventureWorks2012;
GO

CREATE PROC sprocAllTablesIndexREBUILD @FILLFACTOR INT = 90
AS
 BEGIN
   DECLARE @DatabaseName SYSNAME = DB_NAME(),
       @TableName   VARCHAR(256);
   DECLARE @DynamicSQL NVARCHAR(max) = CONCAT('DECLARE cursorForAllTables CURSOR FOR
           SELECT CONCAT(TABLE_SCHEMA,".", TABLE_NAME) AS TABLENAME    FROM ',
@DatabaseName,
       '.INFORMATION_SCHEMA.TABLES WHERE   TABLE_TYPE = "BASE TABLE"');
   BEGIN
    EXEC sp_executeSQL
     @DynamicSQL; -- create tables cursor
    OPEN cursorForAllTables;

    FETCH NEXT FROM cursorForAllTables INTO @TableName;
    WHILE ( @@FETCH_STATUS = 0 )
     BEGIN
      SET @DynamicSQL = CONCAT('ALTER INDEX ALL ON ', @TableName,
          ' REBUILD WITH ( FILLFACTOR = ',
             CONVERT(VARCHAR, @FILLFACTOR), ')'  );
      PRINT @DynamicSQL;  -- test & debug
      EXEC sp_executeSQL
       @DynamicSQL;
      FETCH NEXT FROM cursorForAllTables INTO @TableName;
     END; -- cursor WHILE
    CLOSE cursorForAllTables;   DEALLOCATE cursorForAllTables;
   END;
 END; -- sproc
GO
-- Command(s) completed successfully.


-- Reindex tables with 85% fill factor leaving 15% free space for growth
EXEC sprocAllTablesIndexREBUILD 85;
/*
ALTER INDEX ALL ON Production.ScrapReason REBUILD WITH ( FILLFACTOR = 85)
ALTER INDEX ALL ON HumanResources.Shift REBUILD WITH ( FILLFACTOR = 85)  ....  */
```

User-Defined Functions

Table-Valued Functions

A table-valued function returns a table variable, therefore, it has to be invoked like it were a table in a query. T-SQL table-valued function creates a table from a delimited string of values.

```
CREATE FUNCTION dbo.ufnSplitDelimitedString ( @StringList VARCHAR(MAX),     @Delimiter CHAR(1))
RETURNS @TableList TABLE(ID int identity(1,1), StringLiteral VARCHAR(128))
BEGIN
   IF @StringList = '' RETURN;
   IF @Delimiter = ''
   BEGIN
     WITH Split AS                          -- Recursive CTE
        ( SELECT CharOne=LEFT(@StringList,1),R=RIGHT(@StringList,len(@StringList)-1)
          UNION ALL
          SELECT LEFT(R,1), R=RIGHT(R, len(R)-1)
          FROM Split    WHERE LEN(R)>0  )          -- End of CTE
     INSERT @TableList
     SELECT CharOne FROM Split
     OPTION ( MAXRECURSION 0);
     RETURN;
   END; -- IF
   DECLARE @XML xml=CONCAT('<root><csv>',replace(@StringList,@Delimiter,'</csv><csv>'),
                            '</csv></root>');
   INSERT @TableList
   SELECT rtrim(ltrim(replace(Word.value('.','nvarchar(128)'),char(10),'')))     AS ListMember
   FROM @XML.nodes('/root/csv') AS WordList(Word);
RETURN;
END; -- FUNCTION
GO
```

```
SELECT * FROM dbo.ufnSplitDelimitedString ('New York, California, Arizona, Texas, Toronto, Grand
Canyon, Yosemite,   Yellowstone, Niagara Falls, Belgium, Denmark, South Africa, Sweden', ',');
```

ID	StringLiteral
1	New York
2	California
3	Arizona
4	Texas
5	Toronto
6	Grand Canyon
7	Yosemite
8	Yellowstone
9	Niagara Falls
10	Belgium
11	Denmark
12	South Africa
13	Sweden

Table-Valued Function for PRIME Numbers Generation

Transact-SQL table-valued function generates prime numbers up to the input parameter limit.

```
USE AdventureWorks2012;
GO

CREATE FUNCTION ufnPrimeNumbers ( @Stop INT)
RETURNS @Result TABLE  (Prime INT)
BEGIN
WITH CTE ( SeqNo)
   AS (SELECT 0
      UNION ALL
      SELECT SeqNo + 1
      FROM   CTE
      WHERE  SeqNo < @Stop)
INSERT @Result
SELECT PrimeNo = N2.SeqNo
FROM   CTE N1
      INNER JOIN CTE N2
   ON  N2.SeqNo % N1.SeqNo > 0
      AND N2.SeqNo % 2 > 0
      AND N1.SeqNo < N2.SeqNo
      AND N2.SeqNo > 1
      AND N1.SeqNo >= 1
GROUP  BY N2.SeqNo
HAVING ( N2.SeqNo - COUNT(*) ) = 2
OPTION ( MAXRECURSION 0);
RETURN ;
END;
GO

SELECT * FROM dbo.ufnPrimeNumbers (1000);
GO
-- (167 row(s) affected) - Partial results.
```

Prime
3
5
7
11
13
17
19
23
29
31

Inline Functions

An inline user-defined function, returns table, can be used as a parameterized view.

```
USE AdventureWorks2012
GO

CREATE FUNCTION Sales.ufnStaffSalesByFiscalYear (@OrderYear INT)
RETURNS TABLE  AS
RETURN
SELECT
    CONVERT(date, soh.OrderDate)                                          AS OrderDate
    ,CONCAT(p.FirstName, ' ', COALESCE(p.MiddleName, ''), ' ', p.LastName)    AS FullName
    ,e.JobTitle
    ,st.Name                                                              AS SalesTerritory
    ,FORMAT(soh.SubTotal, 'c', 'en-US')                          AS SalesAmount
    ,YEAR(DATEADD(mm, 6, soh.OrderDate))                          AS FiscalYear
FROM Sales.SalesPerson sp
    INNER JOIN Sales.SalesOrderHeader soh
        ON sp.BusinessEntityID = soh.SalesPersonID
    INNER JOIN Sales.SalesTerritory st
        ON sp.TerritoryID = st.TerritoryID
    INNER JOIN HumanResources.Employee e
        ON soh.SalesPersonID = e.BusinessEntityID
    INNER JOIN Person.Person p
        ON p.BusinessEntityID = sp.BusinessEntityID
WHERE         soh.OrderDate >= datefromparts(@OrderYear, 1, 1)
            AND soh.OrderDate < dateadd(yy,1, datefromparts(@OrderYear, 1, 1));
GO
-- Command(s) completed successfully.
```

```
SELECT * FROM Sales.ufnStaffSalesByFiscalYear (2007)
ORDER BY FullName, CONVERT(money, SalesAmount) DESC;   --  SalesAmount (string) does not sort
correctly
--( 1476  row(s) affected) -- Partial results.
```

OrderDate	FullName	JobTitle	SalesTerritory	SalesAmount	FiscalYear
2007-08-01	David R Campbell	Sales Representative	Northwest	$101,609.29	2008
2007-07-01	David R Campbell	Sales Representative	Northwest	$93,397.64	2008
2007-04-01	David R Campbell	Sales Representative	Northwest	$75,104.65	2007
2007-07-01	David R Campbell	Sales Representative	Northwest	$74,149.95	2008
2007-04-01	David R Campbell	Sales Representative	Northwest	$73,963.26	2007
2007-08-01	David R Campbell	Sales Representative	Northwest	$71,283.24	2008
2007-09-01	David R Campbell	Sales Representative	Northwest	$66,871.84	2008
2007-01-01	David R Campbell	Sales Representative	Northwest	$63,864.71	2007
2007-11-01	David R Campbell	Sales Representative	Northwest	$63,339.26	2008
2007-10-01	David R Campbell	Sales Representative	Northwest	$60,519.95	2008

Scalar Functions

A scalar user-defined function returns a scalar value. It can be used in a query wherever a single value is required.

```
USE AdventureWorks2012;
GO

CREATE FUNCTION dbo.ufnNumberToEnglish (@Number INT)
RETURNS VARCHAR(1024)  AS
 BEGIN
   DECLARE @Below20 TABLE    ( ID  INT IDENTITY ( 0, 1 ),   Word VARCHAR(32) );
   DECLARE @Tens TABLE  ( ID  INT IDENTITY ( 2, 1 ),    Word VARCHAR(32) );
   INSERT @Below20  (Word)
   VALUES('Zero'), ('One'),('Two'), ('Three'), ('Four'), ('Five'), ('Six'), ('Seven'), ('Eight'),
       ('Nine'), ('Ten'), ('Eleven'), ('Twelve'), ('Thirteen'), ('Fourteen'), ('Fifteen'),
       ('Sixteen'), ('Seventeen'), ('Eighteen'), ('Nineteen');
   INSERT @Tens
   VALUES('Twenty'),  ('Thirty'), ('Forty'), ('Fifty'),  ('Sixty'),  ('Seventy'),  ('Eighty'), ('Ninety');
   DECLARE @English VARCHAR(1024) = (SELECT CASE
        WHEN @Number = 0 THEN ''
        WHEN @Number BETWEEN 1 AND 19 THEN (SELECT Word FROM   @Below20 WHERE  ID = @Number)
        WHEN @Number BETWEEN 20 AND 99 THEN
    CONCAT((SELECT Word FROM   @Tens WHERE  ID = @Number / 10), '-',
dbo.ufnNumberToEnglish(@Number%10))
     WHEN @Number BETWEEN 100 AND 999 THEN CONCAT((
        dbo.ufnNumberToEnglish(@Number / 100) ), ' Hundred ', dbo.ufnNumberToEnglish(@Number%100))
     WHEN @Number BETWEEN 1000 AND 999999 THEN CONCAT((
        dbo.ufnNumberToEnglish(@Number / 1000) ), ' Thousand ', dbo.ufnNumberToEnglish(@Number%1000))
     WHEN @Number BETWEEN 1000000 AND 999999999 THEN CONCAT((
        dbo.ufnNumberToEnglish(@Number / 1000000) ), ' Million ', dbo.ufnNumberToEnglish(@Number%1000000))
     ELSE ' INVALID INPUT'  END);
   SELECT @English = RTRIM(@English);
   SELECT @English = RTRIM(LEFT(@English, len(@English) - 1))
   WHERE  RIGHT(@English, 1) = '-';
   RETURN ( @English );
 END;
GO
-- Command(s) completed successfully.

SELECT dbo.ufnNumberToEnglish (9999);   -- Nine Thousand Nine Hundred Ninety-Nine

SELECT dbo.ufnNumberToEnglish (1000001); -- One Million One

SELECT dbo.ufnNumberToEnglish (7777777);
-- Seven Million Seven Hundred Seventy-Seven Thousand Seven Hundred Seventy-Seven
```

Dynamic PIVOT Script

Static PIVOT has pretty limited role since it has to be changed when data changes effects the PIVOT range. Dynamic SQL makes PIVOT data driven. Instead of hard-wired columns, dynamic PIVOT builds the columns from the data dynamically.

```
USE AdventureWorks;
GO

DECLARE @OrderYear AS TABLE
 (
   YYYY INT NOT NULL PRIMARY KEY
 ) ;
DECLARE @DynamicSQL AS NVARCHAR(4000) ;

INSERT INTO @OrderYear
SELECT DISTINCT YEAR(OrderDate)
FROM   Sales.SalesOrderHeader;

DECLARE @ReportColumnNames AS NVARCHAR(MAX),  @IterationYear    AS INT;

SET @IterationYear = (SELECT MIN(YYYY)     FROM   @OrderYear);
SET @ReportColumnNames = N'';

-- Assemble pivot list dynamically
WHILE ( @IterationYear IS NOT NULL )
  BEGIN
    SET @ReportColumnNames = @ReportColumnNames + N','
                + QUOTENAME(CAST(@IterationYear AS NVARCHAR(10)));
    SET @IterationYear = (SELECT MIN(YYYY)
              FROM   @OrderYear
              WHERE  YYYY > @IterationYear);
  END;

SET @ReportColumnNames = SUBSTRING(@ReportColumnNames, 2,
            LEN(@ReportColumnNames));

PRINT @ReportColumnNames; -- [2001],[2002],[2003],[2004]

SET @DynamicSQL = CONCAT(N'SELECT * FROM (SELECT [Store (Freight Summary)]=s.Name,
        YEAR(OrderDate) AS OrderYear,  Freight = convert(money, convert(varchar, Freight))
        FROM Sales.SalesOrderHeader soh
        INNER JOIN Sales.Store s
        ON soh.CustomerID = s.CustomerID) as Header
        PIVOT (SUM(Freight)   FOR OrderYear IN(', @ReportColumnNames,N')) AS Pvt ORDER BY 1;');
```

```
-- T-SQL script continued

PRINT @DynamicSQL; -- Testing & debugging
/* SELECT * FROM (SELECT [Store (Freight Summary)]=s.Name,
        YEAR(OrderDate) AS OrderYear, Freight = convert(money, convert(varchar, Freight))
        FROM Sales.SalesOrderHeader soh
        INNER JOIN Sales.Store s    ON soh.CustomerID = s.CustomerID) as Header
        PIVOT (SUM(Freight)   FOR OrderYear IN([2001],[2002],[2003],[2004])) AS Pvt ORDER BY 1;*/


-- Execute dynamic sql
EXEC sp_executesql @DynamicSQL;
GO  -- (633 row(s) affected) - Partial results.
```

Store (Freight Summary)	2001	2002	2003	2004
A Bike Store	921.55	1637.24	NULL	NULL
A Great Bicycle Company	142.08	114.34	15.24	NULL
A Typical Bike Shop	976.61	1529.08	NULL	NULL
Acceptable Sales & Service	12.58	25.17	NULL	NULL

INSERT, UPDATE & DELETE through a View

Underlying table can be modified through a view, thus adding flexibility to security access since a view can be permissioned independently of the table.

```
USE tempdb;
SELECT CONVERT(INT, ProductID) AS ID, Name AS ProductName, ListPrice, ModifiedDate INTO
Product
FROM AdventureWorks2012.Production.Product;
GO -- (504 row(s) affected)
CREATE VIEW vProduct AS SELECT * FROM Product;
GO
UPDATE vProduct SET ModifiedDate = '2018-01-01';
GO -- (504 row(s) affected)
INSERT vProduct VALUES (2000, 'Three-Wheeler Bike', $999.99, getdate());
GO -- (1 row(s) affected)
DELETE TOP (10) FROM vProduct;
GO -- (1 row(s) affected)
SELECT TOP (1) * FROM Product;  -- 322 Chainring      0.00      2018-01-01 00:00:00.000
GO
DROP VIEW dbo.vProduct;
DROP TABLE tempdb.dbo.Product;
GO
```

Sensitive Data Audit Trigger

Triggers can be used to track sensitive data changes into an audit table. The OUTPUT clause is an alternative, but not exactly equivalent.

```
USE Payroll;
GO


CREATE TRIGGER uTrgEmployeeUpdate
ON Employee
AFTER UPDATE
AS
  IF ( Update(Salary)
     OR Update(SSN) )
   BEGIN
    INSERT INTO CorpSecurityEmployeeAudit
           (auditlogtype,
            auditEmployeeDeptID,
            auditEmployeeID,
            auditEmployeeSalary,
            auditEmployeeSSN,
            auditUpdatedBy)
    SELECT 'PREVIOUSDATA',
         DeptID,
         EmployeeID,
         Salary,
         SSN,
         User_name()
    FROM   DELETED

    INSERT INTO CorpSecurityEmployeeAudit
           (auditlogtype,
            auditEmployeeDeptID,
            auditEmployeeID,
            auditEmployeeSalary,
            auditEmployeeSSN,
            auditUpdatedBy)
    SELECT 'NEWDATA',
         DeptID,
         EmployeeID,
         Salary,
         SSN,
         User_name()
    FROM   INSERTED
   END;
GO
```

Automatic Timestamp Trigger

Whenever the Person.Contact is updated, the ModifiedDate will be updated to current time by the update after trigger. NOTE: disable/drop other update triggers on this table, if any, for the test.

```
USE AdventureWorks;
GO

CREATE TRIGGER uTrgContactTimestamp
ON Person.Contact
FOR UPDATE
AS
  BEGIN
  IF TRIGGER_NESTLEVEL() > 1      RETURN;
   UPDATE Person.Contact  SET    Person.Contact.ModifiedDate = CURRENT_TIMESTAMP
   FROM   Person.Contact c
       INNER JOIN INSERTED i
         ON c.ContactID = i.ContactID
  END
GO
-- (1 row(s) affected)


SELECT *
FROM   Person.Contact
WHERE  FirstName = 'Kim'   AND MiddleName = 'B'      AND LastName = 'Abercrombie'
GO
-- ModifiedDate: 2000-02-10 00:00:00.000

-- Updating a column will automatically update the ModifiedDate
UPDATE Person.Contact    SET   Phone = '299 484-3924'
WHERE  FirstName = 'Kim'   AND MiddleName = 'B'      AND LastName = 'Abercrombie'
GO

SELECT *
FROM   Person.Contact WHERE  FirstName = 'Kim'   AND MiddleName = 'B'   AND LastName =
'Abercrombie'
GO
-- ModifiedDate: 2018-08-11 07:22:01.157

-- Cleanup
DROP TRIGGER Person.uTrgContactTimestamp
```

Recursive Product Assembly

Recursive Common Table Expression (CTE) is used to assemble a bike frame based on the BillOfMaterials table.

```
USE AdventureWorks2012;

DECLARE @ProductID int = 831;
WITH CTE(AssemblyID, ComponentID, PerAssemblyQty,  AssemblyLevel) AS
(        SELECT bom0.ProductAssemblyID, bom0.ComponentID, bom0.PerAssemblyQty,
                0 AS AssemblyLevel
        FROM Production.BillOfMaterials AS bom0
        WHERE bom0.ProductAssemblyID = @ProductID
                AND bom0.EndDate is null
        UNION ALL
        SELECT bom.ProductAssemblyID, bom.ComponentID, p.PerAssemblyQty,
                AssemblyLevel + 1
        FROM Production.BillOfMaterials AS bom
                INNER JOIN CTE AS p
                        ON bom.ProductAssemblyID = p.ComponentID   AND bom.EndDate is null   )
SELECT pp.Name AS ProductName, AssemblyID, ComponentID,
        p.Name AS AssemblyName, PerAssemblyQty, AssemblyLevel
FROM CTE
        INNER JOIN Production.Product AS p
                ON CTE.ComponentID = p.ProductID
        INNER JOIN Production.Product AS pp
                ON CTE.AssemblyID = pp.ProductID
ORDER BY AssemblyLevel, AssemblyID, ComponentID;
```

ProductName	AssemblyID	ComponentID	AssemblyName	PerAssemblyQty	AssemblyLevel
ML Mountain Frame - Black, 44	831	324	Chain Stays	2.00	0
ML Mountain Frame - Black, 44	831	325	Decal 1	2.00	0
ML Mountain Frame - Black, 44	831	326	Decal 2	1.00	0
ML Mountain Frame - Black, 44	831	327	Down Tube	1.00	0
ML Mountain Frame - Black, 44	831	399	Head Tube	1.00	0
ML Mountain Frame - Black, 44	831	492	Paint - Black	8.00	0
ML Mountain Frame - Black, 44	831	532	Seat Stays	4.00	0
ML Mountain Frame - Black, 44	831	533	Seat Tube	1.00	0
ML Mountain Frame - Black, 44	831	534	Top Tube	1.00	0
ML Mountain Frame - Black, 44	831	803	ML Fork	1.00	0
Chain Stays	324	486	Metal Sheet 5	2.00	1
Down Tube	327	483	Metal Sheet 3	1.00	1
Head Tube	399	485	Metal Sheet 4	1.00	1
Seat Stays	532	484	Metal Sheet 7	4.00	1
Seat Tube	533	478	Metal Bar 2	1.00	1
Top Tube	534	482	Metal Sheet 2	1.00	1
ML Fork	803	316	Blade	1.00	1
ML Fork	803	331	Fork End	1.00	1
ML Fork	803	350	Fork Crown	1.00	1
ML Fork	803	531	Steerer	1.00	1
Blade	316	486	Metal Sheet 5	1.00	2
Fork End	331	482	Metal Sheet 2	1.00	2
Fork Crown	350	486	Metal Sheet 5	1.00	2
Steerer	531	487	Metal Sheet 6	1.00	2

Percent on Base Calculation

When deriving percent on base, we need to calculate the overall total in a single value subquery to use it as denominator in the percentile calculation.

```
USE AdventureWorks2012;
```

```
SELECT YEAR(OrderDate) AS [Year],
    FORMAT(SUM(TotalDue),'c0','en-US') AS YearTotal,
    FORMAT(SUM(TotalDue) /
        (SELECT SUM(TotalDue) FROM Sales.SalesOrderHeader),'p0') AS Percentile
FROM Sales.SalesOrderHeader
GROUP BY YEAR(OrderDate)
ORDER BY YEAR ASC;
```

Year	YearTotal	Percentage
2005	$12,693,251	10 %
2006	$34,463,848	28 %
2007	$47,171,490	38 %
2008	$28,888,198	23 %

Adding a Grand Total line with ROLLUP.

```
SELECT COALESCE(CONVERT(varchar,YEAR(OrderDate)), 'Grand Total') AS [Year],
    FORMAT(SUM(TotalDue),'c0','en-US') AS [SalesTotal],
    FORMAT(SUM(TotalDue) /
        (SELECT SUM(TotalDue) FROM Sales.SalesOrderHeader),'p0') AS Percentage
FROM Sales.SalesOrderHeader
GROUP BY YEAR(OrderDate)   WITH ROLLUP
ORDER BY YEAR ASC;
```

Year	SalesTotal	Percentage
2005	$12,693,251	10 %
2006	$34,463,848	28 %
2007	$47,171,490	38 %
2008	$28,888,198	23 %
Grand Total	$123,216,786	100 %

CHAPTER 12: Exporting & Importing Data

Saving a T-SQL Script as .sql File

Any T-SQL script can be saved as .sql file. One easy way is saving from Management Studio Query Editor. Here is the script we will save.

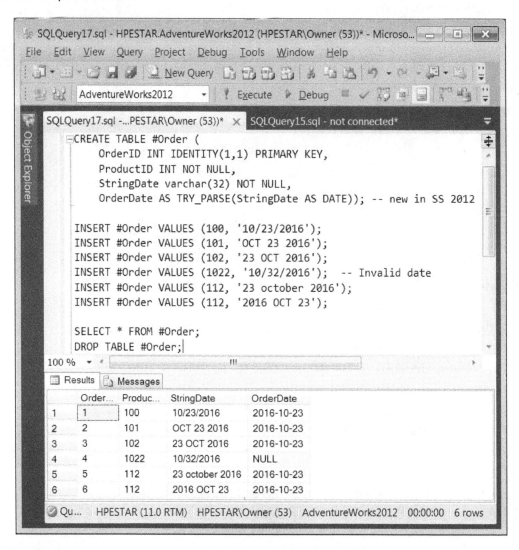

Click on File, click on Save .. As, choose a path and enter the file name for the script.

To load it back: click on File, click on Open File, locate file in Open File dialog pop-up.

Executing a .sql Script File Using SQLCMD

The SQLCMD command line utility can be used to execute a .sql script file typically with the -i (input) and -o (output) options. **Note: with any of the Command Prompt utilities the command line should not be broken with carriage return or line feed (CR/LF), it has to be one long line.**

SQLCMD -S"HPESTAR" -Uyourlogin -Psecret007 -i "f:\data\sql\tryparsedemo.sql" -o"f:\data\result\tryparsedemo.txt"

"HPESTAR" is the name of the SQL Server. With Windows authentication:

SQLCMD -S"HPESTAR" -i "f:\data\sql\tryparsedemo.sql" -o"f:\data\result\tryparsedemo.txt"

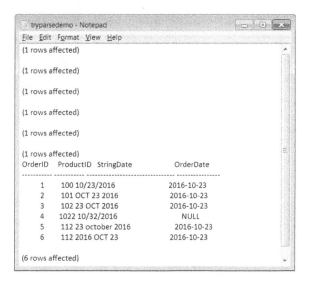

The output file collects warnings, messages, errors and results.

Making a T-SQL Script Rerunnable

It takes special attention to make a T-SQL script re-executable as many times as desired. A CREATE VIEW script can only be executed once.

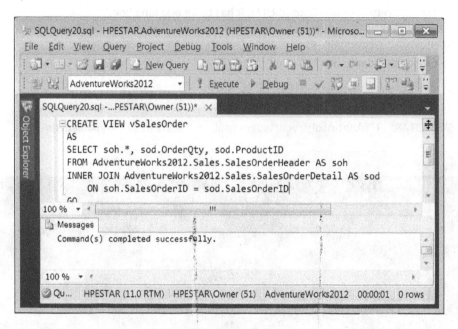

Repeat execution gives an error.

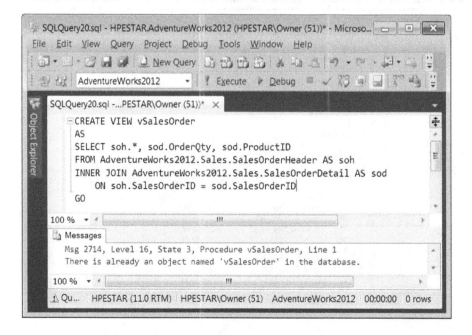

IF...ELSE Conditional Way to Make a Script Rerunnable

IF...ELSE is frequently the solution to prepare a rerunnable script. In this instance, first we check if the view exists. If it doesn't exist, we just go ahead and create it. If indeed it exists, we drop it first, then create it again.

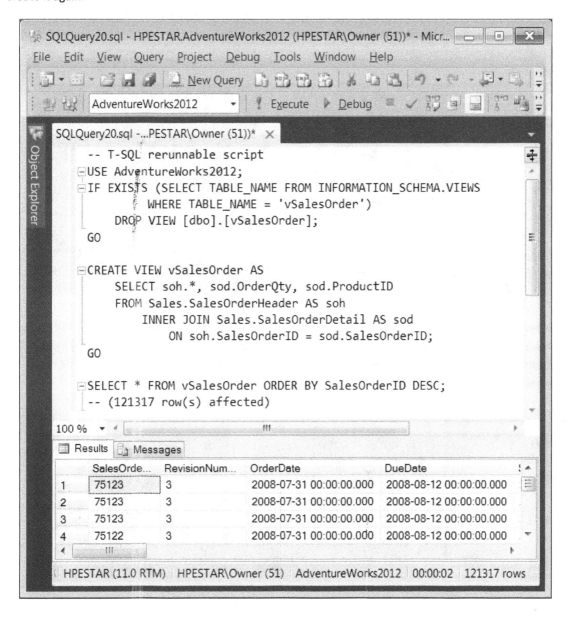

bcp Usage for Exporting & Importing Data

bcp (Bulk Copy Program) is a command line utility for moving data. The Production.Product table is exported to a flat file with bcp using Windows authentication.

For SQL Server authentication, add the "-Uyourlogin -Pyourpasswrd" parameters. **Note: the command must be one long line without breaks.**

```
■ Command Prompt                                                    _  □  X

Microsoft Windows [Version 6.1.7601]
Copyright (c) 2009 Microsoft Corporation.  All rights reserved.

C:\Users\Owner>bcp AdventureWorks2012.Production.Product out F:\data\export\prod
uctz.txt -w -T -S"HPESTAR"

Starting copy...
SQLState = S1000, NativeError = 0
Error = [Microsoft][SQL Server Native Client 11.0]Warning: BCP import with a for
mat file will convert empty strings in delimited columns to NULL.

504 rows copied.
Network packet size (bytes): 4096
Clock Time (ms.) Total      : 125    Average : (4032.00 rows per sec.)

C:\Users\Owner>
```

The **results of a query execution** can be exported with bcp as well using the queryout option. Rule is the same, no carriage return or line feed in the command no matter how long is it. The command can be edited in SSMS Query Editor and pasted into Command Prompt with Right Mouse Click Paste. CTRL-V does not work.

```
■ Command Prompt                                                    _  □  X

C:\Users\Owner>bcp "SELECT × from AdventureWorks2012.HumanResources.Department"
queryout F:\data\export\departmentz.txt -w -T -S"HPESTAR"

Starting copy...

16 rows copied.
Network packet size (bytes): 4096
Clock Time (ms.) Total      : 453    Average : (35.32 rows per sec.)

C:\Users\Owner>
```

Importing Data with the bcp Utility

Importing is very similar to exporting. For better control though it is necessary to use a format file. First we create an empty table for the data.

```
use tempdb;
select  TOP 0 * into product1 from AdventureWorks2012.Production.Product;
go
```

We are ready to execute the bcp import command.

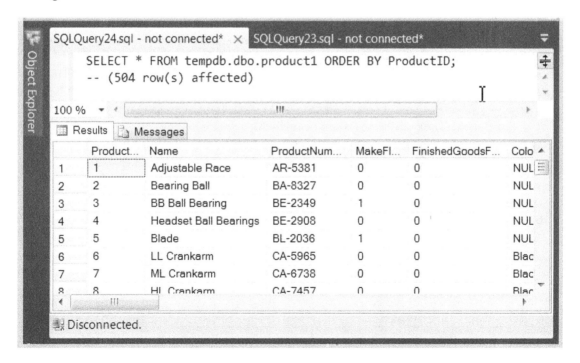

Checking the results.

Exporting Data with SQL Server Import and Export Wizard

We will export a view query results to a new Excel worksheet. The SELECT query returns 8,914 rows from the vPersonDemographics view.

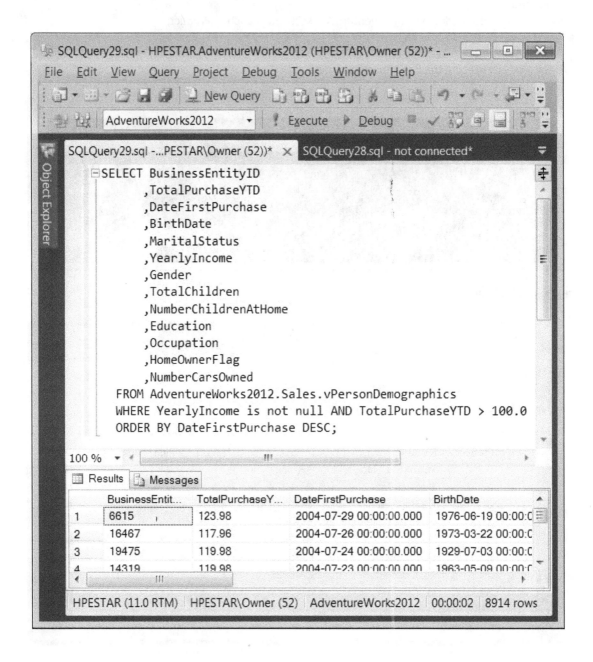

Starting the SSIS Import and Export Wizard

We start the SSIS Import/Export Wizard by a Right Click on the database in Object Explorer. It does not matter much if we choose Import Data or Export data since it only presets the destination or source pages respectively.

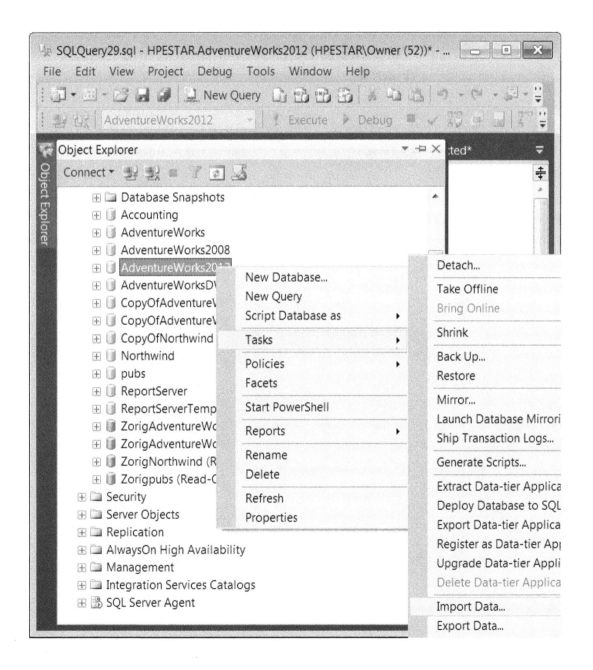

Optional Wizard Starting Welcome Screen
There is a checkmark option on the bottom to turn it off.

Configuring the Data Source Page

The data source is a database, therefore the server and database must be set up on this page.

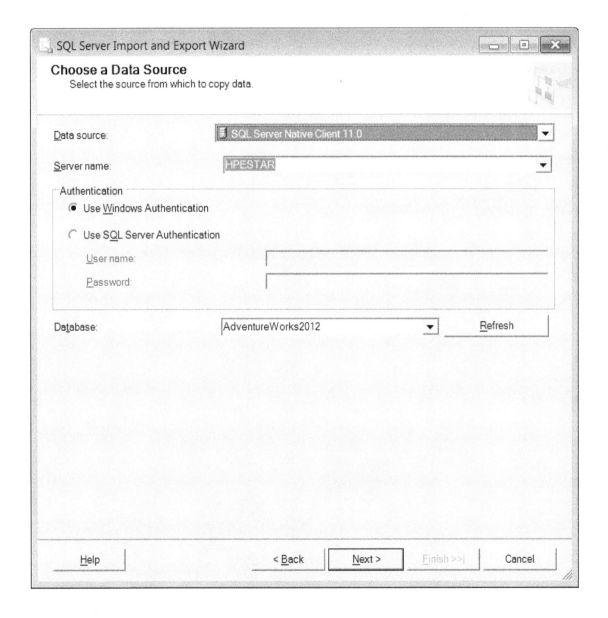

Configuring the Destination Page

The destination is a new Excel worksheet. Path & name must be given.

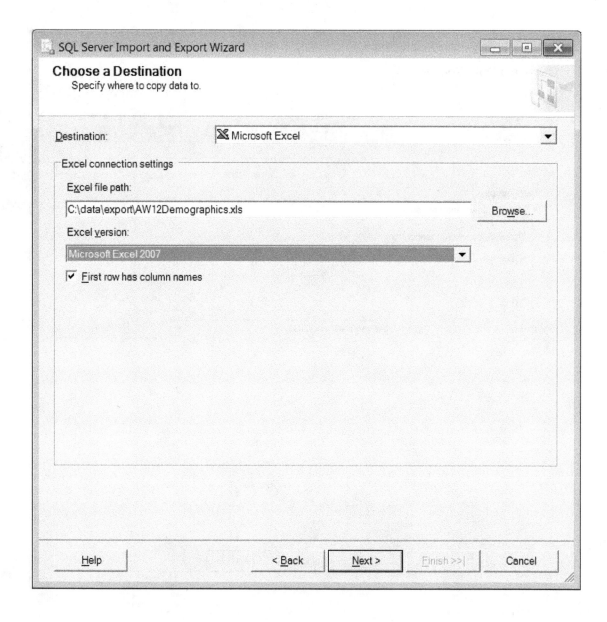

Specifying Table/View or Query Source

The Wizard logic branches based on what radio button we choose. If the choose table/view source, the next dialog box offers the entire list of tables/views in the database for checkmark selection.

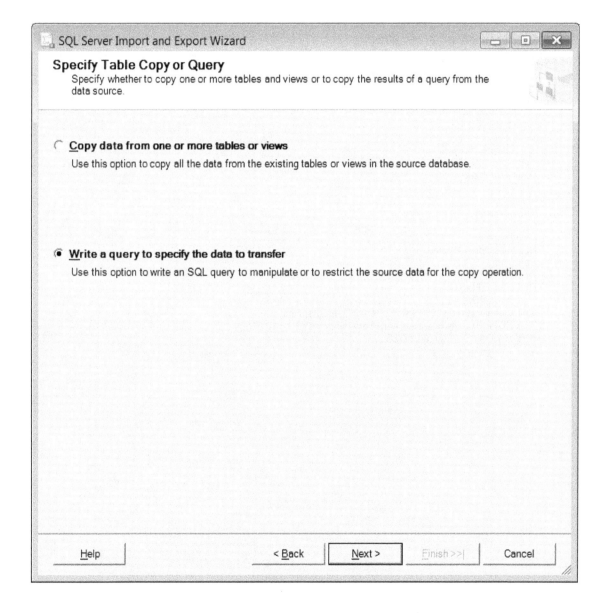

Entering the Query Source

We should use a tested query in order to avoid a failure in the execution of the generated SSIS package. Parse option is available for syntax checking.

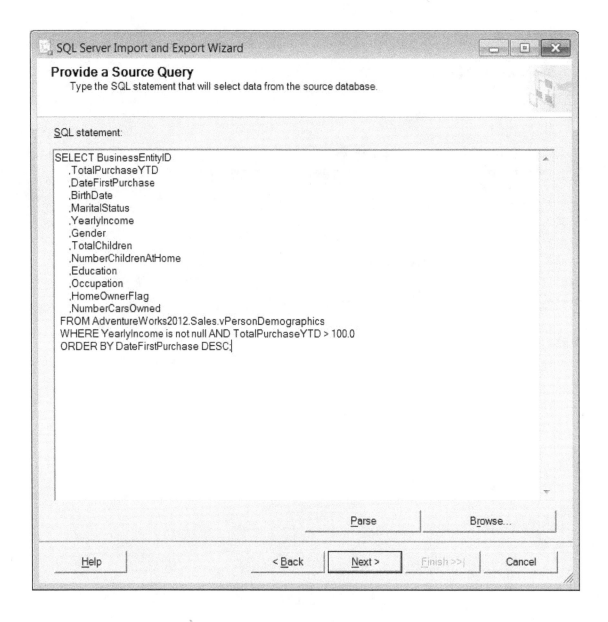

Option to Edit Mappings & Review Data
If you trust the Wizard, you can just click "Next". Otherwise, you can edit column mappings and review the data.

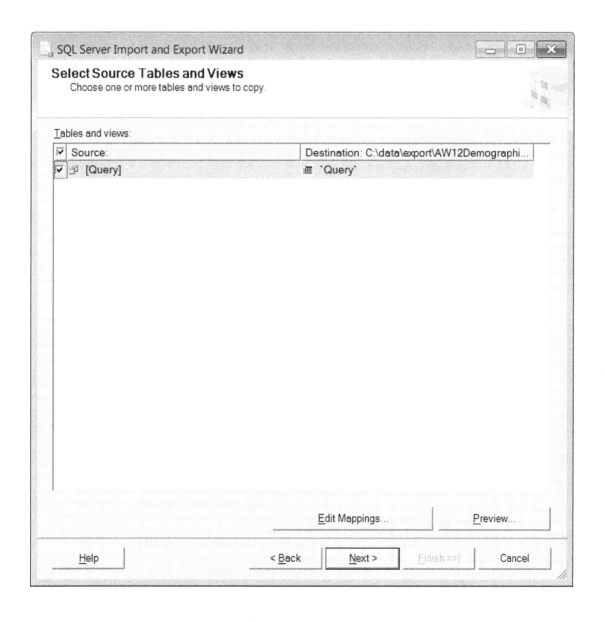

Edit Mappings & Preview

The next Wizard screen offers popup windows for editing the column mappings, changing the CREATE TABLE SQL and preview the data. We don't perform any change.

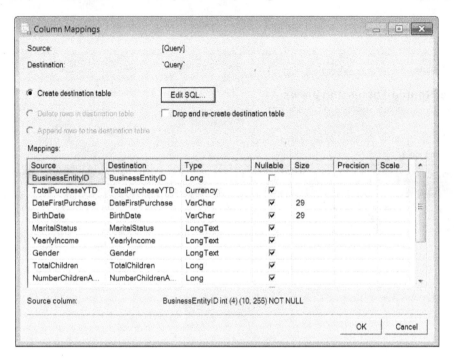

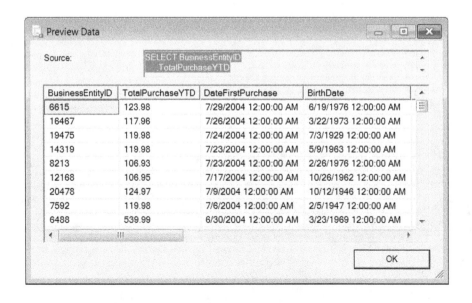

Review Data Type Mappings

Column data mappings can be reviewed in detail on this dialog box.

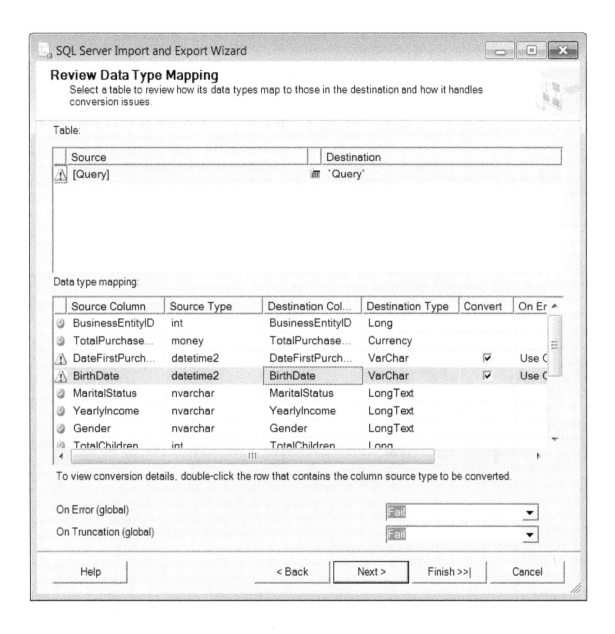

Save and/or Run Package

The Wizard generated SSIS package can be saved for future use or enhancements. If we run it immediately without saving, it will just go away after execution.

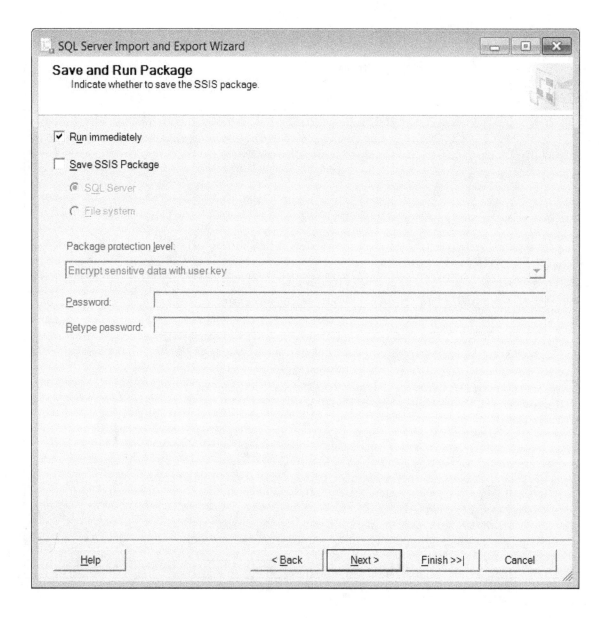

Verification Screen before Execution

At this point we still can go back and make changes should it be necessary. Once we click on Finish and we did not checkmark Save, the package will execute and goes away on success or failure.

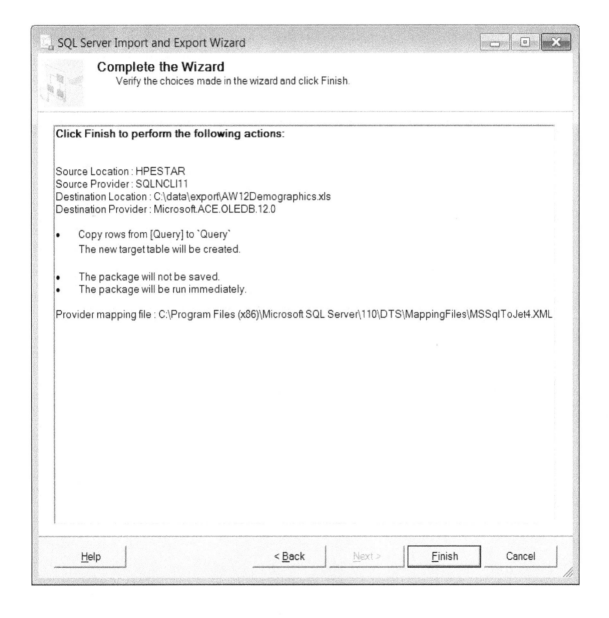

Execution Results Screen

If there are errors in the execution of the package, they will show in this window. The current Wizard generated SSIS package executed successfully.

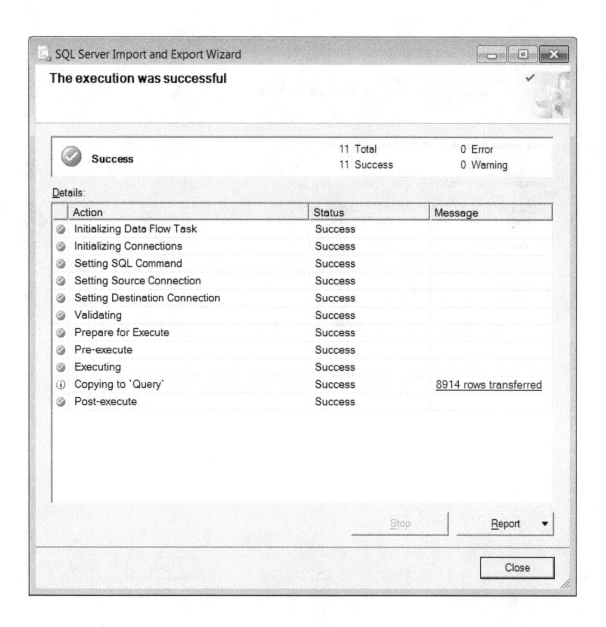

Checking Results in Excel

If the double click on the destination filename, the transferred data is displayed by Excel.

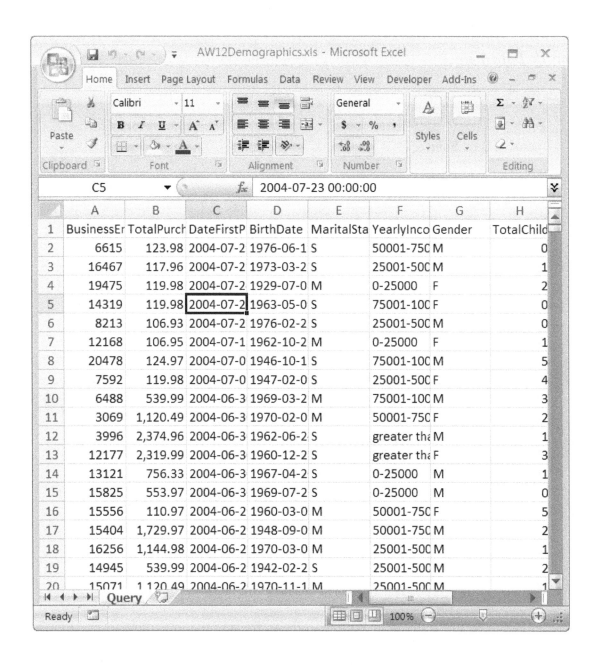

Importing Data with SQL Server Import and Export Wizard

Importing with the Wizard is very similar to the exporting process. We are going to import the just created AW12Demographics.xls Excel worksheet into a new database table. We start the Wizard the same as for export. First we configure the source as Excel worksheet.

Specify Data Source

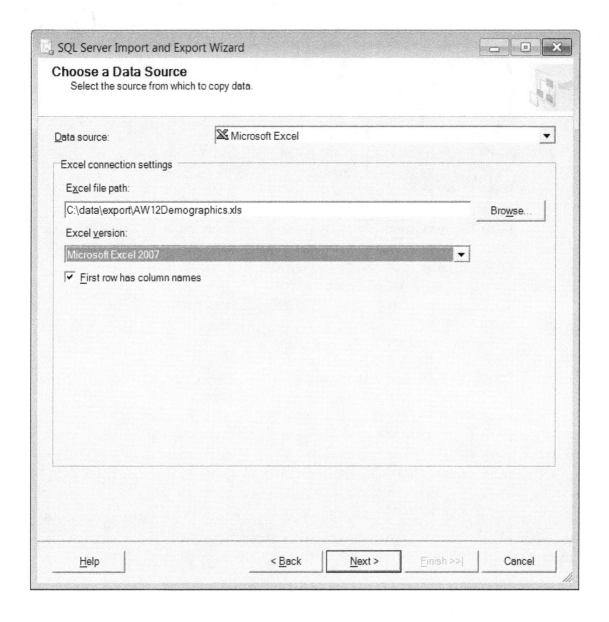

Specify Data Destination as Database

AdventureWorks2012 is the destination for the data movement.

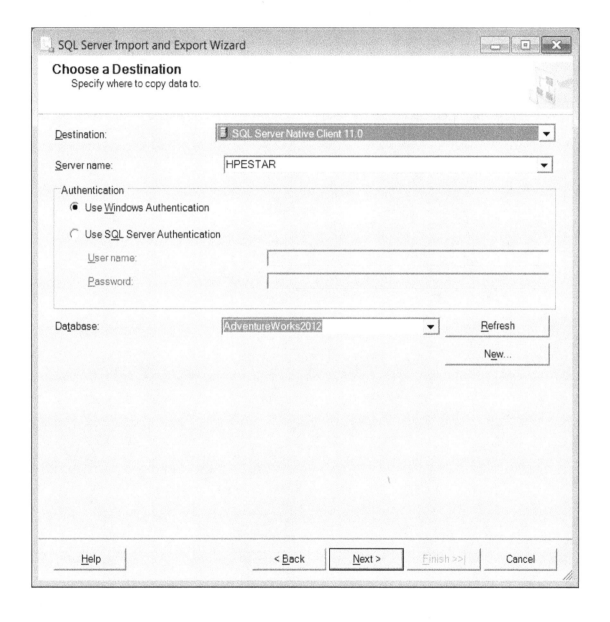

Excel Worksheet Source Is Considered a Table

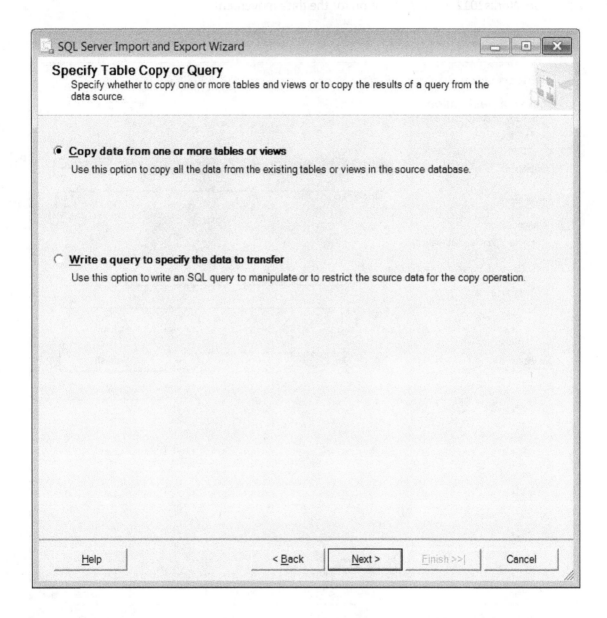

Select Excel Sheet and Assign Database Table Name

All the data is on the 'Query' sheet.

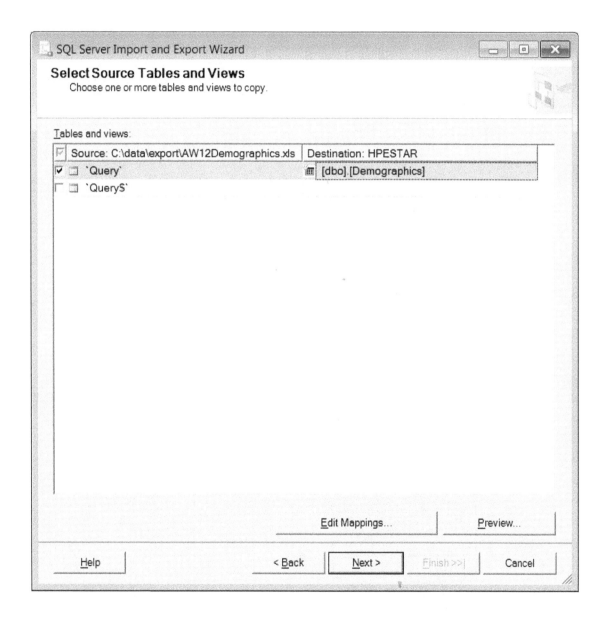

Column Mappings & CREATE TABLE Edit Panels

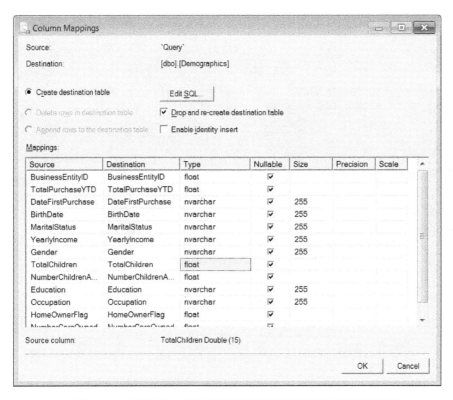

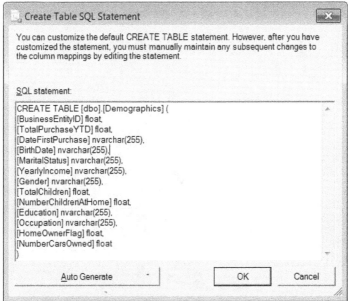

Source Data Inspection with Preview Data

This is a very important step. If the data does not look correct here, it will not be correct in the database table either.

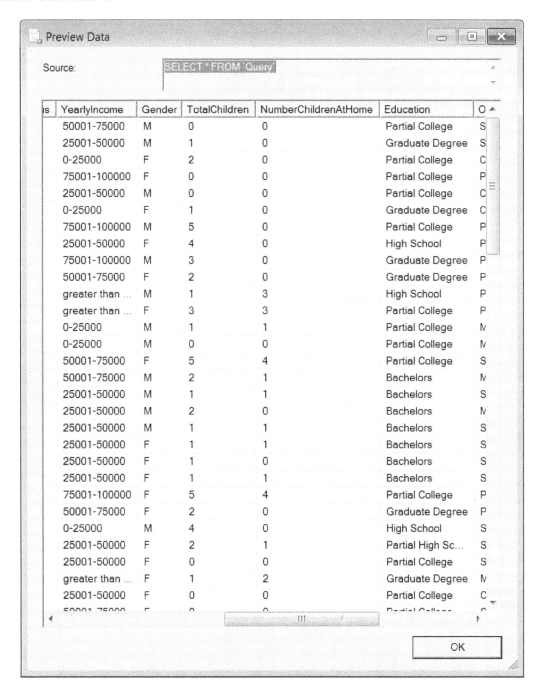

Indicate Saving and/or Run the SSIS Package

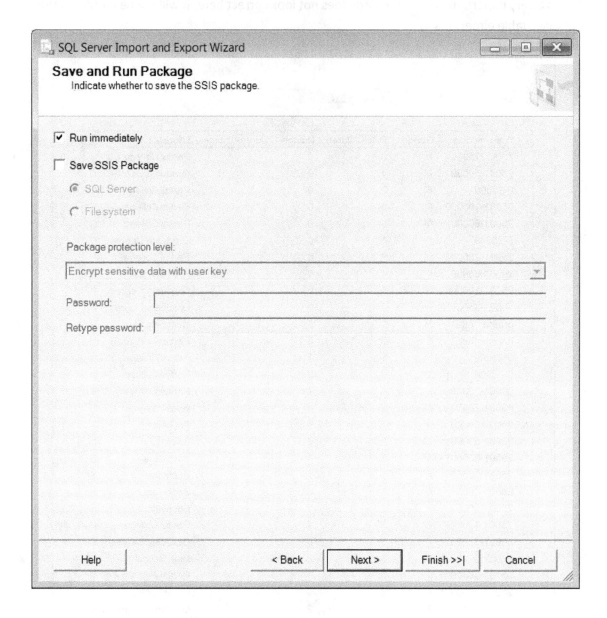

The Final Release Screen for Execution

Successful Execution Screen

In case of errors, hyperlink to errors will display.

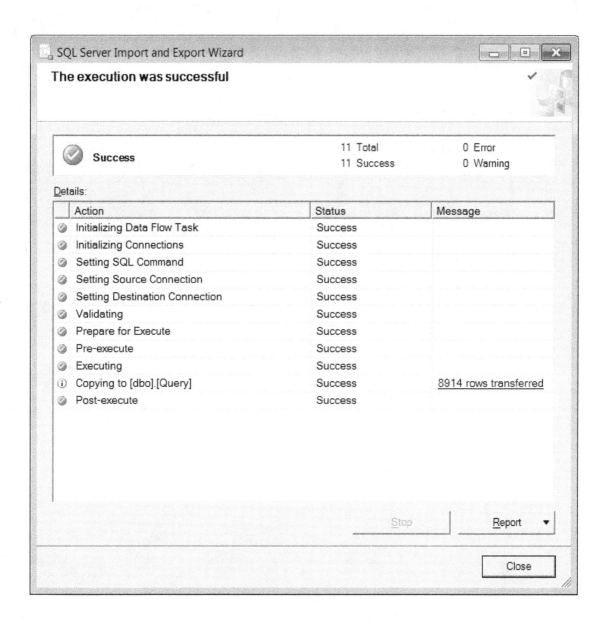

Check New Table in Database

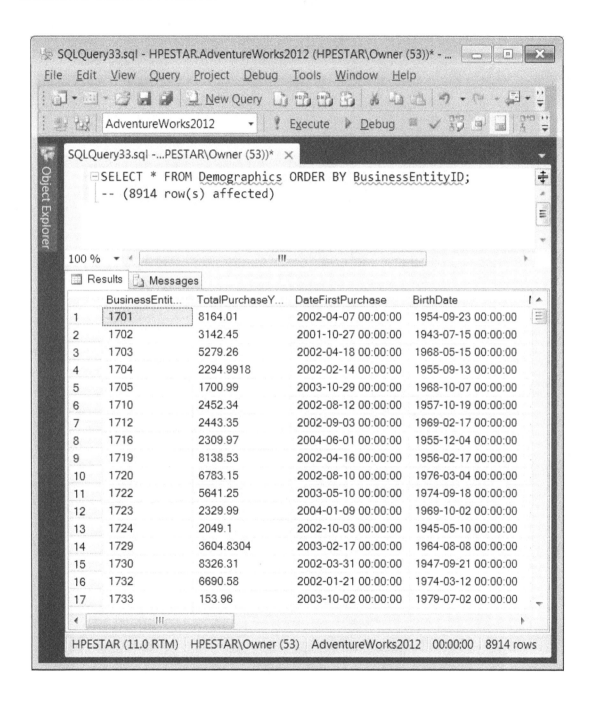

Exporting Database Table to Excel

The Wizard sequence is very similar to exporting query results. We shall export Sales.SalesOrderHeader table.

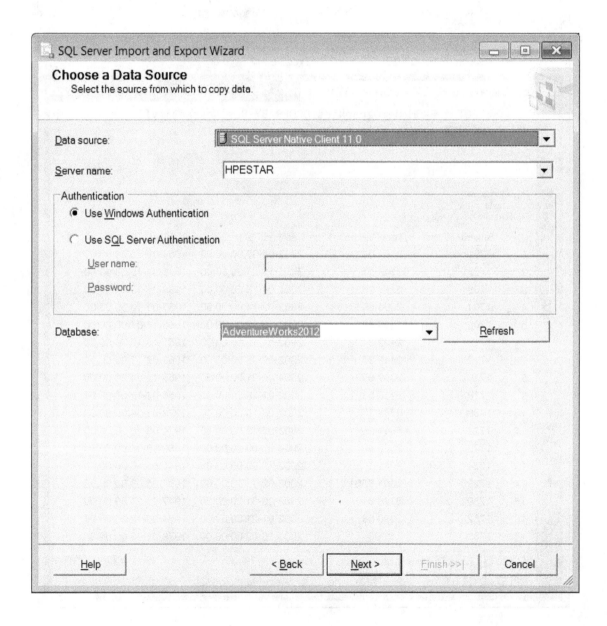

Specify Destination

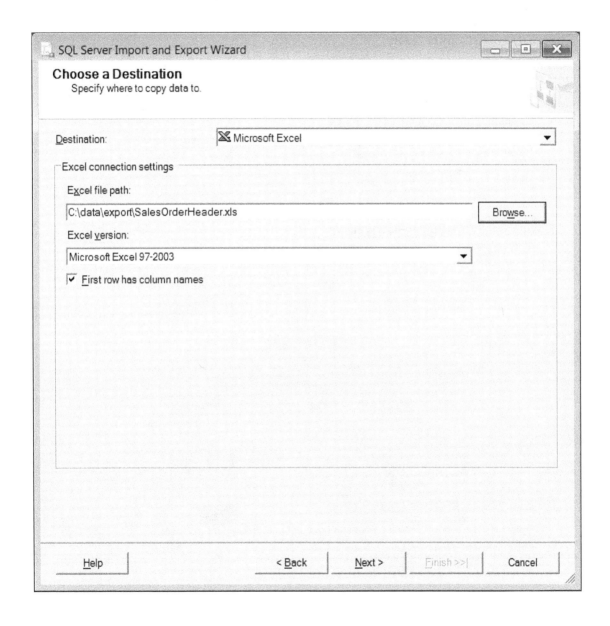

Choose Table Copy or Query

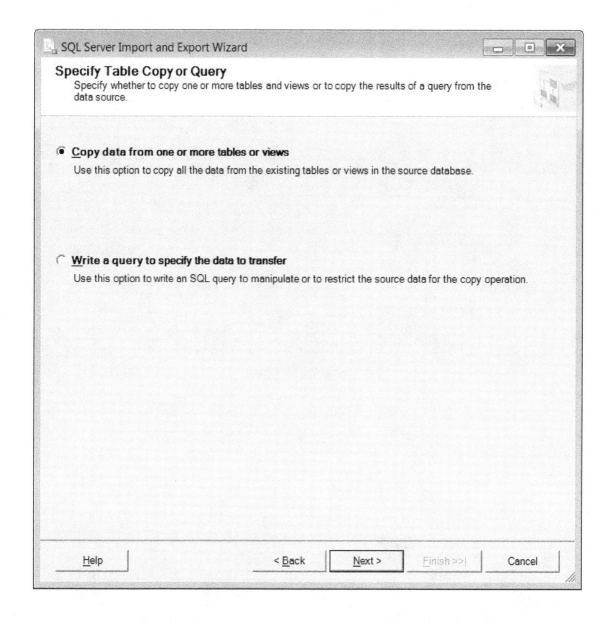

Checkmark Source Table

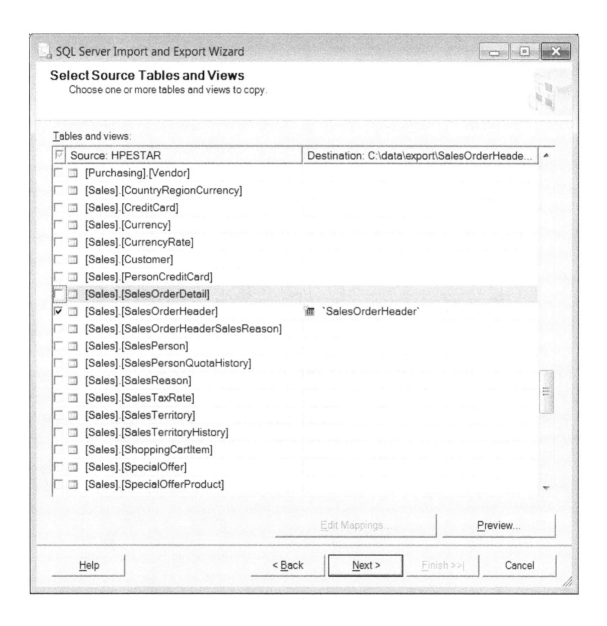

Check Data Type Mapping

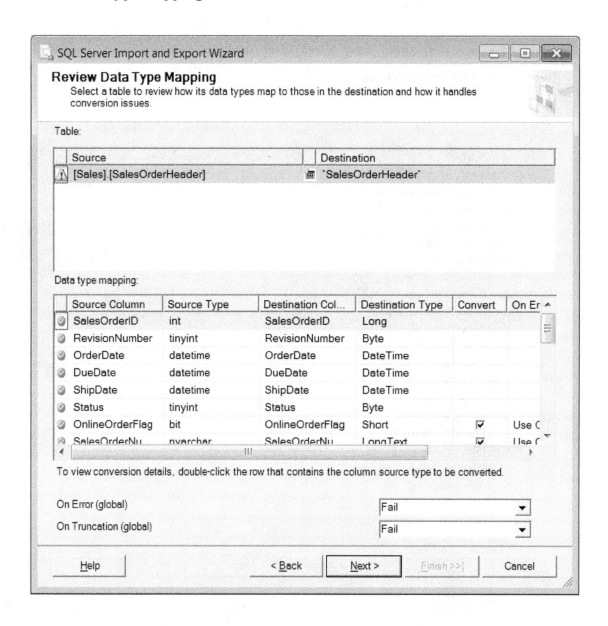

Save and/or Run Package

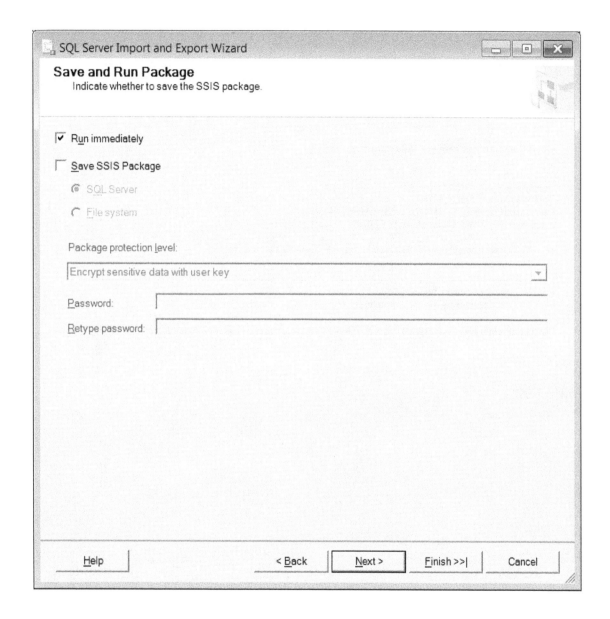

Complete the Wizard

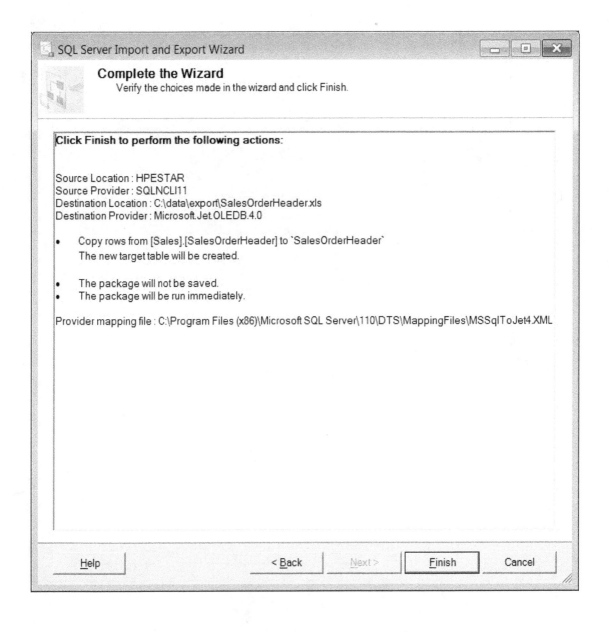

Successful Execution Screen

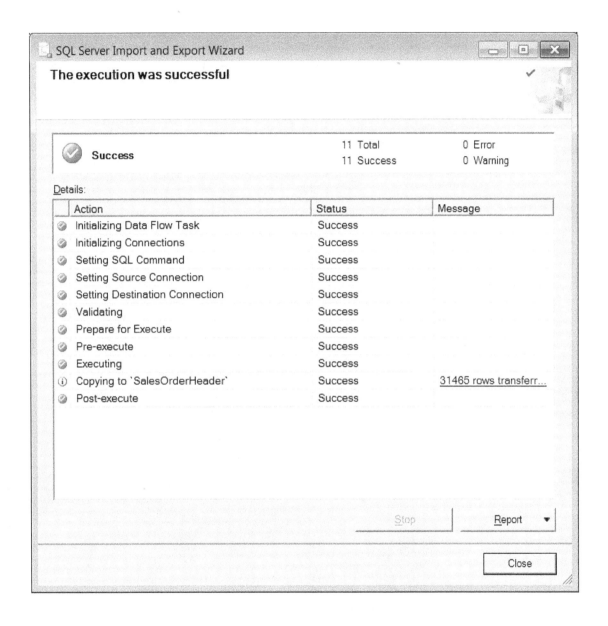

Check File in Folder and Data in Excel

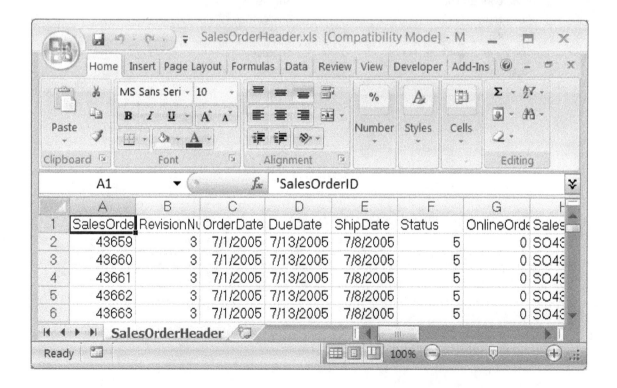

This page is intentionally left blank.

APPENDIX A: Job Interview Questions

Selected Database Design Questions

D1. What is your approach to database design?

D2. Some of our legacy databases are far from 3NF. Can you work in such an environment?

D3. Can UNIQUE KEY be used instead of PRIMARY KEY?

D4. Can a FOREIGN KEY be NULL?

D5. Can a PRIMARY KEY be NULL?

D6. Can a PRIMARY KEY be based on non-clustered unique index?

D7. Do you implement OrderQty > 0 condition as a CHECK constraint or in the application software?

D8. What is a heap?

D9. Can a table have 2 IDENTITY columns, 2 FOREIGN KEYs, 2 PRIMARY KEYs and 2 clustered indexes?

D10. Should each table have a NATURAL KEY or is INT IDENTITY PK sufficient?

D11. How can you prevent entry of "US", "U.S", "USA", etc. instead of "United States" into Country column?

D12. How would you implement ManagerID in an Employee table with EmployeeID as PRIMARY KEY?

D13. How would you implement the relationship between OrderMaster and OrderDetail tables?

D14. The Product table has the Color column. Would you create a Color table and change the column to ColorID FK?

D15. Can you insert directly into an IDENTITY column?

Selected Database Programming Questions

P1. Write a query to list all departments with employee count based on the Department column of Employee table.

P2. Same as above but the Employee table has the DepartmentID column.

P3. Write an INSERT statement for a new "Social Technology" department with GroupName "Sales & Marketing".

P4. Same query es in P2, but the new department should be included even though no employees yet.

P5. Write a query to generate 1000 sequential numbers without a table.

P6. Write a query with SARGable predicate to list all orders from OrderMaster received on 2016-10-23. OrderDate is datetime.

P7. Write a query to add a header record DEPARTMENTNAME to the departments listing from the Department table. If there are 20 departments, the result set should have 21 records.

P8. Make the previous query a derived table in an outer SELECT * query

P9. Write an ORDER BY clause for the previous query with CASE expression to sort DEPARTMENTNAME as first record and alphabetically descending from there on.

P10. Same as above with the IIF conditional.

P11. The table-valued dbo.ufnSplitCSV splits a comma delimited string (input parameter). The Product table has some ProductName-s with comma(s). Write a CROSS APPLY query to return ProductName-s with comma and each split string value from the UDF as separate line. ProductName should repeat for each split part.

ProductName	SplitPart
Full-Finger Gloves, L	Full-Finger Gloves
Full-Finger Gloves, L	L

P12. You need the inserted lines count 10 lines down following the INSERT statement. What should be the statement immediately following the INSERT statement?

P13. What is the result of the second query? What is it called?
SELECT COUNT_BIG(*) FROM Sales.SalesOrderDetail;   -- 121317
SELECT COUNT_BIG(*) FROM Sales.SalesOrderDetail x, Sales.SalesOrderDetail y;

P14. Declare & Assign the string variable @Text varchar(32) the literal '2016/10/23 10:20:12' without the "/" and ":".

P15. You want to add a parameter to a frequently used view. What is the workaround?

This page is intentionally left blank.

APPENDIX B: Job Interview Answers

Selected Database Design Answers

D1. I prefer 3NF design due to high database developer productivity and low maintenance cost.

D2. I did have such projects in the past. I can handle them. Hopefully, introduce some improvements.

D3. Partially yes since UNIQUE KEYs can be FK referenced, fully no. Every table should a PRIMARY KEY.

D4. Yes.

D5. No.

D6. Yes. The default is clustered unique index. Only unique index is required.

D7. CHECK constraint. A server-side object solution (if available) is more reliable than code in application software.

D8. A table without clustered index. Database engine generally works better if a table has clustered index.

D9. No, yes, no, no.

D10. Each table should be designed with NATURAL KEY(s). INT IDENTITY PK is not a replacement for NATURAL KEY.

D11. Combination of Lookup table and UDF CHECK Constraint. UDF checks the Lookup table for valid entries.

D12. ManagerID should be a FOREIGN KEY referencing the PRIMARY KEY of the same table; self-referencing.

D13. OrderID PRIMARY KEY of OrderMaster. OrderID & LineItemID composition PK of OrderDetail. OrderID of OrderDetail FK to OrderID of OderMaster.

D14. Yes. It makes sense for color to be in its own table.

D15. No. Only if you SET IDENTITY_INSERT tablename ON.

Selected Database Programming Answers

P1. SELECT Department, Employees=COUNT(*) FROM Employee GROUP BY Department ORDER BY Department;

P2. SELECT d.Department, Employees = COUNT(EmployeeID)
FROM Employee e INNER JOIN Department d ON e.DepartmentID = d.DepartmentID
GROUP BY d.Department ORDER BY Department;

P3. INSERT Department (Name, GroupName) VALUES ('Social Technology', 'Sales & Marketing');

P4. SELECT d.Department, Employees = COUNT(EmployeeID)
FROM Employee e RIGHT JOIN Department d ON e.DepartmentID = d.DepartmentID
GROUP BY d.Department ORDER BY Department;

P5. ;WITH Seq AS (SELECT SeqNo = 1 UNION ALL SELECT SeqNo+1 FROM Seq WHERE SeqNo < 100) SELECT * FROM Seq;

P6. SELECT * FROM OrderMaster WHERE OrderDate >='20161023' AND OrderDate < DATEADD(DD,1,'20161023');

P7. SELECT AllDepartments = 'DEPARTMENTNAME' UNION SELECT Department FROM Department;

P8. SELECT * FROM (SELECT AllDepartments = 'DEPARTMENTNAME' UNION SELECT Name FROM HumanResources.Department) x

P9. ORDER BY CASE WHEN AllDepartments = 'DEPARTMENTNAME' THEN 1 ELSE 2 END, AllDepartments DESC;

P10. ORDER BY IIF(AllDepartments = 'DEPARTMENTNAME', 1 , 2), AllDepartments DESC;

P11. SELECT ProductName, S.SplitPart FROM Product P CROSS APPLY dbo.ufnSplitCSV (Name) S WHERE ProductName like '%,%';

P12. DECLARE @InsertedCount INT = @@ROWCOUNT;

P13. 121317*121317; Cartesian product.

P14. DECLARE @Text varchar(32) = REPLACE(REPLACE ('2016/10/23 10:20:12', '/', SPACE(0)), ':', SPACE(0));

P15. Table-valued INLINE user-defined function.

This page is intentionally left blank.

This page is intentionally left blank.

INDEX for Beginner SQL Programming Using Microsoft SQL Server 2016

Index of the Most Important Topics

D

E

www.ingramcontent.com/pod-product-compliance
Lightning Source LLC
Chambersburg PA
CBHW080144060326
40689CB00018B/3844